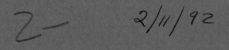

Z—   2/11/92

HAPPY BIRTHDAY   JOE

YOUR GRANDFATHER WAS

A CLOSE FRIEND OF

DEANE DAVIS AS WELL

AS HIS FAMILY DOCTOR.

LOVE
        DAD & Mom

Deane C. Davis

Deane C. Davis

An Autobiography

Deane C. Davis
with Nancy Price Graff

The New England Press

Shelburne, Vermont

© 1991 by the Estate of Deane C. Davis
First Vermont Bank and Trust Company (Brattleboro, Vermont), Executor
All Rights Reserved
First Edition

Designed by Eugenie S. Delaney
Cover photograph by Jym Wilson/The Burlington Free Press
Printed in the United States of America

Davis, Deane C., 1900-
   Deane C. Davis—an autobiography / Deane C. Davis, with Nancy Price
Graff.—1st ed.
      p. cm.
      Includes index.
      ISBN 0–933050–91–7 : $24.95
      1. Davis, Deane C., 1900- .   2. Governors—Vermont—Biography.
3. Vermont—Biography.   I. Graff, Nancy Price, 1953- .
II. Title.
F55.22.D38A3 1991
974.3'043'092—dc20
[B]   91-52770
                                                                          CIP

For additional copies or for a catalog of our other New England titles, please
write:

The New England Press
P.O. Box 575
Shelburne, VT 05482

for my children
and stepchildren
and their children

Contents

Foreword

When Robert Stafford retired after eighteen years in the U.S. Senate, dinners were held all around the state honoring him for his service to Vermont. I met with Governor Davis the morning after he had attended one such dinner in Rutland. As we ended our weekly editorial session, Governor and Mrs. Davis stood at the door chatting about the dinner.

"You would think Bob would be getting tired of hearing all those accolades," Mrs. Davis remarked.

"He's a politician," Governor Davis replied. "He will never get tired of hearing how wonderful he is."

"Oh, Deane," Mrs. Davis said, "wouldn't you be tired of it all by now?"

Governor Davis raised his hands to his chest in a gesture of pathos.

"Try me!" he told her.

We all laughed.

Deane Davis's was a great and long life during which he earned many times over the right to testimonial dinners far into the next century. But as he began these memoirs, he simply meant to document, as his father had before him, the struggles undertaken and lessons learned during an active life. Friends who read the result urged Governor Davis to widen his manuscript's scope and its audience. Yet, as the book grew, he retained both its original tone and its original purpose.

The night Deane Davis died, Mrs. Davis, her son, his wife, one of their daughters, and I sat in the Davis's living room telling stories and taking comfort in each other's presence. Mrs. Davis asked me to read the obituary that Richard Bottamini, a long-time friend, had prepared. It recorded officially some of the professional highlights of Governor Davis's distinguished national career in law, insurance, management, and government. We briefly discussed whether the record was too detailed. I demurred, saying that if this record did not appear in print at this juncture, it might never come to public notice.

"Why, isn't it in the book?" Mrs. Davis asked me in surprise.

"No, it's not," I told her. "This sort of information is not in the book."

Anyone who comes to this book expecting to find an annotated listing of achievements will be disappointed. Governor Davis was fond of repeating his father's words that "struggle is the law of life." He meant not only that life is often difficult and sometimes heartbreakingly painful, as Deane Davis learned himself, but that life is about pushing oneself toward goals not easily reached.

For all of its stories and humor, this book is about struggle, difficult decisions, hard choices, and ultimately the growth of a man and a state, for Deane Davis and Vermont grew into the twentieth century together. It is not about achievements and awards, although Deane Davis earned many of these, and some of them will be evident in these pages.

I came to believe as we worked together once, twice, three times a week for nearly a year and a half, that Deane Davis never included anything that did not have a larger significance, a lesson, a bit of wisdom gleaned from a full and hard-worked life. My respect and affection for him grew exponentially as we toiled and laughed together.

A close mutual friend of ours advised me as I deliberated taking on this project that if I did not do it, I would regret it for the rest of my life. He was right. I will always cherish the brief spell during which I basked in the glow of Deane Davis's illuminating light.

Nancy Price Graff

Preface

These recollections were originally written for my children and grandchildren. After my father's death I found in the attic of his home a book in his handwriting in which he had recorded many interesting facts of his own life and that of members of the family. I remember how much I cherished that book, as did those with whom I shared its contents, and so I decided to put together incidents of my own life in the hope that some of my children or grandchildren might feel the same way about my record. As the work progressed, the scope of the book widened, both in the period of time covered and the material included.

When the book was finished, I shared it with a number of friends who urged me strongly to seek its publication. Thinking over their suggestions at some length, I found myself being easily persuaded. I recognized that the twentieth century was and is a very special time in history. Kenneth Crawford, the highly perceptive and highly regarded observer of the American scene, said in *Newsweek* on the occasion of his retirement that "anyone who has lived as an adult through the last half of the twentieth century has seen more history in the making than anyone who ever lived before him. There has been more change, more cataclysm, more invention, more progress, and more deterioration than ever happened in any previous fifty years." He might have added that there had also been more controversy and disagreement concerning fundamental issues affecting the state and nation. Since I have lived through nine-tenths of the twentieth century, I thought I might be considered an acceptable witness to the events of that extraordinary time.

This book is a description of life in Vermont as I saw and experienced it during that period. It was not written to entertain or persuade, only to testify. I hope that it may be an acceptable addition to the fast-growing library of writings about Vermont.

April 18, 1990

Acknowledgments

If Deane Davis had lived another month, it would have been possible to thank by name all the people who helped bring this book to print. Unfortunately, this was a loose end left untied at his death. I know from our work together that at least half a dozen people had the opportunity to read the manuscript in its various early forms and make suggestions. I do not know your names, but I know that Governor Davis would have wanted to thank you for your encouragement. You kindled the spark that became this book.

For my part, and on behalf of Governor Davis, I would like to thank Tom Slayton for his advice and criticism; Gregory Sanford, state archivist, for supplying dates and other elusive but necessary information; Joelen Mulvaney, Verbena Pastor, and Karen Lane of the Aldrich Public Library and Museum for photographic and research assistance, particularly for the history of Barre; the Vermont Historical Society and the University of Vermont Special Collections for opening up their photograph collections for our use; Bob Davis for helping us to locate photographs we thought had been long lost; Mrs. Gelsie Monti, Craig Line, Norman MacIver, Robert Babcock, Tom Calcagni, Ruth Nims, Toby Talbot, John Belding, and Noel and Janet Induni for their contributions to the photographic sections; and Carol McKee for typing and retyping the manuscript with patience and good humor. I am especially grateful to Tom and Dolly Davis for having the foresight a decade ago not to throw away a box of old family photographs Tom's father had deemed worthless and for generally maintaining a family archive that enriched the photographic sections of the book. I would also like to thank particularly Al and Maggie Rosa, who nurtured this book from its beginnings, and Brian Vachon, for his wise counsel and generosity of spirit. Finally, I thank Marjorie Davis, whose contributions to this book are immeasurable.

N.P.G.

1

Love and Lessons

*My grandmother took me in her arms and sat
down in the kitchen rocker. I cannot remember all
that she said, but I can still feel her rough shirtwaist against my face and the love that she so
patiently expressed. She mended my broken world.*

In 1905, when I was five years old, I went to live with my grandparents. My brother Raymond was seriously ill, terminally ill, although we did not know that at the time. My father's mother took
me in to ease my mother's burden of caring for my brother while she
ran our large household. I have little memory of the long twenty-
mile buggy trip from Barre that first brought me to my grandparents' farm on Pike Hill in the Town of Corinth. I do know that it was
a long trip, between four and five hours, and that I slept part of the
way. But as far back as my memory goes, my world began right there
and then on the farm.

My grandfather took me with him whenever and wherever he
could as he went about the routine of daily chores and occasionally
to Waits River in the buggy. He was a strong, muscular man, a little
above average height, with snow-white hair and pink cheeks. His
countenance had a serious but kindly expression, and his eyes twin-
kled whenever he was amused or pleased. I hung on to his every

word. He had great patience and a talent for explaining why things were done as they were, and he handed down many lessons, both practical and moral.

One particular lesson stands out clearly. One day my grandfather asked me to take a message to Uncle Will, whose farm was about a half mile away. I was to tell Uncle Will that Grandfather could not take the butter to the creamery the next day and to ask him to do it in Grandfather's place. The nearest creamery was located on the main road between Waits River and West Topsham, about four miles from the farm. The milk was separated each day after the cows were milked, and the cream was held in a tub of running water until it was taken to the house to be made into butter. Grandfather and Uncle Will took turns carrying the butter from both farms to the creamery. Normally, their shared system made it unnecessary for either to make more than one trip per week.

I set out on my errand with confidence and great pride. But as I rounded a turn in the road at a point where Uncle Will's house could be seen, my confidence vanished. In the road ahead of me was Uncle Will's dog, a shepherd-like animal of diverse origin, the kind that used to make such good farm watchdogs. He was standing in the center of the road facing me. His hair bristled, and he made a kind of low growl. It was clear that he regarded me as an untrustworthy character and that he understood his duty was to protect the house from intrusion by the likes of me. He left me no doubt, even as a five-year-old, that I was pushing fate to contest the right of way. I tried my best to coax him into a better understanding. He would have none of it. Then he set up a fearful barking, full of menace. My fear multiplied. Desperate, I crossed the fence into the field on my right to make a big arc around him. He followed, placed himself in front of me, and began to make threatening passes at me with bared teeth and even more menacing growls. Then I tried a big arc to the left. Same result. I was shaking with fear. Finally, when it became obvious that he was not going to let me pass and that no one at Uncle Will's house had heard the commotion, I gave up and started my unhappy journey back to Gramp's. My courage was in shreds, and my pride a pool of shame. How could I tell my grandfather that I had failed my first great mission?

"Did you tell him?" he asked.

"Yup," I said in a small and guilty voice.

The next day I faced my inevitable moment of truth. How I suffered in the meantime contemplating what was to come!

When Uncle Will failed to show up at the proper time, Gramp hitched a horse to the buggy intending to drive to Uncle Will's and find out what was wrong. I watched him, consumed with shame and fear. When Gramp finally climbed into the buggy, I could not stand it any longer. I ran to him, choking with my tears, and told the truth—that I hadn't delivered the message.

"Why?" asked Gramp.

So I told him about the dog. He listened patiently as I told the whole story.

Then he asked, "But why did you lie to me?"

I had no answer. I just stood there, shaking with sobs.

Slowly, but quite deliberately, Gramp got out of the buggy, hitched the horse to a fence post, took me by the hand, and led me up to the woodshed. I felt very much like a prisoner on his way to the gallows. Not a trace of anger showed on Gramp's face. Quietly, he said, "It's really not important that you didn't deliver the message. What is important is that you lied to me. I've got to show you that in the long run lying never pays. I want you to remember that all your life." Then he proceeded to give me the worst spanking I ever got in my life—and I've had my fair share. When it was over, I ran sobbing into the house. My wonderful world had crashed.

My grandmother took me in her arms and sat down in the kitchen rocker. I cannot remember all that she said, but I can still feel her rough shirtwaist against my face and the love that she so patiently expressed. She mended my broken world.

My grandfather's farm was a big one. The largest part was pasture and woods, and all of it, including the meadows, was rather steep and rolling. Not too steep to work with machinery drawn by horses but certainly too steep for tractors. The house was located on a little plateau between the two barns and overlooked the meadows. From the house you could see Mount Moosilauke in New Hampshire. Behind the house was my grandmother's garden, and behind that the big pasture rose steeply. I once asked my grandfather why the house was built where it was. He told me it was because the view was so good from the front and the steep hill behind the house protected it from the westerly winds. South of the house was a large orchard with many kinds of apple trees: eating apples, cooking apples, summer apples, and winter apples, and a lot of cider apples that my grandfather took to Bradford to have squeezed for cider. And there was always a barrel of cider, sometimes two, in the small cellar under the house. My grandfather used to trim the apple tree branches with a saw, but he never sprayed the trees as farmers do now.

There were dairy cattle, hogs, sheep, chickens, and horses on the farm. Morgan horses. They were unregistered, for the Morgan Horse Registry did not exist until later. But a registry was not really needed in those days—everybody who knew horses could distinguish a Morgan on sight.

For a youngster like me, life on a dairy farm was busy and mostly fun, particularly with grandparents like mine who gave me jobs within my capacity and made me feel that both the jobs and I were important. In the summer we got up around five in the morning, and my grandfather and I would go down to the cattle barn to do the feeding and the morning milking. The cows would be waiting at the pasture gate, and my job was to go and let down the bars and drive them to the barn. They would go immediately to their stanchions for their grain, and each one knew its own stanchion. I would lock the stanchions while my grandfather was feeding them grain. Then he would get his three-legged stool and his milk pail and milk the cows. He milked them by hand, as he did not have a milking machine, and he carried the milk from each cow to a big metal bowl on top of the separator. When all fifteen cows had been milked, I would turn the crank on the separator, which separated the cream from the milk. After this was done I would unlock all the stanchions, drive the cows back to the pasture, and put up the bars. Late in the afternoon the cows would be back waiting at the bars to be milked again for the day. The cream was carried to the buttery where it was stored until my grandmother churned it and made butter. The skim milk was fed to the calves in the barn and to the hogs who lived in the barn's basement. When the chores were finished at the barn, we went back to the house for breakfast. This would be about seven o'clock. For breakfast we had oatmeal, eggs, bacon, and sometimes griddle cakes with maple syrup. Best of all were Graham muffins, made in a thick black iron muffin pan. They would melt in your mouth, especially when liberally laced with butter. Since then I've never been able to appreciate Graham muffins unless they were made in a black iron muffin pan.

After breakfast there was never any lack of jobs to do. My memories are mostly of haying, since I was taken back to my home in Barre each fall so I could go to school. In summer we mowed, raked, and tumbled the hay into tumbles to be pitched on to a haywagon and then to be brought to the barn and pitched off into the haymows. I hung around my grandfather waiting for a chance to help, and he saw to it that there were plenty of chances.

If it rained, my grandfather would sharpen the sections on the mowing machine and the blades on the hand scythes. He would hold the edges against the grindstone while I turned the handles. This would have been a tedious chore except that my grandfather always used the occasion to tell me interesting stories about his life and things that had happened in the neighborhood. On other rainy days he mended harness, greased all the wheels on the wagons and machinery, and cleaned the cow stable and the horse barn. There was no telephone on the farm. It was not till shortly after he died that the farmers in the area organized a cooperative telephone company.

The house had no bathroom, and we all took a bath, one by one, on Saturday night in a large washtub in the buttery. Nor were there any toilet facilities except the old-fashioned wooden three-hole facility. It was located across from the front yard, and in stormy weather or bitter cold one's need for relief and level of courage had to be strong and high to overcome the discomfort and inconvenience of the trip. There were two wood-burning stoves, but only the kitchen stove was used in the summertime. My bedroom was upstairs, heated through a hole that had been cut in the ceiling of the kitchen, which allowed the heat to rise and warm my room in cold weather. The kitchen was the center of activity and communication. It was a big room with several chairs, a bench, and a small table where we ate meals even though there was a small dining room, rarely used, behind the kitchen. I loved the evenings there after supper, listening to my grandparents talking while I got gradually drowsier until I was either sent to bed or sometimes carried to bed sound asleep.

A few of the farmers in the neighborhood had a hired man, but my grandfather never did except when some man was out of work with no place to stay. Then my grandfather would take him in and the man would work for his room and board until he could find a paying job. Earlier, long before I was there, my father and his three brothers had done the work of a hired man. Farmers used to say, "The best way to get hired help is to raise it."

Gramp loved horses, all horses, his own and those of others, Morgan horses most of all. But like every other living thing on the farm, they had to earn their living. The horses were the only horsepower on the farm, long before the arrival of the tractor. My grandfather used his horses with utmost consideration. Even as useful as they were, he never worked a horse beyond its strength or comfort. He kept them clean and his stable immaculate. When a horse was injured or sick, he treated it himself out of the abundance of horse knowledge that he, like other Vermont farmers, had accumulated from experience out of sheer necessity.

One day I was marching along behind the plow that was hitched to a pair of Grandfather's mares. I watched every detail of the turning of the turf, the straight, uniform furrows, and the way the horses responded to his voice at each turning at the end of the furrow. Suddenly he stopped the horses, unhitched them from the plow, and took them to the barn. The next morning when we went to the barn for morning milking, we had a new foal! Grandfather used the occasion to fill me in on how animals mate and give birth. From time to time he followed up on that lesson by letting me watch the breeding of the mares and of the cows. Two days after the foal was born, the new mother was back on the plow with her new baby tagging along beside her. That day my grandfather was most solicitous of the mare. He stopped the team frequently to rest and every time the baby showed the slightest inclination to nurse.

This is not to say Morgans are not tough. They are. In good weather, after a day with the horses in the fields, my grandfather would turn them out into the pasture instead of putting them in their stalls. As he slipped their bridles off, they would trot away a few steps and then fold their front legs under them, lie down and roll, first one way and then another to scratch their backs. Then up they would get and go to grazing.

Grandfather explained to me that one of the most precious

things to a horse, as to humans, is a feeling of being at liberty; that horses stay healthiest when least confined. Even in winter, when the horses were not being worked, they were turned out to pasture or let loose in the meadow near the barn where they would paw the snow until they could eat the winter grass that had already died and turned brown. They seemed to like this just as well or even better than the clean, early cut hay from the haymow. I don't know about the comparative food value of the grass and the hay, but the horses looked and acted much happier with a maximum amount of freedom. They stayed out in the rain or snow and only came in twice a day to get their grain. If a strong wind combined with sleet or extremely low temperature, the horses would come in, but not for low temperature, rain, sleet, or wind alone.

My grandfather had a beautiful Morgan stallion and kept a few mares that served the double duty of doing the farm work and giving birth to a few foals each year. In addition to using the stallion for breeding, my grandfather used him for driving to the village store, to church, and on any other errands that came up. He liked fast horses, and this stallion had plenty of speed. When the occasion permitted he raced his best horses, including this stallion, just for fun. One of his neighbors, Miller Richardson, raised some fast ones, too, so the opportunity for him to indulge in this sport was readily available. They liked to race each other down the flat roadway from Waits River Village up to the creamery.

When they became two years old, all young horses, if they were not sold before, were broken both to single and double harness and to work in pairs. Eventually they were sold, usually for driving horses. My grandfather was a good trainer of horses. He had a way of communicating with a horse that is the secret of a good trainer.

He used to let me watch him training a colt, and when we had the horses hitched to a hay wagon, he let me drive them. Of course, he was right there beside me, and they stopped and started mostly in response to his voice commands, but he let me hold the reins. I could turn the horses to right and left, and it gave me the feeling that I was driving them.

Measured by the standards of his time, my grandfather had a good education, and he used it in many ways. He had been a teacher in the district schools of Corinth and at one time served on the school board. One of the tests of a teacher in those days was whether he could prevent himself from being physically thrown out of school by the older boys who felt it their duty to try out every new teacher who came along. He survived many of these tests and established a reputation for being a good teacher.

My grandfather was also a very religious man and a regular attendant at church. He read the Scriptures daily, had prayers at breakfast, and sometimes even started a discussion on a point raised in the minister's Sunday sermon.

However, sometimes my grandfather's preoccupation with horses blinded him to everything else. One time my grandmother had been away for a while on one of her frequent errands of mercy. The husband of her patient brought her back in a buggy pulled by a beautiful pair of high-stepping chestnut Morgan horses. By coincidence, my grandfather passed them on the road on his way to the creamery. That night at the supper table he extolled the beauty of the horses. It soon became clear that he had not even noticed his wife in the buggy!

Before she married my grandfather, my grandmother had been married to Dr. A.F. Evans, a practicing physician in Marshfield. Dr. Evans died when their two children were very young, but before he died my grandmother learned much about the basics of medicine as it was practiced in those days and much about the care and nursing of patients. She was in great demand for miles around since there were no doctors within reasonable distance from that part of Corinth. She never refused unless there was a reason beyond her control, and she never accepted money for this service.

One night I woke up to hear voices downstairs in the kitchen. It was during the latter part of February on one of the occasions when I had been taken to my grandparents' farm during spring vacation. I went down to investigate and found a man talking with my grandfather. He had driven five miles through a blizzard and drifting snow to ask my grandmother to come to care for his wife, who was very ill with pneumonia. My grandfather had already taken the exhausted horse to the stable, rubbed it down, blanketed, and fed it. He had also hitched one of his own horses to the sleigh. While my grandmother was bundling herself in her warmest clothing and in my grandfather's bearskin coat, she had been warming a freeze stone in the oven of the kitchen stove. The freeze stone, wrapped in heavy pieces of cloth, was put in the bottom of the sleigh, and without any apparent qualms, my grandmother got into the sleigh. Tucked in with several blankets and a bearskin lap robe around her feet, legs, and lap, she drove away through the five miles of blizzard to the home of her patient. We didn't see her for a week.

Like my grandfather, my grandmother was a religious person. Together they regularly attended the Methodist church in Waits River Village. The church is still there, in the very center of the village on Route 25 on the road to Bradford. It is one of the most often-painted and photographed churches in Vermont and is almost unchanged, except for a small addition in the rear and the removal of the horsesheds.

My grandmother was a serene lady, calm but not placid. She always seemed confident of herself and in control of her surroundings. She had a mobile face, dark brown eyes and hair, and when she greeted anyone her whole countenance would light up and her smile made her look beautiful.

She and my grandfather were of about the same height, around five feet eight inches. He had an extremely rugged frame, but she was of slight build, weighing around 120 pounds. She was always busy about something from morning till night. After the supper dishes were done, we used to sit for a couple of hours in the kitchen and talk of the happenings of the day or one of them would tell me stories. During this time she sewed, knitted, or mended clothes. Her fingers seemed to move automatically even when she was engrossed in conversation. Both my grandparents were good storytellers and knew how to awaken the interest of a youngster.

My grandmother loved her garden. Caring for it did not seem like work to her. She was happy digging in the dirt and doing things to her vegetables and flowers, and she did everything about the garden except the plowing and spreading of fertilizer.

The summer I was seven I noticed that she was not quite so active and that her garden was only partly planted. She began to lie down and rest every afternoon, something I had never seen her do before. Soon I could see that my grandfather was worried about her. He asked me to watch when she was in the garden and to help her with the weeding. Then one day he took her to Bradford in the buggy, and they were gone all day until late in the evening. I learned a bit later that they had gone to see a doctor. It was obvious that Grandfather's worries had increased, but my grandmother seemed her usual serene self. If she was worried, she surely didn't show it by her countenance or by anything she said.

I spent about two years altogether with my grandparents, actually two full summers and part of a third as well as spring vacations. The doctor had diagnosed my grandmother's illness as Bright's disease. Ironically, although all the worry was concentrated on my grandmother, it was my grandfather who died first, early in that third summer.

On the Sunday before he died, Gramp went to church as usual, driving his beloved stallion in the best buggy. He took me on the seat beside him, and I was proud as punch as we drove into the churchyard, hitched the horse under the shed, and walked into church. The next day, Monday, my grandfather and I did the morning chores as usual, and then he took me with him into the upper woods to cut fenceposts. We rode in a lumber wagon, and he worked all forenoon cutting the posts. I tried to help by dragging away the brush and helping load the posts on the wagon. At noon he drove the horses back to the barn, put them up, and went immediately into the house and to bed without eating any dinner. As my grandfather grew rapidly worse the doctor was called from Bradford, but he was unable to diagnose the cause of the illness. On Wednesday, my grandfather died.

Five days later, my grandmother died.

That was eighty-two years ago. I am still grateful for the wealth of memories they gave me, for the confidence and belief in myself. I am grateful for the manner in which they introduced me to work, for the knowledge that work can be fun as well as a means of accomplishment, and for the awareness that accomplishment brings deep satisfactions. They showed me that the variety of jobs I did were important to the running of the farm, and that I was important too. I could feel their approval when it was earned and the absence of it when it was not.

They taught me to love the land, the woods, the fields, and the little brooks. They taught me to listen to the birds when they sing and to watch the sky for its warnings of bad weather and its promise of good weather, to enjoy both the sun and the rain and to appreciate their relationship to life and growth on the farm. They taught me to love animals and particularly horses. And my grandfather showed me how humans and horses communicate. He taught me to use body language as well as my voice to talk to horses and to watch for the signs of body language which they use in return. In this way he laid a foundation for my association with horses that has lasted all my life. He also gave me my first lessons in what today we call ecology—the interrelationship among humans, animals, and the environment.

Perhaps because both my grandfather and my grandmother had been teachers in one-room public schools, they knew exactly how to arouse and direct the interest of youngsters. I learned later in life that all education begins at the point of interest. They both taught me more by actions than they did by words.

And finally they gave me a belief in God. Here, too, it was far more by what they did than what they said. Their regular attendance at church, their prayers, and their Scripture readings at mealtimes convinced me of their belief, and I felt that if wise people like them believed in God, then there surely must be a God. I was impressed, too, by the fact that the only book in the kitchen was the Bible, which lay on a shelf within easy reach of my grandfather's chair. And he used it too. He would often discuss at the table on Sunday some point in the minister's sermon, sometimes agreeing and sometimes disagreeing. The Christianity of the time was the fundamental version, and that was their kind too. Over the years I have come to know that you cannot take literally everything in the Bible, but it has not changed my belief that the world was created by a Supreme Being, which we call God, and that the forces that He set in motion continue to rule the world and are the basis upon which it is preserved.

My grandfather showed me the joy that comes from creativity. I could see it in his countenance as he worked with his crops and his animals. My grandmother showed me the joy that comes from service. She showed it by all the things she did in church, in the home, and particularly in the many times she sacrificed her own pleasure and comfort to go long distances to nurse people who were desperately ill, never charging for her services. These memories of my grandparents are keepsakes I cherish still.

2

At Uncle Will's

*It smelled like home, and a lovely home it was.
After a long day in the sun or the snow it was a
delicious haven. The sense was strong of family,
comfort, and home. For a youngster, it was a security blanket beyond compare.*

After my grandparents died, I often pestered my parents to let
me go to visit Uncle Will, Aunt Effie, and my cousins. Living as they
did next to Gramp's farm and having taken over Gramp's farm to
operate along with their own, they represented a tie to the two years
of joy that I had experienced there. To us kids in Barre, Pike Hill in
Corinth was a haven and a heaven of country life. And none of my
brothers or sisters loved it more than I.

To make these visits possible without causing too much extra
burden to Aunt Effie, our parents swapped kids from time to time,
and we had our frequent taste of country life while my cousins had a
chance to live in "the city," at least for short periods. Dad would
hitch up old Mary Ann, the family driving horse, and take a couple
of us kids to the top of Orange Heights, so named because it was the
height of land between Barre and Waits River. Uncle Will would do
the same with a couple of his children, and we would all meet at
noon in a sandpit beside the road, a spot about halfway between our

home in Barre and Uncle Will's farm. There we would have a picnic lunch. Dad and his brother would chat about grown-up affairs for a couple hours, while we kids romped and played and yelled, as kids always do when having fun in a group. Then Dad and Uncle Will would hitch up their horses, swap children, and start the three-hour drive back home. Looking back, I feel sure that Dad and Uncle Will, as well as Mother and Aunt Effie, were not doing this just to humor us kids but because they believed it would be an educational experience for us. And indeed it was. Perhaps, in this day of the automobile, some people will think that this exchange of kids was a rather trivial exercise, but far from it. These were horse-and-buggy days, before hardtop road or even gravel roads, when horsepower was real horse power, not gasoline horsepower. The trip from Pike Hill to the top of Orange Heights and back would take from five-and-a-half to six hours, some of it over very steep roads, and it was hard work for a horse to pull a buggy for that many hours. Also, Uncle Will's cattle had to be milked and the other animals and chores tended to at both ends of the trip. I have never ceased to be grateful to Uncle Will, my dad, my mother, and Aunt Effie for being so understanding of a small boy's heart's desires.

It was great fun to be at Uncle Will's. The farmhouse was located against a slightly rising hillside and faced east, with a long view of wooded country. A traditional horse barn was connected to the house. This was a common occurrence on Vermont farms in the horse-and-buggy days, and a practical one too. The horses were kept in straight stalls. Behind the horses in the stable floor was a "scuttle hole," with a square plank cover with a ring in the top. By grasping the ring and pulling up the cover, we could uncover the scuttle hole, through which we could easily fork or sweep the horse manure and other residues into a manure pit. There each offering was eagerly greeted by the pigs. Later the manure would be disposed of by spreading it on the land for fertilizer. In addition to enjoying their share of skim milk from the dairy cows, the pigs constantly rooted the manure and salvaged any undigested corn or oats which had been fed the horses. This constant rooting of the manure by the pigs kept it from heating or losing its fertility, and it also minimized the smell. Vermont farmers were, and still are, masters in the science of energy utilization.

At Uncle Will's the kitchen was the center of the home. Access to the kitchen from the horse barn was up several steps through a short passageway that opened directly into the kitchen. Aunt Effie kept her kitchen immaculate. It always smelled of savory cooking odors lightly tinged with good old horse-barn smell. In winter and early spring the added smells of heavy clothing, overalls, boots, and heavy socks made a special contribution of their own. This combination of odors cannot be described—it can only be experienced. It smelled like home, and a lovely home it was. After a long day in the sun or the snow it was a delicious haven. The sense was strong of family, comfort, and home. For a youngster, it was a security blanket beyond compare.

Uncle Will had one of the first registered Jersey herds in his area. It was great fun to be in the cow barn at chore time and even more fun to be part of the action there. During my late summer visits, the cows were in the barn only at milking time. The rest of the time, night or day, they roamed a large pasture. One of the cows wore a bell to indicate where the herd was, but since the pasture was large and partly covered by trees, the process of finding the cows when milking time came was a job for which youngsters with strong legs and eager hearts were especially fitted. We loved it. Usually the cows were easy to find, but sometimes—perverse creatures that they are—they would seem to delight in hiding themselves and making our task more difficult. That was even more fun. It was a challenge and a game. Eventually, we would hear the cowbell. There is nothing quite like that sound, a lonely kind of sound in the quiet countryside, that denoted the end of our search and the accomplishment of our mission.

Today in Vermont, the old hilly, partly wooded pastures are gone, for the most part. Many of them have reverted to brush and woodland since they no longer fit the farm economy of our day. Instead, the cow pastures are usually meadows or rolling fields close to the barn, where heavy tractors and other machinery can be used, where they can be carefully tended and heavily fertilized, causing lush growth and discouraging much walking by the cows to fill their stomachs. This is not by accident, but by a design that fits the modern trend toward larger milking cows, predominantly Holsteins, that produce greater quantities of milk with proportionately less butterfat. These smaller, well-fertilized pastures keep the cows from walking off their energy, thus lowering their milk production. The cow today is a manufacturing plant in every sense of the word.

In the old days the farmers used to separate the cream from the milk, market the cream, and feed the skim milk to the pigs and calves. Today, in our nutrition-conscious age, skim milk sells in the market for almost as much as whole milk. The heavy emphasis on low fat and cholesterol has made it possible for vegetable oils, of the margarine type, to compete and even to take over much of the butterfat market. Perhaps we are approaching a day when the cream will be fed to the pigs and the skim milk marketed!

Even the Jerseys that have evolved are much larger animals, with greater capacity for volume of production. The former Elbert S. Brigham farm in Franklin County is an example. During the 1930s and 1940s his Jersey cows looked nearly as large as Holsteins and maintained a world's record for production and butterfat content. But those big cows of the Brigham farm—like cows on most modern farms—were not fitted for the old-fashioned hillside pastures, where the small Jerseys climbed hillsides sometimes so steep that the cows could only graze horizontally around the hill. Once it was common to see from Vermont highways the circular paths made by this constant horizontal grazing. Now we rarely see them. The hillside pastures have gone back to brush and trees. Instead, we see the cattle grazing or lying down chewing their cuds in the smaller, level meadows beside the roads. This is certainly more efficient, but it is not half so much fun getting the cows at milking time as it was in the hillside pastures far from home!

The haying season is, in some ways, the most exciting time on the farm. I was not privileged to enjoy the haying at Uncle Will's, for when I was eight years old my father got me a job on the Kelley farm on West Hill in Barre Town, and I worked on that farm, as well as others, during the summer haying until I turned eighteen and went away to law school. But I continued my trips to Uncle Will's at other times of the year. Usually I arrived during late summer, after haying was over, when in addition to sharing myriad other activities, my cousins and I would pick wild raspberries and blackberries in prodigious quantities and take them by horse and express wagon to East Barre, where we peddled them from house to house. And I was almost always able to get there during the spring school vacation. By that time the snow had usually started to melt and settle a bit in the daytime, crusting over the surface each night as the temperature fell below freezing.

Life on the farm was never dull. My cousin Leland (John L., as he was usually called), who was about my age, contrived all sorts of fun. Usually when I arrived in the spring, the sap would be running and the sugaring process in full swing. We helped empty the sap buckets into the big wooden tub on the sled that carried the sap to the sugarhouse where it could be boiled down into syrup. For this task, oxen were used to draw the sled because they could maneuver in the deep snow. Oxen could wade through snow up to their bellies quietly with no fuss, while horses tended to become excited and begin plunging.

Each spring, Leland and I trained a new pair of calves to wear a yoke and draw a sled as the oxen did. This was great fun. Uncle Will had made Leland a small yoke and sled, and in the process of training the calves we were often dragged over much of the terrain as the calves tried to escape from our training. But we always succeeded in the end. By the time our two weeks' school vacation was over, we could drive the calves as a team with ease and had a pair of young potential oxen for Uncle Will. All of Uncle Will's stock were trained to be led by a halter, and many of them were really pets.

We helped with all kinds of farm chores, including the milking night and morning. Uncle Will didn't have a milking machine then—the cows were still milked by hand—but he did have a hand-powered DeLaval cream separator, and again I was allowed to turn the crank that furnished the power to separate the cream from the milk. The skim milk frothed up like a milk shake and was a real treat to drink while still warm. I also helped feed the calves and pigs. A cow stable has its own special smells. The odors from the cattle, the hay, the silage, and the grain, as well as that special component—cow manure—all blend into a smell that is one of so many other impressions of early farm life that are pleasant to recall. This was fun, not work. As the number of Vermonters born on farms has declined, so has one of the best educational opportunities for growing kids.

We had no radio, television, or newspapers. The telephone,

however, was a quite adequate communication system. The system was a much less sophisticated one than we have today, but it worked. All the chores had to be finished, all hands washed and hair combed, and everyone seated at the breakfast table to await the daily seven o'clock call from "Central." This call rang simultaneously in every home on the system. When the call came, one of us would go to the dining-room wall and pick up the telephone receiver while the rest of us went on eating, waiting with eager anticipation for a report on the news. "Central" would first announce the correct time. I've often wondered where she got it and how she knew it was correct, but every watch and clock was religiously set by that time. Then she would tell us what the weather was and was going to be. She was usually about as right as the weather forecasters today, and she was never taken to task when her projections proved incorrect. Then "Central" would recite the news of the area, which she had collected from listening in on numerous telephone calls among the subscribers and in other ways unknown. The news was followed by a pause, which was a signal for any subscriber to pitch in with anything of interest that had not been included in the "Central's" rendering of the "official" news. The news thus pretty well covered the whole spectrum of happenings in the area: who was ill and with what; who had died, if anyone; who had visitors or was traveling; upcoming community events, church socials, and meetings; upcoming town meetings; and to some extent, what the issues were. Everyone on the system was alerted by the seven o'clock ring, and everyone listened unless prevented by reasons beyond their control. For the time it was a good system, and it worked remarkably well.

This telephone system was a cooperative system built, owned, and operated by the subscribers on an extremely cost-effective basis. Each subscriber was responsible for supervision and repair of the part of the line that ran from his house to that of the next subscriber. To make it easier to discover and repair trouble spots when they developed, the line for the most part followed the road rather than the shortest distance between two points.

The roads were handled in much the same way. The road commissioner, appointed by the board of selectmen, was officially responsible for building and maintaining the roads, but the custom was to make arrangements with farmers to take care of certain stretches of road for agreed-upon compensation, either to be paid in cash or credited against the farmer's taxes.

The schools in the town were the old-fashioned district one-room schools. A town would have several districts within its large geographical area. My cousins went to the one-room schoolhouse in what was called the Rhobee neighborhood, about two-and-a-half miles from their home. They walked both ways and were expected to be in school no matter what the weather. They had to make their way through big snowfalls many times, since these back roads on Pike Hill had a lower priority than the main roads and were not plowed but rolled with the old-fashioned snow rollers, which often could not get around the whole town in one day.

As in many other Vermont towns of those days, there was a strong cohesion to the community life of the area. The church was the social as well as the religious center. Tradition, too, played a large part in the lives of these people. Tradition had in many respects the force of unwritten law, and was indeed a force stronger than the law. Fiercely independent in thought and action, people nevertheless recognized that they had a social duty toward others, particularly in time of trouble. The rest of the time they minded their own business. But when they were wanted or needed, they were always there. If someone was sick or disabled and without hired help, neighbors promptly took over his chores and, if necessary, planted or harvested his crops as the occasion required. Where illness was prolonged, neighbors would drop by to "set awhile" with the patient or with the troubled family. If a barn or house burned, the neighbors formed barn raisings to restore it. People cared. This helped to make the isolation and loneliness of farm life more tolerable.

People set their own standards of good farming, as well as of morality. If a farmer failed to mow his fence lines, he dropped a peg or two in public esteem. If he became shiftless or lazy, he dropped many pegs in public esteem. When such a person couldn't buy food or clothing for his family, he went to the overseer of the poor. From the overseer he would receive, not cash, but a written order to the town merchant for a specified dollar value of groceries or other goods. But he would also be ordered to appear "next Monday" at seven o'clock at the town woodlot. After working a day or two with ax and saw, he would usually decide that there was a better way to make a living and would somehow quickly find a job that relieved him from such indignity.

At one time a majority of the towns had these lots. Usually, the incentive to restore a bit of lost prestige was as much responsible for mending one's ways as was the hard work on the town woodlot. When, on the other hand, the cause of the inability to provide necessities arose from illness, accident, or mental incapacity, the neighbors took over and solved the problem in some practical way without sacrificing the recipient's dignity. Local opinion was a powerful stimulant to good morals as well as to good farming and good habits. This approach did not cure all social problems, but for its time it succeeded as well as, and usually better than, the welfare system of our industrial age.

As young people were born into this system of values, they came quite naturally to understand its merits and to accept its validity. They didn't try to change the world, but they did try hard to improve their education and skills and to "get ahead." They believed, as my father often said, that "it's not good enough to be good; you must be good for something."

How did the kids feel about life on the farm? Was it hard work? Yes. Was it fun? Definitely. And one more thing is certain: children of those days truly participated in running the farm. They were important, and they knew it. No one had to pat them on the head to tell them they were important in the scheme of things. Nor did they spend any time searching for their identity, as so many young people do today.

They learned early that life on a dairy farm calls for good organization. Good organization calls for a boss. The children had one, more than one: mother in the house and father outside. No one questioned the rightness of their authority, much less the kids. There were no runaway shelters for protesting children, and no runaways to be sheltered. The rare case of parental abuse would become quickly known in the neighborhood and was just as quickly corrected by the weight of public opinion or, if necessary, neighborhood action.

Uncle Will and Aunt Effie had five children: Bernard, Bernice, Evelyn, John Leland, and Shirley. I loved them all. Uncle Will and Aunt Effie gave them a good education and a good "bringing up," all from a hillside Jersey dairy farm. All my cousins turned out to be able, talented, self-sufficient citizens of excellent character. They contributed much to my outlook on life, and I deeply cherish my relationships with them.

3

My Allen Street Years

*. . . Billy Milne was a born leader. He under-
stood boys, and we admired, respected, and loved
him. In the basement of the Baptist church, he
taught us the meaning of citizenship, patriotism,
moral conduct, and the proper attitude toward
others.*

My father was admitted to the Vermont bar while he was serving
as principal of the Island Pond High School. Upon his admission, he
gave up his job as principal and moved with his family to East Barre.
I was born there on November 7, 1900. After practicing law in East
Barre for approximately a year and a half, he moved his family to
Barre City, and there he established his office on the second floor of
the Wood Block on North Main Street (which is the building now
occupied by Ormsby's store and the First Vermont Bank). He purchased a house and several acres of land on Allen Street on West Hill
on the outskirts of the city, about a mile from the center of the city.

Although at different times my family lived in three different
houses in Barre, I always think of the Allen Street house as my
home. I lived there from the time I was a year old until I went to law
school in 1918. The two-story house, built just before the turn of the
century, had eight rooms—four downstairs and four upstairs. A long
veranda with a spool railing ran the length of the front of the house.

The barn behind the house, another two-story building, housed Mary Ann, Dad's driving horse, two cows, two buggies, and a sleigh, as well as several tons of hay in the loft above. Beside it was a small hen house that housed twenty or thirty laying hens and a Rhode Island Red rooster, who each morning loudly proclaimed the beginning of the day. Dad's garden was on the rear of the lot, where each year he planted all kinds of vegetables and introduced each of his children to the virtues of hard work. I can remember him, bare-chested and wearing his derby hat, hoeing the weeds with great vigor while sweat ran down each side of his red face. The garden furnished a surprising amount of the food consumed by his large, growing family. Although it was not pretentious, it was a happy home that fit naturally into the neighborhood. The house is still there, although the neighborhood has greatly changed.

We had one luxury—indoor plumbing and a bathroom facility. It was shared by Dad and Mother, their six children, and occasionally by a hired girl or visitor, but it was still a luxury. The outdoor kind, to which I had become accustomed at Gramp's farm, was still quite common.

The Allen Street property was bounded on its back line by a pasture that was part of the adjacent Allen farm and on its front, directly across the street, by a large field, that was also part of the Allen farm. The field in front of the house, the pasture in back, and the adjoining cultivated land all included hills of differing degrees of slope that were great for tobogganing and skiing. We spent many winter days tobogganing when the snow was crusted, and many more days trying to ski downhill with skis made from barrel staves, to which we attached simple leather straps to hold our feet in place. We spent more time picking ourselves up out of the snow than we did on skis. Allen Street itself was very steep in part, as was Prospect Street, with which it intersected, and we slid down these streets quite recklessly and happily on traverse sleds. On clear cold nights when the moon was out, we organized sledding parties. After an evening sliding down those hills and pulling the traverse back up the hills, we had no trouble sleeping.

The Allen farm was operated on lease by William Rogers, who had three grown sons, Charles, Leslie, and Eldon, and a stepson, Clarence Carpenter, all living on the farm. I spent many hours and days there, sometimes playing with the boys but more often helping with the farm work, which in itself was fun. In those days farmers controlled the weeds, or tried to, by hand hoeing and horse cultivators. The Allen farm was covered with "witch" grass, the hardest known variety of garden or field weed to control or eradicate.

Mr. Rogers usually planted six to eight acres of field corn to feed his cattle every year, and with the boys and Mr. Rogers I walked many miles back and forth hoeing these rows of corn, trying to keep the witch grass down. In between the rows the horse cultivator would be run, but between the stalks of corn the witch grass could only be reached by hand hoeing. We chopped the stuff and covered it with dirt as we walked those unending miles up and down the rows, and as soon as we turned our backs it seemed as though the weeds would promptly reappear. What a boon to weeding are liquid chemicals to the farmers of today! They have been saved the back-breaking work of hand hoeing for days on end, but I'll bet they don't learn as many swear words as we did.

The Allen Street house was considered to be within walking distance of the center of Barre, and all members of the family walked to and from the city whenever there was occasion to go "to town." This constant walking was taken for granted and built strong legs, lungs, hearts, and bodies.

If all this exercise failed to provide those results, we had a hospital in Barre, but in my younger days hardly anybody went there as a patient except for surgery or as an accident victim. Childbirth was almost always at home, and so were most terminally ill patients. I believe that my brothers and sisters and I were all born at home. Gradually the arrangements for treating illness changed, however, and by 1920 it was common practice for many kinds of illness to be treated at the hospital.

Our family physician was Dr. John H. Woodruff. Those were the days when doctors made house calls, and when anyone in the family was ill, it was always comforting to see Dr. Woodruff come driving into the yard behind one of his beautiful driving horses. I used to count it a privilege to be allowed to go out and help him hitch and blanket his horse. My feeling about doctors was that they were the wisest men anywhere and knew everything about the human body, and that if you could get the doctor in time, he could surely cure whatever was wrong. Even the medicinal smell of Dr. Woodruff remains in my solid store of memories.

Dr. Woodruff, and before him Dr. Chandler, performed several minor operations on our kitchen table, some of which required etherizing the patient, and all were carried out without untoward incident. These were always exciting occasions. It took a man with rugged character and physique to respond to the many demands made upon a physician in those days. He was expected to come, and did, in any kind of weather, even heavy drifting snow or howling blizzard. He had to be, and was, a scientist, a physician, a surgeon, a psychiatrist, and a friend. A physician was not allowed the luxury of being ill himself, and he almost never was unless it was a major illness.

As children, my brothers and sisters and I were constantly thinking up things to do for fun. One of them was planning and putting on plays. We used to get the kids in our immediate neighborhood together to plan a play, and often the planning was more fun that the execution. The hayloft in our barn was perfect for a theater when it was empty of hay in the summer. The writing and the production were a bit crude, but the execution, we thought, was quite commendable. In any event, we carried them out with much enthusiasm. We would argue over whether to charge one cent or two cents for admission. In the beginning we more often used buttons or safety pins, but this was before we had worked our way up in the difficult world of the theater. An even more difficult exercise was to decide who was to be in the cast, a ticket seller, a manager, or a business consultant. Those not chosen for one of those functioning categories found themselves members of the audience. This was considered something of a humiliation, but those to whom this lot fell were allowed free admission. For our audience we relied heavily on our parents and the kids from outside our immediate neighborhood. But our parents were our best customers. They purchased many tickets for admission but rarely attended our performances, which did not bother us, particularly as the tickets had been paid for.

All of us children were expected to do our share in caring for the animals on the place, which included two cows, a couple of pigs, a driving horse, and hens. We also helped care for the large lawn and the garden in summer, and we shoveled snow in the winter. The girls did their share of housework in addition to working outside. Dad parceled out the jobs from time to time, but we kids often traded and swapped jobs as occasion permitted.

When I was ten, and when I was not working on a farm during the summer, one of my jobs was to drive the two family cows to and from the pasture each morning and night. The pasture was located on the Perrin farm on Upper Prospect Street about two miles from home, so this job added about eight miles of walking in addition to all the other walking I did each day.

After following that routine for some time, I undertook to train one of the cows to let me ride on her back and save a lot of what I considered unnecessary walking. While this, I may say, was obviously a brilliant idea, it was not a complete success. On one occasion during the training process enough rumpus was created that both cows took off and bolted through Mrs. Ranney's greatly prized flower garden. Needless to say, this performance wrought havoc with Mrs. Ranney's flowers. Things happened so fast and furiously that somehow I didn't get a chance to apologize. The next day, she dressed me down in no uncertain terms, winding up her tirade by asking, "What in the world is your father thinking of, sending a child like you to drive the cows? Why doesn't he drive them himself?" She later claimed that my answer was, "Well, you know he doesn't do any work. He's only a lawyer." Apparently this defense tickled her enough that she forgave me, and we remained friends. But after that episode I gave up training the cows to be ridden, except at home or in the pasture where no damage could be done.

The summer I was eight years old, my father arranged a job for me on the John Kelley farm. The farm was about two and a half miles from our Allen Street home. My pay was to be twenty-five cents a day and three meals. I was to continue to sleep at home, get up at 4:30 A.M. and walk to the Kelley farm, being sure to be there by 5:30 A.M. at the latest. I was much excited about the opportunity and did my level best to make good. The most unpleasant part was being pulled out of bed by my mother at 4:30 A.M. and sent on my way. This often made me wonder what I had thought was so great about my job! But that feeling never lasted long. As I set out on my walk each morning, with the air crisp and clear, the sun shining, and the bobolinks singing, I would soon recover my sense of well-being. Six days a week I would meet the Paquet brothers, Joe and Fred, who lived on and owned a dairy farm near the Kelley farm, as they were driving to their blacksmith shop at the corner of Merchant and Summer streets. The Paquet brothers always drove a smart, snappy-looking pair of Morgan horses, and they presented a beautiful sight trotting along the level road where we usually met. One could almost set one's watch by the regularity of their appearance at 4:45 A.M. at nearly the same spot. The Paquet brothers had a large herd of Holstein cows, and by the time we had met on the road, they had already milked them, finished the other chores, eaten breakfast, and started for a day's work in the shop. Something about that regular early morning meeting brightened the day a bit for me. The Paquet brothers are a good example of the French-Canadian people who came to Vermont and found a way to successfully operate a dairy farm while holding another full-time job at the same time.

When I arrived at the Kelley farm, my job was to groom the three work horses and the Morgan driving horse. I also performed a variety of other duties—namely the boring ones, the ones the oldsters did not want to do.

Mr. Kelley was an exacting boss. Frequently, he would come out to the horse barn as I was finishing my grooming and run his hand along both sides of the back of each horse. If dandruff residue adhered to his hand, I had to groom the horse all over again. By this time the milking would have ended, and I would drive the cows to pasture, a chore for which my experience driving cows at home had well prepared me. One of the pastures was a rented one, just above the Morrison farm, about a mile from Kelley's. Around four-thirty in the afternoon I again collected the cows from pasture. Adding these two trips together with the morning and evening walk I made to and from my home, I walked a total of nearly nine miles each day, not counting any additional walking I did daily in pursuit of my other duties.

The next year, Mr. Kelley asked me to work for him again, and I promptly accepted. He raised my pay without being asked from twenty-five cents a day to two dollars per week for six days' work, and I was very proud. I had it made. I experienced the satisfaction and confidence that come from knowing that your services are wanted and appreciated, an important requisite in the education of boys and girls. But I began even then to understand that people who work solely for money never achieve their full potential. Money is important for many reasons, one of which is that it is evidence of your own worth and ability. But that's not enough. We need the inner drive that is essential to long-term success, and we need to get joy out of the work itself.

In my second summer at Kelley's, my responsibilities were increased. For example, I was assigned the responsibility of hitching up and unhitching Mrs. Kelley's driving horse and keeping her buggy clean and polished, and the wheels greased. I was permitted to drive the horse that pulled the hay rake in the fields and to help mow away the hay when it was brought into the barn from the fields. At times I was allowed to pitch on to the load in the fields. A hired man would work on one side of the hayload and I worked on the other, picking up the hay from the tumbles and lifting it to the top of the load. Mr. Kelley balanced on top of the load, distributing the bundles as they came up to make a square load that would be secure enough to stay on while it was transported to the barn. Mr. Kelley kept up a running exposition on how fast he could pitch on a load, giving specific examples of occasions when these feats of strength and speed happened. I finally caught on that most of these stories were fictitious, but they served to make both the hired man and me pitch hay faster. That was a type of leadership to which I was unaccustomed. It worked though, after a fashion.

That year I also took over the task of feeding the pigs and cleaning their pens. I had more than thirty pigs to look after, plus I still groomed the horses and drove the cows to and from pasture. I also still turned the grindstone to sharpen the hand scythes and the sections of cutter bar on the horse-drawn mowing machine. The third year, Mr. Kelley wanted me again. I accepted and received another raise, which brought my salary to $2.50 per week. Among my new responsibilities was learning to milk cows by hand, a talent that served me well later in life, when I owned a dairy farm of my own. I was sure I was on my way to success in the world. It was still just as hard to get up in the morning at four-thirty, but that year I achieved one of my principal goals. I was allowed all alone to take old Dan, one of the work horses, and drive two miles with the express wagon to the village of South Barre for grain. The grain store was operated by Guy Howard as an adjunct to his general purpose store. The grain was stored in the ell of the building, which in later years became the post office. It was unusual for a boy of ten to be given the responsibility of driving a horse and express wagon all alone, and I was a proud lad to drive up to the platform, present a note from Mr. Kelley, and have my wagon loaded with several one-hundred-pound bags of grain. I tried to act nonchalant about the whole affair, but I had suspicions that Mr. Howard guessed how excited and proud I was to be entrusted with such heavy responsibilities.

In late summer, when the days shortened, I dreaded my trips home at night after work. By seven o'clock or seven-thirty the quarter-mile stretch through the Allen woods had become a nightmare. In the darkness and shadows, in my childish imagination, I saw lions, bears, and desperate villains lurking behind every tree. My heart pounded like a triphammer, and sometimes it was almost more than I could do to keep walking on toward home.

On nights when Mr. and Mrs. Kelley attended Grange meetings in South Barre, they would ask me to sleep at the farm in case anything happened that needed attention. I would be alone, of course. The Grange always seemed to meet on nights when there were severe thunderstorms. I was deathly afraid of thunder and lightning. With every crash of thunder, I ducked under the bedcovers and cringed in fear. I was greatly ashamed of myself but could not get over my fears. That was part of growing up, however, and when morning came, I looked forward with excitement to another day on the farm.

During the next few years I worked summers for different farmers in the area. I hayed, threshed, hoed corn, and hauled wood. The summer after I turned sixteen, I got a job on a farm owned by Irving Bates, a successful farmer who lived a couple of miles above East Barre. Bates was a well-known Guernsey breeder who lived on a back road leading from East Barre Village to Washington. I used my bicycle to get to and from the farm, where I stayed during the week. On Saturday nights I came home in order to have each Sunday with my family.

Mr. Bates kept a Belgian stallion. It was not long before I was able to prove to him that I could safely handle the stallion, and then he turned the feeding and care of this horse over to me. The stallion was used for breeding purposes by many farmers living in the area. Even as late as 1916, horses were still furnishing the major part of the horsepower on Vermont farms, and quite a few Vermont farmers bred their mares to raise their own horse replacements. The Belgian stallion was in great demand, and Mr. Bates soon allowed me to assist in the handling of the stallion during the breeding process— hardly a task for an inexperienced youngster. Mr. Bates also had an ox team composed of one steer and his very special Guernsey bull. They made a great team, and Mr. Bates taught me to drive them. I plowed and harrowed many acres of ground with that pair, and they never gave me a bit of trouble. The next year, however, during the winter when the ox team was not being used, the bull tackled Mr. Bates in the barnyard and injured him so badly that he never fully recovered.

While still in my early teens I had my first experience in breaking colts all by myself. Arthur Campbell raised Shetland ponies. They were kept in the barn attached to the Campbell home (which is now the Country House restaurant on North Main Street in Barre. The large party room in the rear of the restaurant was formerly the stable where the ponies were kept.) Laurence Campbell, son of Arthur Campbell, was my classmate in school and a close friend, so when I was ten or eleven years old, Mr. Campbell worked out an arrangement with my father and me which was to give me much joy. Each year he would bring me a two-year-old unbroken pony colt that I would keep for a year until it was thoroughly broken to ride and drive. Then I would return it, and he would give me another. This arrangement benefited us both. I got a pony to ride and drive, and he got free training services. For Christmas one year my father presented me with a pony-size sleigh made by Mr. Benedict, the local cabinetmaker, and a pony harness made by Mr. Parker, the local harnessmaker.

During this period my father kept a driving horse, Mary Ann, which he used primarily for trips he made in connection with his law practice. Whenever it was convenient, he took me with him on these trips, some of which took several hours and some all day. Those were happy and instructive occasions. If Dad knew he had a trip to make on a certain day, he would take the mare with him when he went to the office in the morning and hitch her to a telephone pole beside the sidewalk in front of the office in the Wood Block. The mare had a very uncertain disposition. When people walked by her on the sidewalk she would squeal and kick the front axle of the buggy. This attracted a lot of attention from passers-by, and frightened many of them. People soon formed the habit of giving her a wide berth as they passed by. Another idiosyncrasy she had was the way she approached her task of going up steep Hooker Hill on Prospect Street on the way home. A wooden bridge straddled the river at the approach to the hill. Invariably, unless she was strongly restrained, she would start into a gallop just as she came to the bridge and stay in a gallop until she reached the top of the hill. When she went across the bridge at a gallop, the loose planks made a terrific noise. Frequently, people unacquainted with her thought she was running away. I don't know whether her purpose was to make the noise or, more likely, to be able to pull the buggy up the steep hill with plenty of momentum.

During my preteen years, as later, I made a practice of hanging around my father's office in the Wood Block and trying to make myself useful. I swept the floor, cleaned spittoons, ran errands, and did the best I could to be of sufficient use to be allowed to stay there. When I was around twelve years old, I formed a little club of boys my age. Our clubroom was an unlighted back room used for storage. I was delegated the task of writing the bylaws because I was the only lawyer's son in the club. Among the bylaws were requirements such as: "There shall be no unnecessary swearing," "There shall be no unnecessary fighting," and "Meetings shall last only a reasonable length of time." My father found a copy of the bylaws patiently pecked out on an old discarded Olliver typewriter and was sufficiently amused to show them to his friend George Tilden, a local shoe merchant. Tilden was equally amused. He made several copies of the bylaws and passed them up and down Main Street among the merchants. They in turn passed the story along until it was pretty well known around town, at least in the downtown area. Shortly, my ears were burning, and I was greatly humiliated. I couldn't see anything funny about it. The words *necessary* and *reasonable* are core words in the law. Obviously, necessary fighting would be "reasonable," as would necessary "swearing"! Later, when I was in general practice, I often thought of those bylaws while arguing before juries that my client's conduct was "reasonable."

Sometime between nine and ten years of age, I discovered the Boy Scouts. It added a happy new dimension to my life. The Boy Scout movement, which started in Great Britain, was very strong in Scotland. William (Billy) Milne, a native of Aberdeen, had been a dedicated scouter in Scotland and had served as a scoutmaster there. When he came to Barre to work in the granite sheds, he missed this activity and decided to start a Boy Scout troop here. He was a member of the Baptist church and persuaded a number of his fellow parishioners to join with him in sponsoring this new troop. As a result, in 1909, he became the first scoutmaster in the United States. A beautiful Rock of Ages monument in front of the Baptist church on Washington Street in Barre now records the formation of that troop as the first in the country. This was before the Boy Scouts were chartered by the United States Congress, so Billy Milne was free to run the troop according to his own rules. Fortunately, I was permitted to join even though I was only nine. The minimum age for Boy Scouts was set at twelve soon after. The Boy Scout movement was dedicated to teaching boys of immature years the basic principles of good conduct, good citizenship, crafts, the skills of outdoor life, and self-discipline. It has been a great force for good in the past in this country, and Billy Milne was a born leader. He understood boys, and we admired, respected, and loved him. In the basement of the Baptist church, he taught us the meaning of citizenship, patriotism, moral conduct, and the proper attitude toward others.

Billy Milne also taught us the methods and fun of outdoor camping. He took us on overnight trips and taught us about the woods, the trees, the sun, the sky, and the interrelationship of these things to each other and to God's plan. Shortly after the Barre Baptist Boy Scout Troop was organized, legislation was passed in Congress to establish the Boy Scouts of America on a national basis and to provide a formal method of granting charters to individual clubs around the country. At that time or shortly thereafter, a troop was formed in my own church, the Hedding Methodist church in Barre, and I joined that troop.

The Boy Scout movement was intentionally competitive. One of the ways I participated in the competition was by learning how to make fire without matches. (My wife says that I can't make fire now *with* matches!) This competition took place after I had transferred to the new troop at the Methodist church. After a number of lessons in which all the boys were taught how to make fire by rubbing two sticks together, a contest was set up that in effect lasted from January to April. We boys were to select the best wood and practice the technique of producing a fire, and then in April we would compete in the basement of the Methodist church to see who could make fire this way in the shortest time.

This contest kept me busy all winter. I roamed the hills around Barre hunting for different kinds of wood to find exactly the right combination. The technique we were taught was fairly simple, but getting just the right kind of wood was not. We were taught to use a bow—a simple piece of flexible wood such as you would use in a bow and arrow. The string to the bow was a piece of rawhide. Then we fashioned a round piece of dry wood like a spindle and a flat piece of wood twelve to eighteen inches long and four to six inches wide. In this flat piece we would gouge out a hole near one edge and then cut a notch adjacent to the hole. One loop of rawhide was wrapped around the spindle, and then the spindle was inserted in the hole in the flat piece. In this manner, we could pull the bow back and forth, which turned the spindle. The resulting friction created small grains of sawdust, and if they were produced at the right speeds and with the right kind of wood, they would be so hot that eventually they would burst into flame. In my explorations and practice during the winter I found just the right combination of woods to make the sawdust burst into flame quickly. I can't even imagine how many times I roamed the hills, how many different woods I tried, or how many different bows I constructed during those winter months. I found that a cedar rail from an old, well-seasoned cedar fence for the flat piece and a dead branch from a cedar tree for the spindle made the best combination. I'm sure the scoutmaster could easily have told us all this, but he was setting up a situation to make us discover it by the long task of searching, testing, and discovering. My work paid off, and I won the contest.

4

My Schooling

*I came home on the train, traveling from Montreal
on the old Central Vermont Railroad in a car that
had an observation deck. The weather was mild
and warm, the sun was shining, and Vermont was
in its greenest glory. I have never forgotten how
those hills, fields, pastures, rivers, and lakes
looked, and how lucky I felt to live in Vermont.*

My school experience began at the Church Street School in
Barre, when I entered the first grade. The school building was located next easterly from the Congregational church. (The building
still stands but has not been used for a school for many years and is
currently used as an office by the Barre Granite Association.) Miss
Tracy, the teacher of the first three grades, was a strong disciplinarian, but she liked children and they liked her. Doubtless we learned
something in those early classes, but for the life of me I couldn't tell
you what, except, perhaps, that it pays to behave. While at Church
Street I walked to school. There were no school buses or other public
school transportation at that time, and as far as I can remember, all
the other pupils walked too.

After three years at Church Street School, I entered the fourth
grade at Matthewson School on Jefferson Street. Those of us who
lived at greater distance from the school carried our lunches. Usually
I carried a couple of sandwiches, which were stored in lockers in the

hallways. The hallways were not heated, and in the winter by lunchtime the sandwiches were often frozen.

It was while I was attending Matthewson that my friendship for Laurence Campbell began and matured. He often invited me to walk with him to his house, where I would spend an hour or so before walking home. The ponies that his father had there were part of the inducement.

When I was in the sixth grade at Matthewson my father arranged with the principal of Goddard Seminary that I should be allowed to take typing lessons in one of the seminary's regular classes. Goddard Seminary was located on a hill that was an extension of Seminary Street and was a private institution furnishing high-school-level courses. It later became Goddard College, now located in Plainfield, Vermont. After eating an early breakfast, I would walk the mile and a half or so from home to the seminary and attend a typing class that began at 7 A.M. The class lasted about forty minutes. Then I would rush to Matthewson School for the opening of school there. I learned enough at Goddard so that I continued taking typing lessons when I was later in high school in New Richmond, Wisconsin, and there I won a first prize in typing offered by the Remington Typewriter Company.

In later years I came to know how wise my father was to insist that I acquire this skill. In law school I found the ability to type invaluable. There I typed up my lecture notes, thus making them available for repeated review and study. For forty years after graduating from law school I rarely typed at all, yet when I retired, the ability came back to me at once, just like riding a bicycle.

In the sixth grade at Matthewson, I received the worst licking I ever received in school. It was in spring, and I had walked home for lunch that day. As I started back to school, I noticed great clouds of smoke coming from the grass and wooded area of Upper Prospect Street. I ran over to that vicinity and found a grass fire raging over a large area and threatening the nearby houses and the woods as well. It seemed natural to pitch in and help the small group of men who were fighting the fire. We successfully put the fire out, but by that time I was at least an hour late for the afternoon session. I did not realize how black my face was, and when I entered the classroom, my classmates broke into loud laughter. This angered the teacher, and she told me to report to the cloakroom at once, where she joined me and administered punishment with a vengeance. I tried to explain the circumstances, but the teacher would not listen. I was crushed by the feeling of utter helplessness and despair.

I entered Spaulding High School when I was fourteen years old. In my freshman and sophomore years there, I competed in prize speaking, which was a popular part of the curriculum in those days. I won a second prize in my freshman year and a first prize in my sophomore year. Looking back, I realize that this type of activity was then and could now be a valuable part of high school activities. Teaching young people to stand on their feet and talk to a public gathering improves their confidence and gives them a boost along the road to good communication skills. Once, when I was much older, I asked Dr. Ernest Martin Hopkins, former president of Dartmouth College, what he considered to be the principal purpose of a college education. He replied, "To make men articulate." This answer surprised and puzzled me at the time, but thinking it over later, I came to understand what he meant. If one is to be articulate, one must first have something to say—a fact, an argument, an idea, an analysis, or even a personal experience—then one must be able to organize one's thoughts so that they are clearly put together and perceived in one's mind. Finally, one must build the confidence to speak both in public and in private with clarity and poise. Public speaking helps to make men and women articulate. This is what I gained most from my first two years in high school.

During my junior year my father sent me to New Richmond, Wisconsin, to attend high school, as my brother Ralph had done before me. Dad believed in pushing boys out of the nest early to broaden their viewpoints and to teach them to begin making more decisions for themselves. One of the reasons he chose New Richmond was because his brother, my uncle Frank, lived there and could keep an eagle eye on me. I did not live with my uncle though, but roomed for the school year at the home of Mrs. Epley, a kindly widow who rented out rooms. I boarded there, too, and earned part of the cost of my room and board by taking care of her furnace.

I also took care of the furnaces in the post office and the Congregational church. The furnaces were completely unlike each other, and they were antiquated as well. Hence, I became something of an expert in antiquated furnaces at an early age. The church furnace was fired by wood. I do not mean sticks, but four-foot logs. The church was not heated except on Sunday. I had to get up at four o'clock in the morning on Sundays and start the fire in order to get the church warm enough for the services, which began at 10 A.M. In addition to firing the furnace, I had to ring the church bell by pulling a rope that hung from the bell into the foyer of the church. The bells needed to be rung at a quarter to ten and at five minutes to ten. Since I was simultaneously tending my temperamental fire in the basement, I came upstairs to ring the bell in my overalls. Several complaints were made to the minister that I was not appropriately dressed to appear in the foyer of the church as the congregation was gathering. I solved the problem by keeping my second-best suit in the cellar and changing from work clothes when it was time to ring the bell. I thought it was a stupid complaint. I couldn't see that a difference in dress had anything to do with religion, but I had to comply because I needed the money. I wondered if it was this sort of thing that my father was trying to teach me by sending me to New Richmond.

The previous year, my brother Ralph had distinguished himself on the high school football team. The team had an outstanding season, and Ralph was picked for the All-State Championship Team. Ralph played center, and his friend and classmate Lloyd Lynch played quarterback. Lloyd had a brother my age, and when I arrived in New Richmond it was soon decided that Lloyd's brother, Ed, as quarterback and I, as center, would duplicate the shining examples of our respective brothers and thus bring great glory to both the high school and the town of New Richmond. I had considerable doubt that I had inherited much of the same skill as my brother, but I went along with the idea. My doubts were soon confirmed. Neither Ed nor I showed any signs that we had inherited our brothers' skills. We were a terrible team. On one occasion we went to Cumberland, Wisconsin, to play the high school team there and found them all to be big, strapping fellows much heavier and taller than any of the players on the New Richmond team. The game was a disaster. We were beaten 87 to 0. The hopes of the New Richmond townspeople and undergraduates were crushed, and Ed and I were greatly humiliated.

I had a chance to partially redeem myself later in the school year. Basketball had not yet become widespread in the Midwest, but I had played some in Barre. Since this was the first year that the New Richmond High School had had a basketball team, I had a leg up. I got along well enough to get my letter in basketball, and the team had a fairly good season. But those experiences convinced me that my career would not be in professional sports.

While in New Richmond, I augmented my income by selling Vermont maple syrup. I had written to my father and asked him to buy and send me one hundred gallons of Number 1 Vermont syrup. He bought them at three dollars a gallon and shipped them to me, and I began a house-to-house canvass to solicit orders at four dollars a gallon. This would have given me a profit of seventy-five cents a gallon after repaying my father for the syrup and the cost of the freight. But I quickly found I had a problem. The Number 1 syrup was so light in color that people thought it was a mixture of syrup and white sugar. I tried to convince them that the light color was the hallmark of the highest quality maple syrup, but I couldn't make them believe me. So I wrote to my father and asked him to rush me one hundred gallons of Number 3 syrup, which was the poorest grade of syrup and the darkest in color. This sold like hotcakes for four dollars a gallon, while I had to sell the good syrup for a dollar a gallon in order to get rid of it. This was my first connection with the fantastic world of merchandising.

The school year at New Richmond High ended during the first week in June. I came home on the train, traveling from Montreal on the old Central Vermont Railroad in a car that had an observation deck. This was an open area, somewhat like the deck of a boat, that made it possible to see in all directions. The weather was mild and warm, the sun was shining, and Vermont was in its greenest glory. I have never forgotten how those hills, fields, pastures, rivers, and lakes looked, and how lucky I felt to live in Vermont.

The following September, I reentered Spaulding High School in Barre and met the girl who would later become my wife. My class, 1918, was made up of vigorous and active members. It took the lead in starting the *Sentinel*, the first school newspaper or magazine in the history of the school. The newspaper still exists today, seventy years later, although in a different and improved format. All four classes in the high school were represented on the staff, and Corinne Eastman of the class of '20 was elected associate editor. She was the daughter of William Eastman and Mrs. Thomas H. Cave. Laurence Campbell, my close friend, was the elected business manager, and I, the least qualified of any of the elected officers for the job I held, was elected editor-in-chief. Laurence should have the principal credit for holding the paper together during the first year. We had major financial difficulties, and without his management skill I doubt if we could have made it. He had to personally guarantee to the printer the cost of printing in order to get the issues out on time! And he did all of the work of soliciting advertising from the local merchants. At times it was touch and go, but before the year was over the paper was running in the black. It was, of course, necessary to hold frequent meetings of the officers and staff, and these meetings gradually developed into semisocial affairs. In this way the editor-in-chief and the associate editor came to know each other, and soon it was publicly recognized that Corinne was "my girl."

By this time, my father owned a Model T Ford. It came in handy during my senior year. Most evenings that school year there was something going on. The gasoline tank of this Model T, incidentally, was under the front seat. It had no gasoline pump as in modern cars, and the gasoline ran by gravity directly into the carburetor. Because the carburetor was farther front than the gasoline tank, when the car was climbing a hill and only a small quantity was left in the tank, the gasoline could not flow uphill into the carburetor and the engine would stall. Money was tight, and the price of gasoline was high—twenty cents a gallon! Thus, as you might expect, there were times when, coming home late at night, I discovered the gasoline level was low. In fact, there were many such occasions. But I found a quick answer to the problem. If the motor sputtered as I started up the steepest portion of Prospect Street, I simply pushed the clutch into neutral and coasted backwards far enough to back into the first dooryard I came to. Then I pointed the car downhill and reengaged the clutch. The motor restarted. Now with the gasoline tank higher than the carburetor, power was instantly restored, and I would back the car the half mile or so to the top of the hill. I soon developed real skill in this maneuver and could negotiate the hill backward almost as well and as fast as Mary Ann at the gallop.

My father often commented that he thought the car was using a lot of gasoline!

I finished my fourth year at Spaulding and graduated in the spring of 1918. World War I was in progress. For several years, I had been watching successive units of recruits marching down the street on the way to the trains that would take them to their training centers. The street would be lined with cheering people and flying flags. Patriotic emotion was running high.

The phenomenon doubtless seems strange to young people of today. Public attitudes toward military service have changed so much over the years. It had changed perceptibly even by the time of World War II. During World War II, there were no parades, no people on the street, no flags, and little appreciation or emotion shown by the public other than that from family and close friends. The practice during World War II was to assemble each quota of recruits from Washington County at the Washington County Courthouse in Montpelier, where a brief program was held, composed usually of a speech by a dignitary, quite often a clergyman. Very few people attended except the recruits, relatives, and friends. After this bit of ceremony the recruits would walk to the Central Vermont Railroad station to board the train. To one like myself, who was accustomed to the exhibition of public appreciation in World War I, it seemed that something was missing. During the Vietnam War, however, even this bit of ceremony was dispensed with.

Looking back to those earlier growing-up days, I am amazed by my consummate ignorance. Certainly Barre, Vermont, was a parochial place in which to grow up. Today even a casual reading of history makes it clear that during the first quarter of the new century events were occurring that would reshape the economic, political, and social values of the future, for this was the period when the United States became the dominant nation of the world. It began in 1900, when leaders in Congress and elsewhere saw the country as a trustee of the world's progress and as guardian of world peace. For a brief period this country gloried in its strength. The policy was, of course, expressed in such noble terms as "the white man's burden" by the leaders of the nation, but it actually contained a generous portion of imperialism. It is fortunate that this policy soon lost favor with the public, and soon the country did a complete about-face and decided against further expansion—a policy to which it has adhered ever since. It was this about-face and the resulting foreign policy of the past eighty years that has earned our country its rightful reputation as a nonimperialistic nation. By 1914, when we became involved in World War I, the United States had not the slightest desire for new territory. We entered the war to "make the world safe for democracy." Democracy was then our ideal and it still is, although its shape and form have undergone some rather drastic alterations.

Several members of my Spaulding graduating class were already in the service in June, having been accepted by the Army immediately after graduation. But I could not enlist. The minimum age for enlistment was eighteen, and I was under age. My failure to get into military service was disappointing, not just because it posed financial problems about how I would support myself. I suffered a disappointment bordering on shame. Young men of my approximate age were expected to be in military service in time of war, and we were at war. Patriotic feeling was running high. I knew people would wonder why I was not in the service, and they did. Always when this question was raised in later years, I was embarrassed and uncomfortable. Somehow it has never seemed a satisfactory answer to tell them that I did not turn eighteen until November 7, 1918, four days before the armistice was declared.

After graduation, then, I began to think about college. I was working for the R.L. Clark Feed Store driving its delivery truck that summer and spent many of my evening hours with Corinne. Consequently, I did not pursue my plans for college until late in the summer. Eventually, however, I decided on Boston University and made a successful application for admission. I don't remember when, where, or how Corinne and I became formally engaged, but when I left for college in late fall, she was wearing my high school class pin, and that was pretty clear evidence that we both had "intentions."

5

My Dad and Mother

"At Montpelier I found a deep and lasting attachment for the girl whom I later married. She, like myself, was wholly dependent on her own efforts, but in spite of her obstacles she was one of the leaders of her class in scholarship. She had a far brighter mind than I."

My father, like me, was a country lawyer. He was born on Pike Hill in the Town of Corinth, then and now one of the most rural spots in Vermont. He was educated in the one-room schoolhouses of the time, went on to attend Montpelier Seminary (now Vermont College), and eventually received his bachelor's degree from the University of Vermont in June 1895. All his life he was justly proud of being the first Davis in my family line to graduate from college. I can remember attending with him his fiftieth reunion at UVM and enjoying how excited and vivacious he was all day as he met one after another of the graduates and talked with them of their college days.

At Montpelier Seminary, Dad met my mother, who was also a student there and the daughter of the school cook. Mother worked as a waitress in the seminary dining room, receiving the sum of ten cents per day plus her board, room, and tuition. At that time there were no public high schools in Vermont. To get the equivalent of a high school education, it was necessary either to go outside of the state or to attend one of the private seminaries or academies. As was true of my father, only my mother's own hard work made her high school education affordable and possible.

I never heard either of my parents talk about how their romance began. I was delighted to receive some years ago a letter from a Mr. Eaton of South Royalton, a former Montpelier Seminary student and a contemporary of theirs. He gave me a bit of information about that romance. It seems that my mother and the girl who later became Mr. Eaton's wife were roommates. These two girls decided to invite a couple of boys to dinner, which they would cook in their room, a practice permitted even at that time. My mother invited my father, who promptly accepted. Apparently the dinner was an outstanding success, which I can well understand if Mother could cook as well then as she could during my growing-up days. Almost immediately, Dad and Mother were "going together," a status of true significance in those days. I have always regretted that I never had sense enough to question my parents concerning the details of their romance. In later years it would have meant a great deal to my brothers and sisters and me to know more of the details.

My memories of Mother, as well as pictures taken shortly after her marriage, confirm that she was a beautiful woman. She had dark brown eyes that looked black, jet black hair and eyebrows, and a clear complexion. She was a lady through and through, and she walked, talked, and carried herself at all times with quiet dignity. My dad wrote in his journal that "she had a quick mind—quicker than mine." I recall Dad using the expression "quick mind" many times with reference to other people, and to him it denoted a high degree of intellectual capacity. My mother also had a tremendous capacity for love and affection. I was never conscious of any dissension between my parents, and I am positive that they loved each other deeply all their lives together.

After her graduation from Montpelier Seminary in 1891, Mother taught for a time in Windsor, Vermont. Among the courses she taught was German, which she had studied at the seminary. After Dad graduated from UVM in 1895, he and Mother were married. They went to live in Island Pond, Vermont, where Dad had accepted a position as principal of the Island Pond High School. While there, he decided to study law and to eventually try to pass the

Vermont Bar examinations for admission to practice law in Vermont. It was a long shot at best. It was quite common in those days for young men to study law in the office of some practicing lawyer, without benefit of formal law school education. This usually required actual attendance in a law office, with the opportunity not only to observe what goes on and to some extent to participate in the activities of the office, but more important to have the benefit of guidance and daily discussion with a practicing attorney. Dad did not have any of those advantages. He registered as a law student in the office of Porter H. Dale, who stayed in practice just a short time before he secured a position with the U.S. Customs Office at Island Pond and later was elected a United States Senator. This made it necessary for Dad to transfer his registration to the office of Porter H. Dale's father, George N. Dale, an elderly lawyer, a man of far more than ordinary ability but who at that time was not actively practicing. By the time evening had arrived, therefore, and Dad had finished his day's school duties, Mr. Dale was seldom in his office. Dad had access to plenty of law books, however, and with those—but without contact with any other law students and far removed from any of the courts—he plugged along many a dreary day.

On those lonely nights in Mr. Dale's office, he read Blackstone, the first of the great books on the history and content of the English common law, upon which most of our law is founded. By the time I went to law school, Blackstone was not prescribed reading nor were its contents discussed. I doubt that more than 1 percent of lawyers now practicing have ever read it. It is difficult reading and even more difficult to fathom without someone with whom to discuss it, someone experienced in the law and hence with a rounded perspective to help interpret the ponderous sentiments embodied in that great book. My father also read the work of many other modern authors, such as Wigmore on evidence, Thompson on negligence, the *General Statutes of Vermont, Robert's Vermont Digest,* and the opinions of the Vermont Supreme Court. Looking back, I have to give my father the very highest marks for having the courage, the fortitude, and the self-discipline to prepare himself in that unorthodox way and actually to pass the bar, practice law, and earn a living for himself and his family. And he did it in less than four years from the time he started.

When he was admitted to the bar in October 1899, my father had never attended a trial or entered a courtroom. It is no wonder that the elation he felt at passing the bar resulted in the following incident. As he and the other successful candidates left the courthouse where the examinations had been given and where they had heard the happy news, they decided to celebrate. My father was a man who practically never touched alcohol. But that night, he and his lucky associates had procured some alcohol and celebrated by marching up and down State Street in Montpelier. None of them were feeling any pain, and my father met a most dignified gentleman coming down the street wearing a very handsome and expensive derby hat. In his elation, Dad walked up to the dignified gentleman and for no reason at all except high spirits banged his hands down on the top of the gentleman's derby hat, crushing it beyond recognition. The next day, when told what he had done, my father was shocked and humiliated. He immediately went in search of the gentleman, found him, apologized profusely, and bought him a new and better derby.

Now my father gave up his secure job as school principal and embarked upon the uncertainties of law practice without any financial backing. As Dad wrote in his journal, "With this meager preparation for practice, I moved to East Barre in the month of August 1899 with the hope of making a living for myself and family," which then consisted of a wife and two children. It was not a bright prospect. But as he also wrote, "Here my experience with the realities of life in some degree supplemented my inexperience with the practice of the law, so by extreme economy and ably assisted by my wife, we never went hungry or cold, nor were our children ragged or dirty. We kept up a front, maintained our self respect. Not however without many discouragements and some days dark and gloomy!"

When my father wrote of his experience with the "realities of life" that he felt made up somewhat for his lack of formal education, he was referring to the troubles and struggles he had had in getting an education. It is quite an extraordinary story. To begin with he was in school very little between the ages of ten and sixteen. This was not uncommon for farm boys of his day, but neither was it a good foundation upon which to build a higher and more specialized education in the law. But as I often heard him say, "Not all our lessons are learned in school." He did learn to work and had the advantage of intelligent, strict, clean-living parents. Also, he had determined early in life to make something of himself, and he clearly saw that more and greater education was indispensable to success in that endeavor.

In the fall of 1885, when he was sixteen years old, my father attended one term of school in the town of Corinth. The school was called, somewhat ambitiously perhaps, the Corinth Academy and Cookville Graded School. It had before that time been an academy, but by some kind of reorganization it had later become part of the public school system, doubtless because of its emphasis on the elementary grade curricula. Referring to that school, my father wrote in his journal, "The teacher was better than average. He had somehow the ability to inspire his pupils with ambition. His name was A.E. Perkins, now [1922] an M.D. living in some part of Massachusetts."

Dad's struggles to get an education are best told in his journal, which I found in the attic after his death. He did not make daily entries, but he wrote in it from time to time when the occasion permitted. It prompted my interest these many years later in making some record of my own life. The book is in his own handwriting, and he there recorded the course he followed after leaving the Cookville Graded School in 1885.

"The following winter," he wrote, "I somehow secured a certificate or license, and taught the winter term at East Orange, Vermont. It was along in this period of my life that I formed the firm intent of securing more than a common school training and also, the notion of becoming a lawyer, though having no very clear idea just how it was to be accomplished. And from that time, the general course of my efforts were along those lines, although with more or less delays and deviations, by reason of financial and other obstacles, which had to be met and removed or passed around. During the winter of 1886 I again taught the winter term of the East Orange school. I got $5.00 per week and my board. However, it may be that in addition to the wages I also received more value in other ways, in fact I feel sure that I learned much more during both of those terms of school than any of my pupils."

This comment of Dad's has always interested me because I

often heard him say that everyone ought to teach at least one term of district school (as he called it) as part of their education. But having had this experience, my father was now ready for other things.

"In the autumn of 1887 I entered the Seminary at Montpelier, Vermont," he continued. "When I entered I had with me $35.00, but with close economy and by working Saturdays and odd jobs during the week I somehow managed to get through the fall term. I got a chance to teach a term of school in the winter, and the wages therefrom enabled me to get through the spring term at the Seminary. So by working on a farm during the summer vacation and teaching winters, I graduated from Montpelier Seminary in June 1891. At Montpelier I formed a deep and lasting attachment for the girl whom I later married. She, like myself, was wholly dependent on her own efforts, but in spite of her obstacles she was one of the leaders of her class in scholarship. She had a far brighter mind than I.

"After graduating from the Montpelier Seminary I decided to enter the University of Vermont, and to secure funds to begin, I taught the fall term of school at Corinth of ten weeks, thus securing $100 to begin a college course, leaving Corinth direct for Burlington, the day school closed, entering College about Thanksgiving, (and so several weeks late) and with no other funds in sight. However, soon after I reached college an opportunity opened for me to teach an evening school in Burlington, for a few nights, in place of another college boy who had the position, he being called away by sickness in his family. This temporary job became permanent, and I held it for three winters, so by teaching a fall term of school each year, and going back to college late, and at once taking up the evening school which usually was kept open from Thanksgiving till about April 1st, I managed to get through college in June 1895. During my college course I taught in Corinth, Topsham, and Georgia, besides teaching the evening school at Burlington."

Dad secured the position of principal of Island Pond High School immediately after getting through UVM. He held that position for four years, during which time he studied law and was admitted to the Bar in the fall of 1899. But he did not begin the practice of law until the next summer, when he came to East Barre with his wife and two children, about thirty-five dollars, and a few law books. My parents left behind the grave of my brother Paul, who had died in infancy.

After living a year and a half in East Barre, Mom and Dad moved to our Allen Street home in Barre City in November 1901. Dad had borrowed the money to buy this new house. I had been born on November 7, 1900, while Dad was practicing in East Barre, so now he had a wife and three children to provide for.

Over the next ten years our family grew by another five children. Ours was a big family, but my mother loved us all. If she loved one more than the others, she never showed it by word or deed or expression or countenance. She slaved night and day for her family, at times beyond her strength.

With a family of that size, Mother had no time for social affairs and little time to spend with her closest friends. She did attend church and some of its associated activities, and she was always in attendance whenever any of her children were on the program at church or school affairs. Occasionally she exchanged visits with some of her closest friends. These were high moments in her life.

Most of her time was spent in doing housework, cooking, cleaning, washing, knitting, and mending our clothes. She loved to knit and crochet, and not once but many times knitted mittens, caps, and sweaters for us all. My sister Ruth seems to have inherited her love of crocheting and knitting.

Strangely enough, I cannot remember my mother ever having any kind of illness. I hope it was not because I didn't notice. Most likely, she just didn't have time to be sick.

My mother was an excellent cook and she knew how to cook tasty and nutritious food from the most common and inexpensive ingredients. On the income of a country lawyer of those days, she needed this skill to feed such a large family with such voracious appetites. The memory of what she could do with vegetables from our garden and apples from our own orchard makes my mouth water even now. In the spring she used to send some of the children out to pick cowslips, those tender, succulent leaves that grow in the swamps in the spring. After she boiled them with salt pork and a variety of other mysterious ingredients, they were a real delicacy. She cooked on a large Glenwood kitchen stove that was fueled with wood and later with coal, and that seemed constantly in need of replenishment. It contained a large oven in which she baked delicious bran muffins in a black iron muffin pan; apple, pumpkin, and cream pies; and a variety of sugar cookies and many other delicacies. The garden, the orchard, the eggs from our hens, the pork from our own pigs, and the milk, cream and butter from our two cows made up a very large part of the diet for our hungry family. Salt pork and milk gravy on her delicious baked or mashed potatoes were often served and much appreciated. No one was diet conscious then. Weight was controlled by the expenditure of energy, and no one had ever heard of cholesterol. The stove oven, we found, was a wonderful place to put our stockinged feet after being out in the freezing weather. Mother seemed to have any and every talent when it was required. It was a happy home for us kids.

Mother taught us to say our prayers at bedtime as soon as we were old enough to talk, and she made sure we did it regularly. She made God seem very real and near. And she made sure that we went to church and Sunday school regularly. Then later, as we reached high school age, she sent us back to church at night to attend what was called Epworth League, because by that time night religious services had been discontinued except for the league, which was designed for young people of high school age. She didn't have to work all that hard to get us to go after we discovered girls, an incentive whose power should not be underestimated. Naturally, some of the girls needed to be safely escorted home after the services, and there were plenty of willing recruits.

Having been a teacher herself, my mother found it natural to spend many evening hours overseeing us while we did our homework and watching us closely to see that we received decent grades. She was quite proud of the fact that three of her children—Doris, Ruth, and Helen—became teachers. I doubt that I would have passed my courses in Latin in high school without her constant help. She would have been mortified if any of us had failed her in this respect. She was a very proud woman and a wonderfully good woman too.

In one incident that impressed me greatly, Mother heard indirectly that a second cousin of hers was living in the poorhouse in South Northfield, Vermont. She hadn't seen this second cousin for years. Nevertheless, she was greatly agitated. It was a disgrace for a member of her family, no matter how distant, to be taken care of by public charity. She asked me to take her to South Northfield to see what could be done, and I did. The result was that she made arrangements for him to be taken care of in a private home, and she and my father paid the full expense until he died. That was an example not only of her pride but also of her idea of the length and breadth of family responsibilities.

Discipline was one of her responsibilities that she took very seriously. Alcohol was not allowed in her home, although in the fall Dad always bought a large barrel of sweet apple cider that we kept in the cellar. All of us sampled it liberally, but sometimes we did not get around to finishing the cider while it was still in its sweet, pristine state. This did not prevent the adults from consuming the balance, even if by that time it had something suspiciously like an alcohol taste or effect. After all, Vermonters do believe in the old maxim, "Use it up, wear it out, make it do, or do without."

One of the things that gave Mother much pleasure in life was music. She loved it, although she did not sing or play an instrument herself. She saved money for a long time, in bits and pieces, until she could buy a piano. She tried to interest her children in music, and some of us made periodic attempts to please her by taking either voice or piano lessons, but none of us became proficient except Doris, who learned to play the piano beautifully and who gave Mother many hours and days of satisfaction and delight. If Mother could have had the benefit of televised concerts as we know them today, it would have been a great joy in her life. Or if she could have known that two of her grandchildren would become professional musicians, it would have delighted her even more.

I had a paper route for a while when I was ten, and it was necessary for all of us newsboys to wait for the paper to come off the press. The timing of this was never regular, so we often kept watch from the window of Dad's office, which was diagonally across the street from the *Barre Daily Times* office and printing presses. If the weather was good we would play marbles outside on the sidewalk while we were waiting. But I soon came to enjoy spending more time in Dad's office. In the same office suite as Dad were Herbert Slayton, a deputy sheriff, and Mr. and Mrs. Waldron Shields, who rented office space and a desk from my father. Waldron Shields operated a small brokerage office for the sale of granite monuments. I remember well that finances were sufficiently tight that Mr. and Mrs. Shields used to save, clip, and stack all the incoming envelopes to use as paper on which to figure the costs and sizes of monuments. Fifteen years or so later, Mr. Shields greatly enlarged his business and started manufacturing monuments himself. It was not long before he had built a large, modern manufacturing plant that was as good as any in Barre at that time. When I was later admitted to the bar, Mr. Shields became one of my loyal clients, and I'm sure it was the result of our close contact when I was a boy hanging around Dad's office.

Dad took a close interest in everything his children were doing. He was particularly zealous to see that each of us kept busy doing something constructive. He was not above establishing "work projects" that were either unnecessary or unimportant in order to teach us how to work and, as he believed, to ingrain the habit of work, which he thought was a necessary part of an education and a curative for many of the ills of mankind. And I admit that he was quite successful, for not a single one of my brothers or sisters could ever be called lazy.

One of these work projects involved my becoming a shoe peddler for a couple of weeks during spring vacation when I was fifteen. At that time my father was keeping two driving horses. He and his friend George Tilden, the shoe merchant, hatched up a scheme to send me over into the hills of Corinth with a horse and pung sled full of outmoded shoes that Mr. Tilden couldn't sell in the local shoe market in Barre. I have long since forgotten the precise financial arrangement—it was essentially a commission deal—but I have never forgotten the experience. I knew nothing about shoes or salesmanship, but I managed to stick it out for most of the two weeks and sold enough shoes to provide my bed and board during that period. Wherever I found myself at mealtime or at night, I negotiated with the farmers for meals and lodging, just as in the back-peddling days. Most often the farmers were paid in shoes.

Before the two weeks were up, a heavy thaw came that made the back roads treacherous. The heavy snowdrifts, which during the winter had been packed down by the snow rollers, now became too soft to hold up the weight of a horse. Suddenly and without warning, the horse would sink into the thawing drifts up to her belly. Then I would spend an hour or so, sometimes more, unharnessing the horse from the sled, digging out the snowdrift with a shovel, and hitching up again. After a succession of these experiences, I thought I had a valid excuse for cutting my two-week assignment short and drove home to Barre with horse, harness, sled, and myself still intact and with almost as many shoes as I had started out with. The whole experience was hardly a howling success and convinced me that I was not cut out to be a salesman, but it was another good lesson in self-reliance and how to get along with people. I suspect that this was all that George Tilden or my father really had in mind. They were most understanding or at least appeared to be so.

I have often speculated about where in my father's education or experience his understanding of people derived. His understanding of why people do things and how they are motivated was a real talent. Even more often I have wondered how he came to understand children to the extent he did. He knew when not to spare the rod, and he knew when it was best to deliver punishment in some other way. Always he was a teacher at heart—but not a preachy one.

One Saturday afternoon I failed to work in the garden as I had been instructed. The truth is, I had forgotten my instructions. The reason I had forgotten them was that Charlie Beck had asked me to go canoeing with him. We had canoed several times before on the Stevens Branch, and we both found it great fun. The Stevens Branch ran by the Trow and Holden Fork Shop on South Main Street and supplied the water for power through a sluiceway to a water wheel in the shop. We both failed to take note of the fact that this particular occasion was a Saturday, and that on Saturdays the shop was closed. When the shop was closed, so was the sluiceway, so that all the water ran over the top of the dam instead of being diverted. On the earlier occasions, we had enjoyed letting the canoe bump up against the top of the dam to see the water cascading below. On this Saturday I was in the front of the canoe, and as we slowly let the canoe come up to bump the top of the dam, we were astonished when it started to go over the dam. We paddled frantically backward, but it was too late. The canoe, with its two occupants, went over the falls and down eighteen feet. I was trapped under the cascading water and had no way to get out because of the pressure of the falling water. I nearly drowned before Charlie braved the tons of water pouring down over me and saved my life by pulling me out. In the process I broke a small bone in my foot. It was never treated, then or afterwards, because I didn't want to admit what had happened or where I had been when I should have been hoeing the garden. But somehow my dad got hold of the fact. He said nothing for days, while I did my best to conceal my limp. Later, when both of us were hoeing in the garden and I was still trying to conceal my limp, he looked at me with a knowing look and said, "Do you think it was worth it?" I replied in a very small voice, "No." And that was the end of it. It was punishment enough.

Another example of his understanding and consideration for children was the occasion when my sister Ruth contracted an intense fear of all policemen. As a child in graded school she had broken a bottle on the sidewalk and that had initiated her fear. She would never go by the police station on Prospect Street unless my father had her by the hand. She would go to his office after school and wait hours, if necessary, so she could go home with him because the route home passed in front of the police station. One day Dad took her into the back door of city hall, which led to the police station by an indirect route. Ruth became suspicious that he was taking her to the police station and tried to beg off, but to no avail. When they got into the police station, Dad introduced her to the chief of police, Jerry Donahue, and to several other police officers. Dad had arranged for the chief and the other officers to have candy available, which they quietly gave to Ruth, and the chief gently talked with her and convinced her that policemen were friends of children, not enemies. It was another well-taught lesson carried out with finesse.

By 1917, my father's law practice had increased to what, in his journal, he described as "comfortable." That year he was appointed state's attorney by then-Governor Graham.

During his term of office, he was confronted with the task of prosecuting several murder cases. One of these was a case that attracted national attention. In addition to receiving widespread press coverage, it was the subject of at least one book and several articles in magazines of national circulation. The reason for its notoriety was the circumstantial quality of the evidence and the many peculiar things that happened during the investigation. In fact, it was some time before the state was able to identify the suspect.

The murder took place in a house on South Main Street in Barre that, according to the evidence, was operated by a Mrs. Parker as a house of ill fame. Early one Sunday morning the dead body of a woman was found in a vacant lot on Keith Avenue right in the center of the city. (Today on this lot there is a brick building formerly occupied by the Barre Electric Company.) About the only clue that was found in the early stages of the investigation was a tire track in the dirt beside the curb adjacent to the spot where the body was found. It had rained hard the night before, which accounted for the clear marks left by an automobile tire, which obviously had parked there after the rainstorm. Too much time and space would be required to describe all the details in full. Suffice it to say that my father employed the services of the Wood Detective Agency in Boston, and after a long and intensive investigation, sufficient evidence was found to incriminate a man named George Long. The evidence placed Mr. Long in the Parker House with the victim—a Mrs. Broadwell. The victim had been strangled with a handkerchief, which by a series of strange coincidences was traced back to Mr. Long. The tire mark was conclusively traced to a car from a garage on South Main Street that had been loaned to George Long the day before the murder. These pertinent pieces of evidence, together with many others, were sufficient for the grand jury to indict Long for first-degree murder, which it did in October 1919. The trial lasted a month and ultimately resulted in a conviction of second-degree murder and a sentence of life imprisonment.

My father, however, was concerned as to whether he really did have the right man. To satisfy himself, he had a dictaphone set up in the jail outside the locked cells in the common corridor where all inmates were permitted to be in the daytime. The dictaphone was connected to a listening device in a room in the adjacent Washington County Courthouse.

I was working in my father's office at the time of the trial and took a small part in the actual trial. My job was to keep track of the long list of witnesses so that they would be on hand at the proper times to testify without requiring them to be in court for the whole length of the trial. The state's witnesses numbered more than one hundred. My other task was to man this dictaphone at certain hours when Long would be in the corridor of the jail. It was arranged that one of the detectives of the Wood Agency would intentionally get himself intoxicated in Northfield and make sufficient display of himself on the streets to be arrested and brought before the justice of the peace in Northfield. He would plead guilty to intoxication and indicate that he was without funds. In such cases the law provided that a convicted alcoholic could work out his fine in jail at the rate of two days for each dollar of the fine. And the jail for Northfield at that time was the Washington County jail in Montpelier, where Long was being held. All this happened as it had been preplanned. Neither the arresting officer nor the justice of the peace knew that this was a trumped-up arrangement to provide the conditions necessary to use the dictaphone.

My job was to listen and record things that were said when the other inmates engaged Long in conversation. The idea was that perhaps enough information could be elicited to convince my father of Long's guilt, or perhaps the contrary. My father did not expect that any of the evidence so elicited would be used in court. He hoped only to salve his own conscience and assure himself that he had the right man. Over a period of three weeks, sufficient admissions came out of these conversations to convince Dad of Mr. Long's guilt, and the dictaphone setup was discontinued.

On the whole, Dad had a very successful term as state's attorney. His only real disappointment was in connection with a homicide that occurred in Middlesex in which a recluse was bludgeoned to death. Despite months of detective work, the guilty person was never found.

Dad used his own philosophy of life in his law practice, and much of the legal advice he dispensed to clients was liberally laced with philosophy. Many of his clients were Italian and Spanish immigrants who spoke little or no English and often communicated with him through an interpreter. These clients developed great confidence in him and sought his advice on a variety of matters quite unrelated to the law: personal affairs, family troubles, quarrels between neighbors, where to bank and which doctor to consult, and help in carrying on correspondence with old friends or officials in Italy and Spain. He settled many a neighborhood quarrel right in his office, and he kept many a dispute from ending up in court.

The fact that I did not have a liberal arts degree was a great disappointment to my father. To him the law degree I obtained and the two years of liberal arts I received during law school have never really made up for the liberal arts degree I did not receive. When I came home from law school after graduation, he brought up the subject again and told me of his disappointment and of his belief that it would be a handicap all of my life. "Now," he said, "there's only one way you can overcome it. If you have the guts to create the habit and stick to it of reading one hour a day, outside of the field of the law, you can partially make up for the loss of a degree and perhaps you can entirely make it up."

As a result of that advice I did form the habit of reading an hour a day in non-legal fields, and I followed the practice for over twenty-five years. I know it has been a great help. Again I came to realize my father's great understanding of life and people.

In November 1922, shortly after I was admitted to the bar, Dad ran for the office of probate judge. He was nominated by the Republicans in September and was elected in November. This was a disappointment to me. I had graduated from Boston University Law School the preceding spring and had anticipated going into some kind of partnership with my father. The position of probate judge is a full-time job, so his election put an end to that hope. I was proud that my father had been elected, however, since the political pros were all saying that he could not be elected. Their pessimism was not an indication of their lack of regard for him but rather an acknowledgment that Dad was running in the primary against a very distinguished lawyer who had a wide acquaintance in the county. But Dad was favorably well known in Barre and had many friends among influential people in the rural sections of the county, from which many of his clients had come. All this, plus the added recognition and acquaintance given him during his term of office as state's attorney, turned the trick, and he was elected by a large margin. He served for twenty-one years and was reelected every two years without opposition. He loved the job. He suited it, and it suited him. The informality of much of the work was his cup of tea. He had ample opportunity to help solve the problems of people involved in settling estates, and his common sense served him in good stead.

One day while I was general counsel at National Life, I picked up the *Times-Argus* and read a front-page article about my father. He had quietly announced that he would not be a candidate for reelection. I was surprised and puzzled. I grabbed my hat, went to my car, and drove down to the courthouse to find what this was all about.

"Dad," I asked, "have you lost your mind?"

"Not yet," he said.

"Is it true? Are you going to give up this job?"

"It's true," he said.

"Well, I don't understand it. You have done an excellent job. All the lawyers and the public say so. You love the job better than anything you have ever done. Why now?"

"It's very simple," he said. "I don't want to be sitting in this chair someday when they are all saying I have lost my buttons and don't have sense enough to know it. I want to leave while I'm ahead."

I did my best to change his mind, but to no avail.

After his retirement, Dad kept quietly busy helping old friends with matters legal and semilegal, and he seemed to enjoy life to the full. Years before, he had purchased the old Davis homestead on Pike Hill in Corinth and had been leasing the place to farmers to operate. He had built himself a cabin on the farm, and whenever possible, both before and after he retired, he drove over there for a day or so at a time and lived in memory of the days of his boyhood on the farm. He would work in the fields with the men for a few hours until he tired and then go and sit on the porch of the hillside cabin and look out over the fields as far as his eyes could see, which included a view of Mount Moosilauke. Those were truly sunset years.

One day during this period, I received a telephone call from my mother telling me that Dad had become ill. I went immediately to my parents' home on Washington Street in Barre and found that Dad had suffered a severe heart attack. He was being treated at home by Dr. Woodruff. His recovery was slow, and when he was finally allowed to begin activity again, he was told by his physician that his condition was such that he should not drive a car. What a crushing blow this was! Most young people have no real idea what it means to an active, self-reliant elderly person who has driven himself for years to come and go as he pleased. For a time, Dad hired a boy to drive for him, but this did not overcome his sense of frustration. One day, without saying anything to any of the family, he went over to Waits River and negotiated a sale of his beloved farm on Pike Hill for a shockingly low figure. Within ten days after the sale was consummated, the house on the farm burned. The new owner collected twice as much insurance as he had paid for the farm and still owned nearly five hundred acres of land. Dad never went near the farm again.

The last entry in Dad's journal was made on January 3, 1943. "I may say that while none of my children were perfect," he wrote, "they are all capable of taking care of themselves, without charity. This gives me a degree of satisfaction, as I realize that for me the sands of time are nearly run.

"It is better to consider at this time in life for what one may be thankful than grieve over lack of achievements. I can look back over more than seventy-five years of active zestful life—some of the things I hoped to achieve I can only hope my children and their children will achieve.

"We are in the midst of another great war. I do not expect to live to see it through."

He did live to see the end of the war, but not much more. On December 29, 1945, while at my home in Barre, I received a telephone call from Arthur Theriault, a lawyer in Montpelier, informing me that my father had passed away. I drove immediately to Mr. Theriault's office, which was located on the second floor of the Capital Savings Bank Building. I found my Dad's body sitting in an overstuffed chair, and Art told me the story of his passing. The stairs leading from the street to Art's office were very steep and long. Dad had gone to Art's office to transact a routine piece of legal business, climbed the steep stairs, calmly walked into the office, greeted Art cheerfully, sat down, and immediately expired. He had shown no visible sign of illness or distress. He just sat down and died. Dr. Chandler, whose office adjoined Art's office, came immediately to render assistance if he could. He explained that Dad's tired and impaired heart had been over stressed by the climb up the stairs and had just stopped. All of us in the family were grateful that his passing was unaccompanied by pain and for the fact that Dad had truly died in harness, as he had hoped to do.

Later, I learned from Dr. Woodruff that my father had had an impaired heart for more than thirty years before his death. Dr. Woodruff had sent him to Boston for consultation with the famous cardiologist Dr. Paul Dudley White, who had carefully and fully explained to Dad the details of his condition. Dad had asked Dr. Woodruff to say nothing to anyone about his heart condition, and none of the family were aware of it until after his death. Dad preferred for all those long years to live alone with his problem.

My father was a powerful individual. His philosophy of life and his wisdom pointed my life in the direction it was to go, and his advice and understanding were constant sources of strength. He often said that "struggle is the law of life. When you stop struggling, you are dead—or ought to be." He lived his life in accordance with that code and inspired a number of young men to do the same.

My mother lived on alone for seven years after Dad's death, in the home she loved so much on Washington Street in Barre. It was a quiet and sometimes lonely existence for her at the end of a long and active life. She had borne nine children—Paul, Ralph, Raymond, me, Doris, Ruth, Hugh, Wayne and Helen—six of whom lived to maturity. The deaths of Paul, as an infant; Raymond, as a young boy; and Hugh, as a teenager of infantile paralysis during the 1924 infantile paralysis epidemic in Vermont, took a heavy toll on her health and spirit. She always seemed a bit frail, tired, and somewhat sad.

Until she died on January 8, 1952, at the fairly advanced age of 82, however, she continued to find joy in the things around her. She loved flowers and her canary birds, and several of her children lived close by enough to make frequent drop-in calls. She was a dedicated mother to us all, and we all owe her a great deal.

6

Barre: The Granite Capital

There was much group singing and some dancing
with the green grass for the dance floor. It was fun
to watch the fathers and mothers teaching their
youngsters how to dance. They sang the songs of
their homeland with gusto and ate and drank
throughout the day. It was joy unrestrained . . .

On the graceful, sloping lawn of the old Spaulding High School, overlooking the center of the Barre business district, the Barre City Park, and the five surrounding churches stands the famous Robert Burns granite monument. Its midsection features four side panels of raised carving, depicting scenes from the works of the famous poet, and above that rises a life-size statue of him. The monument, erected in 1899 by the Scottish citizens of Barre, is considered one of the ten best granite memorials in the world, and many regard it as the best of all.

During my high school years I regularly walked up the main sidewalk that passes this distinguished piece of artistry. Its arresting quality never failed to impress me then, as now.

Across the city, in the North End of Barre, at the busy intersection of North Main Street, Maple Avenue, and the entrance to I-89, stands another granite monument. It is a twenty-six-foot-high carving of a stonecutter, complete with the tools of his profession: leather apron, hammer and chisel in his hand. Cut from a thirty-ton piece of granite furnished by the E.L. Smith-Rock of Ages quarry, it, like the Burns statue, has the best of Barre's granite-carving talent in its design and sculpture. And it, too, is rapidly earning its own recognition for excellence. In 1985 it was dedicated by the Italian American Memorial Committee to honor all Italian Americans whose accomplishments have contributed so much to the social and cultural life of the city and state. When I first saw the carving, I was startled by the fidelity with which the figure portrays the stonecutters enveloped in stone dust that I so often saw during my early days.

Nothing could be more appropriate than these two granite works of art to memorialize the two ethnic groups that in their separate ways were so responsible for transforming Barre from an agricultural region into a thriving industrial area. Their grand statements of ethnic roots and diversity convey eloquently the social and cultural characteristics that made Barre a melting pot unique among all towns and cities in Vermont.

The town I grew up in was a rapidly growing, bustling community. It was tightly knit and unselfconsciously segregated. The stonecutters' families had their homes on the north side of the city, while most of the more traditionally "Yankee" families lived on the south side of Barre, where my own family lived. The graded schools were neighborhood schools, and the children from the different sides of town did not mix regularly until we were all united at Spaulding High School. Nonetheless, the strong presence of the Scottish and Italians in Barre was felt by everyone, young and old, by all nationalities and by those from all socioeconomic backgrounds. They influenced the food that was sold in the markets, the shipments that came in on the trains, the city's celebrations, the public schools—both in educational content and in the social life that prevailed—the competitive sports of the city, its artistic life, particularly its music, and its general flavor. One would have had to have been blind, deaf, and dumb to grow up in Barre during the early decades of this century and not be affected by this city's unique cultural mix.

It was the immigrants from the Aberdeen vicinity of Scotland who first brought their exceptional skills in stoneworking and their native acumen and entrepreneurial skills to Barre, and who owned and operated many of the early quarries and manufacturing plants.

In fact it was two Scotsmen, Pliny Wheaton and his son Oren, who owned the first quarry to be opened in Barre. The quarry was located just off the back road from Cobble Hill in East Barre and furnished the granite for the portico and the seven magnificent columns of the first Vermont statehouse, built between 1832 and 1836. The original columns and portico are still intact in the present statehouse. In 1840, from the same quarry, Pliny Wheaton built the first stone house in Barre. It still stands in its original location on Cobble Hill Drive and appears to be in perfect condition.

Around 1880, Italian immigrants began pouring into Barre in steadily increasing numbers until it was estimated that over 25 percent of the population of Barre was of Italian origin. Between 1880 and 1890 the population of Barre more than tripled. The largest proportion were stonecutters, carvers, letterers, and designers who found ready employment in the granite manufacturing sheds and plants that were already established. They came from northern Italy, long known as one of the largest producing areas of memorial stones, where a large proportion of the population were men skilled in cutting, carving, and designing marble memorials. At first these Italian immigrants were slow to take over the business end of the granite business, but as time went on some started small businesses of their own, usually in a rented corner of a shed owned by someone already engaged in the granite business. This trend kept growing until eventually first- and second-generation Italians predominated, not only as workmen but as owners and operators.

The stonecutters loved their work, but the occupational hazards exacted a frightful toll on their health and lifespans. In the early part of this century most Barre stonecutters did not survive their mid-forties, and many died even younger. Silicosis was known in other granite-producing areas but was far more prevalent in the Barre granite area, probably because of the unique hardness of the Barre granite. Other prevailing conditions also contributed to the risk. The early stonesheds in the area had low ceilings and were poorly heated and ventilated, all of which increased the risk. Before automobiles were in general use in the winter, stonecutters walked long distances to their work, often in bitter cold, wet, and windy weather, then subjected themselves to long hours of exposure to clouds of granite dust saturated with siliceous particles. Breathed into the lungs, these particles could not be broken down, and they accumulated over time. Eventually, lung capacity was so much reduced as to interfere with the ability of the lungs to dispense oxygen into the bloodstream. Although it was sometimes a fatal disease in itself, silicosis was, in addition, a predisposing cause of tuberculosis.

Stonecutters and their families lived in constant dread of both these diseases. Many wives begged their husbands—usually to no avail—to leave the granite sheds and find other work. But these stonecutters were artists. They loved their work as all artists do, and they were untrained for other work. They felt trapped. And so they went on, hoping against hope and most often losing, with tragic consequences to themselves and their families. As the incidence of tuberculosis became more prevalent, then dramatically escalated, the state built the Washington County Sanitarium on Beckley Street. Although it rendered a great service and gave much-needed care and comfort to many afflicted with tuberculosis, the San, as it was called, cast a dark shadow over the North End of Barre. Situated on a high hill and widely visible, it was a stark reminder to those not yet afflicted of the hazards of their occupation.

The granite industry eventually sought and obtained the help of state and federal agencies to solve the problem. Only after years of study and experimentation, however, were dust-removing devices finally designed that were capable of removing the finely textured silica from the air. Fortunately, during this same period new stonesheds were being built of more modern design, with improved ventilation, lighting, and heating, which assisted in the long-awaited solution. Since the middle of the 1930s no new cases of silicosis have occurred, and as the patients at the sanitarium gradually passed away, the San was no longer needed. It was taken over by the Catholic church and is now used to house healthy and vigorous members of the Carmelite monastery, an important order of the church, and certainly a most fitting use for the San, which symbolized the agony of those earlier years.

I first came to know the Italians the summer I was ten. I was working my third summer on the Kelley farm on West Hill. One of the Kelley pastures included a large area of relatively flat land covered with trees that were sufficiently separated to make a nice park. By way of the Berlin Street extension, the pasture was readily accessible to much of the North End, where the Italian community lived, and Mr. Kelley permitted the Italian people to use the pasture for picnics whenever they wished.

The Italians are a pleasure-loving people. In Barre, they were isolated because of language difficulties, but they were adept at making their own fun. They loved picnics and had several picnic locations in and around the city. The trotting park, on the southwestern part of the city (where the new Spaulding High School building is located), was one of them. Mr. Kelley's pasture was another. As Mr. Kelley's hired man, I was made welcome at their picnics there, and I availed myself of the opportunity. Mountains of delicious food were always available, which the women packed in wash baskets and transported to the site by horse and express wagon borrowed from friendly grocers. Bottles of wine were packed with huge chunks of ice in washtubs and made available throughout the day.

The picnics were Sunday and holiday affairs, for the stonecutters worked six days a week. They were also family affairs in every sense of the word. The children loved them as much as the grownups, and they romped and played and shouted with obvious joy. The older boys played baseball. The adults gathered in small groups and chatted in their native language. Musical instruments were abundant, and some kind of music seemed to be playing all through the afternoon. There was much group singing and some dancing with the green grass for the dance floor. It was fun to watch the fathers and mothers teaching their youngsters how to dance. They sang the songs of their homeland with gusto and ate and drank throughout the day. It was joy unrestrained, and by early twilight when they packed up their belongings and started the long walk back to their homes, they were a tired, relaxed, and happy group.

Pleasure-loving as they were, they quite naturally enjoyed group activities. They organized a number of Italian clubs and organizations for social and other purposes. The Italian Pleasure Club had a large membership and was very active in sponsoring social events such as dinners, dances, and musicals, and the Italian Athletic Club also had much success in furnishing public entertainment. Its baseball games quickly attracted spectators from a wide area, and it soon developed some outstanding athletes among the membership. Some of the players, such as Kio Granai and Crip Polli, both of Barre, became so good that they earned contracts with national baseball teams. Kids of my generation used to save our money to pay ten cents to ride on the trolley car to see the local games, which were played at Inter-City Park, a large, level, open area near the present Lums Restaurant on the Barre-Montpelier Road in Berlin. Another of the Italian clubs was the Società di Mutuo Soccorso, originally organized as a self-help organization but which became eventually the leading Italian social club of the area. It is still in existence and has a club room on Beckley Street in the North End.

Although the Italians had emigrated from an area that was over-whelmingly Catholic, they did not join the Catholic church in Barre. The reasons were not entirely clear. Doubtless this absence of church connection increased their need for social opportunities, for when I was a child the church played a more important social role than it often does today. The Methodist church of Barre, in an attempt to fill this void, set up the North Barre Community House, later known as the North Barre Mission. The activity was carried on by deaconesses of the Methodist church, but much more was offered than religious worship and instruction. Classes in American forms of cooking, sewing, knitting, and in the English language were a few of the secular activities carried on there. Also, there was an attempt to meet the social and religious needs of young people. Among those young people were Cornelius O. Granai, who became a well-known lawyer, was later elected mayor, and even later was elected to serve a term or two in the Vermont legislature; Aldo Polletti, a graduate of Harvard Law School and later governor of New York; Gelsie Monti, who became a lawyer in Northfield and Barre; Ugo J. A. Carusi, who became U.S. Commissioner of Naturalization after long service in the U.S. Attorney General's office under five different attorneys general; and Dr. Michael Cerasoli, who practiced medicine in his native Barre and was a very popular and able physician.

I had further opportunity to get acquainted with the Italians at my dad's law office, for they constituted a sizable proportion of his clientele. There I met both clients and their interpreters, who were necessary because many of Dad's Italian clients did not speak English, and those who did spoke it imperfectly. Later, my father had a succession of young Italian students who worked after school and functioned as secretaries and interpreters. Among these young men were Robert Susena of Montpelier, Gelsie Monti, and Ugo Carusi, all of whom were in this way inspired to study law and become lawyers.

I used to talk with these Italian clients in Dad's waiting room. They would talk in a combination of English and Italian, and the interpreter would help by interposing an interpretation when either of us showed signs of not understanding what was being said. It was during this time that my father made an arrangement with an Italian woman living on Blackwell Street to give me Italian lessons. This arrangement lasted less than a year; hence I learned a bare minimum of Italian. I often later wished that I had pursued that opportunity more earnestly. I did, however, find that it helped me in catching on to the pronunciation of Latin, which was a required subject in high school.

There were few Italian children in my classes at Matthewson Graded School. Most of them went to graded school in the North End, either at Beckley Street School or Woodchuck Knoll, as it was called, on High Holborn Street. Since there was only one high school in Barre, all the Italian young people came to Spaulding, and by that time they spoke perfect English as well as Italian. They were excellent students. They did their homework. Their parents saw to that, and they carried off a large proportion of the scholastic honors.

After my freshman year at law school, I took a year off from school in order to earn some money for tuition and expenses. I came back to Barre and landed a job with the R.L. Clark Feed Company, which sold animal feeds, fertilizers, garden supplies, and paints both to farmers and to city dwellers. Italians of the North End were among the company's best customers for many of them kept hens and often a cow and a pig and had small gardens in the backyard. Among other responsibilities, my job included driving a three-ton truck to make deliveries of grain, fertilizer, and paint within the city limits. In this way, I came to know the Italians even better. Grains and fertilizer were kept in the cellar so I was in and out of their homes many times. It gave me a front seat view of their lifestyle.

The Italian women were immaculate housekeepers. Everywhere—both upstairs and in the cellar—was clean and orderly. They were good cooks, and the cleanliness of the houses and the tantalizing smell of good cooking enhanced by the herbs of their native land gave these houses a delightful smell and sense of home. Occasionally, when I was late making my rounds, I would be invited to dinner. My hosts were most hospitable and these dinners were delightful events. The whole family would enter into the occasion. At first I was sometimes a bit embarrassed by my inability to understand the language, but we always found ways of making each other understand enough of what was being said to carry on an interesting conversation. And where there were children in the family, they would act as interpreters since they could understand and talk English. I treasure the memories of those occasions.

Wine was always present at dinner. I was brought up in a Methodist home where alcohol in any form was completely forbidden. It was with some trepidation, then, that I first tasted wine at these meals. And it was some time, too, before I remembered to tell my parents about it. But to the Italians wine was a necessary and usual part of the dinner meal, part of the culture they brought with them from their homeland. They knew how to use wine: sparingly and tastefully.

I used to watch the public carters unload grapes at the freight station during the grape season. They delivered the grapes to the different homes by horse and express wagon. Although later some of the Italians had their wine come already made and curing in barrels, most of them made their own wine, and they aged it well before using it. I can remember, when carrying grain to the cellar in Italian homes, seeing eight or ten barrels of wine aging in the cellar. The Italians pooled their resources and had the grapes shipped from California in carload lots, thus greatly reducing the cost of shipment. They were quite proficient in winemaking and produced several runs from the grapes, then distilled the residues of grape skins, seeds, and stems to produce what was called *grappa*, a smoky, white or graying substance that was the very essence of potency.

To sit at dinner with an Italian family, enjoy a delicious meal of Italian-cooked food, in the presence of the whole family, and to be accepted as one of them was a memorable experience. I was surprised how easy it became to talk with them. We covered many subjects, but there was one subject we never discussed: politics. It was well and generally known in Barre that Italians had strong feelings about politics—influenced partly, no doubt, by the political movement that took place in Barre during the first decade of the 1900s.

It was called by many names. I remember standing on the sidewalk in front of the Socialist Hall on Granite Street when I was around ten years of age and watching with great interest the people coming and going to the hall and the excitement that prevailed. I was trying to see what went on in the hall. The fascination came from the fact that the hall was known as the headquarters of the IWW. I had no idea what the letters *IWW* meant, but I did know it was something taboo from hearing my elders talk about it. I do not know whether it ever was the home of the IWW, but I did know that it was definitely the center for propagation of the outer reaches of libertarian political thought at that time. The hall had over the doorway a granite carving of the arm and hammer, the symbol of the Socialist Labor party. Mari Tomasi, who understood Barre and the Italian community so well and who wrote extensively and sympathetically about the life and times of the Italian community, said that "Barre was one of America's two hotbeds of anarchism," which she went on to say, "died to grey ashes" in 1909. But during this peak period of agitation, such well-known agitators as Eugene Debs, Mother Jones, Bill Hayward, and Emma Goldman visited Barre and spoke to large gatherings in the hall.

One of the leaders of the movement was Carlo Abate, whose manifold services to the city and to the Italians caused the Italian American Monument Association to erect a granite memorial honoring him at the site of his former studio on Blackwell Street. Abate came to Barre in the prime of his life in 1899, at the age of forty, after losing his wife and three of his five children in an epidemic in Italy. He had earned an honorary degree from the School of Fine Arts in Milan and medals of honor from the Museum of Fine Arts also of Milan. Almost immediately upon coming to Barre, Abate became the editor of an Italian-language newspaper, the *Cronaca Sovversiva*, which became the strongest voice of the movement. I believe that the rank and file of Italians were concerned principally with the help they could receive to advance the cause of unionism in Barre.

Abate opened a private school in Barre to teach young and old alike the art of drawing, design, carving, and sculpture. His school was so popular and successful that the Granite Manufacturers and

Quarriers Association and the city of Barre soon joined in sponsoring the effort. The additional financial help made it possible for other good teachers to be recruited and thus for the school to handle the growing demand for instruction. Among the teachers I recall was Charles Pamperl, known far and wide as "the dove man" because he fed the doves regularly on the public streets. Soon the doves were following him in droves. The drawing school was first held in the basement of the Matthewson Graded School on Elm Street and later in larger and better quarters in one of the buildings at Goddard Seminary. The school met an ever-increasing need for more granite designers and carvers during the days when the granite monumental business was flourishing.

Abate was an eccentric. I remember him walking the streets of Barre always well dressed, wearing a beard, a peculiar hat always set at a jaunty angle, and a toothpick between his teeth, apparently in deep thought and oblivious to his surroundings. He was an eloquent voice for socialism both in speech and in his paper. He was sincere to the core. He truly believed that capitalism was wicked and that workers everywhere were badly mistreated. But while he had a clear idea of what was wrong with capitalism, he was quite imprecise, even fuzzy, about how the wrongs could or should be righted. The movement, self-described by its leaders as anarchy, sounded more like socialism as it came to be described in the United States. It had its day and faded away, but it left in its aftermath the fertile soil that elected two self-declared socialists as mayor of Barre, Fred W. Suitor and John W. Gordon. Ironically, both were not only good mayors but can be numbered among the most conservative mayors Barre ever had.

Thus, Carlo Abate—the strongest intellect among the political leaders of the movement, eccentric or not—left two lasting impressions upon Barre. He helped to make Barre the granite center of the world by increasing the numbers of stoneworkers and improving the artistic quality of their work, and he influenced a large segment of the Italian community toward liberal political thought, which is one of the reasons that Barre, politically, has been Democratic ever since.

However, credit for the phenomenal growth of the granite business and of Barre must not be reserved solely for the Scottish and

Italians. Immigrants from a variety of countries supplied the ranks of the granite workers, among them Canadian, French, Irish, German, Swede, Polish, Finn, and Welsh. All furnished material for the melting pot for which Barre became famous.

In 1922 and in 1934–35 there were two bitter and disastrous strikes in the Barre granite industry. French Canadians began immigrating as a result, and many of them filled the jobs left open by the strikes. Many had worked in the stone quarries and granite manufacturing plants in Quebec. Most had been raised on the farms of Canada in big families where the work ethic has been practiced almost from birth.

After the strikes were settled, the Canadians stayed on, joined the union, and bought farms in the outlying areas of Barre. Thrifty, hard workers that they were, many carried on their farms in addition to working in the granite sheds and quarries. For them, sixteen-hour days became commonplace. They were successful farmers. Their wives helped with the farm work, as did the children as soon as they were old enough to carry a half-filled milk pail. Gradually, the French Canadians, too, began to accumulate capital and to establish their own businesses, and today they have become a predominating factor in the granite business, surpassing the influence even of the Scottish and Italians.

7

The Law School Years

A large, rotund, pink-faced individual with a walrus moustache and pure white hair, he was an imposing figure. It didn't take the students long to realize that he was a man not only of superior intelligence but of unusual warmth, and it was easy to see why he had been elected president.

Late in September 1918, I was on my way to Boston University Law School. My registration was delayed a few weeks while I recovered from a bad attack of influenza. A nationwide epidemic of that year had struck Vermont unusually hard and many lives were lost. At the height of the epidemic in Vermont, doctors, nurses, and undertakers could not keep up with the demand for their services. Many victims became ill, died, and were buried without medical, nursing, or professional undertaking attention.

I had chosen Boston University Law School for a number of good reasons. One important reason was that by the time I had recovered from the flu, it was the only remaining law school in the East that had not yet filled its quota for the Student Army Training Corps (SATC). The United States government had introduced the SATC program in order to expedite the supply of recruits for the army. This plan permitted recruits to be trained without interrupting their studies while they waited to be needed for active service. The program was enthusiastically received because the recruits could go on with their college studies without cost to themselves. This program also helped many young men to get started on a college education who otherwise, because of financial considerations, would have found it impossible.

I looked forward with keen anticipation to these new experiences. I was a country boy who had never been outside Vermont except in my junior year in high school in Wisconsin. Boston was a large city, and I knew absolutely nothing about military life. It was an exciting prospect.

Gelsie Monti, who had been working as a secretary in my dad's law office for the previous four years, had decided to go to law school with me. He was influenced by my father to become a lawyer. Monti and I left together, roomed together, went into business together, and graduated together.

Upon our arrival in Boston we found a room at Ma Chase's at 70 St. Stephens Street, where a number of Vermont boys were already rooming. Ma Chase was a kindly lady, widow of a sea captain who had been lost at sea. The day following our arrival, the city of Boston enacted a quarantine law for one week due to the influenza epidemic, and we were not allowed to leave our rooms during that time. You can imagine what a bedlam these boys caused cooped up together for that length of time. On the night of the first day of the end of the quarantine, we went out on the town and lived it up.

We immediately registered the next morning at the law school and reported to the recruiting center, as instructed, for induction into the Student Army Training Corps. Monti went through with flying colors and was immediately assigned to a unit that had barracks in the old St. Botolph Garage. I filled out the necessary forms, took a physical examination, and waited for hours in a waiting room for news that I would be accepted, but my hopes were dashed. My eighteenth birthday was still about six weeks away. The military personnel at the recruiting center told me to return on November 7 and I would be inducted without delay. My hopes were revived—but only partly. How was I to support myself in the meantime and pay my tuition at the law school? I had no money, little talent, and no acquaintances in Boston. It was a dim prospect.

I decided to talk over the problem with the dean of the law

school, Homer Albers. Albers was a distinguished lawyer who maintained an extensive practice and also functioned as dean of the law school. He was a lawyer's lawyer and very much a scholar. After listening to my story, he said, "Don't worry. You'll make out all right. To begin with, you can work here for me until you are accepted by the army. That will pay your tuition. Your duties will be simple. You will sit in the outer room of my office in the afternoon after morning lectures and answer the telephone. You can study at the same time, and there won't be interruptions enough to bother you much. This will relieve your evenings, and you can hunt around and get some light job for a few hours in the evening that will pay for your room and meals. It's only about six weeks. You'll get by. Don't give up your chance for a legal education."

His confidence was contagious. I began my afternoon office work the next day. On my second day in the office, while I was hard at work studying the day's assignment, the telephone rang. On the line was a professor of mathematics at the Massachusetts Institute of Technology, who, like me, had just registered as a first-year law student. He was studying law for fun, he said. He was blind and needed someone, preferably a member of the freshman class, to read to him in the evenings. The job would be for five days a week, and the pay would be a good dinner, carfare to Cambridge on the subway, and a dollar each evening. Without hesitation, I told him I knew just the student for him and would send the student out that evening to be interviewed. So I sent myself and met this distinguished, scholarly, and warm-hearted man who ultimately helped me much more than I helped him. I should have paid him the dollar each evening! He was unmarried, about sixty years old, and lived with his mother, who was in her middle eighties. She was equally warm-hearted and a good cook besides. The dollar I received every evening paid for my breakfast and lunch for the next day, so I was financially on my way. My breakfast cost me ten cents for toast and coffee, and my lunch cost thirty-five cents at one of the houses on upper Beacon Street, immediately behind the statehouse and within a few minutes' walk of the law school on Ashburton Place.

For three weeks I watched my pal Monti marching with his unit to and from classes in his smart-looking uniform. I envied him. Then suddenly he was transferred to Camp Lee in Virginia, where he began the initial preparatory phases for officers' training.

When November 7 finally came, I promptly reported again at the induction center. Again my hopes were dashed. The induction center staff seemed quite uninterested in me. I was told I would be called when needed. The tone of voice suggested that would be never. Four days later, the armistice bells rang all over Boston, and the reason for their lack of interest became clear.

So my financial problems had to be reviewed again in the light of the fact that Uncle Sam was not going to be my benefactor. If I was to get an education, I would have to do it on my own. For a time after the armistice I carried on as usual, awaiting Monti's return from Camp Lee. After a month he was sent back to Boston with his unit and mustered out of service immediately. Then we engaged in some serious financial planning.

One night while we were making a list of the possibilities for survival, Monti told me about some of his experiences at Camp Lee, among them how the recruits used to shine each other's shoes. As a joke, Monti had announced that he was going to set up business as a shoe-shiner in the barracks. He found an old chair, elevated it by placing it atop an old packing case, and was ready for business. Business thrived. He started by charging two cents a shoe.

This story ripened into a discussion between us as to the feasibility of starting a real shoeshine business of our own in Boston. We had noticed that a number of shoeshine parlors in Back Bay had closed, either because the operators had joined the Army or because they had found better jobs during the short labor supply caused by the war. We found just what we needed on Huntington Avenue. It was within a few minutes' walk of our rooming house and right next to the old Putnam Hotel, where the Boston Red Sox were quartered. Across Gainsborough Street was the New England Conservatory of Music, and across Huntington Avenue was Northeastern University, as it was when it first started, before its incredible growth. A short distance north on Huntington Avenue was Wentworth Institute, and further out on Longwood Avenue were the Harvard Dental and Medical schools. Within a block was the Boston Symphony Orchestra hall, the Mechanics Building, and the St. James Theater. Thousands of students lived in this section of Back Bay within easy walking distance of our shop.

Our shining parlor, as we called it, was a one-story wooden building. (The site is now occupied by the Back Bay post office.) The building was owned by Mr. Andropolus, a Greek fruit merchant. He occupied half of the total floor space on one end, and the parlor occupied the opposite end. A partition separated the two halves. The parlor was fitted with six shoe-shining chairs for men and two for ladies. We rented the shoe-shining parlor space for forty dollars a month. Unfortunately, we did not have forty dollars, so Monti gave Mr. Andropolus a check drawn on the Quarry Savings Bank and Trust Company in Barre. At the time the check was drawn, there were not enough funds in Monti's account to cover the forty dollars, but Monti was anticipating a check for the final payment for his military service, which he was sure would come in before the check went through. Moreover, we were both sure that our income from the shoe-shining business would materialize with sufficient speed and in sufficient amount before the expiration of the time allowed for the check to clear.

We were mistaken on both counts. The place was much dirtier and required more repairs than we had anticipated, and it took us a full week to get it cleaned up, repairs made, and the brass polished to our satisfaction. One day Mr. Andropolus came striding into the parlor with his hair standing straight up on end, waving the check in the air and threatening, in part Greek and part English, to have us in jail forthwith. I concluded then and there that Monti would make a great lawyer: He talked Mr. Andropolus out of his rage and gave him another check! It took a real mouthpiece to do that. By the time the second check had cleared, our business was in full swing, and enough money had come in to Monti's checking account in Barre to cover the forty-dollar check—and more.

Mr. Andropolus became our true friend. For years afterward when I was practicing law, whenever I went to Boston on business I made it a point to stop and visit him.

We painted a new sign on the front of the parlor, which in large letters advised the world that these were the CONSERVATORY SHINING PARLORS and in small letters announced that "our shines put a polish on you." Several of our college friends wanted to know where the "other" parlors were, but we ignored them.

During this period large numbers of troops were returning from

Europe and passing through Camp Devens to be mustered out of service. Among them was the famous Twenty-sixth New England Division. Officers in those days wore high leather boots, much like riding boots, and military regulations required that the boots be highly polished at all times. While waiting for the mustering-out process, many of these officers came into Boston from Camp Devens for evening entertainment. They became an excellent source of patronage, and since we charged twenty-five cents for shining a pair of high boots and the officers were generous tippers, they made a substantial contribution to our business success and to our law school expenses. For shining an ordinary pair of shoes we charged ten cents, but almost everybody tipped us more.

We learned how to put on a high polish and worked hard at it, and soon we had a reputation for good work. In addition to this kind of patronage, we also had a steady stream of customers from among those living in the vicinity, particularly college students from nearby colleges. The Conservatory of Music girls were also customers, and most of them came from affluent homes and dressed well. Being next door, they sort of adopted our parlor.

One Saturday morning while I was on duty alone, an attractive middle-aged lady came in for a shine. While I was shining her shoes she asked me how I happened to be doing this kind of work. I explained that my partner and I were students from Vermont who were working our way through law school. She was intrigued by my story and asked many detailed questions. When she left, she tipped me a quarter. The following Monday afternoon two photographers and a reporter from the *Boston Post* appeared. They took many photographs of us and of our shop, inside and out. The reporter asked a lot more questions. At that time, the *Boston Post* had just started using color photographs in a new-style rotogravure section of this widely read paper. On Thursday we were delighted to see in the *Post* a whole page of color pictures and a long story about our shining parlor and our business. The paper played up beautifully the story of two boys working their way through law school. Our volume of business immediately surged. New customers came in, and many mentioned the story in the *Post*. We hired an extra boy weekday evenings and two extras for weekends. One of these boys had a marvelous tenor voice and liked to sing, so when business was a little slow he would get out on the sidewalk and sing, which attracted more people to our place. We found it true that advertising pays, and we would not hide our light under a bushel. I found out later that the lady whose shoes I had shined was secretary to the editor of the *Boston Post*. Fate is often a generous benefactor.

To further broaden our patronage, we began taking in shoes for repair. We knew absolutely nothing about repairing shoes and of course had no equipment or other needed facilities, but I slipped around the corner onto Massachusetts Avenue and made a commission deal with an established shoe repairer. It was easy for us to take the shoes there and pick them up when finished, and this became a profitable adjunct to our business. Soon we were clearing a net income of eighty dollars a week, giving us forty dollars a week each, which was more than adequate for our needs. But it was hard work.

We became well acquainted with the members of the Boston Red Sox who lived next door at the Putnam Hotel. Several of them became not only regular customers but friends as well, as many of them hung around our shop during their hours off. I had a baseball autographed by all of the Red Sox regular players, including the celebrated Babe Ruth, who was then at the height of his popularity. My son Tom, an avid baseball fan, now has that baseball, which he greatly cherishes.

Our new and growing business made it necessary for me to give up all the other jobs I had in order to do justice to the shoe-shining business and my studies as well. Monti and I took turns manning the shop, one in the afternoon and one in the evening. While one of us was working at the shop, the other would be home studying. We kept the shop closed in the forenoon because there was little business at that time of day, and we were both in classes at that time.

At the time we entered law school, the entrance requirements included a provision that students had to complete two years of study in liberal arts. These requirements were waived during the war, provided students would enroll and complete the two years at some liberal arts college. At Boston University we were permitted to take these courses at the same time we were taking law school study, and we made arrangements to take them at Boston University College of Liberal Arts. Moreover, Boston University had made additional arrangements for some of these courses to be given at the law school by professors from the liberal arts college. I doubt if many of the students got much out of courses taken under such pressure. I know I didn't, with the single exception of the course in logic. That course fascinated me, and since logic is so closely associated with the work of a lawyer, I found it a great help during my years of practice.

At that law school we had professors who were good teachers of the law and who had a talent for enlisting and sustaining interest. The curriculum combined lectures and casebook study. The lecturers would cite decisions of various appellate courts, and we were required to read them and abstract them. We were taught the five-point system for abstracting a court opinion. I found this system so helpful that I used it in my practice and later when I was on the bench. The system includes the following elements: (1) the kind and nature of the case; (2) a summary of the pertinent facts; (3) a simple statement of the issue; (4) the decision and; (5) the reasons for the decisions. This system, if painstakingly followed, can reduce a hodgepodge of legal statements and narrative into an orderly and logical content that gives the true meaning of the decision and is quickly comprehended. The virtues of this system are that it aids— and indeed requires—close concentration, it helps the student to master the logic and the reasoning involved, and it focuses on the key elements of the case. Later, when I was a superior court judge in Vermont, I used the five-point system to abstract all the cases reported in the *Vermont Reports* beginning with the establishment of the Supreme Court in 1789 and taking it up to the time I was doing that work. It took me nearly five years in my spare time to finish the task. I found it, however, a profitable exercise.

Our pressing schedule left little time or opportunity for recreation or social activities. Since the various colleges constituting the university were then spread out in many parts of Boston, there was a dearth of central activities with which to build a sense of alma mater that existed in so many other colleges and universities. Our work and study kept us busy all day, and most evenings we were content to drop into bed at eleven o'clock and sleep soundly until seven in the morning. We usually walked from St. Stephen Street in Back Bay to 11 Ashburton Place each morning partly for the exercise and partly to save carfare. So each day we grabbed a breakfast of toast and coffee at Norris Drug Store around the corner from our room and set out for school. Our course took us down Huntington Avenue and Boylston Street to the common, where we cut up across the common and past the statehouse to the law school. This was a walk of over two-and-a-half miles, and I still remember some of those winter mornings when the wind was blowing hard and the temperature down to or below zero. We hadn't heard of "wind chill" in those days, but we experienced it. This kind of weather surely increased our speed, and when we arrived at school, we were fully awake.

In due time, Monti and I accepted an invitation to join the legal fraternity Delta Theta Phi. Since that fraternity had no fraternity house, its minimal social activities consisted of occasional dances. At one of those dances I met the sister of a fraternity brother who lived in Cambridge, and she invited me to dinner a few times at the home of her parents. Her father was a prominent manufacturer, and these dinners usually included many guests and were quite formal affairs. Each time I was compelled to rent a dinner jacket from Hirsch the tailor. One day, alone on duty at the shining parlor, I was horrified to see her approaching the shining parlor. I was dressed in the appropriate uniform of a professional shoe-shiner, but this was not the image she had of me, nor the image I wanted to project at that particular moment. What could I do? Nothing but see it through. I did this by keeping my head down with great concentration on her shoes, mumbling monosyllables in reply to her conversation, and trying my level best to keep her from recognizing me. False pride? Yes. But very natural and real for a Vermont country boy. She showed no sign of recognition, and I thought I had successfully concealed my identity. But I noticed that the dinner invitations ceased, which was probably just as well, for obviously I was out of my proper element.

Monti and I were getting only average grades at law school. Whether we could have done better with more time for both study and leisure is a moot question. Certainly we thought we could. But we did acquire an adequate knowledge of the fundamentals of the law and the legal system. Many of our professors were practicing lawyers, or had been. This was a real advantage to students who wanted to get into active practice immediately upon graduation. Among our professors were the scholarly Professor Simpson, who taught torts and criminal law; Professor Bowman, who taught real estate; and Dean Homer Albers, who lectured on contracts. There were many others of like stature whose names I can no longer recall.

On the first day of school Dean Albers lectured the whole class on contracts. He began by saying, "Now I'm going to start at the beginning. I'm going to give you a definition of law. This is fundamental, so get out your notebooks." We did, with great anticipation. He continued, "Law is something which everyone is presumed to know"—he paused while we diligently wrote these deathless words of wisdom—"and which no one in fact does know." Again he paused, while we stared at him and at each other, somewhat puzzled. But he had a straight face so we dutifully wrote down his words. And then he wound up his definition by saying, "But which the Supreme Court gets paid for having the last guess." Only after this introduction did he proceed to give us some practical advice:

> Now if you're going to be lawyers the first thing you must do is destroy your memory. Kill it off. Before it destroys you. If you don't you'll find yourself using it, and the more you use it the more you will strengthen it. But you must learn never to rely on your memory when an important principle of law is involved or the exact wording of a statute is required. Go and look it up. If you try to rely upon your memory, the first thing you know, you'll discover too late that some legislature or some appellate court has repealed all you know. Make an index of your mind. Try only to remember that there is a statute or a decided case on the particular point. That is the index. Then go and look it up. You'll be surprised how often a statute will read differently than you remember it. And the same is true of case law. Memory is a dangerous tool for a practicing lawyer. Keep it dull. Don't try to sharpen it.

Legal ethics was a short but important course. At Boston University Law School it was given by former president of the United States William Howard Taft, who was immensely popular with the students. A large, rotund, pink-faced individual with a walrus moustache and pure white hair, he was an imposing figure. It didn't take the students long to realize that he was a man not only of superior intelligence but of unusual warmth, and it was easy to see why he had been elected president. The aura of leadership surrounded him

79

like a mantle. Not a single student missed his classes. They were the highlight of the year. His lectures were scholarly but not sticky. It was a joy to watch and listen to him or even to be in the same room with him.

His style was an effective combination of manuscript and extemporaneous delivery, but his mastery of the use of humor gave another important dimension to his delivery. Every lecture was generously sprinkled with humor. Using it to drive home a key point, he would carefully and slowly build up to his climax. Then just before the punch line he would pause, and from the subterranean depths of his lower abdomen you could actually see and hear his inimitable chuckle, which carried you to the punch line and culminated with a great laugh which broke upon the audience with devastating effect. His was truly the art of communication.

Reams have been written by experts on the relative merits of manuscript speaking or extemporaneous speaking. Which is superior? The question has never been settled. My experience has convinced me that extemporaneous delivery is usually the best for me—with one exception. Manuscript delivery is best if the subject is highly technical and if the audience is composed of professionals. It is not so difficult to hold the attention of a professional audience on a technical subject. Moreover, in these circumstances accuracy and precision clearly should have priority. They are too important to be left to the vagaries of extemporaneous delivery.

But for most speechmaking, the extemporaneous mode is best. One reason lies in the comparative *pace* of delivery between the two modes. Manuscript delivery is much faster because it does not require the time lag of thinking on the part of the speaker at the moment of delivery. If listening is a passive exercise, so is manuscript delivery. Most manuscript delivery involves only the use of the eyes and the lips of the speaker. Extemporaneous delivery, on the other hand, is an active exercise. The extemporaneous speaker must think while he speaks. This slows delivery and permits the audience more easily to keep up with the pace and train of the speaker's thought. A former governor of New Hampshire, speaking at a Dartmouth convocation, read one page of his manuscript three times, happily unaware of what he was doing, wholly oblivious to his triple repetition. Why? Because only his eyes and his lips were involved. It would be interesting to know how many of his audience were equally oblivious to the triple repetition! Some speakers, it is true, do become expert in manuscript delivery. They do it by purposely slowing their pace, by skillful use of emphasis, and by rethinking the words as they are uttered. But these experts are rare.

The best reason I have heard for the superior advantages of the extemporaneous method is found in a quote from Daniel Webster: "There is a magic in actually watching the process of thought as it rises in the human mind." This magic, I believe, involves the mobility of countenance and natural gesture present in extemporaneous delivery that are important elements in communication both in the human and the animal world. Today we call it body language.

In the early part of our second year, I sold my interest in the shoeshine parlor to Monti. He wanted to take his friend Joe Leddy, another Boston University Law School student, into the partnership. I felt strongly that the business was not large enough to split the profits three ways. I guess we were both pretty stubborn about it. After many tempestuous discussions that almost brought our long friendship to the breaking point, Monti made me a buy-or-sell proposal. He set the figure at which I would have the option to either buy his interest or sell mine. I elected to sell. That saved our friendship. Not long after, Monti sold his interest to Leddy, and not long after that, Leddy closed the business out as it was not doing well.

As a result of this series of events both Monti and I were back in the labor market. I found a job with the Norris Drug Store working on the soda fountain from 5 P.M. until midnight and another job at Ginter's Restaurant, then on Lower Washington Street, working as a bus boy and general handy boy from 12:30 P.M. till 2 P.M. My job at Ginter's kept me in the basement taking orders from the waitresses upstairs, who shouted to me below through a speaking tube. I collected the food from the chef or from the storage shelves and brought it to one of the four automatic elevators that by electric power took it up to the waitresses, who served it to the customers. The lunch period was a hectic affair. I learned all the best and most lurid swear words at that time from the waitresses, who knew them all and could articulate them with great skill. In later years, I often thought that the experience of taking their verbal abuse was great preparation for holding political office.

Graduation for both Monti and me was delayed a year in order that we might take a leave of absence from school at the end of the second year to earn a little money for school and living expenses, which were rising rapidly and making it difficult for us financially. Monti spent his year and a half selling Fuller brushes in Maine. During the first summer of that year and a half, I worked for the R.L. Clark Feed Store in Barre, driving a truck to deliver grain. Handling those one-hundred-pound grain bags all day long was great exercise, and I really enjoyed that summer. In the winter and spring I worked for my father in his law office. Living at home permitted me to save a nice nest egg for the next year's school expenses. That made my senior year much easier and gave me more time to study.

Monti did so well selling Fuller brushes in Maine that he persuaded me to join him in that occupation during the summer of 1921 preceding our return to law school for our senior year. It was a profitable summer both financially and in experience. Our territory included both Penobscot and Aroostook counties, but we spent the summer mostly in Aroostook County. I learned a great deal about salesmanship. We found that if we could get inside a person's home we could usually make a sale. But the Aroostook and Penobscot county housewives were as reluctant to let salesmen in as most housewives are anywhere. We realized that we had to come up with a technique to facilitate getting invited into the house.

We experimented with various techniques that didn't work. Finally we hit on a solution. It was quite simple. We went to the telephone book in each town where we were to work and made a list of names. At first, we picked them pretty much at random, but later learned to check the streets where the most prosperous-looking homes were and eliminate from the list all names in the book that were not on those streets. We then mailed postcards to the selected names advising them that as representatives of the Fuller Brush Company, we would be in town on a specified date to introduce the Fuller Brush Company products to the community and that the addressee had been selected as one of the people to receive a free brush and a demonstration of the full line of products. When we arrived at a specified address, we would ring the doorbell. When the housewife answered the bell, we would ask her if she had received a card from the Fuller Brush Company. She would, of course, answer in the affirmative and invite us in. The small potato brush we gave away was a nice brush and a most useful tool in the kitchen. Quite frequently we would learn from talking with our customer that she had learned from another customer what a nice brush the potato brush was. In those cases we found that sales were made even easier.

These potato brushes could not be purchased in the stores because Fuller Brush Company's policy was to sell exclusively through door-to-door salesmen. All of the company products were excellent. The whole line of brushes covered every use anyone would have for cleaning house. Most of our territory had never been covered by a Fuller Brush salesman before. And we came at a good time. The preceding year had been a bumper potato-crop year in Aroostook County. It was always feast or famine in Aroostook County, depending upon the abundance of the potato crop. The people were big spenders in the feast years and cautious in the famine years. In some houses we sold as much as ninety dollars' worth of brushes.

While we were working in the Millinocket area, we became quite conscious of Mount Katahdin. That majestic mountain seemed to dominate the landscape in every direction and for hundreds of miles around. We could hardly keep our eyes from it. We decided that, like Mount Everest, it was there to be climbed. It was no simple feat in those days to climb to the top and back. There was a road, of sorts, for about ten miles in from East Millinocket, where a small building was used as an office in the summer by a registrar who registered those visitors who proposed to climb the mountain. From that point on, only a dim and narrow trail wound in and out among the trees and boulders, through brooks, swamps and rocky terrain, growing fainter and fainter as it wound up the mountain. It was approximately thirty miles from the point where the trail began to the top of the mountain. No human being lived anywhere in the area, and there was no shelter except a small unoccupied fire warden's cabin partway up the mountain. Hence, to reach the top meant sleeping in the open several nights.

Monti had some of the skills of a woodsman. I had only my short Boy Scout training. But we took a few days off in the middle of the summer and set out with great confidence, carrying as little weight as possible. We had a small amount of concentrated food and little else, except sharp knives, a small hatchet, a canvas canteen, and drinking cups. We had no blankets or changes of clothing or footwear. For the first day it was great fun. The sun was shining and we saw an abundance of wildlife, including those special birds that sing so gloriously in the deep woods. We lost the trail once, which cost us about two or three hours. Late in the afternoon, we spotted a huge moose on the trail, which fascinated us because neither of us had ever seen a moose before. He gazed at us with the same interest that we displayed in him, then quietly slipped into the thick woods and was gone. We kept on until dark, not even stopping to eat but munching sandwiches as we walked.

Monti was convinced that we could reach the top and return to the registrar's office fast enough to break the official record existing at the time. When dark descended, it came all at once, so we stopped and made a small fire and cut some soft wood brush to make beds. We ate a light meal, curled up on top of the evergreen boughs, and fell promptly to sleep. In a couple of hours we awoke amid pouring rain. To protect ourselves from the rain, we girdled two large white birch trees with our hunting knives to get a couple of long strips of bark about five feet long and wide enough to curl around our bodies. This shielded us quite a bit from the soaking rain, although our clothes were already soaked by the rain that had fallen while we slept. The rain kept pouring until around three o'clock in the morning. As soon as the sun rose we did likewise and tried to build a fire, but everything was so wet, we gave that up and ate another cold meal. Then we set out on our journey soaking wet and somewhat subdued. We took it a little easier this day because we were still tired, and our first day had taught us that we were pushing too hard.

About halfway up the mountain we discovered the fire warden's cabin and stopped there for a rest and to eat. It had grown hot, and our clothes were fast drying out. We found many initials and dates carved on the walls of the cabin by former hikers, so we followed suit. I carved not only my initial but also the letters and numerals to indicate my class in law school—B.U. '22. Years later I received a letter from a young man who had climbed the mountain and found my initials and school symbols. He wrote that he had corresponded with the law school and had identified me as the only person either in the law school or the other schools constituting Boston University who had those initials and who had graduated in 1922. An interesting correspondence followed in which we compared notes on our experiences climbing the mountain. I concluded that this young man would be a good recruit for the FBI.

As we pushed on toward the top of the mountain, the sun kept getting hotter, and our clothing became much drier and quite bearable. But as the heat continued to increase from the radiation from the rocks, we became excessively thirsty, and exhaustion began to overtake us. We drank all the water in both canteens. About five-hundred feet from the top, we found a huge mass of rock with a needle's-eye opening at the base through which the trail ran. There was no way around this mass except through the needle's-eye opening. Monti, who weighed much less than I, wiggled through without difficulty. I was less successful. Halfway through, my hips became wedged in a manner that made it impossible for me to move either forward or backward. The more I struggled the tighter I became wedged. The tighter I became wedged, the weaker I became as the hot sun poured down. It was a frightening feeling, and I began to panic, which made the situation worse. Monti tried to help by pulling, but that, too, only made matters worse. Finally, completely exhausted, Monti convinced me that I should try to rest awhile in the hope that relaxation would help. So, trying as best I could to calm my racing heart, I rested and even dozed off for a while. When I awoke I felt much better and somewhat relaxed. Again the struggle started. Relaxation apparently was the answer, for in a short while I was able to twist my hips in just the right way. I was through! My trousers were in tatters, but my spirits were again in full repair. We finished the remaining distance to the top without incident.

There we felt fully repaid for all our troubles. The air was incredibly clear and visibility was excellent. What a sight! It seemed as though we could see all over the State of Maine. We tried to count the hundreds of lakes but had to give it up because we thought we might be counting some of the most distant ones twice. I do not recall ever seeing a panorama equal to it.

Coming back, I refused to try the needle's eye again. This presented a problem because the mass of rock through which the needle's eye ran was so huge and the sides so steep and smooth that there was no way to get a foothold or a handhold on the lower side of the rock where the land sloped off so rapidly. It was easy enough to get on top of the rock from the upper side, but we could see no way around the mass. Finally, Monti wiggled through safely, and after much discussion I got on top of the rock mass and slid down the side about fifteen or eighteen feet into Monti's arms. This broke the shock of the fall somewhat, but left my trousers in even more tatters. I looked quite a sight and was glad that we did not encounter any humans on the way back.

From there on, things proceeded without difficulty until we reached the lower elevations. Then I began to have trouble with my feet. In my ignorance of woodcraft, I had worn sneakers instead of boots, thinking that because they would grip rocks better, they would be better. This was a bad mistake. I took off my sneakers and found the soles of both feet were forming large blisters. The pain was intense. I walked through every brook and swamp we came to, attempting to get momentary relief from the heat and pain. I took off and put on my sneakers scores of times. We finally arrived back at the registrar's office sore, exhausted, and lame but nevertheless ecstatic that we had made it to the top and returned. Since we arrived back at the registrar's office after office hours, the registrar was not there, but we recorded the time of our arrival. Some weeks later, Monti told me he had corresponded with the registrar, and on the basis of the time Monti gave him, the registrar confirmed that we had made the trip up and back in the shortest time up to that date. I don't remember what our time was, and of course it was wholly unofficial because we had arrived at a time when the registrar could not see us. And I'm not at all sure that it was a record. But I can give some sound advice: Don't hike long distances in sneakers!

I understand that since those days the trail has been greatly improved and that over much of the distance some kind of vehicle can travel. I remember reading of a commercial movie being made of the trail and the mountain, and at that time much heavy equipment was transported up the mountain.

Our summer in Maine was a memorable one and ended all too soon. While we were in Maine we had purchased an inexpensive secondhand Model T Ford touring car. And I mean secondhand! We were tinkering with it and patching tires much of the time. Our plan was to take Fuller brush orders right up to the time we started back for Vermont. This meant that the orders we took during the last week could not get delivered by hand because it took about a week to get orders shipped from the factory in Hartford, Connecticut. We arranged with the customers that these last-minute orders would be shipped by parcel post COD.

Just before we started our journey home to Vermont, we drove to Caribou to do some last-minute selling for a couple of days. Business was excellent, and we were sorry that we were at the end of our summer. Many French-Canadian people lived in the area, many of whom couldn't speak English. We had learned a few French words in and around Aroostook County, and that came in handy, especially up there. Phrases such as *"une bonne brusse pour la plafond"* and *"une bonne brusse pour la mur"* we repeated often enough so that our customers readily understood us. The French I had learned in high school was nowhere near as useful as these few words learned in Aroostook County!

While in Caribou, we drove up to Edmunston across the line into Canada, and each of us purchased three bottles of Canadian whiskey. This was during Prohibition. Neither Monti nor I drank hard liquor in those days, but we had school friends in Boston who did, and we thought they would appreciate some real whiskey, which was hard to obtain in Boston.

In our first year at school none of our classmates had been much interested in liquor. In our senior year, with the advent of Prohibition, use of hard liquor had become widespread among students. Most of it was moonshine of one kind or another, and much of it was downright dangerous. It is another indication that all you have to do to stir up interest in a commodity is to make it illegal.

Monti and I gave little thought, if any, to the details of the law regarding the importation of liquor. Enforcement at the border must have been pretty casual. We drove into Edmunston and back with the liquor without passing any customs office. When we arrived back in Boston, we found that first-quality Canadian whiskey was more valuable than we had suspected. We kept the liquor safely stored for months, and along toward spring I traded my three bottles for a new Hart, Shaftner, and Marx suit of clothes, which I badly needed. This new suit of clothes had just been purchased by a more affluent student friend of mine. He said he had paid sixty-five dollars for the suit, which was quite a price in those days. He needed the liquor worse that I did, and I surely needed the suit worse than he did. It was a fundamental basis for a good swap.

Near the end of August, Monti and I packed our bags and headed for Vermont greatly anticipating the short vacation we had planned before returning to law school. In one of our bags were the COD orders and our joint cash net returns for the summer amounting to over twelve hundred dollars in cash. Yes, in cash—Monti did not believe in banks in those days. Our summer's net earnings were rolled in bills wrapped in brown paper secured by rubber bands and carefully concealed in the bottom of a traveling bag with clothes and other traveling utensils.

Off we started along the northern border of Maine on our homeward trip in our antique Ford. When we arrived at Fort Fairfield, we stopped at a rooming house for the night. When we alighted and went to pick up our bags, the bag with the money was missing. We were crushed. We decided that it must have fallen out of the car where it was resting on the rear seat, probably on the last part of our trip. There was no point in going back to law school without money. We decided we would stay in the area and search for the bag. Perhaps we could find it. It was a forlorn hope, but the only one we had. We had little cash in our pockets, so we decided to go and see Edward Hopkins, a friend who lived in Fort Fairfield, whose father owned and operated a large country store. Ed Hopkins had been going to school in Boston, and we had met him there and were quite friendly with him. We thought one of us might possibly get a job in the store while the other spent the days searching for the bag. Ed had a better idea. He had heard me play my tenor banjo in Boston and was impressed with my musical ability—more than I was. He said he would get me a job with the Country Harmony Band, a local group that played for country dances, which were very popular then. "Fine, but I don't have my banjo with me," I said. "Don't worry," he said, "I'll borrow one for you." And he did. He also got me the job. I was to receive five dollars per night, which was ample for our room and meals.

And so the search started. We put ads in every country newspaper for miles around and spent our days making inquiries at garages, police stations, sheriff's offices, and newspaper offices, all to no avail. Then Monti got the idea that possibly our bag had been found by one of the hoboes who had an outdoor camp in a large sandbank just outside of town. This was the time of the year when the potatoes were being harvested in Aroostook County, and annually large groups of these tramps would congregate and work for high wages picking up potatoes. So Monti and I decided that we would join the hobo camp and live with these men in the hope of picking up some news of our bag. It is surprising how silly one can get when one is desperate, as we were. Properly dressed in ragged clothing, we joined the hobo camp. We lived in complete filth for two days, which was all I could stand, and then left, even though we had discovered nothing. Back I went to the Harmony Band and my five dollars per night, while Monti danced with the pretty girls to the tune of our music.

I was not much of a banjo player, but I carried some unearned prestige since Hopkins had built me up with the band leader as a famous banjo player from Boston. Almost immediately, I began to see in store windows posters advertising country dances on which were printed little gems like "With the Country Harmony Band featuring Deane Davis, famous Boston banjo player." My embarrassment increased when the band leader began asking me to play solos. Fortunately, I was better at finding excuses than I was at playing the banjo. When the full band was playing, the racket was sufficient to keep anybody from a true appraisal of the level of my competence.

Four days after my return to the band, Monti and I received a letter from the manager of the Maine district office in Portland of the Fuller Brush Company informing us that our bag had been found and asking instruction as to where to ship it. We immediately called the manager and asked him to ship the bag to Fort Fairfield, where we waited three days for its arrival, all the time biting our fingernails and wondering if the money would be intact. It turned out that the bag had been picked up by a driver of the car which had been following us the night we arrived in Fort Fairfield. Just as we had concluded, it had fallen out of our car into the road. The driver of the car who had picked up the bag had opened it and found some correspondence with the Portland office that gave the company's district address. It happened that he had an office in the same building. So he took it along to Portland and promptly delivered the bag to the manager. When the bag arrived, we opened it hardly daring to breathe. There in the bottom of the bag, obviously undisturbed, was the twelve hundred dollars that meant we could finish our senior year at Boston University Law School.

Now, our money miraculously recovered, we were on our way back to Barre. It was a long, tiring trip in our ancient Ford. We traveled three hundred miles, much of it over dirt and gravel roads with twists and turns that bore no relation to that route as it is today. The route then did not have any hard surface except in the towns and cities it went through. We made the trip with only one minor breakdown and immediately prepared to leave for law school. We had no time for the vacation we had planned with such keen anticipation. The minor breakdown occurred in the middle of a twenty-mile stretch on which there was not a single dwelling house. The car suddenly stopped. Jumping out to investigate, we found gasoline trickling down onto the ground from the carburetor. I got down under the car and found that a small screw on the bottom of the glass bowl on the carburetor was missing. Apparently it had shaken out somewhere before the car stopped. We diligently searched the area for the screw, even walking a quarter of a mile back over the road we had just traversed. No luck. We were not keen for walking the next ten miles for help. Finally, in a burst of unexpected genius, we cut a short twig about five-eighths of an inch in diameter from the bushes beside the road, pushed it into the hole where the threaded screw should have been, and screwed it into the threads as far as it would go. I grabbed the crank and gave it a few rapid spins. Lo and behold, the car started! What a relief. With much self-congratulation we drove on ten miles through the woods to a small village where we found an automobile shop and a mechanic. He didn't have a new screw of the type we needed, but he retrieved one from an old Ford car of similar model and year that was parked in his yard, and we went merrily on our way. When I have had trouble with modern cars in the years since, I have often wished for the same mechanical simplicity.

During my senior year in Boston, I worked part time in the well-known and prestigious law firm of Hermanson and Silverman. Hermanson was on the faculty at Northeastern University, and Silverman was city attorney for the city of Boston. Both of these men had been protégés of the famous Boston firm of Jacobs and Jacobs.

I worked a few hours each afternoon as a docket clerk for the firm. Each day I went to the bankruptcy court and represented the firm at the docket call. This task was essentially a messenger's job because the list of cases and status information that I was to report to the court were all prepared by others in the firm office. My job was simply to stand up when any one of the firm cases was called and orally inform the judge from the material already prepared. Occasionally, I would be questioned by the judge about a specific case, and when that happened I was supposed to know enough about the case to make an intelligent answer. At first it was frightening, but after a few weeks it became more or less routine. In addition, I was occasionally called upon for other minor and unimportant chores around the office. Despite the relative unimportance of my duties, I greatly enjoyed the experience because of the opportunity it gave me to absorb the atmosphere of a large city law office as well as the atmosphere of the courtroom.

As a result of this exposure, the firm offered me a job as a salaried associate when I finally graduated from law school in the spring of 1922. I was tempted to accept because I enjoyed living in Boston and the salary was attractive—certainly more than I could expect to earn during my first few years practicing law in Barre. But as I pondered the offer, I kept seeing the hills, valleys, woods, and streams of Vermont and the very special kind of people I had grown up with in Vermont. I found that I really wanted to return to Vermont. So did Monti. We packed our things and came home. I have never regretted that decision.

8

Getting Launched

I expect, but do not remember, that we were a somewhat bleary-eyed group when we filed into court and faced the justices. But if we were, I'm sure those justices were quite understanding, for there had once been a day when they too had filed into court after an evening of celebration for passing their exams.

When I was twelve, my father took me to hear Teddy Roosevelt, who had come to Barre during his campaign for the presidency. It was a big day in Barre, and people turned out by the thousands to crowd the area around City Park and the adjoining streets to catch a sight of Roosevelt and hear him. I never saw a larger crowd in Barre in all the years I lived there. He spoke from a high platform in front of the Church Street School. There was no amplification system, of course, and the crowd pressed right up against the platform on which the famous man stood. I saw nothing resembling Secret Service protection as we know it today, but our local police were there in full force striving valiantly to keep the people from trampling each other as they pushed and shoved, hoping to get a bit nearer the platform. I have no memory today of a single word Roosevelt said, but I do remember of how he looked as he spoke in his usual clear, loud, and penetrating voice, and of the effect it had on me.

On the way home from Roosevelt's speech, my father explained some of the issues involved, and I marveled that he knew so much about national affairs. I'm sure his idea of taking me to hear Teddy Roosevelt was to further my education in a part of life that he thought was important—politics. He understood kids, and he understood education.

My twelve-year-old imagination was fired with enthusiasm by my first exposure to politics. I vowed I would someday find a way to be involved in politics—without the slightest notion, of course, of how I could achieve it. I imagined the role of the politician as one fighting for justice for the downtrodden people. That evening I even composed a few choice paragraphs as to what I would say when my opportunity for political service came. Those paragraphs have long since gone the way such compositions should, but the thrill of my simple involvement that day is with me still.

Other than campaigning in high school class elections and occasionally doing legwork supporting candidates at the local and state level—and once helping in a campaign for Stanley C. Wilson, who was running for the United States Senate—I had no further involvement in politics until I had graduated from law school and started practice. Even then my involvement was principally to help convey voters to the polls, a practice that was followed much more intensively then than it is today. I also helped to man the checklists at the polling booths to make sure that known supporters of our candidate had actually voted. If, near closing time, we noticed that certain known supporters had not voted, we dashed outside to send cars for them. A higher percentage of eligible voters actually voted in those days, and the practice of transporting voters contributed to that result.

Occasionally, we had torchlight processions up and down Main Street in Barre with a snappy band in the lead. Then we would march back to the opera house to listen to our candidate try to convince us of what we were already convinced. A lot of effort was spent in building enthusiasm—much more effort than was spent arguing over issues. In that regard, our campaigns were not much different from those of today except that there was a lot more excitement and emotion then than we have today.

Without radio or television to give us instant news, we had to wait for voting results until they were written in big letters and numbers on brown paper and pasted to the window of the *Barre Daily Times* office.

Transporting voters to the polls taught me a few things about what motivates people to vote for a particular candidate. I enjoyed talking with the voters on the way to the polls about the issues and who they were going to vote for and why. It became clear that motivations for supporting a candidate were of many kinds, but that the one that led the list by a wide margin was self-interest of the particular voter. And in the case of the candidates running for the United States Senate, voters were usually for the incumbent because he had done some particular errand for them in Washington.

This tainted somewhat my idealistic view of politics as a noble profession. But in later years I gradually came to understand that democracy as a working process is founded upon the notion of self-interest and its expression at the ballot box. As I read more deeply into the subject, I discovered that the founders of our nation and the political system supporting it knew this quite well and accepted and endorsed it as a sound basis for representative government. Out of the variety of individual self-interests generally comes a consensus that approximates the national interest. Senators and congressmen must maintain offices in their home districts to serve the self-interests of their constituents. This is expected of them, and it is in their own self-interest—and there is nothing wrong with it. In a nation and a government as vast as ours, there is no other practical way for most individuals in Vermont, for example, to satisfactorily transact business with the Washington bureaucracy. And what holds true for senators and congressmen at the federal level holds true to a lesser extent at home, for officeholders on the state level. In a very practical sense the officeholder is indeed the "representative" of the members of his constituency.

I was hardly thinking about any of this, however, when both Monti and I learned that we had survived our senior year at Boston University Law School and would graduate. My mind was solely on the diplomas we would receive and the looming challenge of the Vermont Bar examinations. We took our bar examinations in September 1922 in the usual fashion of the times: eight written examinations and four oral, in which all members of the examining committee participated.

I approached the ordeal with considerable trepidation, for while both Monti and I felt we were fairly well grounded in the basics of the common law as taught at Boston University, Vermont law was not taught in that law school. My approach to solving that problem was twofold. First, I obtained copies of previous written examinations for a number of years and tested myself with these. Whenever I was not sure of the answer or the reasons behind the court's conclusion, I went to the *Vermont Reports* and researched the question. While the written examinations varied from year to year, I found that there was a consensus of questions that in one form or another involved the same subjects from year to year. Second, I took *Robert's Vermont Digest* and read every word it contained. *Robert's Vermont Digest* was then only a one-volume book, and it contained a brief summary of every decision the Vermont Supreme Court had rendered up to that time. If the summary was not wholly clear, I went to the opinion itself and read the actual decision in full and tried to master not only the meaning of the result but the reasoning behind it. It sounds simple as I write it, but it took me nearly all summer from the beginning of June until September to finish the task. I still had butterflies in my stomach each time I thought of the upcoming examinations.

The examinations were held in the Hall of Representatives at the statehouse, and they lasted three days. I was a nervous wreck before it was over. No one could have been more surprised or pleased than I was when my name was called as one who had passed. I am sure my excitement closely matched that of my father when he had taken the examinations back in 1899.

Monti passed too, and the following day we appeared in Supreme Court—then in session for the regular September term—and solemnly took the oath of office before the distinguished justices of the court. And they were distinguished and looked the part. I was tremendously impressed. The justices in their flowing black robes with solemn countenances were to me the personification of the law and its institutions in all its grandeur. It was an exciting event, and the oath of office that I took to become a member of the bar has always seemed a sacred obligation.

I do not recall any formal celebration by our class for the exams except a rather hilarious evening the day our passing was announced. Many candidates had been housed in the Pavilion Hotel during the examinations, and we were a pretty sober, scared, and hardworking group until that last night. Somehow, I can't even remember what we did to celebrate. There was no liquor, which is probably hard to believe nowadays, but Prohibition was in effect, and besides the use of liquor for social occasions was far less common than it is today. So it was not liquor that caused my mental blackout on that occasion. All I remember is that we spent a hilarious evening at the Pavilion Hotel that ran into the early hours of the morning. When it was over, we dropped into bed for a few hours of sleep before appearing in Supreme Court for the oath-taking. I expect, but do not remember, that we were a somewhat bleary-eyed group when we filed into court and faced the justices. But if we were, I'm sure those justices were quite understanding, for there had once been a day when they too had filed into court after an evening of celebration for passing their exams.

Now it was Monti's wish that we go into partnership. I gave this proposal long and careful consideration. I genuinely liked him and much admired his fighting spirit. He was determined, driven, persistent, and confident. These qualities were clearly evident both in the way he walked and in the way he tried a lawsuit. On the trail or on the sidewalk, he walked rapidly with a long, purposeful stride with his head thrown forward in a posture that clearly showed that he knew what his goal was and where he was going and that he intended to achieve his purpose come what may. He was not given to compromise of any kind, and this characteristic led some to call him stubborn.

Having lived with Monti for several years while in law school, I was fully conscious of the strengths of his personality and equally conscious of the incompatibility of our temperaments. We had had many rough times during those school years when our temperaments clashed, and I felt that such a partnership would be unwise for both of us. When I declined, it cast a cloud over our friendship for quite a few years.

My intention had always been to begin practice in partnership with my father, who had practiced law in Barre for about twenty-one years. It was a real disappointment for me, therefore, when in 1922 he became a candidate for the office of probate judge and was elected. Consequently, I began on my own. I took over the office he had occupied in the Gordon Block. Fortunately, Dad elected to keep office space there, too. He was there nearly every weekday evening, and I thus had the opportunity to pick his brains and practical experience, the value of which cannot be described.

Early on, he asked me how I was getting along. "Fine," I said, "except that I can't seem to solve the problem of how much to charge." "That's no problem," he said. "Don't waste your time and energy worrying about what you are going to charge. Concentrate on trying to do something for your client. When you have, you'll have something tangible to measure it by. You'll know what to charge. Charge what the traffic will bear."

My office in the Gordon Block had an additional benefit. John W. Gordon, the owner of the block, was a practicing lawyer with long experience and an established reputation. His office was just across the hall from mine. His knowledge of the whole breadth of the law and his understanding of its history both of case law and the statutes were prodigious. Always ready and willing to help a scared and confused beginner at the law, he was a powerful source of support in those days.

In the beginning my practice consisted largely of collecting bills for local merchants. This type of practice was not greatly remunerative. The fee was invariably 15 percent of the amount collected and nothing if no collection was made. Young lawyers wore out a lot of shoe leather in the early stages of their practices and made little money but learned a lot. My father had given me some sage advice about collecting bills. He told me that collecting bills was a natural way for a young lawyer to show the public what kind of stuff he was made of. "And you learn a lot about human nature too," he said. "You haven't anything else to do, so put everything you have into doing the best job you can. You'll find that a lot of merchants will send you bills that have previously been in the hands of some other lawyer who failed to collect them. Make an earnest attempt to collect them, and if you find they are uncollectable, send them back to the merchant with a letter carefully explaining what you have done in an attempt to collect and why they are uncollectable. If you collect even as little as one dollar, send your client the one dollar immediately, less your 15 percent, and make your report. When merchants send bills to lawyers for collection and hear nothing about what has been done, some of them get to wondering if the bills have actually been collected and not paid to them. You'll wear out a lot of shoe leather and it will seem to you that you are wasting a lot of time and effort, but it's a natural way to begin building a reputation for honesty and diligence."

Years later, after I had given up general law practice and was serving as general counsel for National Life, I learned how true this was. Joseph Sanguinetti, a distinguished figure in Barre and a solid citizen, called me at my home and asked me to make a will for his wife, Modesta. Modesta had operated a grocery store at the corner of Main and Seminary streets, and I had collected many bills for her during my early beginnings. I explained to Joe that I was not in general practice and advised him to get another lawyer to do the job. He pressed me, and I still refused. Reluctantly, he hung up. A couple of days later he called me again and said, "Deane, if you don't make Modesta's will, she says that she is not going to make a will." I gave up and made the will. I called at their home on North Main Street to supervise the execution of the will. When it was completed, I said to Modesta, "Now Modesta, do me a favor. Joe said that if I didn't make your will, you were not going to make a will."

"That's right," she responded.

"Well, I want to know why you felt so strongly about that," I said.

"Because when you were a young lawyer and collected bills, you were prompt and careful and sent me reports of what you were doing, and you sent me the money just as soon as you had collected. I knew you were an honest lawyer and a good one," she replied.

I soon learned that collecting bills required in many cases bringing suit in court. Consequently, it gives a young lawyer his first actual experience in court practice. My dad was indeed a philosopher.

I had hardly opened my office to practice law, however, before I became involved in politics on a personal basis. Frank Langley, the owner and publisher of the *Barre Daily Times*, was a powerful figure in politics behind the scenes. He came to my office and asked me to run for the office of alderman from Ward Three. I was so flattered by the attention of this leading figure in Barre that I did not even inquire why I should run or what it was that I would do for the good of the city. I promptly assented, feeling quite sure that with Langley's support, election would be assured. And it was. I served for several years, and the experience taught me a great deal about politics at the local level and how a city is run. I must note here that at no time did Langley ever try to influence me on a vote or to dictate to me in any way.

After a time, the office of city attorney became vacant, and I discussed with the members of the city council my desire to hold that position. It is a position filled by the city council. By long practice it had become established that whoever held the position of city attorney would automatically be appointed grand juror. The position of grand juror in those days was a statutory one in which the grand juror had the duty to prosecute criminal offenses within the city limits. Since the city attorney worked closely with the city council and attended most meetings of the council, I could see where I could continue to enjoy most of the advantages I had enjoyed as an alderman and in addition would be involved in legal matters of importance, both civil and criminal, which was my first love. Moreover, the actual prosecution of criminal offenses would give me a widening experience in trial work.

Not all of those experiences were pleasant ones. It was my responsibility as city attorney, for example, to prosecute violators of the Volstead Act. The act gave muscle to the eighteenth amendment, which outlawed the manufacture, sale, and transportation of intoxicating liquors. Many of the Italians living in Barre received special permits that allowed them to continue to make wine and *grappa* for private consumption, but there were others, often women, whose houses acquired reputations as places where customers could buy liquor. From my experience making deliveries for the R.L. Clark Feed Company and from my friends in the Italian community, I knew that a number of these rum runners were widows who had lost their husbands prematurely, many to silicosis. With children to raise and no insurance to help them, they turned to manufacturing and selling *grappa* out of desperation. Moreover, I knew that most of the residents of

Barre opposed the law in the first place, including many people who did not use liquor themselves.

Those were difficult times. As a professional sworn to uphold the law, I knew I had a duty to enforce it or face being kicked out of office in disgrace. But I had seen the dilemma these widows faced and my heart went out to them. I never did find a satisfactory way to resolve all the offenses, so I just handled each case individually as it came along. If it was a first offense as far as the court records showed, I would always ask for probation on the theory that maybe the practice would stop. But I never had the remotest idea how they could stop until their children grew old enough to support them. In the worst cases, I guess people blinked and looked the other way. That's what I did.

Law practice is not built primarily on publicity, but for young lawyers it helps. A practice is primarily built on demonstrated competence. First you have to get a chance to demonstrate your competence, however, and a prosecutor's job not only tests your mettle but gives you a chance to demonstrate competence if you have it. If you have the stuff, a period in the public eye puts you in the position of being sought out by individuals with legal problems. From there on, if you are lucky—and competent too—you become favorably known to more and more people by word of mouth of satisfied clients.

My next step into participatory politics followed in due course. I ran for the office of state's attorney. This time I ran on my own motion, although I had the wise counsel of my father. He recognized that I was developing a taste for trial practice rather than office practice, and he pointed out that as state's attorney I would have a greater opportunity for trial work as well as a modest salary to help pay living expenses. The state's attorney's job was still, at that time, a part-time job, and the state made no allowance for expenses for office rent, secretarial help, and all the other administrative costs incident to running an office.

The work as state's attorney gave me a feeling of being more in the center of things. Moreover, it gave me lots of trial experience, and I began to feel much more comfortable and at home in the courtroom. It widened my acquaintance in the county and gave me an opportunity to know most of the lawyers in the county intimately. I worked hard at the job. As my father had predicted, my practice began to increase not only in numbers but in the importance of the cases. I prosecuted any and all types of criminal cases including a few homicides. The courtroom exposed me to the public as in those days the newspapers covered major court trials much more thoroughly than today, when political matters are the chief subjects for newspaper fare. At that time, there was no cadre of reporters primarily devoted to political matters.

Although considered a part-time job, in one sense it was a twenty-four-hour-a-day job since the state's attorney was always on call. Moreover, at that time there were no trained investigators or detectives and no state police, so it was the custom of the sheriff and the police departments to call upon the state's attorney to help them in the investigations of the more important criminal complaints.

One homicide that I prosecuted occurred in Montpelier, right across the street from the Washington County Courthouse, while I was trying a case in that court. The courtroom doors suddenly opened, and in walked Sheriff Henry Lawson, breathless and obviously agitated. Without ceremony but in a loud voice, he informed the presiding judge that a murder had just been committed across the street and the presence of the state's attorney was urgently needed. The judge promptly recessed court, and I accompanied the sheriff across the street. He piloted me upstairs to the second floor of a building that at that time adjoined the Episcopal church. I followed him into a bedroom. On the bed was the dead body of a woman. Sitting upright on the couch was a man, covered with blood running down over his face, neck, and chest. Much of the bed, the couch, and floor was covered with blood. It quickly became apparent that the man had shot the woman in the head and then tried to commit suicide. A doctor was immediately called, who took one quick look at the patient and ordered him removed to the hospital. The doctor informed me that it was doubtful that the patient would survive.

Since all the evidence as to what had happened was circumstantial, I was anxious, if possible, to get a statement from him, just in case he should live. He had shot himself above the temple, and the bullet had penetrated his skull and emerged at the top of his head. He was conscious but very weak and unresponsive. I asked the sheriff to send a deputy to accompany the man to the hospital and to stay with him until I could prepare the necessary papers to place him officially under arrest. I completed the papers and gave them to the sheriff, who went to the hospital and went through the motions of placing the man under arrest. Again at the hospital I talked with the doctor, who now thought the man could not possibly survive. I then asked the doctor, the hospital superintendent, and the attending nurse to stand by while I questioned the man. He was conscious and apparently heard and understood me and my questions, but he was so weak that his responses were barely above a low whisper.

This was before the days when the law required that a suspect must be warned in great detail as to his rights, including the right to remain silent. I explained to the suspect that I was the state's attorney and asked him if he understood what that meant. After a long pause he nodded his head. I then asked him if he shot the woman, whose name was Lottie. There was no reply so I repeated the question several times, and he finally whispered, "Yes." Then I wrote affidavits out in longhand for signatures of each of the three witnesses who had heard this somewhat unusual conversation. I felt sure the man would not live. But to everyone's surprise, after hovering between life and death for many weeks, he began to improve and eventually was tried on a charge of first-degree murder. He was defended by William Lapoint, a Barre lawyer who put up quite a fight to keep the whispered confession out of evidence. When this failed and the court admitted the evidence of the confession, Lapoint tried just as valiantly to prove the accused was insane at the time he committed the act, but the evidence on this point was so weak that the jury turned down this line of defense also. If I had not obtained this whispered confession, there would have been no direct evidence of the commission of an offense, and the man might easily have escaped conviction. He was convicted, however, and sentenced to life imprisonment. He started to serve his sentence in the state prison at Windsor, but he lived only about a year and a half because of the injuries to his brain caused by the shooting. It was a tragic case, but most homicides are.

During my term of office as state's attorney, I worked closely with Sheriff Lawson. This involved much traveling around the county to assist in the investigation of criminal complaints. On one of these trips the sheriff received an urgent phone call informing him of trouble at a farmhouse in a remote section of the town of Plainfield. We immediately terminated the investigation we were pursuing at the moment, and I accompanied the sheriff as he responded to this call.

As soon as we arrived and found what the problem was, I wished I were elsewhere. The owner of the farm was up with a shotgun in the haymow of the barn, badly intoxicated, yelling and threatening destruction to anyone who came near him. His housekeeper was in the house, crying and greatly frightened. Every few minutes, the man would shoot his gun just to emphasize that he was in earnest. By that time, a small crowd had gathered, carefully remaining—as I did—out of range. After surveying the situation, the sheriff announced that he could see no alternative except to go in and subdue the man before he did something desperate. I advised against it, but Lawson disregarded my advice. The sheriff called to the man, told him who he was, and informed him that if he didn't come down in five minutes, he was coming after him. He also explained carefully that he would get off much easier if he would come down voluntarily than if he were taken by force.

The man refused to budge and kept up a running fire of threats against the world in general and the sheriff in particular. Thereupon, I saw one of the most unusual exhibitions of raw courage I have ever witnessed. Lawson had a pistol in a holster on his belt, but he never touched it. He walked straight for the ladder to the haymow, talking all the time to the man in the mow, who yelled to Lawson that if he came any closer he would kill him. Lawson walked up to the foot of the ladder directly beneath the man and ordered him to throw down his gun at once. There was a brief pause, and then to everyone's amazement the gun came clattering down. Lawson put handcuffs on the man, I made out a warrant for his arrest, and together we drove to Washington County Jail where Lawson locked his prisoner in jail. Then we drove back to Plainfield to complete the investigation we were pursuing when we had been interrupted by the telephone call. Such was the life of a sheriff in those days before state police.

Another case I remember well began with a telephone call around midnight to my home. It was Sheriff Lawson calling. He explained that he was calling from Plainfield, that there had been a bad fire in the adjoining town of Marshfield, and that a farmhouse and barn had burned under most suspicious circumstances. Lawson explained that he was holding several persons for questioning and needed help. I dressed and went to Plainfield, where Sheriff Lawson was waiting for me. After questioning his witnesses at length, I failed to get any clear evidence sufficient to hold any of the witnesses, and they were released. The next night, another farmhouse burned in the same general area, and we found that we had a difficult and tricky problem on our hands. Arson, the crime of burning a building without right, is a difficult offense to prove, and prosecutors generally hate such cases. Then began a long course of burning buildings. Each night, or sometimes after two or three intervening days, another fire would break out.

It was obvious that a dangerous criminal, probably unbalanced, was at large, and a reign of terror began in the community of Marshfield and adjoining Plainfield. The newspapers began to criticize "the authorities" and pontificated that there must be some easy way to stop this series of fires. Lawson and I dropped everything else and devoted our full time and energy, day and night, to the task of solving this mystery. We had very little sleep for a period of three weeks, and on several nights we did not even take our clothes off. We would drop down on a couch for an hour or two of sleep and then go back to work. The fires persisted until nine sets of buildings had been burned. False clues were turning up by the dozens, each of which had to be investigated and scores of witnesses interviewed. We were literally at our wits' end, tired and discouraged. The townspeople were terrified, and many were complaining because we had not solved the mystery.

This, of course, was long before we had a state police organization in Vermont, with a sophisticated and capable detective service. We were alone and very much on our own. Neither of us had any professional training in criminal detection, much less in detection of the crime of arson.

Finally, we had a stroke of luck. At the scene of one of the fires, Sheriff Lawson found several clear footprints in the mud immediately outside the place where the fire had apparently started. We took drawings of the shape of the prints and a design of the impressions made by the sole and heel. Fortunately, these prints had been undisturbed by the crowd milling around the fire. Even before this fire, we had become suspicious of two young men who were living in the vicinity and always seemed to show up at each fire, but we had no real evidence to connect them with the fires. Often they valiantly helped to put the fires out. Neither of these young men had a criminal record or had shown any signs of psychiatric disturbance, which are typical of the kinds of people who set fires. As soon as we had developed the impressions of the footprints, we brought the two young men to Montpelier for questioning. After hours of questioning that accomplished nothing, we took each man aside separately and compared the size and contours of the prints with the shoes that each suspect was wearing. In one case the shoes matched the shape and size and design of the prints. The match was not conclusive, but it was close enough to make us reasonably sure that we had the right man. We confronted the man with the matching shoes, and he began to weaken. After a half hour or so, he broke down and confessed and told the whole story—even the part that his friend had played in setting the fires. Armed with this confession, we confronted the other young man, and he too confessed. Both men were convicted and sentenced to long terms of imprisonment. They were obviously of that class of humanity that is sufficiently abnormal to get some kind of visceral satisfaction from watching a fire they have set.

One of the most unusual cases I tried involved Mr. D. Fumagalli. Mr. Fumagalli lived on Granite Street in Barre in a four-story brick building that he owned and rented to a variety of tenants for living quarters. During a pronounced thaw of snow late in the winter of 1926, an explosion occurred in the building. To those in the vicinity, it sounded and felt like an earthquake. An elderly couple who were living in the building were killed, as were several people on the sidewalk in front of the building. Mr. Fumagalli, who was in the building at the time and was horribly burned, died weeks later of his injuries. A suit was brought on behalf of the family of Mr. Fumagalli and the families of the others who had lost their lives against the Vermont Gas Company, which had been a client of mine for some time. The estates of the injured people and of Mr. Fumagalli claimed that the explosion had been caused by illuminating gas escaping from gas lines in the building under the control of the Vermont Gas Company.

Soon after these original suits were filed an insurance policy was found issued by Aetna Insurance Company that insured Mr. Fumagalli against liability for death or other injuries to any person caused by negligence or mismanagement of the building in which the explosion occurred. This information became known to representatives of the families of those who had lost their lives in the explosion and caused them to bring actions against the estate of Mr. Fumagalli as well. The Aetna Insurance Company thereupon entered the suits against Mr. Fumagalli and took charge of the defense. The result was that I found myself involved in a large and tangled court case representing the gas company. I was in association with S. Hollister Jackson, a Barre lawyer of excellent standing who was later elected lieutenant governor of Vermont, and with Bruce Wyman of Boston, a noted utility lawyer with a national reputation who had also achieved prominence as the author of several textbooks on utility law and the law of explosions. Given the high value of the building and the loss of so many lives, millions of dollars were involved, which was a new experience for a young Vermont lawyer like me.

The principal facts were agreed to by all. During the afternoon of the day of the explosion, one of the tenants had noticed a strong smell of gas fumes that seemed to be coming from the cellar. The day was dark, foggy, and overcast due to unseasonably high temperatures and thawing snow. Water had overflowed the banks of an adjacent river and had flooded the basements of some of the buildings in the vicinity, including that of the Fumagalli building. The cellar was not lighted, and when the tenant smelled the fumes he and his wife lit a kerosene lamp and proceeded to go down the stairs into the cellar to investigate. Almost immediately the terrific explosion occurred, demolishing the building and throwing debris out into the street.

At first everyone assumed that the explosion had been caused by the illuminating gas. The building, including all the rooms rented to tenants, was lighted by illuminating gas supplied by the pipes of the Vermont Gas Company. But as the investigation proceeded a surprising discovery was made. In the backyard some fifty feet behind the site of the demolished building a two-thousand-gallon gasoline tank was found buried in the ground. Two pipes ran from the tank into the cellar. Both were about an inch and a half in diameter, and one was about eighteen inches above the other. The ends of the two pipes were open. The gasoline tank was dug up and found to contain several hundred gallons of high-test gasoline. Further investigation disclosed that at the time Mr. Fumagalli bought the property, an old machine in the cellar had been connected to the two pipes. By that time the building was lighted by illuminating gas, so neither Mr. Fumagalli nor anyone else knew that this machine had been used many years before to convert high-test gasoline into a mixture that could be ignited and used for lighting.

On the basis of this discovery, we claimed that the explosion had been caused by gasoline fumes escaping from this old gasoline tank. We theorized that the water that had flooded the basement had come into the cellar and run into the open end of the lowest pipe and back into the gasoline tank. Since gasoline is lighter than water, we further theorized that the gasoline had come to the top of the water in the tank, and when the water and gas had reached the right height, the mixture had run back into the cellar and distributed itself over the top of the water in the cellar. Gasoline—not illuminating gas—we claimed, had given off the highly explosive fumes that caused the explosion when the two tenants came down the cellar stairs with a kerosene lamp.

Our contention was disputed by the other parties to the litigation. Since the whole case would now turn on whether illuminating gas or gasoline fumes had exploded, we engaged one of the most famous explosive experts in the country, Professor Gill of the Massachusetts Institute of Technology. He had written on the subject of explosives for many years. Shortly after we had engaged Professor Gill, we obtained evidence that the old machine in the basement had been sold to a junk dealer for $2.00 by Mr. Fumagalli. This was the fatal act that made possible the sequence of events detailed above. The other side hired another explosive expert, and we were ready for trial. The number of cases involved complicated the matter somewhat, and counsel in the case and the various parties involved were able to agree to submit the case to the presiding judge of Washington County Court without benefit of jury.

Immediately after Professor Gill entered the case, he asked what kind of smoke, if any, had been observed immediately following the explosion. He explained that an explosion of large quantities of gasoline produces a thick cloud of black smoke, whereas an explosion of illuminating gas leaves only a very little smoke, and it would not appear to be black. Thereupon I searched for people who might have been in places where they could observe the smoke. This included passersby, neighbors, and people living within a half mile or so on all sides. I interviewed more than 150 people, and out of that number found thirty people who qualified as good witnesses on the point and who told me in sworn affidavits that they had observed the site at the time of the explosion, and that immediately thereafter heavy clouds of black smoke had risen from the wreckage.

Not only did our opponents claim that the fuel that had caused the explosion was illuminating gas, but that according to their expert, it would be impossible for a casual observer to recognize the difference in the degree of blackness of the smoke. To counter this we decided upon an experiment quite unusual in courtroom procedure. We hired a contractor and had him build two models of the Fumagalli building. One of these models was fitted with a pipe into which illuminating gas could be piped and the other with a pipe into which fumes produced from high-octane gasoline could be piped. Each model was about fifteen by fifteen feet. We then sought the permission of the judge to move these models to the lawn of the courthouse where the trial was in progress. We also sought permission to explode both of these models so that the judge and all interested parties could observe for themselves what, if any, difference in color could be observed between the different smokes.

Opposing counsel fought this request valiantly. After several days of testimony as to how the models were built and after testimony by Professor Gill as to the relevance and importance of the volume and color of the smoke, the judge granted the request. The fateful day set by the judge for the exhibition arrived. Clients, attorneys, and court attendants gathered on the lawn. As the word quickly spread, a sizable crowd of the public gathered. Butterflies were flying around inside my stomach. Everything now depended on how this demonstration came off. As agreed, both models were to be fired at the same time in order that a true comparison could be made. The judge gave the word. Professor Gill fired the two models. A tremendous cloud of black smoke poured outwards and upwards from the model fired by gasoline. A few spirals of brownish- or gray-looking smoke emerged from the model exploded with the illuminating gas. What a relief!

I watched the judge like a hawk. He turned and without a word went back to the courtroom. He sent word by the court officer that he wanted to see all counsel in chambers. We responded promptly. He minced no words. "Gentlemen," he said, "as you know, the whole case depends upon whether it was gasoline or illuminating gas that exploded and caused the damage. You could see as well as I. It was gasoline. We could go on with the trial, and I will if counsel wishes. But since, in my opinion, this demonstration is determinative of the case, it looks like a waste of time. Let me know tomorrow morning."

The next morning counsel for the other side came into court and reported that they saw no reason for continuing the trial and would await the judge's final written order and findings of fact. It was a heady experience for a young lawyer.

One other event stands out clearly in my memory of my days as state's attorney: the flood of 1927. The cities of Montpelier and Barre were badly hit by the flood.

During the afternoon of November 2, I was involved in trying a case at Montpelier in the Washington County Courthouse. Rumors began to trickle into the courtroom that the rivers were overflowing their banks and flooding highways and bridges. No one seemed to take the warnings very seriously until later in the day. The rumors persisted, and the court decided to adjourn early in case travel might be impeded by the rising waters. This was around four o'clock in the afternoon.

Lieutenant Governor S. Hollister Jackson, who lived and practiced law in Barre, was drowned later that afternoon as he was driving home from the office. At a point not far from his home, a small brook had become swollen with the flood waters and had overrun the street, leaving a large chasm that made the street impassable. In the gathering twilight Mr. Jackson stepped out of his car to determine what was holding up traffic and stepped too close to the raging brook. The bank caved in, and he was swept away. None of the people standing around the site even knew that he had fallen into the brook. His body was not found for several days, a half mile or so from where he had fallen.

On that day, Gerald Drock and Ralph Winter, both friends of mine, were lost in the basement of the F.H. Rogers store on Main Street in Barre, where they had volunteered to go to help save merchandise in the cellar. As the flood waters rose, the pressure had become so great that it pushed over one of the division walls in the cellar, and they were overwhelmed by the rushing waters.

All bus and railroad service between Barre and Montpelier was suspended because of major washouts in the highway. Electric, gas, and water lines were broken, leaving much of Barre and Montpelier without heat, light, or water for several days. No mail came into Barre for about a week, and telephone service was unavailable for most residents. When the waters subsided, the main streets of Barre were filled with large deposits of clay and silt, in some places four and five feet in height. A Red Cross station was set up in the armory on Elm Street in Barre to provide food and shelter for the homeless and ill. The National Guard was sent into Barre, and for a time it was the only law we had. Martial law was not formally declared, but there was such chaos and confusion that people obeyed the on-the-spot orders of the Guard members without question. There was very little crime, if any.

The first news of the flood from elsewhere around the state was delivered by those who walked into Barre. In that fashion I received an urgent message from the sheriff that something had to be done for the inmates of the Washington County Jail in Montpelier. The water in Montpelier was higher than it was in Barre. It had flooded the Courthouse nearly to the ceiling of the street floor, and the swift waters had pushed in a large section of wall where the county clerk's office is on the south side of the building. Large objects had gone through the gap on the swirling tide and out the other side through the probate office. One eyewitness reported seeing the dead body of a horse atop a large piano sweep through the courthouse in this fashion.

The message from the sheriff was that the twelve inmates of the jail were without food, heat, or warm clothing. They had saved their lives during the worst of the high water by holding on to the bars of their cells and letting their bodies float horizontally on the waters. Death had been a near thing for them.

I decided that the best thing to do was to bring the twelve prisoners to Barre and house them in the Red Cross facility at the armory. But how? Washouts had made the usual Barre-Montpelier route impassable to cars. I borrowed the new Black Maria patrol wagon from the Barre city police and drove it alone over the back roads through East Montpelier. I will never forget that experience. Several times I had to build temporary bridges of stone where culverts were washed out. When I finally arrived at the jail I explained to the twelve prisoners that if they would come to Barre voluntarily and work faithfully as volunteers to help clean out the mountains of mud and silt in the streets for a period of ten days, they would then be permitted to go free. In the meantime, I explained, they would have a warm place to stay, good food, and warm clothing. They were glad to accept the arrangement, and they did work faithfully for ten days. Then one by one they disappeared. Of course, I had no legal authority to make this arrangement with the prisoners, but something had to be done for them, and when there is a vacuum in the government, somebody has to take over. If the right thing is done, no one questions it. And no one did.

Mail service was eventually restored to Barre and Montpelier by a small, single-motored plane that flew daily to Montpelier and landed on Towne Hill (close to what is now Greenock Avenue, just a couple of hundred yards from where I now live at 5 Dyer Street). On the last trip, the small plane overturned while making a landing on the rough grassland, and the pilot was killed. It was still another of the tragedies that befell Vermont during these dark days.

In view of the widespread damage to highways, bridges, railroads, homes, and commercial properties, Vermont made a remarkably rapid recovery from the devastating 1927 flood. Vermont received much publicity from the statement of Governor Weeks when offered help from the federal government: "Thank you, but Vermont will take care of its own." This self-reliant position had to be modified later when it was found that in spite of the state's first major bond issue, Vermont would need to accept over two million dollars in aid from the federal government in order to complete its recovery. But one good result of the disaster was that it provoked public officials and the private sector to seriously study ways to prepare for a reoccurrence. Consequently, the state was better able to cope with extensive floods when they did occur later.

9

Corinne

She also had the ability to get everybody singing, even those who couldn't carry a note. At parties she would be called upon to play the piano, and invariably, after a few minutes she would have people gathered around the piano singing away at the top of their lungs.

When I left for law school in 1918, Corinne Eastman and I were engaged—or perhaps it is better described as "pinned." She was wearing my 1918 high school class pin, a convention that in those days was a near equivalent to formal engagement. In any event, neither of us had the slightest doubt that we were engaged and would be married when we had achieved our educational plans and my income was sufficient to set up housekeeping. And after six years, we were married in 1924.

During the winter of 1917-18, while Corinne and I were associated on the editorial staff of the *Spaulding Sentinel*, we had met frequently at staff meetings to ponder the problems of the *Sentinel*. She quickly caught my eye. She was of average height, slim but well proportioned, with sparkling blue eyes, brown almost chestnut hair, peaches-and-cream complexion, a mobile countenance, and a smile that lit up the world. She liked people, all kinds of people, and reacted to them instantly and sympathetically. She never said unkind words to or about people, even the few whom she disliked. She was a sensitive, intelligent person who loved to read and write and listen to good music, and she played the piano brilliantly.

These editorial meetings were quite informal. One aspect of this informality was the way I called the meetings and gave notice. I simply sent each member of the staff a copy of a tentative "program" with the date, place, and time of the meeting and asked for suggestions for the agenda. Since Corinne was the "associate editor," I usually included a short note asking more positively for definite suggestions. She would answer by sending back the same "program" with her suggestions written thereon. In some strange way these messages quickly began to take on a more personal tone. And even later, when we were writing letters during college days, we would often head the letter "program." One day by this means of communication I asked her to go to the movies, which she loved. She accepted, and so began the romance that lasted until her death.

After the first movie I began calling on her regularly. During the year that I took off from law school I was working for R.L. Clark Feed Store and in my father's law office, and my evenings were mostly free. My father's 1917 Model T Ford was in constant use, and most of that use was in diligent prosecution of our romance. We even smashed up the Ford once when we collided with another car on the highway a mile or so south of South Barre. I shall always remember the kindness and understanding that my father exhibited on that occasion. He paid for repairing the car, a sum of no mean consequence to him. Investigation showed that the tracks of the Ford were over on the wrong side of the road at the point of collision, and that it was therefore my fault. Not a word of scolding came from Dad. His only remark was, "You know, you're supposed to keep your eyes on the road part of the time."

Corinne and I picnicked a lot during that summer, and when the Ford was not available, I had free access to the Clark Feed Store horse and surrey. The horse was on well-earned retirement from long service on the feed store grain delivery wagon and needed exercise. He was old enough and quiet enough to require little concentrated attention from the driver, who was thus free to concentrate on more important things. All of this made him a much more appropriate means of transportation than the Model T Ford.

Upon graduating from Spaulding High School in 1920, Corinne applied for admission to Mount Holyoke College and was accepted. Her older sister Doris was enrolled at the same school, and I was not far away at Boston Law School. The summer that Monti and I bought our Model T to sell Fuller brushes in Maine, we offered to take Corinne and her sister to college in the fall on our way to Boston. By September, we had already sold our ancient car for what we had bought it for at the start of the summer, but this opportunity was too good to pass by. Consequently, we negotiated with the new owner to bring the car back for delivery in three weeks.

Unfortunately, on the trip down Route 14 disaster struck. Monti was driving and Doris was seated beside him. Corinne and I were riding in the back seat. Suddenly a rural mail carrier pulled left across the road in front of our car to deliver mail at a mailbox on that side of the road.

The front of our car struck the left rear side of the body of the mail carrier's car. When the cars came to rest a great volume of steam was rising from the hood of our Ford, and the left rear fender and body of the carrier's car was badly crushed. This episode delayed us for nearly three hours while we argued over whose inattention had caused the accident. Then we limped into Randolph, where we had new hose pipes put on the radiator. But there were other leaks in the radiator too. We found we could navigate only if we stopped every half hour and refilled the radiator. When we finally pulled into Northampton, Massachusetts, it was well after midnight. This presented us with another problem. The girls insisted that they would not be allowed to enter the dormitories without registering first, and by this time, of course, the registration office was closed. We looked in vain for a hotel for the night. Finally we approached a police officer who was patrolling the streets and explained our predicament. He told of a hotel where he was sure we would find rooms. We followed his directions and found a small, dilapidated hotel in a very poor slum area. Later, we found that it also had a very unsavory reputation. But beggars couldn't be choosers. All four of us went into the lobby to inquire for rooms. By this time it was about 1:30 A.M. The aged clerk on duty was asleep but quickly awakened and told us that we could have rooms for five dollars each. We all signed the registry, and the clerk produced two keys. Then, taking a careful

To my brothers and sisters and me, Uncle Will's farm on Pike Hill in Corinth was a heaven of country life. My aunt and uncle and my parents would swap children during vacations and let my country cousins have a taste of city life in Barre while I enjoyed the opportunity to work and play on the farm. (DCD)

My father, Earle Davis, was proud all his life to be the first Davis to graduate from college. Pictured here (front row, second from the right) as a member of UVM's football team in 1895, he worked his way through college, teaching school during vacations and in the evening. (courtesy of University of Vermont Special Collections)

The house I grew up in on Allen Street was about a mile from the center of Barre City. It was surrounded by my family's large vegetable garden, a barn where we kept our animals, and leased farmland. It was not a large house for a family of eight, but it was a happy one, and it had two luxuries—indoor plumbing and a single bathroom. (DCD)

I began school at the Church Street School next to the Congregational church in Barre (I am in the back row, fourth from the left). Miss Tracy, my teacher, was a strong disciplinarian, but she liked children and we liked her. (DCD)

Horses have been a part of my life for as long as I can remember. I learned to ride on Mary Ann, my father's driving horse. By the time I was eight, I was working on a neighbor's farm grooming horses. By the time I was a teenager, I was breaking colts all by myself. (DCD)

When Billy Milne (back row, second from left) arrived in Barre from Scotland to work in the granite sheds, he brought the idea of Boy Scouts with him. In 1909 he organized Troop Number 1, the first Boy Scout troop in the United States, and I was permitted to join. I'm directly in front of Milne. (courtesy of Vermont Life)

In 1912 Teddy Roosevelt, running for president on the Bull Moose Party ticket, came to Barre to give a speech. My father and I (lower right-hand corner, with the light-colored cap) and several thousand other people turned out to hear him speak. My twelve-year-old imagination was fired with enthusiasm by my first exposure to politics. (courtesy of the Vermont Granite Association)

Mine was a large and loving family, but death thinned our ranks prematurely. Only five of my eight siblings lived to adulthood. In the back row, to my right, are Ralph and Hugh. In the front row are Ruth, Helen, Wayne, and Doris. Hugh died from polio as a teenager in 1924. I had a light case, not diagnosed for several years, that left me with a slight limp. (courtesy of Tom Davis)

Spaulding High School published its first year-book in 1918, the year I graduated. Even then, my personality was apparent to all. In the notes that accompanied my photograph, someone wrote, "Deane has a marked propensity to procrastination, and to argumentation. He cares not which side of an argument he takes, so long as he's in it." (courtesy of Aldrich Public Library, Barre, VT)

Corinne Eastman followed two years behind me at Spaulding. She caught my eye during her sophomore and my senior year, when she became associate editor of The Sentinel, *Spaulding's first school newspaper. I was editor-in-chief. By the time I left for college, she was wearing my pin, and it was pretty clear that we both had "intentions." (courtesy of Aldrich Public Library)*

Marjorie Phyllis Smith graduated from Spaulding as valedictorian of her class in 1922. We saw little of each other in those days and knew each other hardly at all, but our paths intersected thirty years later after the deaths of our spouses. (courtesy of Aldrich Public Library)

Although I had a job offer from a large Boston law firm, I elected to come home to Barre after my graduation from law school. My hopes of going into practice with my father were dashed after he became a probate judge, so I went into practice alone and became a Barre City alderman. (DCD)

Corinne and I were married on June 14, 1924, on the eve of her graduation from Boston University. (courtesy of Tom Davis)

Our first-born child was a son, Deane C. Davis, Jr. He died in 1929 when he was four years old, in a house fire that he accidentally started by playing with matches. Corinne always bore the signs of a lingering sadness from this tragedy, although our daughter Marian and son Tom brought love and light to her life. (DCD)

Corinne was an excellent mother to Marian and Tom during the years when I was away much of the time. It was Corinne who suggested that the family accompany me to Brattleboro during my first term on the bench in order to maintain a semblance of family life and to provide me with regular meals. (courtesy of University of Vermont Special Collections)

Corinne loved music and was a talented pianist. She played frequently at parties and at home, where Marian, Tom, and I would accompany her. Marian inherited her mother's musical ability. (courtesy of Tom Davis)

In 1945 I left a lucrative private practice with one of the state's most prestigious law firms to become general counsel for National Life. The choice was a difficult one to make, and my life followed a completely new direction thereafter. (courtesy of the Vermont Historical Society)

My father ran for probate judge in 1922 and, following his election, served for the next twenty-one years. He loved the job and it suited him. My mother lived on alone for seven years after Dad's death, surrounded by flowers and canaries and those of her children who remained in the area. She was a dedicated mother to us all, and we owe her a great deal. (DCD)

AFTER TWENTY-FIVE YEARS IT'S STILL
MERRY CHRISTMAS
1949   DEANE AND CORINNE

Corinne and I celebrated our 25th anniversary shortly before she was diagnosed as having cancer. Her death barely a year later was the first time I ever understood what the word heartache means. (courtesy of Tom Davis)

Gelsie Monti was my life-long friend, although several times over the years we came close to parting ways because of our very different temperaments. In 1948 we traveled together to the Republican National Convention. I am on the far left, third row; Monti is third from the left, second row. (courtesy of Tom Davis)

Dr. Ernest Martin Hopkins, interim president of National Life, selected me to take over as president of National Life in 1950. I came to depend on Hoppy's wise counsel and experience, and our fast friendship was one of the cherished privileges of my life. (DCD)

On the day of the groundbreaking for National Life's new headquarters, I climbed aboard a bulldozer alongside Montpelier's mayor, Edward Knapp, to make the first cut. As I drove the behemoth toward the assembled crowd, however, they broke ranks and fled from my path. Their lack of faith in my bulldozing ability was altogether too apparent. (DCD)

Marjorie Smith Conzelman and I were married in the Old South Church in Boston on July 5, 1952. In the years to come, she taught me much about the joy of family relationships and made our marriage a constant love affair. (DCD)

look over his grandfather glasses, he asked, "Who's going to sleep with who?" By this the two girls were visibly shaken. I replied firmly that the girls would occupy one room and Monti and I another. The clerk's surprise at this answer was painfully obvious. Monti and I slept fine, but the next morning we discovered that the girls had promptly moved all of the readily movable furniture in their room against the door. And they didn't look as if they had slept a wink.

While Corinne was attending Mount Holyoke, she became much interested in English and English literature and pursued her writing of both poetry and prose, both of which continued to give her much pleasure as long as she lived. In her senior year in college she transferred to Boston University, which she felt had a stronger writing curriculum.

After we were married in 1924, she became one of the founding members of the Vermont Poetry Society and remained active in its affairs as long as she lived. One of her pet projects of this association was the magazine *The Mountain Troubadour*, which the Poetry Society founded and which published poems written by society members. Both the Society and the *Troubadour* are still in existence and appear to be flourishing.

Our first-born child was a son, my namesake, born January 9, 1925. He was followed two years later by our daughter Marian, who was born on August 5, 1927.

During Deane's short life, he filled Corinne's days with joy—and mine, too. He was a smart little fellow, full of life and with a great capacity for fun. He lived only four years. He died in 1929 as the result of a fire that partially destroyed our house on Hilltop Avenue in Barre.

On the day of the fire I had not been home for lunch. At about 1:30 P.M. I was interviewing a prospective witness on Orange Street very near our Hilltop Avenue home. I heard the fire alarm ring several times but thought nothing of it at first. Suddenly it dawned on me that the number of the alarm rings specified the area of Hill Street and vicinity that included our home. Still, I did not imagine that my own home was involved, and it was not until a couple of minutes later when I rounded the corner at the intersection of Hill Street and Hilltop Avenue that I was horrified to see a large assortment of fire-fighting equipment in front of my house and firemen pouring water on the house. Volumes of smoke were rising from the house through the doors and broken windows.

Just as I arrived, Mert Emerson, one of the firemen, came out of the house bearing my unconscious son in his arms. He saw me and shouted at me to follow him to the hospital. In the confusion and crowd, it took me a few minutes to find Corinne. I found her in the home of the next-door neighbor, grabbed her, and rushed her into my car, and we drove rapidly to the Barre City Hospital on Washington Street. I don't remember where Marian was, but doubtless she was at the neighbor's, too. Fortunately, Dr. Woodruff, our family physician, was at the hospital at the time making his rounds when the unconscious lad reached the hospital and gave emergency treatment at once. Dr. Woodruff strove valiantly to resuscitate little Deane long after signs of life were gone. I recall that, as a last resort, he injected a stimulant by hypodermic needle through the boy's back directly into the heart, attempting to get it going again. It was all to no avail. I believe that Deane was dead even before the fireman found him.

Later I assembled all the facts, and it appeared that little Deane had learned to play with matches. On the day of the fire he was doing this down in the cellar, out of sight and hearing. He had apparently ignited a match, which in turn ignited some combustible material, from which the fire spread to the woodwork in the cellar. As the fire began to spread, little Deane must have been frightened, and knowing that he had done something wrong, he dashed unnoticed up two flights of stairs and hid in the closet of one of the bedrooms, where he was found. He was not missed during the early minutes of the fire as Corinne thought he was playing with one of the children outdoors, where he had been not long before. By the time it was learned that he was nowhere outside, the house was completely filled with heavy smoke. When the firemen arrived, the smoke was so dense inside the house that it was impossible to see. In spite of this, several of the firemen donned gas masks and searched each room in the house trying to find him. Mert Emerson found him by entering the bedroom from the outside and crawling on his hands and knees all over the room until he opened the bedroom closet and found Deane's inert body. The boy was not burned in any way.

Thus began a sad chapter in our married life. Corinne was

crushed. She was overcome by a deep depression and at times seemed to be going through the motions of life in a trance. As she began at long last to slowly improve, she told me that she wanted to have another child and hoped desperately it would be a boy. The moment she knew she was pregnant she began to improve rapidly, and when Tom was born on November 30, 1931, she was ecstatic, and lavished Tom with love and attention.

While she always bore the signs of a lingering sadness, she rapidly began to appear and act more like herself. Even her friends noticed it and remarked on it. A very religious person, she had prayed constantly for this third child, and when Tom was born, it made all the difference for her between a life of undue sadness and a normal one.

Corinne had many friends, and she now began to take more interest in them and in doing things with them. Her two closest friends were Kathy Beck and Elizabeth Campbell. These were the ones with whom she shared confidences. They were most helpful in getting Corinne through this difficult period.

After the fire the Hilltop Avenue house was uninhabitable for many months while it was being restored, so I decided to buy another. Moreover, I became convinced that Corinne would never be happy going back into the house that had been the scene of the tragedy. Time proved that to have been a wise decision. Fortunately, a house at 25 Tremont Street was on the market, and I quickly negotiated for it. It would be our home for the next eighteen years. Situated as it was—immediately in back of and within a minute's walk of Corinne's mother's home—it was possible for Corinne to spend much time with her parents and her sister Doris. Corinne was close to her mother, and I know she received much reassurance and comfort from these increased opportunities to be with her.

By nature Corinne was a happy person, happy with her friends and her family. She was sensitive, always kindly, and most considerate of others. Although she was an outgoing person, she had a strong, secure inner life, too. She loved to read and to attend the theater and movies. Among her greatest joys were the trips to Boston and New York we made to go to matinees in the afternoon and other performances at the theater at night.

She was an excellent mother. In the days when we used to go

once or twice a week to the movies, we always had a reliable babysitter. Yet when we arrived at the theater, usually about five minutes after leaving home, she would insist on going into the adjoining drug store and calling back home to make sure that young Tom had settled down and was not crying because of her absence. And when the movie was over, she never wanted to stop to have an ice cream soda, which she loved; she wanted to go home immediately to make sure that Marian and Tom were all right.

I took far less responsibility for rearing the children than I should have. During my years in general practice, I was too much occupied with earning a living and trying to increase my earning capacity. And for five years, while the children were young, I served as a superior court judge and was gone five and six days a week, holding court in other parts of the state. While I was in general practice, I went back to the office after dinner nearly every night in the week. Until the children grew older, they were usually in bed by the time I came home.

I came to understand this after Corinne died. Tom was in college then, and Marian was married. By then my rapport with my children was nowhere near as close as I wished it to be, and I came to understand what I had missed.

By the mid-1940s Corinne began having physical problems. Never a strong person physically, she began to have problems of the nervous system and a general malaise.

Dr. Ernest Reynolds, an M.D., and Dr. Thomas Dunleavy, an osteopath, were her physicians. Those were the days when the family physician concept of medical practice was still in vogue, and both of these physicians took a keen personal interest in Corinne. I shall always be grateful for the comfort and reassurance—far beyond professional attention and treatment—that these men gave to her during those troubling days.

In the late 1940s she developed a slight swelling in her left breast. It was not a bunch or a lump but a swelling. Consulting her doctor, she was told that the condition appeared to be mastitis, and treatment was prescribed. As time went on the condition grew gradually worse, and finally, in 1949, Dr. Reynolds sent her to the Lahey Clinic in Boston for more intensive evaluation. Her close friend, Elizabeth Campbell, went with her and stayed with her for a few days while extensive tests were being made.

While Corinne was still in Boston, I received a call from Dr. Hare of the Lahey Clinic asking permission to put Corinne on a highly unusual and new treatment that had not yet had medical approval. I was puzzled by his suggestion and apparently showed it in my voice. He asked me, "Don't you know what your wife's condition is?"

"Yes," I replied, "she has been diagnosed as having mastitis."

"Well," he said, "I'm sorry to tell you that your wife has cancer. It is well developed and we know of no treatment that will effect a cure for this particular condition. We would, however, like to put her on a new kind of radiation treatment that we have developed in association with the Massachusetts Institute of Technology."

The shock of this news left me so unstrung, I couldn't think straight. In fact I couldn't think at all. I could only feel. I told him that I would fly down on the first plane and talk with him. I took the early plane and went immediately to the Lahey Clinic, then at 605 Commonwealth Avenue. Dr. Hare told me bluntly that there was no hope of saving Corinne's life under conventional medical treatment; that this new kind of treatment offered some hope of extending her life for some period of time and possibly might effect a cure, although he doubted that.

He described this new treatment in some detail. He explained that X-ray radiation had a beneficial effect in treating some kinds of cancer although there were definite limitations. One of the limitations was that in certain deep-seated cancers, it was not possible to use a sufficient voltage to effect the benefits without burning the skin of the patient. The new treatment was a machine developed by Dr. Trump of MIT that, it was hoped, would overcome that problem. The technique was to place the patient on a slowly revolving table. The radiation rays would always be hitting the target of the deep-seated tissue involved, but the rays would not be hitting any single exterior spot of the skin continuously for more than a few seconds at a time, thus avoiding serious burning of the exterior skin.

It sounds simple, but in practice it is a highly scientific and complex exercise. It calls for a careful mathematical computation that needs to be made for each patient and carefully monitored and adjusted in accordance with the patient's condition.

This particular machine the Lahey Clinic was using could deliver two million volts without injuring the skin. This was a dosage many times greater than could safely be delivered before that time. I understand now that this technique has been improved and modified so that voltages of three and four million are safely being used and that it is now accepted practice by the medical profession for use in appropriate cases. Corinne was the first patient on the machine, and the machine was the first of its kind ever developed.

Because of the novelty and lack of experience with the treatment, I found great difficulty reaching a decision as to whether we should take the risk. After a long and thorough explanation by Doctors Hare and Trump, the decision became easier. They both agreed, as did other associated physicians at the Lahey Clinic, that Corinne had a very short life expectancy if only conventional treatment were used. They did not promise a cure, but they did give me strong reason to hope that her life could be significantly extended and that she would not suffer any great additional pain or discomfort from the use of the treatment. The decision was further complicated for me because Dr. Hare had not told Corinne of her condition and strongly advised against it. The pressure of the decision weighed heavily on me. It seemed to me that I was making a decision which in such cases should rightly be the province of the patient. However, I finally gave my permission and treatments began. They were given at MIT in Cambridge three times each week.

Corinne had taken a room on St. Stephens Street in Back Bay, almost next door to where she had roomed while attending Boston University. She was familiar with the neighborhood and liked it, particularly the little church across the street, which had a beautiful carillon that was played many times throughout the day.

When I first saw the room at MIT where the radiation machine was housed and patients were treated, I was a bit shocked. I had envisioned surroundings similar to those of a hospital or clinic. Far from it. The room was situated in what appeared to be a storage building. It had a cement floor and walls and a rough exposed ceiling. Only a few old chairs were scattered around to accommodate patients or visitors. The side walls had just recently been constructed of reinforced cement and were now eight feet thick to protect against any escape of radiation. During treatments a small staff was in attendance, including Doctors Hare and Trump, a nurse, and an assistant to Dr. Trump, for mathematical computations. Fortunately, the surroundings did not seem at all forbidding to Corinne, and all the personnel were wonderfully kind and helpful to her. These treatments lasted about eight weeks.

I had arranged with the doctors to have one of her weekly treatments on Friday afternoon late, or early Saturday forenoon, thus enabling me to be with her for one treatment each week and for the rest of the weekend. I would fly to Boston on the late plane Friday from Berlin airport and return either late Sunday night or early Monday morning. In spite of the overhanging shadow, those weekends were happy occasions. We would go out for meals and an occasional movie, but mostly we spent the time in her room. On one occasion she entertained both Doctors Hare and Trump and their wives for dinner, there in her room. It was a festive and memorable occasion.

I will never know for sure whether Corinne knew she had cancer. I think not. At least, I was never aware of the slightest indication that she did. After her death in 1950 I found among her writings an essay that she had written during those treatments, the title of which was, "I Thought I Had Cancer." It was a beautiful piece of writing and described with clarity and detail the reasons that had made her conclude that she did not have cancer. I do know from different things she said that she was very nervous while on the machine. She told me that while on the machine she used to sing to herself the hymn "Be Still My Soul."

Corinne lived for about a year after the treatments were ended. The first eight or nine months were reasonably comfortable and normal for her, but the last three months were extremely difficult. During that period we had nurses around the clock who were able to minimize her pain and discomfort. But during the last two weeks she had attacks that made it difficult for her to catch her breath. I believe that her lungs had become affected by that time. The nurses, every one of them, were wonderful, and so was Dr. Reynolds. Even though she was under heavy medication she was cheerful throughout, even up to the night of her death.

On the night she died I spent the evening with her. Before she went to sleep she asked me to take her in my arms. That is a precious memory. I kissed her goodnight and went to my room across the hall and to sleep. In the middle of the night I was called by the nurse and was told that Corinne had passed away. I had seen, close up, the deaths of relatives, even close relatives, but the effect of Corinne's passing was different. It was the first time I understood what the word *heartache* means. Grief I had experienced several times. This was that and more. A feeling of deep harsh doubling-over with physical pain starts in your throat and goes down into your chest. I remember going outdoors and walking up and down the long driveway trying to ease my pain. I had known for some time that I was going to lose Corinne, that it could happen any day. Yet this heartache hit me within minutes of her death. I have never forgotten the experience.

Corinne's death was a tremendous shock to the children, too. Marian was at home waiting out the Korean War and the return of her husband, Frank Calcagni. Tom, at the University of Vermont, went through a difficult time since he and his mother had always been close. In retrospect, I feel that I did not shore up the children as well as a father should. No doubt part of the reason was that I needed shoring up myself, and I let myself become too preoccupied with my own grief.

I hope I have not unduly emphasized the sadness in Corinne's life because, on balance, she lived a truly happy life. She loved music and was a talented pianist. She loved to play the piano for group singing and had that rare ability to recall old songs not only by title but when a few bars were hummed or lyrics spoken. She also had the ability to get everybody singing, even those who couldn't carry a note. At parties she would be called upon to play the piano, and invariably, after a few minutes she would have people gathered around the piano singing away at the top of their lungs. She traveled with me to conventions when I was general counsel of National Life and came to know personally a large number of the agents around the country. She loved these trips and was always a favorite of the groups. She was soon known as a pianist and song leader and was frequently called upon to "get them started." The trouble was, once they started, the sessions often didn't stop until the wee hours of the morning because everyone was having such a good time, including

Corinne. She had what musicians call "absolute pitch," a capacity to hear a song and immediately play the whole thing through note perfect. Often she would come home from the movies and play a song she had heard at the movies for the first time. Our daughter Marian inherited the same ability.

One other activity that brought great joy to Corinne's life was writing. Although during her life I knew that writing, both prose and poetry, had always been important to her and that she spent much of her time pursuing this hobby, I did not realize until after she died the quantity of her writing. After her death I published a selection of her poems and distributed these booklets to many friends, neighbors, family, and members of the Poetry Society. The central poem in that publication says as much about her skill as a poet as it does about her person, and does so far more eloquently than anything I could say about her.

Love Song
1950

If all the dawns of earth
are blotted out
And every hope and prayer
become a doubt;

If land is swallowed by
a tideless sea,
And night follows night
endlessly;

If planets thunder down
in mighty quake,
And the skeleton of earth
Begins to break;

My love for you, lingering
On in space,
Will listen for your voice,
Will seek your face.

10

On the Bench

*. . . the real job satisfaction was found in court,
principally in jury trials. A jury trial is in some
ways like a theatrical production, one in which the
script has not yet been written. It writes itself as it
goes along, but the drama is there nevertheless.*

In the fall of 1931 Stanley C. Wilson, who was then governor of
Vermont, phoned and asked if I would accept an appointment to the
superior court. This came as a complete surprise. He had previously
sounded me out as to whether I would accept an appointment as
commissioner of motor vehicles, and I had been pondering that proposal when this call came. I told the governor I was greatly flattered,
as I was, but that I would need a couple of days to think it over. I
spent most of those two days discussing the pros and cons with Corinne and my father, whose judgment I greatly respected. I hesitated
because I enjoyed general practice very much and wondered if the
quieter and less adversarial character of life on the bench would
challenge me enough and prove as interesting. But I was, at the
time, fighting exhaustion and stress from the long hours I was working. I felt tired and worn out. Both Corinne and Dad felt that the
more relaxed life on the bench would improve my health. This persuaded me, so I called the governor and told him I would accept

with pleasure.

Governor Wilson appointed me immediately. I made an arrangement to go to Woodstock, county seat of Windsor County, and sit as a spectator on the bench with Judge Bicknell, who was holding a session there. I regarded it as a one-week apprenticeship. It was well worth it as Judge Bicknell was a good judge and had been a distinguished lawyer and a good trial lawyer. I learned a great many practical things from him that helped me get on top of the job quickly. I had, of course, tried many cases in court, of nearly all kinds, and one might wonder why I felt the need of further preparation of this kind when I had been observing judges for the previous nine years. But the perspective is quite different from the bench than it is from the counsel table. I was glad that I took this kind of refresher course. When I left after the week to take up my duties in Windham County, I felt fully confident to do the job.

A couple of discussions I had with Judge Bicknell were especially useful. On one occasion, I asked him why he had taken the job of judge since he had such a remunerative practice. His reply tickled me. He said, "Well, you know my office was on the second floor of the building I was in. There came a time when if I heard a step on the stairs, I knew it was a client coming to me with a problem. When I got to the point where I wanted to jump out the window to avoid clients, I thought it was time to quit." I understood how he felt. And why. I had had some of the same feelings at times. The accumulation of problems, the sense of responsibility that goes with practice are heavy burdens on the physique as well as the spirit.

On my final day of that week in court, Judge Bicknell and I dined together. I told the judge that I had been digesting his wisdom all week but wondered if he had any last pearls of wisdom to throw my way before I took up my new life. He replied, "Yes, as a matter of fact, I have. I've got three bits of advice that may help you more than anything you have learned this week.

> *First*, don't get yourself all in a sweat trying to make lawyers get their cases tried. Relax. If one side presses for trial, then force the other side to trial unless there is some good reason for delay. But you'll find that the majority of the cases that are never ready are the ones in which both sides want them contin-

ued. Don't push the lawyers around. Usually there are good reasons not to try a case when both sides want the case continued. But the reasons are not the kind of reasons that get on the record. In these cases justice is just as likely to be served by not trying the case as it is by forcing both sides to a trial neither wants.

Second, when you rule on a question of law, make your ruling as unmistakably clear as humanly possible. It's in the cases where the Supreme Court can't figure out what you really meant by your ruling that justice often fails. Just remember that you've got a fifty-fifty chance of being right, and you can safely rely on the Supreme Court to correct your mistakes in the other 50 percent.

Third, at all times, and in all events, don't take yourself too damn seriously.

My new career as a superior court judge gave my life a new dimension. Heretofore, my trial practice had been almost exclusively in the Washington and Orange county courts and in the Barre and Montpelier municipal courts, the forerunners of the district courts now in place. Now as a judge I would be presiding in all fourteen of the county courts as my assignments directed. Assignment of judges to particular counties in those days was by a process that is now obsolete. The six superior court judges met once a year at the call of the chief superior judge and performed the most important function for which those meetings were called—the assignment of judges. We had a wheel about two or two-and-one-half feet in diameter that had on the circumference the names of the fourteen counties and the names of the two terms in that county. One by one the names of the judges in alphabetical order were attached to a sprong, and the wheel was given a vigorous turn. Wherever the sprong stopped would be the name of the terms and the counties in which that judge would preside for that year. This was done until all judges had their assignments for the year. It was pretty simple, but it worked. There was no appeal, no discussion, and everybody appeared to be satisfied. In this way, each judge moved from county to county and gradually came to cover the whole state. The theory of the law at that time was that a judge should not preside in one county too long for fear that he would become too well-acquainted with the lawyers of that county, and hence, compromise his capacity for complete impartiality. In the years since, that theory seems to have gone the way that all theories should that rest on such weak premises.

My first assignment, however, was not determined this way. I had taken the place of the Honorable Warnet F. Graham, one of the most scholarly judges on the bench. His appointment to the Supreme Court caused the vacancy, right in the middle of the fall term in Windham County. For that reason I was assigned by the chief superior judge to take over the assignments of Judge Graham, which included finishing up the fall term in Windham County and then moving on to a second term in Lamoille County.

Corinne and I decided that we would rent a house in Brattleboro for the duration of the Windsor County term to provide me with home cooking and a proper diet and our family with a semblance of family life. Our children, Marian and Tom, went with us, and for the rest of that term we lived comfortably and happily in Brattleboro. Marian attended the local graded school, and I attended the sessions of county court in Newfane about twelve miles distant. I found a man who owned a stable of riding horses nearby with whom I became friendly, and he invited me to ride whenever I wanted in order to help keep the horses exercised. I did so and found other riding companions with whom to explore the trails surrounding the outskirts of Brattleboro.

The first case to be tried in the county was an action by a former patient against her surgeon for malpractice resulting from an unsuccessful operation after which the patient suffered chronic and debilitating physical and mental problems. It was claimed by the plaintiff that the doctor as a country physician had undertaken to perform an operation with which he was not sufficiently familiar.

Suits for medical malpractice were almost unknown in the early 1930s. One reason was that the settled case law of the state provided that no recovery could be had for medical malpractice in Vermont unless it was proved that the care and skill utilized by the defendant did not measure up to the standard of skill "prevailing in the community." The only way to prove this was through the testimony of other doctors in the community who would know what that standard was, and not surprisingly, doctors were not inclined to testify adversely to the interests of their fellow doctors. The case was fought vigorously by four lawyers, two on a side. It lasted about a week and called for many rulings by the presiding judge on close and complicated questions of evidence. It became my trial by fire as a judge. Whether my rulings were right will never be known. The defendant was a popular doctor in and around Brattleboro, and the courtroom was filled each day with former patients who rooted silently for their doctor to win. But the jury disagreed, and the question of the judge's rulings was never raised on appeal.

Later on in the term, a school holiday permitted me to take Marian with me to Newfane to watch what went on in a Vermont courtroom. Marian was then between seven and eight years of age and had a wonderful time. She was intensely interested in everything that went on. A jury trial of a civil case was in progress. During the afternoon a motion was made by one of the attorneys that raised a very important and complicated legal issue. The motion was sufficiently fundamental to the case that, if granted, it would end the case right then and there. Since it was obvious that the arguments on the motion would be lengthy, I excused the jury for the rest of the day and adjourned the hearing to the judges' chambers, where we could have the privacy and leisure to give the matter the thorough treatment it deserved. I took Marian with me into chambers so she could see and hear all that went on. Her intense interest was apparent in the sparkle of her eyes and the rhythmic swinging of her short legs as she sat on an adult-size chair. She followed the arguments of the lawyers with great concentration. As the heat of the arguments increased, so did the tempo of the swinging of her legs. When arguments were completed, and it was time for me to make a ruling, I tipped back my head in the chair to gather my thoughts.

It was a close and difficult legal question, and I was not about to make a snap decision. As the minutes went by in silence, Marian's eyes were glued to her daddy. Her legs were swinging at a terrific pace, and her face bore an anxious and disturbed expression. She obviously interpreted my hesitation and concentration as an indication that her daddy didn't know the answer or what to do. Finally, pointing to the side judges, she burst out, "Daddy, why don't you ask one of them?" The group in chambers burst into loud laughter. It took me a long time to live down that incident!

My first term in Windham County Court took so long to complete that it became necessary to officially defer, for a few days, the opening of the upcoming term in Lamoille County, my next assignment. I drove directly from Newfane to Hyde Park to open the Lamoille County term. Mary Cerasoli of Barre was the official court reporter for both terms, and she drove with me. On the way I told her that because I had been working so continuously in Windham County I had not had time to draft an opening charge to the jury panel in Lamoille. It was traditional in those days for the presiding judge to make a General Charge to the whole panel from which each twelve-person jury would be chosen. Such a charge is for the purpose of explaining to the jury panel in considerable detail the nature of their duties as members of each jury, when called. While the charge differed somewhat from judge to judge, it included among other things such matters as procedure, evidence, witnesses, burden of proof, and the differing functions of the judge from those of the jury. Usually, as judges grew in experience they had charges that they could and did give at all term openings.

Mary, sympathetic soul that she was, came immediately to my rescue and suggested that if I would hold up the opening of the court for an hour or so, she would type out from her stenographic notes Judge Sherburne's opening charge from the preceding term. This was done, and at the appropriate moment I took the typewritten transcript and read Judge Sherburne's resurrected charge to the jury panel with all the emphasis and solemnity of which I was capable. At recess Josie Mudgett, county clerk for Lamoille County, came into the judges' chambers and with the greatest sincerity said, "Judge Davis, I've been here as county clerk many years and have heard a lot of charges given at the opening sessions by different judges. I want you to know that the charge which you have just given is the best charge I have ever heard." Since she had already heard the same words delivered by Judge Sherburne at the preceding session, I couldn't figure out whether her words were a tribute to me or to Judge Sherburne!

That same term of Lamoille County Court was the scene for another humorous court incident. Part of the official ceremony at the opening of county court in those days was the opening proclamation, historically given by the sheriff, announcing to the world that court is in session. This practice dates back many centuries to the early days of the common law in England. A new sheriff for Lamoille County had just been elected, and he was taking his duties quite seriously, including his duties as officer of the county court. In preparation for this somewhat formidable duty and to get a few pointers on how to make his own proclamation, the sheriff had attended the opening of the Supreme Court in Montpelier. The form of proclamation then used in Supreme Court was somewhat different from the one customarily used in county court, but that didn't bother the sheriff. He was greatly impressed by the proclamation given by Joseph G. Frattini, clerk of the Supreme Court. Picture the scene. Here's a brand-new judge, second youngest ever to have been appointed a superior court judge in Vermont, a little—indeed, perhaps more than a little—unsure of himself, sitting on the bench attempting to make a good impression.

In my most dignified and solemn manner I announced: "Mr. Sheriff, you will now make the proclamation of the opening of this court."

With equal dignity and solemnity he arose at the sheriff's podium and in a loud, clear voice proclaimed, "Hear ye, hear ye, hear ye, the Honorable, the County Court within and for the county of Lamoille and the Court of Chancery are now open for business. All ye that have business before this Honorable Court draw nigh that ye may be heard." And then with dramatic pause and looking squarely at me, he concluded, "God Save The State of Vermont."

In time, I found the work on the bench less strenuous than trial practice. The joy of the job was increased by the fact that the greater part of the work was performed in the courtroom, where the action was. Even as a lawyer, I had loved the drama and the excitement of the courtroom. Of course, some work of a judge must be performed outside the courtroom—preparing formal written instructions to the jury in each case, drawing up findings of fact and judgment orders in cases not tried by jury, and in some cases investigating thoroughly the course of prior decisions—but the real job satisfaction was found in court, principally in jury trials. A jury trial is in some ways like a theatrical production, one in which the script has not yet been written. It writes itself as it goes along, but the drama is there nevertheless.

The part of the job I liked best was preparing and delivering a "charge" to the jury. The purpose of the charge is to explain to the jury what the law is and how it should be applied to the facts in the case. The facts are what the jury finds as a result of hearing all evidence on both sides. The charge is uniformly delivered after all the evidence has been presented and oral arguments on both sides have been completed.

Practically speaking, a good charge is one that is legally correct and that is presented in such a way as to help the twelve different minds on the jury concur on the facts and law so as to be able to reach a verdict. Legally, the charge must be a letter-perfect exposition as to what the law is because every word of the charge is subject to exception by either side and its validity tested in the Supreme Court upon appeal. Simply put, the jury is told that if certain specified facts are found to be true, then the law provides so and so. They are likewise told if the specified facts are not found by the jury to be true, then a different result is required. In practice, however, the discharge of that responsibility in most cases is far from simple because many cases present a variety of legal and factual issues and each such issue has to be covered by the charge.

I enjoyed this part of the job because I felt a great sense of its importance to the reaching of a just verdict and because as a practicing lawyer I had felt that nonlawyers were often confused by the blunt statements of the law. Consequently, as a practicing lawyer I had tried hard to make complex legal situations understood by clients, and my clients were most appreciative. But anyone who attempts this derring-do of stating complex principles of law in simple terms runs the risk of making an error. Judges are no exceptions. A judge must walk a very narrow and precise line between the exact language of the law and the simplicity that is desired.

The one aspect of the job that I did not enjoy was being away from home so much. Since judges were rotated around the state there was much traveling to and from the fourteen county seats. I would leave home early Monday morning of each week, drive to the county of my assignment, stay in a hotel nights during the week, and drive home late Friday night or early Saturday morning, in order to have the weekend at home. There were no Vermont thruways then, so traveling required more hours of driving than it does today. In winter the driving conditions were often treacherous with ice or drifting snow. Without the kind of snow tires we have today, I often found myself shoveling snow to get my car back on the road. Since judges (including me) are not very adept at changing tires or solving even minor mechanical problems, this was a hazard even in good weather.

But not every judge suffered as I did. One of my peers had his own way of dealing with these inconveniences. Judge Bicknell often picked up hitchhikers on the road, a practice for which he was frequently soundly scolded by Chief Judge Moulton. Once, after a judges' conference in Montpelier, Judge Moulton again upbraided Judge Bicknell for this practice. Judge Bicknell usually accepted these scoldings meekly and did not attempt to defend the practice. He accepted this one in his customary style. After the meeting was over it developed that four out of the six judges in attendance had assignments that took them along the route from Montpelier to Burlington. Judge Bicknell was the first to leave. On the way, he picked up a hitchhiker. Near Williston a tire blew out on his car, so, one by one, the other judges were greeted by the spectacle of a hitchhiker hard at work changing the tire while Judge Bicknell sat comfortably on the bank smoking a big cigar. Judge Bicknell waved his cigar gaily at each of us as we drove by looking straight ahead as though we hadn't seen him or his industrious helper. On the Monday morning following, Chief Judge Moulton received a card from Judge Bicknell asking, ''Now who wins the argument about hitchhikers?'' As far as I know, Judge Moulton never answered the card or scolded Judge Bicknell again for picking up hitchhikers.

One aspect of this job which I enjoyed more than I expected to was my association with the side judges. Side judges are elected by the people of each county and almost exclusively have not been lawyers. Vermont is the only state that still has the institution of elected ''assistant judges'' in its courts of general jurisdiction. The positions are provided for in our state constitution and have survived many attempts to be eliminated.

Why do we have assistant judges? And why are they elected by the people rather than by the legislature, as are the presiding judges of the superior court? The answer lies in history and goes back to the

Boston Tea Party, the Revolutionary War, the voyage of the *Mayflower*, and the conditions existing in Great Britain that caused the immigrants to America to embark on the voyage of the *Mayflower* in the first place: fear of arbitrary government. This was the prevailing drive in the settlement of America, and it is clearly reflected in the constitutions of the earliest of the states, of which Vermont was the fourteenth. It was these historical imperatives that caused all these states to include in the structure of their constitutions checks and balances to prevent the exercise of arbitrary power. The provision of assistant judges, who are elected by and accountable to the electorate and who would constitute a majority of three judges in the court of general jurisdiction, was just one of the many checks and balances that were used.

Only recently have several cases decided by the Supreme Court somewhat narrowed the side judges' authority. In my time on the bench, assistant judges had power to overrule the presiding judge both on factual questions and on legal questions. It was attempted on me only once.

The case was a hotly contested divorce with political overtones. Not being a Rutland County resident, I did not recognize or sense the political aspect, which my two assistant judges clearly did. In our conference after the case was completed, the two assistant judges took a radically different view of the case than I did. I was sure I was right, but I failed to convince them and was overruled. Their judgment was to be the judgment of the court in the case, but since I did not want my name associated with such an indefensible decision, I asked them to write up their own findings of fact and judgment order, and I would do the same. "Mine," I said, "are already written, and I'll put them right here in the drawer. When you get yours finished, give them to me, and I'll file both sets with the clerk, but yours will be the ones that govern." I knew it would be difficult for them to write findings and judgment orders in a case this complicated. They could have asked the attorneys for the plaintiff to help them, but I sensed that they would be embarrassed to do so. Every day for ten consecutive court days, I asked them if they had completed the writing. Each time I asked it became a bit more embarrassing for them. Finally, on the eleventh day I opened the drawer and found that the two assistant judges had signed my findings and order. Thus does justice get served in many queer ways.

Notwithstanding this incident, my five years of experience on the bench led me to believe that, on the whole, the institution of side judges is a good one. For example, in determining the sentence in criminal cases I often found the participation of side judges to be helpful. The wide latitude given to judges of the county courts in prescribing sentences for serious crimes imposes a breathtaking responsibility. In most cases no statutory guideline exists other than a prescribed minimum and maximum. The judge is forced to fall back upon his own experience in life and to construct his own standards to determine what is, in each case, a "just" sentence, taking into account the life and liberty of human beings. No judge worth his salt can fail to feel the weight of that responsibility. Here I found that side judges could and often did make helpful contributions to the decision.

In a sense the same situation prevails when a case is tried without jury. Here the judges perform the same function as do juries as well as determining the applicable law. They become judges of "the facts" as well. In doing so, they need to be able to judge the character of witnesses and the reasonableness of their testimony, and to reach a judgment as to what "the facts" are. Good side judges can add a perspective and a different life experience, which is a real help in reaching sound conclusions.

I do, however, favor the elimination of the side judges' power to participate in rulings that require analysis and application of the law to the facts. This, I believe, is a satisfactory compromise to the issue now raging as to whether the office of side judge should be abolished. I also think that if the political decision is made to retain the side judges as an institution, Vermont should upgrade the job so as to attract more people. When I was a judge, the side judges were paid four dollars per day for actual time spent plus expenses. Back in those days the job was usually sought only by people who had not much to do. And even though good judges were often elected, still, far too many of only moderate talents were elected. Now the state is paying per diem fees many times the four dollars per day and the quality has improved, but even the present stipend is not sufficient to attract enough of the very best men and women qualified for the job. In total government costs, the addition of enough money to truly upgrade the job would be minuscule.

I'm sure that my five years on the bench were not essentially different from those of the other superior court judges of the time. I'm also sure that the ones who got the most satisfaction from their work were the ones who had been active trial lawyers before assuming the bench. Moreover, I believe that the work of the superior court judges of those times was not much different from that of judges of today except in one respect. Today the dockets are far more crowded. In my time we were not actually in court more than seven or eight months of the year. We worked at a more leisurely pace. We had more time to study, to research, and to write our findings and judgment orders. The presiding judge called the shots. He decided when court would convene and when it would recess and had arbitrary authority to do things when and how he wanted to do them. Hence the pace of the action was much slower and easier for a judge than it was for a lawyer in general practice, who had many cases in process at the same time, for all of which he was responsible. I felt this difference immediately and greatly relished it. I even gained weight during those more leisurely years on the bench.

11

A New Direction

*We're happiest if we adjust to the changes going on
around us and to the changes going on inside us
and grow in experience and understanding of ourselves and of the world and people in it. Growth, I
guess, is the critical word, for growth is one of
the fundamentals of a full life.*

I enjoyed being a judge and looked forward to spending my working lifetime on the bench and of eventually being elevated to the
Supreme Court. In those days candidates for advancement to the
Supreme Court were invariably taken from the ranks of the superior
court judges, usually the superior court judge with the longest years
of service. That tradition was unbroken until the Snelling administration, when two attorneys from outside the court system were selected. Both of them were extremely able lawyers and fully qualified
for service on Vermont's highest court. But at that time and considering my age, I had good reason to expect that my hope of being
appointed to the Supreme Court would be fulfilled.

In January 1935, however, when Stanley C. Wilson finished his
second term as governor of Vermont, I was surprised when he and
J. Ward Carver (an extremely able trial lawyer and former attorney
general of Vermont) invited me to join a new law firm that they were
organizing. At the time when the invitation came, I was having some

financial worries. The legislature had reduced the salaries of superior court judges from $5,000 to $4,200. I was not saving money and was worried about how I was going to finance the education of my two children, who were now eight and four. This consideration weighed most heavily in my decision to accept the offer.

Before my decision to retire from the bench was publicly announced, I received a telephone call from Chief Justice George M. Powers of the Supreme Court. Without explanation, he asked me to come to Montpelier for an interview. Apparently he had picked up a rumor of my impending resignation. When I arrived at the judge's chamber, he asked me bluntly if it was true that I intended to resign. I replied in the affirmative. Thereupon he gave me a blistering lecture. I cannot ever remember being scolded more fiercely and more skillfully by anyone, not even by my father, who was an expert in that field. Most of the scolding was directed at pointing out how badly I was letting the state down. When I felt that he had taken off every last shred of my skin, he suddenly paused.

"Is your decision final?" he asked.

"Yes," I replied.

"Then I just want to say that if I was in your place, I'd do the same thing."

I felt better.

F. Ray Keyser, Sr., then a practicing lawyer in Chelsea, also joined the firm, which became known as Wilson, Carver, Davis and Keyser. Wilson had been a practicing lawyer, legislator, superior court judge, and governor. F. Ray Keyser, Sr., had been state's attorney of his county, later a superior court judge, and later still a justice of the Supreme Court. Carver had been an outstanding trial lawyer and attorney general of the state. We established offices in Chelsea and Barre. The four years I spent with the firm were happy and productive ones. I became involved in important litigation over a wider geographical area (which incidentally brightened my financial outlook).

The first days were difficult ones for me, however. Not until the fourth day did a single client came to the office to consult me. I twiddled my thumbs and nervously began to wonder if I had made a mistake in getting off the bench. On the fourth day a client came in with a case that took over a year to conclude. From that day on I can truthfully say that there has never been a day in any job I held in which I did not have more things to do than I could keep up with. But those were three bad days!

During my time with the firm, I became involved in one of the most heart-wrenching and complicated cases of my career. I represented the widow of Deputy Sheriff Gross, who had been an upstanding, quiet, competent, well-respected citizen of Franklin County. One of his duties as deputy sheriff had been to serve for very small fees civil writs, documents, and orders of court. He had had occasion to serve a writ upon a young man in Barre, whom we'll call Brown, who had for some time operated a collection agency. Brown apparently had suffered some financial difficulties and had consequently embezzled certain funds belonging to one of his clients. He merely "borrowed" the funds to begin with, but as often happens he got deeper and deeper in debt and borrowed more and more until his financial situation was desperate. Suit had been brought against Brown by an injured client, and Deputy Sheriff Gross was given the writ to serve with instructions to arrest the defendant unless, in accordance with permitted practice of the times, the defendant furnished bail. In civil cases such as this, that would have meant finding some person willing to sign the writ to guarantee the defendant's appearance in court at all required times.

Gross proceeded to perform his duties promptly. He drove to Barre, took Brown into custody, and informed him that he would have to be committed to jail unless he found someone who would "go good" for him and furnish bail. Then Brown began a frantic search for someone who would offer bail. Gross was most accommodating, apparently feeling sorry for the young man, and he drove Brown sundry places where Brown thought he might have a friend who would be willing to furnish bail. Everyone whom Brown approached was found to be unwilling. Brown was growing frantic. He then asked Gross, as a last resort, to drive him to Brookfield, where he thought he might find a friend who would be willing to furnish bail. But the two men never reached Brookfield. A short distance below Williamstown, on the road to Brookfield, Brown pulled a revolver out of his coat and fatally shot Deputy Sheriff Gross. Afterward, Brown buried the deputy's body under some rotting boards that were part of a collapsed barn, appropriated Gross's car, and drove quickly out of state, having apparently made up his mind to abscond. In the course of his flight he drove through Concord, New Hampshire, where he stopped in front of the courthouse and went to the men's room. As he was coming down the steep steps leading to the sidewalk on his way back to the car, Brown met two New Hampshire state police officers on their way into the courthouse building. The officers knew nothing of the killing of the deputy sheriff, but Brown concluded they had come to arrest him. He pulled his revolver from his jacket and fatally shot himself in the head.

The Vermont statutes at that time provided no pension for deputy sheriffs or coverage of workman's compensation or any other kind of reimbursement for loss of life in line of duty.

In due course I was consulted by members of the Gross family to see what, if anything, might be done to bring some help to the deputy's widow. While I held out little hope for success, I suggested that the Gross family try to get some member of the legislature to introduce a bill to compensate the widow to the extent of $3,500, the amount of money payable under workman's compensation at that time. Sympathy for the widow was running high due to newspaper coverage, and it was easy to find a legislator to draw up and file such a bill.

Almost immediately the bill ran into opposition from the attorney general, Lawrence C. Jones, and from Howard Rice, a stalwart and prestigious leader in the legislature. Before the claims committee, where the first hearing on the bill was held, Jones announced that the bill was unconstitutional. Naturally, the committee was impressed by this announcement and hesitated to take a positive position in favor of the bill. It hung in committee for some time.

Finally, as time was running out, I had an idea. I had found by counting noses that a large majority of the committee favored the bill but were loath to recommend it in the face of the attorney general's opinion. I then prepared a long brief in support of its constitutionality. I gave copies to the members of the claims committee, who were all nonlawyers, and told them that I realized it was difficult for them to pass judgment on a legal question. I suggested that they refer the bill for an opinion to the House judiciary committee, most of whose members were lawyers. Asa S. Bloomer, an able lawyer with much legislative muscle, was its chairman. My idea appealed to the claims committee, and the members voted to follow my suggestion.

On the way out of the claims committee hearing, I happened to meet Bloomer in the hall. I stopped him and explained what had happened. I knew that there was bad feeling between Bloomer and Jones and that it had existed for some time.

"Ace," I said, "I've put some real study into the question and have prepared a long brief on the subject. I'd like you to have a copy of it."

He took the copy of the brief and asked, "What's the issue?"

"They claim that the bill's unconstitutional," I replied.

"Who says it's unconstitutional?" he asked.

"Lawrence Jones," I replied.

Without even looking at the copy of the brief I had handed him, he handed it back to me and said, "It's constitutional."

Sure enough, the judiciary committee reported the bill constitutional by unanimous vote, and in spite of valiant opposition in the House on the floor, the bill passed by a narrow margin.

Unfortunately, our troubles were not yet over. Jones, in his capacity as attorney general, brought a petition for an injunction against the auditor of accounts and the state treasurer to restrain them from paying the proceeds provided in the bill. The action ran its course and finally came to the Supreme Court on appeal, where Jones and I argued the constitutionality of the bill with much heat and some logic. When the Court finally acted, the justices decided the bill was constitutional by a vote of three to two.

It was a lot of work for so little money, but even that amount was greatly appreciated by the widow.

The firm of Wilson, Carver, Davis and Keyser was unique in one respect. It is the only law firm in Vermont ever to supply three superior court judges, two governors, and an attorney general from its partnership. If you add F. Ray Keyser, Jr., who worked in the Chelsea office as a student, the firm supplied three governors.

The firm was prosperous, and we lived together amicably for four years. Edna M. Cheever, who was then secretary to the firm of Theriault and Hunt in Montpelier, was persuaded to join our firm as secretary. Thus I began a professional relationship with Miss Cheever that lasted the rest of her life. She had been my classmate at

Spaulding High School in Barre in the class of 1918. In the 1918 Spaulding yearbook under the section headed "Goal in Life," she had recorded, "I want to be the best possible private secretary." She attained that goal with great distinction and was widely so recognized. When I left the firm to became general counsel for National Life Insurance Company, she was appointed claims officer at National Life. Ten years later, when I became president of National Life, she again became my secretary.

During the last year I was with the firm of Wilson, Carver, Davis and Keyser, I was retained as counsel by Fred Howland, longtime president of National Life Insurance Company and then chairman of the board. I had never met Mr. Howland before this. The retainer came about as a result of a recommendation by George L. Hunt, who was already retained in a lawsuit of considerable size and public interest. The case had no relationship to National Life but was brought by Mr. Howland in his capacity as trustee for a group of stockholders of Wetmore and Morse, a large granite-quarrying company that did business in the Town of Barre. It involved a claim by Mr. Howland and his group that the officers had voted themselves illegal salaries and bonuses to the detriment of the stockholders. After months of negotiations, the case was finally concluded to Mr. Howland's complete satisfaction.

Shortly thereafter, a legal problem arose at National Life at a time when the company's general counsel was incapacitated by illness. Since it was necessary to take action immediately, the executive committee of the company decided to seek outside counsel, and Mr. Howland recommended me to handle the matter. I received a telephone call from Elbert Brigham, who was then president and chief executive officer, asking me to meet with him and the committee. The case, I found, involved the interpretation of the Vermont statute defining the investment authority of the company. A dispute had arisen between the company and the official examiners, who were making a routine five-year audit and examination of the company on behalf of all the state insurance commissioners of the states in which National Life was doing business. The dispute turned on what was the correct meaning of just one word—*more*. Although it was a small word, the correct interpretation would make a difference of millions of dollars to the company. Mr. Brigham asked me to represent the company in the matter, and I agreed. Fortunately, within a short time I was able to conclude the matter in favor of the company.

Shortly afterward, I received another call from Mr. Brigham asking me to come to Montpelier to talk with him. When I arrived, he shocked me by asking if I would consider coming to National Life as its general counsel. The salary proposed was generous, and from that point of view I was tempted to accept the offer.

It was a difficult choice. I loved trial work, was a member of one of the most prestigious law firms in the state, was earning enough money so that I paid off the mortgage on my house, and could now see my way clear to provide a college education for my two children. I asked for time to think it over. After a week's consideration, I went to Montpelier and thanked Mr. Brigham for considering me for the job, but told him that I did not feel I could accept the offer and told him why. I thanked him also for the honor he had conferred on me by thinking of me, and we shook hands. I left believing that had ended the matter.

It hadn't.

A few weeks later, I received another phone call from Mr. Brigham. I went to Montpelier to see him again. I wondered what he had in store for me this time. He had called me down there to ask me to reconsider. We talked the job over in much detail. He painted an attractive picture and raised the salary offer. Mr. Brigham had been so nice to me in several ways that I felt I should at least give the offer a reconsideration. But once again I reached the conclusion that I should refuse. Before I had communicated this decision to Mr. Brigham, however, I went up to visit my father, who was bedridden recovering from a severe illness.

I told Dad of this latest offer. I had not told him of the first offer because I was so sure that my decision was right. Even now, forty-seven years later, I can still see the thoughtful expression on my father's face. For quite a few moments he said nothing. Finally he asked me, "What are you going to do?"

"Turn it down," I replied.

"Why?" he asked.

"For several reasons," I said. "I'm completely happy doing what I'm doing. I think I have some talent for trial work. I'm not getting rich and don't expect to, but I'm earning enough to support my family and educate Marian and Tom. I like the freedom of this work, and I have difficulty seeing myself shut up within the walls of a large corporation subject to the whims of other people and dependent upon their continued good will and support for job security."

"Well," he said, "those are good reasons, but let me suggest another perspective from one much older than you. Sure, you love trial practice, and that's important. But it probably has never occurred to you that the fun of trial work may not last indefinitely.

"Many good trial lawyers have found that as they reach a certain age, a lot of the fun of the adversary character of trial work begins to lose its glamour and fade. It's a process of age and maturity. It doesn't happen to everybody, but it does happen in varying degrees and at different ages to most trial lawyers. By that time, it's too late to build an office practice, which you probably wouldn't like either. So if it does happen to you, you are on the horns of a dilemma. You either have to go on doing what you are doing and not enjoying it or quit, which you wouldn't like either. This job would give you a whole new dimension of experience. Since National Life is doing a national business, you would be required to travel all over the country getting to know all kinds of interesting people and getting involved in all kinds of interesting things. It would be a real mind-broadener. Don't hurry your decision. Take more time, and let all sides of the question sink in. If I had been offered a job like that at your age, I would have grabbed it."

I didn't sleep much that night. His advice gave me a new perspective, and I had great respect for Dad's wisdom. I tossed and turned most of the night. Wrestling with the problem in the wee hours of the morning, I reached a decision. I would follow Dad's advice. Strangely enough, once my decision was made I turned over and went to sleep. I waited a couple of days just to be sure I wouldn't have second thoughts, then went to Montpelier and accepted the offer. I have never regretted the decision.

Occasionally, I did look back to my trial practice days with nostalgia. In fact I still do, but life is a changing, moving process. We're happiest if we adjust to the changes going on around us and to the changes going on inside of us and grow in experience and understanding of ourselves and of the world and the people in it. *Growth*, I guess, is the critical word, for growth is one of the fundamentals of a full life.

As a result of my decision my life followed a completely new direction. I took up my new duties almost immediately during the first week in February 1940. The arrangement included an agreement on Mr. Brigham's part to find a job for my secretary, Edna Cheever, at National Life Insurance Company, with a salary at least equal to what the law firm had been paying her and also an agreement that I would be free to devote the necessary time to clean up all pending unfinished cases that I had been handling for Wilson, Carver, Davis and Keyser.

It is not easy for a lawyer to clean up his desk of pending matters when he gives up his practice. Things have a tendency to drag on and take on a life of their own. My practice was no exception. Perhaps this is one of the reasons so few lawyers ever actually and fully retire. Moreover, I found that I had to fight being dragged into new issues and cases arising out of old cases in which I had been involved for long-standing clients. It took me several years before I was completely clear of old business. I did most of the work after hours, on evenings and weekends. This was no great burden to me, however, because the office hours at National Life were from 8 A.M. to 4:30 P.M., and I had been accustomed as a practicing lawyer to working long hours, including evenings after dinner. But of course some matters did require court appearance or for other reasons could not be handled except during regular office hours.

The law department at National Life at that time consisted of six lawyers in addition to the general counsel and a large staff of paralegal individuals whose responsibility was to handle the matters of settlement options chosen by policyholders or their beneficiaries—a very technical field indeed. We had also a well-stocked library of legal and other books and material relating to fields interesting to or required by life insurance companies, all presided over by Miss Fitts, a well-trained librarian. When I arrived, the law department's six lawyers consisted of John Avery, an expert in federal, state, and municipal taxation; Clifton M. Heaton and Peter Giuliani, both experts in the law relating to investments of life insurance companies; Guy Horton, historian and expert on settlement options and trusts; and David Hoxie and Robert Craythorne, who functioned in all phases of the law department's work. All were extremely capable men. They accepted me as a newcomer and were most cooperative, for which I was truly appreciative.

At the time I accepted the job, the previous general counsel, Mr. Young, was still confined to his home and was thought to be more or less permanently disabled. Mr. Brigham informed me that the directors would designate him as advisory counsel and that he would be available to be called upon when circumstances warranted, but it was not expected that he would be able to come to the office regularly or assume any active responsibility. To my surprise, within a few days Mr. Young showed up at the office. We chatted a bit about how we could work together, but he seemed most interested in where his desk and chair were to be. Apparently, things had not been discussed very fully with him. Here I was sitting at his desk and in his chair, and no other desk or space was available! I promptly rose from the chair and said to him, "You come right around and sit where you always have. I'll sit on the other side of the desk." I went and got a simple extra office chair and placed it on the other side of the desk. We sat down and resumed our conversation. This seemed to mollify him completely, and we continued an amiable discussion about some of the company's legal problems for a half hour or so, whereupon he arose and picked up his coat and derby hat and left the office. I never saw him at the office or anywhere else again. Retirements are not always easy or happy occasions. Not long afterward, he died.

I spent the first few weeks trying to learn all I could about the law department, its activities, its responsibilities, its personnel, and how the department related to other departments of the company and to departments of state and federal government. Until this experience, I had no idea what a complicated business life insurance is or within what a myriad of legal relationships and restraints a life insurance company operates. Every state regulates not only those companies domiciled within its borders but also every life insurance company that does business there.

Among other things, all policy forms and scores of other forms must be approved in all states, and each state has its own peculiarities and requirements as to what can and cannot be included in policy forms. At that time, National Life was doing business in about forty states. This required the department to be familiar with the infinite varieties of the requirements in every one of those states. In the same manner the legal department was required to be familiar with the investment laws and authority in each state. The legal department reviewed all contracts to which the company was a party; handled all litigation against the company (of which there was an annual average of about thirty-five or forty suits arising out of death or disability claims in which the company denied liability); and gave legal advice to the board, all officers of the company, the executive and finance committees, and others. The department was also required to be familiar with the federal and state laws relating to income and estate taxation of life insurance proceeds, which at that time was a rapidly growing field.

As I realized the dimensions of this responsibility in those early weeks, it looked like a monumental task. But my perspective changed rapidly as I watched these six lawyers handling their respective areas with seeming ease and assurance. I soon found myself getting the hang of the work and enjoying it, except for one incident that happened early on and that still stands out in my memory.

John Avery, a veteran member of the department and a former Vermont tax commissioner, had been ill and out of the office for some time. He called me early in February to say that he would be back in a week or so and to please hold open for him the job of preparing the federal income tax return for the company, as he had performed this function in previous years. At that time, although National Life's premiums were heavily taxed by the individual states, the federal tax on life insurance companies was solely on investment income, with appropriate deductions for meeting the company's requirements for reserves held to meet its policy liabilities. In mutual companies, such as National Life, this resulted in no federal income tax liability. All this is changed now, and all companies, both stock companies and mutual companies, are heavily taxed by the federal government as well as by the states. Even when the company had no liability, however, the return had to be filed each year. It was always a voluminous document filled with mountains of figures gathered from the different departments of the company.

One morning shortly after John Avery's return to work, he came into my office extremely agitated and told me that a tentative computation had indicated that, for the first time, the company would be subject to a large federal tax liability. This was disturbing news to a brand-new general counsel. Discussing the situation with John, I found that for years the company had not bothered to include its depreciation on owned real estate, even though the depreciation was a statutory deduction, because no liability ensued without it. It was simply not needed, and for this reason depreciation had not been set up on the company books. Now, apparently, depreciation would be needed and fast, since the return was due in about ten days. John and I agreed that we must set up depreciation accounts on each of the large number of farms the company owned in the West and Southwest, all resulting from the company's long interest and investment in farm real estate. The accounts would be necessary so that we could include the depreciation in the tax returns as a deduction. Time was short, and up-to-date appraisals would have to be made. I went to the executive committee, explained the situation, and asked for authority to hire twenty additional temporary personnel. This request was granted, and I began the task of locating and hiring them.

Two days later John came dashing into my office all out of breath.

"Call it off," he said.

"What do you mean, call it off? Call what off?" I asked.

"We don't need them," he said.

"Why don't we need them?" I asked.

"It's all a mistake," he said.

"What do you mean, a mistake?" I replied.

"One of the adding machines went wrong and made a mistake of a million dollars," he said.

So with a red face, I rescinded the order for the twenty people.

It didn't seem funny at the time, but since then, I have had many chuckles over it. How much can turn on so little!

One area that captured my interest early on was the marketing of life insurance. Agents and general agents who came to the company on business often dropped into my office. I enjoyed getting their viewpoints on marketing the company's product, and from these discussions it soon became apparent to me that fundamental changes were occurring in the marketing of life insurance. Social Security was prompting the changes. The built-in life insurance element in Social Security was taking the place of voluntary life insurance for many small policy prospects, and the result was a loss of a sizable segment of the life insurance companies' traditional market. Consequently, life insurance companies and their agents were beginning to put more emphasis on developing a market with the professional and business segments of the· public. The quality and education of agents needed to be improved to attract this market, and this spurred companies to create training departments and to add sophisticated staff with training talents and education.

I had joined National Life during the early stages of this phenomenon. No training department yet existed at National Life, and agents were turning to the law department for information about advice on how tax laws affected the owners and beneficiaries of life insurance policies. Several lawyers in our law department quickly became competent in this field. The activity grew by leaps and bounds. Soon we were writing articles for our company field force magazine on current subjects of this nature, and this in turn quickly led to requests to write for the *Chartered Life Underwriters* magazine and other insurance magazines that circulated among agents and general agents and managers of all companies. Shortly we were being invited to speak before agents' groups, trust council groups, and estate planners, all of which widened the acquaintance of agents of all companies to the National Life Insurance Company.

This naturally led me to write a book on the use of life insurance as a vehicle for the smooth transition of businesses, particularly partnerships and closely held corporations, in which one of the partners had died. The book, my first, called *Life Insurance and Business Purchase Agreements*, was well received, and our agents gave it to lawyers, trust officers, accountants, and others involved in estate planning. Soon it became a valuable professional tool for them and for the company as well. For my part, it gave me a thorough understanding of the marketing of life insurance.

During my first and second year much of my time was spent in reviewing hundreds of administrative practices, procedures, and documents. I did not originate this activity—it was thrust upon me. The moving spirit in this exercise was L. Douglas Meredith, who at that time was assistant to the president. A very intelligent, able, and alert officer, he would ask me from time to time to review documents and practices in use by the company and to evaluate how effectively they protected the company's interest. I took each request very seriously and made my evaluation carefully. I was surprised at the number of times when a document or a practice from a legal standpoint left the company open to possible legal trouble. Afterward, in every case, I wrote an opinion, offering my advice on improvements and changes to make, and sent copies to everyone involved. Another surprise—again and again, I received back the opinion from the department head responsible for the practice with the comment, "This is the way we've always done it." As if antiquity could justify an improper or insufficient practice! It required considerable tact and patience to implement the numerous changes. Some problems never were corrected. If the case seemed to me a very important one, and if I could not convince the person involved to change the practice, I would finally go to the president, who invariably moved to protect the company's interest. But my persistence did not prove to be any great aid to my popularity! I was beginning to understand some of the human sides of corporate bureaucracy.

In my second year after coming to the company, I was elected a vice president, and my title became Vice President and General Counsel. I slowly began to participate more in day-to-day policy decisions that were not legal in nature. I had mixed reactions to this trend in my work, for I had little experience in business enterprise and none in large corporate organizations.

I was introduced to the investment side of the business after my appointment to the finance committee. Day by day, in turns of two each, finance committee members passed judgment on loans below a certain amount; regularly the committee met as a whole to consider matters of general investment policy and to approve the large loans. A big batch of loans landed on the committee desk each day. A member of the investment staff carefully investigated each loan before it came to us and offered a recommendation, but we had final authority.

I was first introduced to this work at a time when the general level of interest rates was the lowest that I have ever seen in my lifetime. It seems incredible now, in light of our recent history of high interest rates, that we were approving many of the larger loans at 3 percent or even less. At that time National Life policies, like those of most legal reserve companies, provided that the policyholders could borrow the cash value from the company at any time at 5 percent. While there was provision in these loan agreements for payment of interest, no provision was made in the policies for the repayment of the principal except at maturity, either by death or endowment maturity or surrender. Consequently, many were never paid until maturity.

Not surprisingly, National Life began to receive a large number of letters from policyholders complaining that a policyholder should not be required to pay 5 percent for a loan when the company was making real estate loans for 3 percent or less. But the company felt that it could not legally make such loans at a rate lower than that specified in the contract without discriminating unfairly against those who had contracts and loans outstanding at 5 percent. Moreover, if the general level of rates should rise, as it was expected to, outstanding loans at lower rates could not be raised. Later, when the prime rate in the country rose to 20 percent and hordes of policyholders paid off any existing loans they had with banks and came to the company, as was their right, for loans at 5 percent, I often thought of those letters of complaint. Life is indeed a two-way street! Under these conditions, the company was forced to forgo investments up to 15 percent or more in order to have the funds to respond to policyholders' demands for 5 percent loans. The question naturally to be asked is, Why didn't the company change the specified rate in the policies, at least in all new policies issued? The answer is that the law of most states sets a limit as to what rate policyholders could be charged, and in Vermont, National Life had reached that limit. Fortunately, after a long battle the laws of most states have been changed to allow higher rates of interest to be charged for policyholder loans.

During my years in general law practice, I had occasionally represented clients before committees of the legislature, a practice called lobbying. Through this exposure I became aware of a rule of practice that permits chairmen of committees in the Vermont legislature to bottle up in committee in their sole discretion any bill that has been referred to their committee for recommendation. This rule has sometimes been used by chairmen even when a majority of the committee is in favor of the bill. While I have great respect for our state legislature, I have long been bothered by this practice. I realize that there are occasions when bills should be left in committee without action on the floor, but I believed then and believe now that this should only be done by action of a majority of the committee affected. Yet because of a long tradition, members of legislative committees will rarely—indeed almost never—go over the head of the chairman.

A situation like this happened to me once while I was acting as general counsel for National Life on a bill of great importance. The statute involved had been on the books for more than seventy-five years, and in addition to other taxes, it levied an annual tax on National Life of one quarter of one percent on the surplus of the company. The political or practical reason for the enactment of such a statute has been lost in the shadows of antiquity. Whatever the reason for its origin, it was a grossly unfair tax, principally because it violated one of the basic tenets of the philosophy of taxation. It was not a tax on the annual *accretions* to surplus but on the *accumulated* surplus, which thus taxed the same dollars over and over again, amounting to legal confiscation.

One morning upon arriving at the office I picked up a newspaper and read that the legislature, believing that substantially more revenue was going to be needed, had set up a blue ribbon commission to examine the present tax system of the state and to recommend to the legislature what additional sources were available. Buried inconspicuously among the directions to the panel were the words, "to review and determine the relative fairness of existing tax exactions."

This gave me an idea. I went into Mr. Brigham's office, showed him the article, and told him I thought the company should file a petition with the commission and ask that it recommend the repeal of this tax.

"Why, that tax has been on the books for seventy-five years," Mr. Brigham said.

"I know," I replied. "But antiquity doesn't make it right or fair. You'll admit it is completely unfair, and this is just the sort of situation that those words in the statute apply to. I believe I could present a pretty strong case of unfairness."

"You don't really believe you could get the legislature to repeal a tax that's been on the books that long, do you? Particularly when the legislators believe they must have more revenue."

"Yes, Mr. Brigham, I do," I said. "Anyway, I could make a pretty good try. I can't guarantee what the legislature would do. But I've looked over the names on that commission, and there are some pretty fair-minded men on it. And even if I failed, I think it would cool their enthusiasm for trying to get more taxes out of the company."

"But look at the politics of the situation," he said. "A big corporation getting its taxes reduced at the time the state is looking for more revenue."

"I know," I said. "But this is the clearest case of unfair tax exaction that this panel could possibly find in the state. And besides, these taxes are not the company's money. That money belongs to the policyholders in a mutual company."

"But how would you go about it?" he asked. "Just say that it's unfair?"

"No, there are lot of reasons why it's unfair. First, no other company in the United States has to pay this kind of a tax, and no other state has any such law. State taxes on life insurance companies are in all states based on premiums, and in Vermont we pay the highest premium tax of any state. This is a clearly unconscionable tax. It is a competitive disadvantage. And furthermore, it can be demonstrated that it is unfair when measured against non-life insurance companies in Vermont. National Life pays a far higher tax than they do."

Mr. Brigham still seemed doubtful but gave me the go-ahead anyway.

To make a long story short, we presented our case before the panel, and it recommended that the tax be repealed. Two committees in the House to which the issue was referred also recommended repeal unanimously. The full House voted its repeal unanimously. One committee in the Senate recommended repeal, and then we struck a snag. Three men of the five-man committee on finance were in favor of repeal, and the other two, which included the chairman, were opposed. The chairman refused to let the bill be voted out by the majority.

Nothing I said or did could budge him from his position, and time was fast running out. Adjournment was near. The chairman wouldn't even give me a reason for his stubbornness. But, of course, I knew the reason. It stemmed from an old disagreement with one of National Life's agents living in Rutland. The committee chairman's dislike of the agent had spilled over onto the company.

It seemed incredible that one man could kill this bill single-handedly. This seemed such an indefensible perversion of the legislative process that I decided to explore the possibility of appealing to public opinion. But how? The chairman was a senator from Rutland County. I decided to present the facts to Robert Mitchell, who was then editor of the *Rutland Herald*. He was an extremely intelligent person and was without doubt the most knowledgeable man in the state on political and legislative history due to his long years of covering the legislature as a reporter for the *Herald*.

I arranged for an interview, stated my case, and left with him a thirty-page memorandum on the issue that I had used with the panel and also the legislative committees. Mr. Mitchell listened closely and politely but gave no indication of his reaction. He thanked me for coming to see him and terminated the interview. Days went by with adjournment coming closer and closer. I decided that I had wasted my time.

Then one morning I picked up the *Herald* and read a long editorial on the subject. Written by Mr. Mitchell in his usual scholarly style, it was a scathing indictment of the hold-up procedure.

Within days the finance committee reported the bill out favorably with a vote of 3 to 2. The Senate promptly took the bill up for action and pushed it through before adjournment with a vote of 28 to 2. Messaged to the governor, it was promptly signed by Governor Ernest Gibson. My mission had been accomplished.

Never underestimate the power of the press. And never underestimate simple fairness as a weapon in political affairs.

I enjoyed my association with President Brigham. He was a former congressman from Vermont, a well-educated and well-informed man with a deep love for Vermont. After graduating from Middlebury College, he had taken over the home farm in St. Albans at the Bay and gradually bought up farms surrounding the original farm until he operated a large acreage with a Jersey herd of over one hundred cows. This was in the days when herds of that size in Vermont were few and far between. He was famous in the dairy cattle world for his outstanding success as a Jersey breeder. He held the much-coveted title in the American Jersey Cattle Club of Master Breeder, and he held the world's record for nineteen consecutive years for pounds of production of milk for herds of more than one hundred cows. While he was at Middlebury College, he had majored in chemistry, and he became fascinated with the application of chemistry to the management of agricultural soil and the feeding of cattle for milk production.

Mr. Brigham loved the farm. He spent all the time there he could. He lived in Montpelier while he was president of National Life, but he retained his home in St. Albans and spent practically all of his weekends at the farm at the Bay. He loved to talk about farming and cows. Since I was operating a small Jersey farm on East Hill in Barre at the time, we shared a common interest. Often in the forenoon, after he had his desk cleared, he would call me on the phone and ask, "Judge, have you got a few minutes?" Of course I always had time for the president! He would discuss some business matter for a while, then the conversation would invariably turn to farms and cows.

He also had a deep interest in Vermont, part of which doubtless stemmed from his days as a congressman from Vermont. He was regarded by most people as a hard-core conservative, which he was on most matters, but he had a strong innovative streak in his nature, too, which at times put him squarely on the liberal side of a public issue. For example, he favored the controversial legislation that set up the program for federally guaranteed mortgage loans, a position that pitted him squarely against almost the entire life insurance industry. He was also much interested in education and was a firm believer in private colleges and their special mission. Doubtless here, too, his Middlebury experience was responsible for his views.

One day upon entering his office, I found him reading the *Burlington Free Press* with a noticeable scowl on his face. It turned out that he was reading a news item to the effect that the Vermont legislature had just made a biennial appropriation of $250,000 for the support of the University of Vermont. He read part of the newspaper item to me, then rose and paced around the room delivering a most forceful lecture on the impropriety of that action. I remember he wound up with a dour prophecy: "Young man," he said, "you'll live to see the day when the legislature will be appropriating $500,000 a biennium to UVM." It turned out to be a conservative prophecy. The appropriation is now more than $58 million a biennium.

My ten years as general counsel of National Life were active, rewarding, and educational years. They fulfilled completely my father's prophecy. They broadened my knowledge, lifted my horizons, and introduced me to the complicated inner workings not only of National Life but of the life insurance industry as a whole. Moreover, those years gave me the confidence to undertake larger responsibilities when the opportunity came.

12

Onward And Upward

*The challenge of the job appealed to me as, of
course, did the prestige, but there could be no
guarantee of my success, and if I failed it would be
unfortunate for the company and a disaster for me.
I made up my mind to give the job every ounce of
my energy and dedication.*

One day when I had been general counsel at National Life for ten
years, President Brigham notified the board of directors that he
wanted to retire. The events surrounding the selection of a successor
created a sharp division on the board, the like of which I had never
seen during all the time I had been there. Among the candidates
proposed were L. Douglas Meredith and me.

Doug Meredith had been with the company longer than I had.
He was a graduate of Syracuse University, where he had majored in
economics. He had been a professor at the University of Vermont
prior to his service as commissioner of banking and insurance for
the State of Vermont. At National Life he had held, at different
times, the positions of assistant to the president, treasurer, and
chairman of the finance committee. He was a brilliant man with a lot
of drive and self-organization. Mr. Brigham favored Doug, and Fred
A. Howland, longtime member of the board, former president, and
later chairman of the board, recommended me. Both Mr. Brigham

and Mr. Howland were determined and immovable, so the situation quickly deteriorated into a seemingly irreconcilable issue that quickly divided the board approximately evenly. Both Doug and I were uncomfortable in this unfortunate situation, tried to stay out of the dispute, and succeeded fairly well in doing so. As the matter dragged on without being resolved, however, it became obvious that something had to be done.

Finally, Edward S. French, a distinguished member of the board, proposed a temporary solution. He proposed that Dr. Ernest Martin Hopkins, a National Life board member and a retired and much-revered president of Dartmouth College, be persuaded to take the job on an interregnum basis for two years and to return to the board at the end of that time with his recommendation for the permanent new president of the company. Because of Dr. Hopkins's wide reputation as an expert in the field of corporate management, particularly in the field of personnel relations, this proposal was greeted with enthusiasm by the board, and he was promptly elected.

During this period I received a phone call from a member of the board of directors of the Federal Reserve Bank of Boston asking if I would be willing to come to Boston to meet with a special committee of the board searching for a new president for the bank. Naturally, I was more than a bit startled, but since I was then unhappy at National Life over the controversy there, I was curious. I went to Boston and met five members of this special committee at the Union Club on Park Street. During the long interview, I was quizzed at great length about my education, background, experience, and philosophy. Harold Hodgkinson, a member of the committee and the president of Filene's Inc. in Boston, did much of the questioning in his usual thorough manner. It was my first meeting with Mr. Hodgkinson, and so impressed was I by him that I was later responsible for his election to National Life's board.

I told the committee that I had no experience in banking beyond serving for a few years on the board of the People's National Bank of Barre and that I had no education or background in finance or economics, which I thought quite essential for a bank president. The members of the search committee explained to me that they were trying to decide in their search whether to pick a man with banking experience or one who could do a good public relations job. It was in the latter capacity that they had become interested in me. I found out later that my name had been brought to their attention by Roy Patrick, president of Rock of Ages in Barre, on whose board I was serving at the time.

After the meeting was over, Corinne met me at the Union Club, and we walked for a while on Boston Common. It was a beautiful early summer day, and finally we sat down on a bench across the street from the front of the beautiful Massachusetts Statehouse. Corinne wanted to know everything that went on at the meeting. I told her as fully as I could. Then she asked, "What are you going to do?"

"Well, they haven't offered me the job yet," I replied.

"I know that," she said, "but you're nervous as a witch, and you had better make up your mind."

"My guess is that they won't offer me the job," I said. "They'll choose a real banker, which is what they ought to do. But what do you think I should do if they by some chance do offer me the job?"

"It's not my decision," she said. "You tell me what you think you ought to do. Then I'll tell you what I think."

"Well," I said, "I think I could do the kind of public relations job they have in mind. But I have a kind of a gut reaction that I ought not to do it. So if by chance they should ask me, I think I ought to decline."

"Oh," she said, "I'm so glad. And I think you would be doing exactly the right thing. What a wonderful day! Let's go to the movies tonight."

And we did.

As it turned out, several weeks later the members of the committee decided to choose someone else. They chose a good man with banking experience who had an outstanding record and who served the bank extremely well.

Meanwhile, during the presidency of Dr. Hopkins at National Life, I avoided him as much as possible other than meetings that were necessary to carry out my responsibilities as general counsel. I found myself increasingly embarrassed by the situation at the company, and it was repugnant to me to appear to be job-seeking, for in fact I definitely was not. I was happy with my responsibilities as general counsel, and I was sure I was doing a good job there. Moreover, I was not at all sure that I possessed the necessary education, training, experience, or temperament to make a good president.

It was tacitly understood that Dr. Hopkins would serve for a two-year term to discharge his undertaking. But before the two years had expired, he had made up his mind. He came to me one day and said that he had concluded that he was going to recommend me to the board as the next president and that he wanted to know before he did whether I would accept the job. I told him that I could not possibly guarantee that he had made the right decision, but that I would accept on condition that he become chairman of the board. If he would do that, I would do my level best to make the arrangement work. I pointed out that he would not need to live in Montpelier, that he would only have to have an office here, and that he could spend just as much or as little time on company affairs as he wished. His wife was ill at that time, as I knew, and I suspected that he was making his recommendation earlier than he would have otherwise because he wanted to be back home in Hanover. I suggested that he serve as chairman of the executive committee and that meetings be held in Hanover whenever it was inconvenient for him to come to the office in Montpelier. He agreed to this and made his report to the board. It was accepted, and I was elected president and chief executive officer. Douglas Meredith was elected executive vice president and chairman of the finance committee. Dr. Hopkins was elected chairman of the board, to which both Doug and I were also elected.

I approached my new responsibilities with mixed emotions. I knew that if the arrangements were to succeed, my first task would be to heal the wounds that had been inflicted during the two years of turmoil and indecision. The challenge of the job appealed to me as, of course, did the prestige, but there could be no guarantee of my success, and if I failed it would be unfortunate for the company and a disaster for me. I made up my mind to give the job every ounce of my energy and dedication. Whether I did succeed is not for me to say, but the company prospered and grew during my seventeen years as president, which is the best evidence I can offer. Some of the things I did, I would do differently if I had the job to do over again, but I think that is true of almost everybody who assumes a post of that kind for any great length of time. In any event, I satisfied the members of the board, and it was their desire that I remain as president until I reached age seventy, five years beyond normal retirement time. As events unfolded, I did not stay that long, but I did stay until I was sixty-seven, and I served another year beyond that as chairman and chief executive officer while my successor, Dr. John Fey, was taking over.

Certainly the success of my start as president of National Life was due, in part, to the graciousness of Doug Meredith, who came to me immediately after the decision was made and offered his congratulations and his wholehearted support. This became a wonderful help in healing the wounds. He lived up to his promise 100 percent, and we became close friends and still are. For most of the next two decades, we kept in close touch on all phases of company operations and met daily for a half hour on all days during which we were both in the office.

Dr. Hopkins also turned out to be a tower of strength in my support. His wise counsel and long experience, as well as his prestige and his personal charm, were made available to me at any and all times. My understanding of the depth and breadth of his experience continued to grow throughout our long association, which lasted fourteen years. We developed a firm and fast friendship which was one of the cherished privileges of my life. My second wife Marjorie and I spent short vacations with him every summer at his seaside home at Southwest Harbor in Maine, which is how I happened to be with him when he died in his sleep there. The memories of those visits, filled with business and philosophical discussion, are keepsakes I treasure.

During the first year or two of my relationship with Dr. Hopkins after my election as president, I invariably addressed him as "Dr. Hopkins." One day I received a handwritten letter from him in his usual somewhat formal style. He wrote that he had always believed that one should address another person in the form that comes most naturally. However, he wrote, his closest friends addressed him as "Hop" or "Hoppy," and if it came naturally for me to do the same, he would be pleased. I was enormously pleased to receive this touching letter and immediately began addressing him as "Hoppy" and always did during the rest of his life. I felt that I had been admitted to a most distinguished and much coveted society—the close friends of Hoppy. Further evidence of that was soon forthcoming. I received an invitation to attend a birthday party for Hoppy at Hartness House in Springfield, Vermont. I promptly accepted. Upon arriving, I found that those attending, eight or ten, were close friends of Hoppy's who had been meeting this way for years. I was the youngest by many years of any of the attendees. This annual event was purposely held outside Hanover, Hoppy's home town, to avoid the pressure to include many people who otherwise might be offended. I had the cherished privilege of attending these celebrations for ten years. They were always happy and stimulating experiences. The affair invariably consisted of cocktails and dinner and some three or four hours of fellowship and discussion afterward. There were no speeches, no encomiums. We retired around midnight and slept soundly. We awoke to reassemble for a bounteous breakfast served in Hartness House's best style before leaving to go our separate ways. I always felt a deep sense of satisfaction and contentment after those parties.

Hoppy's letters were works of art. I have hundreds of them in my files and occasionally reread a few just for the sheer joy of the experience. He could make words sing. Although his style was a bit formal, he had a well-developed sense of humor. Always, he knew how to make his correspondents feel good with a few simple words. Once he concluded a business letter to me with, "If this letter were being written to Marjorie instead of you, it would have simply said 'I love you, burn this.' "

Hoppy's method of giving advice was equally artful and unique in my experience. When I had a problem that seemed to defy solution, I usually turned to Hoppy. Many times I drove to Hanover and spent time with him wrestling with the problem. I would chat with him for an hour or two, or even longer at times, sometimes staying overnight or for lunch, and then drive home to Montpelier. As we discussed the problem at hand, Hoppy would ask questions to keep me talking. He would intersperse his questions with anecdotes of his experiences in other organizations, which always seemed to have a bearing on the problem at hand. Before the session was over, I invariably talked myself into what appeared to be the solution. Hoppy almost never gave a word of direct specific advice, but it would soon dawn on me that his Socratic method of teaching had shown me the path to the solution. I have come to realize that this is an effective way to build self-reliance and the ability to make decisions and sleep with them, which is the principal job of a chief executive in any line of work. What a man Hoppy was!

One of the first and thorniest problems I tackled as president of National Life was the matter of rising field expense. General agents in many companies, including National Life, have historically been compensated by commissions and an expense allowance. The general agent's duties are to recruit, train, and supervise the agents who do the actual selling. It is common within the business that new general agencies need special expense allowances for a few years until the agency is well enough established to generate sufficient commissions to operate the office. These special allowances are arrived at by negotiations between each general agent and the home office merchandising department officials, taking into account the peculiarities of each agency. At National Life in the early 1950s, however, this practice of negotiation had been extended to embrace agencies that were well established. For several reasons, I did not like this method of fixing expense allowances for well-established general agencies. For one, it took up too much time on the part of the home office agency department officials as well as of the individual general agents. Also, I felt the system was inherently unfair because the strongest and best negotiators and not necessarily the best agencies were getting the most generous allowances. This was causing jealousies among our general agents, and the method, I thought, contributed to the rapidly rising field costs.

Much of the competition among the better life insurance companies in the United States was based on the lowest net cost of the product. National Life had always stood well up toward the top in this respect, an edge that our agents used aggressively in the market. So, in addition to costing the company income, our rising field expenses had caused our position to slip. I felt it might slip even more unless we could correct the problem. Conversely, if we could substantially improve our net cost position, I felt that agents would sell more life insurance and hence make more commissions, which would more than offset any reduction in the general agent's expenses.

After studying the problem at the home office, we decided that a more equitable and cost-effective method for fixing expense allowances of the established agencies would be by formula. Once we determined that a formula method would be better, we undertook to settle the question of how it could or should be implemented. Our concern was how to get the general agents to accept the formula without losing too many of them. Too much opposition would likely cause resignations, which might result in a situation worse than the one we were facing. Moreover, I was aware, too, that all but two of these general agents had signed a petition in my behalf directed to the National Life board asking that I be selected as the new president. I could see myself through their eyes as a new president, one who had been supported by the general agents, whose first act was to attempt to reduce their compensation, and I was embarrassed.

I talked the matter over with my associates at the home office, and we agreed that we would invite all the general agents to the famous Greenbriar Hotel in West Virginia to discuss the matter. Archibald McAuley, an actuary at National Life who had worked on the formula, Doug Meredith, and I prepared ourselves for the task of presenting the situation in detail. To emphasize what we were doing we all donned Scottish tam-o'-shanters and wore them throughout the daylong presentation. We three acted as a panel, each covering a separate phase of the problem. In the afternoon much of the time was taken up by questions by individual general agents and the opportunity for them to make statements or arguments. By five o'clock most of us were quite exhausted. I had planned on taking a horseback ride in the late afternoon but gave that up and took a sauna treatment instead, my first.

We had presented the general agents with an option. We told them that if they would accept the formula graciously and unanimously, we would improve the net cost immediately. If they did not, then we would implement the formula anyway, but more gradually. We pointed out that if the latter course were taken, we would not be able to lower the net cost until the formula had been fully implemented.

I had kept the National Life directors fully informed of our intentions and of the risk involved in case any of the directors wished to disapprove of the action. None did. On the contrary, one went way out of his way to help put it across. Dr. John Thomas, then of

Mendon, Vermont, was highly esteemed as a clergyman who had been the president of five different colleges and universities in the United States. He is the only man then or since to achieve that honor. Fortunately for us, he had a good understanding of the intricacies of field management and life insurance merchandising. He was also a very persuasive gentleman. Without informing me, or as far as I know anyone else at National Life, he made a reservation at the Greenbriar and came by train unannounced and unexpected to do what he could to further my cause. It was a service well beyond the line of duty for a director. He was well along in years and under some physical handicaps, which made it more of a chore. He circulated among the general agents during recesses, at meal times, and in the evenings, quietly using his considerable powers of persuasion with them. He was most effective. When I learned what he was doing, I was greatly touched. I have thought of this many times since and always with deep appreciation.

The second day of the convention the general agents met by themselves to determine what as an association their position would be. Late in the second day they sent word that they were ready to report, and the home office officers joined their meeting. We were delighted when they informed us that they had voted unanimously to accept the formula method immediately. What a relief!

The toughest problem I faced during my incumbency, however, was a local issue. Later, it became a statewide political issue, but it began in my own backyard and occupied much of my time and energy during my first decade in office. The problem was how to provide additional office space to meet National Life's rapidly increasing space requirements.

When I became president of National Life in 1950, the company occupied the granite building on State Street to the west of the statehouse. The building had been built in 1921. It was the sixth home office building for National Life since its incorporation in 1848. All six offices had been in Montpelier. The 1921 building had been originally designed to include seven floors. The company, however, had ordered the plans redrawn for a five-story building when it became apparent that the sixth and seventh stories would throw out of balance the statehouse quadrangle. Thirty years later, the company was seriously discussing the need for additional space and was beginning to feel not only crowded but actually pinched.

The north end of this 1921 National Life building had been left in brick to allow for the later building of a second wing running parallel to the wing on the Baldwin Street side. As soon as the issue was opened up, however, we found that some of the directors felt that the company should not add to the 1921 structure or build new space in Montpelier. Most of the directors agreed that we should not put on the new wing conceived in 1921 because of the traffic problem that had developed on State and Main streets due to increases in the numbers of employees at the statehouse, at National Life, and at the two fire insurance companies housed on State Street. Some directors went even further and believed we should not build in Montpelier at all because National Life's growth was outpacing the population growth in Montpelier and immediately surrounding communities. In a short time, they feared, the company would not be able to supply its clerical staff requirements from Montpelier and environs. The directors, or some of them, also believed that because National Life's business was nationwide and because many investment and agency department visitors were coming to the home office, the company should be located where more attractive airline service could be had.

All of us realized that a new wing or a new building in Montpelier would increase company taxes substantially, particularly because tax rates in Montpelier were much higher than in many other locations due to the large amount of land and number of buildings in Montpelier that were owned by the state and hence free from taxation. It was also quite obvious that the state was going to have to take over much more property in Montpelier, thus contributing to further raises in the tax rate. Consequently, pressure was building up on the National Life board to consider some location outside Montpelier and possibly out of the state. On the other hand, the home office had been located in Montpelier for more than one-hundred years. The company began there and grew there, and some of its best agents thought the Vermont image to be a help in merchandising. National Life had grown to be the twenty-fifth in size out of more than seventeen hundred legal reserve life insurance companies in the United States. It was the only life insurance company in the country that had grown to any real size in a completely rural setting.

I was not convinced that the company should move out of Montpelier, yet I realized that I might be prejudiced. In fact, I admitted to myself that I probably was. I was determined to keep that prejudice out of consideration as far as possible and comforted myself with the knowledge that, after all, this was a question for the directors to decide. So for four years while the board was considering the matter, I did not tell anyone how I felt about it. I intended to do a thorough and unprejudiced job of investigating all sides of the question and to present the evidence fairly and fully to the board. Since I steadfastly refused to tell anyone how I stood on the question, my friends on both sides assumed that I was on the other side. Most of my friends, of course, were from the Montpelier area and some felt that I was a traitor to the area. But I stuck to my guns and kept my views to myself. I knew from the start that it would take years to solve this problem and get the building built.

As part of the planning process, I felt the first question to be decided was whether National Life would consider moving out of Vermont. This was the easy part. To dispose of that option and decide right off whether National Life would move outside Vermont, I asked the executive committee and the board of directors to decide this larger question immediately and declare the company's intention of staying in Vermont. Both the executive committee and the board were unanimous in voting to stay in Vermont.

The second thing we did was to buy land in Burlington, just in case the decision should be to build in the Burlington area. We picked a beautiful site straddling Shelburne Road on Route 7 adjacent to Bartlett's Bay on Lake Champlain. We bought the site, which included eight or nine parcels and amounted to several hundred acres, as a precaution. We knew that if we went to Burlington later, we would find it impossible to secure a good site without paying an inflated value. Also, we knew that the rapid pace of rising land values in the Burlington area would make it easy for us to sell the land for more than we paid for it if we should decide not to relocate there.

We hired an outside real estate firm to make the purchase without disclosing the name of the real purchaser. Immediately afterward, we made an announcement that the land had been acquired. We fully realized that such an announcement would be taken to signify that a decision had been made to move to Burlington. We also included in the press release a statement that no decision to move had been made, but I'm sure at first no one believed it. As we expected, the public reacted strongly. For months papers were full of the story, most of it speculation.

Next we hired a Washington, D.C., site specialist to study the problem and advise the company. His report was a lengthy portrayal of the problem and was filled with statistical evidence. He recommended that we move to Burlington. His report relied most heavily upon the argument that the company was growing more rapidly than Montpelier and the surrounding area were, and hence within a few years the company would be unable to fulfill its requirements for staff, principally clerical staff. The report was duly presented to the board through the building committee and discussed at great length. I was not happy with the report, not only because of its conclusions but because of the reasons given for moving. I insisted on a second opinion. We then hired an exceedingly prestigious site-selection firm from New York City. Its report, too, advised us to move to Burlington, for many of the same reasons.

While these studies were going on, an organization of citizens was formed in Montpelier for the sole purpose of trying to prevent the company from moving. It was spearheaded by Robert Ryan, an able lawyer who was president of the Capital Savings Bank in Montpelier. The activities of this committee were carried out aggressively but with commendable dignity and efficiency. In an excellent report, the committee marshaled the arguments against moving and presented us with a report that likewise was circulated among the members of the building committee and the board and discussed at length. Shortly after this report was presented, Bob Ryan came to my office to make a proposal. The proposal was that the City of Montpelier would give National Life a real estate tax exemption for a period of ten years if the company would stay in Montpelier. He told me that he had discussed the proposal with enough people, including members of the city council, to be sure the proposal could be implemented if we agreed.

I turned the proposal down immediately without even presenting it to the board. I well knew that a company the size of National Life could not comfortably live in Montpelier paying no taxes. I told

Bob, however, that I would look favorably upon an arrangement whereby the amount of the taxes to be paid for ten years would be agreed upon. I also told him I thought it would help the cause of staying in Montpelier.

After the report of the second site-selection firm was received, I decided that it was time for me to take a position on the question before the building committee and the board. I again reviewed the mass of evidence that had been collected (only a fraction of which is mentioned here), and it appeared to me that the only substantial argument in favor of moving was the matter of whether the Montpelier area could supply our needs for future increased staff. But even this argument, up to this point in the debate, was based almost exclusively on projected population growth in various regions compared to National Life's projected needs for increasing numbers of staff.

Such a mathematical comparison left out of consideration any changes that might occur as the years went by, and if experience teaches us anything, it is that things don't stay the same. For example, we knew that eventually Vermont was going to have an interstate thruway, and it was reasonable to expect that this road would greatly enlarge the geographic area from which National Life might expect to recruit staff. We were also aware of the developing field of computers, which offered the possibility of slowing down the rate of growth of clerical personnel needs.

Neither of the reports touched upon the subject of what other life insurance companies were experiencing in the matter of filling their clerical staff requirements. Both reports had proceeded on the assumption that high-density areas would offer better potential for recruiting large numbers. But was that theory sound? I felt we should see how companies in high-density areas were doing in this regard, so I personally made trips to Boston, New York, Hartford, and Newark, New Jersey, to see what I could learn from the companies in those well-known life insurance regions.

I was surprised by what I found. Every company I visited was having trouble filling its needs. I remember particularly that Metropolitan Life Insurance Company in New York City had sixteen hundred desks unfilled in a region that was about as densely populated as any we were likely to find. All the companies had found it necessary to solve the problem of empty desks by expensive methods. In Hartford, one company was running two shifts so that it could hire back former employees who had married and had children. The two shifts made it possible for these employees to work in the evening after their spouses were home and able to take care of the children.

By this time I had made up my mind that National Life should not move, and I became an advocate for staying in Montpelier. In addition, National Life now had an offer of a real estate tax agreement to consider from the City of Montpelier. The effect of the offered agreement would be to maintain for ten years the amount of appraisal on the proposed new building at a figure 50 percent higher than the appraisal figure then in effect on the company's old building. Before the offer was made to the company, the Montpelier City Council approved the proposed agreement unanimously. Shortly afterward, the question was presented and explained in great detail to a meeting of the Montpelier voters and again was unanimously approved.

When the evidence was all in before the board at National Life, the question was presented for action. After painstaking consideration and discussion, the board voted to remain in the Montpelier "area." It was a great relief for everyone when at a special meeting of all National Life staff held in the State Street Theatre, I was able to announce that a final decision had been made and that we would remain in the area.

Vice President Roy Johnson was delegated the task of investigating and helping the building committee choose a site in the area. He came up with a list of eleven sites worthy of consideration, upon which we took immediate options. Some were in Berlin, some in East Montpelier, and some in Montpelier. We then hired a firm of site selectors from Watertown, New York, who had done a lot of work for the State of Vermont and who knew the area well. We gave the selectors the list of eleven sites and asked them to make a careful review of each, list the advantages and disadvantages of each, and rank them in the order of their preference. When their report arrived, the covering letter described how they had followed instructions and listed the advantages and disadvantages of each site in the order of their preference, but it concluded with the statement, "But we wouldn't build on any of them." This was a shocker. I immediately called the firm and talked with the man who had done the principal work and asked him why he had made that statement. "Because you have a much better site right under your nose than any of the eleven," he said. "Where is it?" I asked. He tried to tell me, but because he was not familiar with the names of streets, we had some difficulty in communicating. Suddenly it dawned on me that he was talking about a site that Roy Johnson and I had favored during a scouting trip in an airplane but that we had eliminated when we saw it from the ground because it was rough and much rock would have to be removed.

The core land of the site was owned by Robert Ryan and his brother William. The evening of the day I received the Watertown report, I went to Robert Ryan's home and asked for an option. We agreed on a purchase price of $75,000. The option was executed, and I called the Watertown people and asked them to come back to Montpelier and do an on-the-ground evaluation of the site in comparison to the other eleven. They did, promptly. When their report came in they were still enthusiastic and placed it first, far ahead of all others. They admitted it would cost roughly an additional million dollars to fit the site over the cost of other sites, but they said, "It's well worth it."

When the building committee had examined all the sites and the reports, it could recommend only two sites to the full board. One was the Ryan site. The other site was known as the recreation field, although it was owned by National Life. Years later, long after this decision had been made, National Life donated the land to the city on which to build its new high school. Even with the strong recommendation of the site-selecting firm, however, the board was divided on the choice of sites. None of the members who lived outside of Vermont had seen the Ryan site, and they asked to do so. The board recessed so everyone could climb atop the rock ledge. The day was beautiful, clear and warm. They took one look at the breathtaking view of the mountains, and the argument was all over. The Ryan site won by acclamation! I have since wondered what would have happened if the day had been cloudy.

After the site was partially cleared of trees and rocks, we had a simple outdoor groundbreaking ceremony attended by the mayor of Montpelier, the city council members and other dignitaries, and our entire staff. Everyone was seated in newly built and erected bleachers for the occasion. Roy Johnson, who supervised the construction, had persuaded me to "break the ground" not with the usual gold-plated spade but by driving a thirty-ton bulldozer.

For a week I went out secretly once a day for my driving lesson. By the day of the ceremony, I was proficient enough at handling the behemoth to perform my simple part.

During the speeches and other parts of the program, the audience was surprised to see a horse ridden by a man attired in the formal clothing of the mid-nineteenth century. The rider was Heber England. He was posing as Dr. Dewey, commonly called the founder of National Life. He rode down to the crowd, stopped and looked carefully over the proceedings, and rode on without uttering a word.

After the speeches I mounted the bulldozer, and after making a couple of passes up and down in front of the seated office staff, I turned the bulldozer directly toward the crowd and started to drive it to the spot where I was to drop the blade and break the ground. To my astonishment, up they jumped almost to a person and scampered in every direction away from the path of the bulldozer. Their lack of faith in the bulldozing ability of the president was altogether too apparent!

There were many decisions to make and steps to take on the road to erecting our new headquarters. In recognition of the city's traffic problems, it was decided to build a road from Winooski Avenue to Mountain View Avenue, thus connecting with Northfield Street and the Northfield Road. This would permit many employees to drive to and from their homes without going through the thickest traffic in Montpelier and thus reducing the congestion on Northfield Street, a street too narrow to handle much more traffic without expensive alteration. The road to be built would be used by the public when coming south into Montpelier en route to Northfield. The road was built at a cost of $250,000 and given to the city. As the years have gone by, the wisdom of this decision has become increasingly clear. The new road also created a site for building a new guest house, now called the Hopkins House, which has served the company well.

We also had to solve the problem of what to do with Montpelier's worst eyesore, a dozen or more tarpaper shacks on the western side of Winooski Avenue. So ramshackle was the area that it was known derisively as "Little Hollywood." Squatters had appropriated the location and built out of boxing boards, tarpaper, and discarded secondhand lumber the worst looking mess of housing anyone could imagine. They held no deeds or leases, written or oral. They were just squatters, squatting on land that we had bought from the Ryan brothers. When we were ready to start building, I called Peter Giuliani, then a lawyer in the law department, and asked him to join me in my office. "Peter," I said, "we've got to get rid of those shacks, and we've got to do it fast. We can't wait for legal proceedings. We need the space now. Would you be willing to undertake the job?" He agreed that he would. "Go down to the treasurer's office," I said, "and get a bunch of signed blank checks. Then go down there and get quit claim deeds just as fast as you can. Don't give the company away, but pay what you have to." Peter did that and came back in a week with quit claim deeds for every one. He had paid $200 each, and he had done it in a week. Except for that, we might have been held up in court for a year or more fighting nuisance cases. No wonder Peter made such a good politician after he retired.

Cram & Ferguson were the architects of the new building. This firm enjoyed an international reputation as architects of cathedral-type construction. They were chosen largely because they were also the architects of the State Street granite home office building. They drew a set of plans that were unacceptable to the board. They drew several more, all of which were also unacceptable. Finally, a young apprentice architect in their office took his work home with him and conceived a completely new approach. The next morning, he showed it to his bosses, who liked it and put it into production. What emerged was a design of a wrap-around building. This design the board accepted by acclamation. It is, I believe, one of the most beautiful and functional office buildings in northern New England.

We had an excellent building committee. From memory I would say that the committee consisted of Dr. Hopkins; Edward S. French, long-time president of Boston and Maine Railroad; Robert S. Gillette, formerly president of Rock of Ages, and later chairman of the board of National Life; Doug Meredith, executive vice president and chairman of the finance committee; and me. Although we frequently had spirited discussions, there were no bad feelings or controversies that didn't get "hammered out on the anvil of discussion."

At one time, when the projected cost of the building looked pretty high to me, I suggested that we reduce the length of the building by thirty feet. Mr. French, looking at me with an eagle eye, said, "Think big, young man, think big." I subsided and abandoned my proposal. From the perspective of thirty years or so later, I have to say how right he was.

Roy Johnson did a superb job supervising the company's interest during construction and taking the leading part in handling the questions as they arose, investigating them and referring them to the building committee for decision. There were hundreds of these questions. The building cost $16 million, which seemed high to everybody, and it was, but we had a quality building. Today it is estimated that it would cost between $50 and $60 million to build.

Then came the day in 1960 when we moved into the building—ten years after I had become president and had first faced the company's problems of overcrowding. Six years had passed in reaching this solution. The beauty and comfort of our surroundings was an immediate lift to our spirits. Many of the young women who had been wearing jeans and sneakers at work in the old building now donned dresses and spike-heeled shoes. They walked faster, lifted their feet higher, and smiled oftener. Ringing laughter was more often heard in the halls. And then we found that those spike heels were punching dents in the new vinyl floors. We solved that unexpected problem not by outlawing spike-heeled shoes, but by buying and distributing thousands of rubber caps that pulled easily over the heels.

We deferred the final dedication until we had settled in. It was a gala day. Over fifteen hundred people came, including the staff, their families, and many people from around the state. Proceedings were held in the specially decorated new garage. The National Life Chorus never sang more lustily nor more beautifully "The Battle Hymn of the Republic." Our speaker was Dr. Wernher von Braun, then the outstanding expert on nuclear fission in this country.

Dr. Hopkins, as chairman of the board, presented to me the key to the building by passing it to Mike Davis, my six-year-old grandson. Mike walked across the stage and presented it to me, still resting upon a beautiful silk-embroidered pillow. In accepting the key I tried briefly to explain what moving into this building meant to those of us who worked there, to the City of Montpelier, and to the State of Vermont. After all these years I cannot remember anything I said except two sentences: "Already we have been in the building long enough to know what it means to work in these surroundings. When we run up against a seemingly unsolvable problem we go to the nearest window and there, we do indeed, 'lift up our eyes unto the hills from whence cometh our help.' " This was not a platitude. It was a solid truth. It was testimony to the emotional and spiritual impact that we had already experienced from moving into the new building.

In the thirty years since, the building has served the company well and the city, too. It has helped in a substantial way to sustain the Montpelier economy and to improve the city's bad traffic problem. Our choice of site made it possible for National Life to give the city prime land for a modern high school and to sell land on the eastern side of Winooski Avenue to the state for its Employment Security Building and liquor control warehouse and to Green Mountain Power Company for its office building. Moreover, the company now pays the city annually many hundreds of thousands of dollars in property taxes.

Time has also shown that the concern about availability of staff was unwarranted. At the time the decision to build was made National Life had a waiting list of approximately two-hundred applicants. The last I knew a short time ago, that list had grown to include eleven hundred names. The building of the interstate, the enlarging of the geographical area for recruiting, the growth in population in Central Vermont, and the fantastic achievements in data processing all contributed to this result and has produced a pool of staff people that any company would be proud to have.

Of course, in politics everything has a dark side, and National Life's new building did not escape this eclipse. Nearly thirteen years later, during my first campaign for governor, my opponents accused me of selling the City of Montpelier an unfair tax agreement. It was difficult for them to make this accusation politically effective, however, in view of the fact that the tax agreement offer was made after free and open negotiations initiated by the city officials and after the unanimous approval of the city council and the Montpelier voters present at a legally constituted city meeting at which the subject was again presented and discussed openly and thoroughly.

I wish I could say that every issue I faced as president of National Life was so satisfactorily resolved, but I cannot. Sometimes the inexorable march and changes of time upset the equilibriums we are able to achieve. This is certainly true of the questions of how insurance companies should be taxed under federal law. Continually changing political and technical issues have kept the controversy raging on this question since well before 1942, even though it appeared in 1957, however briefly, that peace was at hand.

Life insurance companies have for long been taxed at the state level by a flat tax on gross premiums. Originally, the premium tax was established not for general revenue but to compensate the state for its cost of regulating and supervising life insurance companies. But today that is only a fiction. The revenue in all states far exceeds the cost of regulation and has for many years. At one time early in the history of life insurance, no tax was levied at all. This was based on the theory that life insurance companies were serving a governmental purpose by providing benefits to families whose breadwinners died prematurely. In the absence of life insurance death benefits in such cases, the government realized it would have had to step in to care for the families.

When life insurance companies were first taxed at the federal level, the tax was measured by investment income. This was because the nature of the operations of life insurance companies are such that their financial dealings do not logically fit into the theory of the "net income" concept in the federal income tax. In a mutual company where there is no such thing as an annual "profit or loss," an actual "profit or loss" cannot even be determined on an *annual basis*. A life insurance policy is a long-term contract measured not only by the life of the insured but also by the lives of any beneficiaries who may elect to have the death proceeds paid out as an annuity. Hence, contracts can run fifty or sixty years or possibly even more.

The operations of a life insurance company can be divided into two separate and distinct aspects, an investment operation and an insurance operation. Income can be readily determined on the investment of funds temporarily set up and held as reserves in order to ensure the future proceeds of a policy, but no such simplicity exists in determining what if anything is a profit or loss on the insurance operations because new policies are continually being sold and old ones maturing.

From 1942 until 1959, the federal income tax on life insurance companies had been on a "stopgap" basis. No permanent tax was enacted; the complexity of the problem defied solution. No one could come up with a basis for a permanent tax that was both logical and fair. Consequently, every few years Congress and the life insurance companies would enact or extend the temporary stopgap tax, but at a different rate. The rate was always determined by negotiation, and a compromise for that year would be reached. These compromises came down essentially to the life insurance companies asking, "What is the least you will take?" and Congress responding with, "How much will you give?" It was Yankee horse-trading actually, and surely an unsatisfactory way to tax any group of taxpayers.

When I became president of National Life in 1950, I became directly involved in the controversy. Around 1955 or 1956 someone put forward a new theory for the taxation of life insurance companies. It was called the dividend method. The tax would be measured by "dividends" paid by the company to its policyholders. The big problem, however, was that a dividend in a life insurance company is not what is usually a dividend in all other companies. That is, it is not a measure of profit or loss. Rather, it is a return of a portion of the premium originally charged by the company after it has been determined that it is no longer needed. In other words, the company charges a conservative premium and agrees to return what it doesn't need. Moreover, in stock life insurance companies the substance of what constitutes "dividends" is entirely different from what prevails in mutual life insurance companies.

I felt strongly that such a method of taxation would discourage efficient operation and encourage inefficient operation. My vehement opposition was expressed at both board and committee meetings of the Life Insurance Association of America. The Life Insurance Association of America and the American Life Insurance Convention, now combined into the American Council of Life Insurance, represented both stock and mutual life insurance companies in their relations with the federal government. Each had an independent board of directors, and the two boards created what was called the Joint Committee on Federal Income Taxation of Life Insurance Companies. This committee consisted of fifteen members representing both stock and mutual companies.

In 1957 I was asked to become chairman of that committee. I appreciated the confidence that the insurance community was showing in me, but had I fully anticipated what I was getting into I would probably have declined, for the next two years found me in the center of a storm of controversy not only between life insurance companies and the government but between stock companies on the one hand and mutual companies on the other. Additional controversy swirled among mutual companies themselves. This is not the place to describe the intricacies of the many issues that developed and the technicalities involved. Suffice it to say that during those two years I made many trips to Washington in an attempt to work out a solution, chaired many meetings of the tax committee, testified many times before congressional committees, negotiated with officers and staff of the government and congressional committees, and made many friends and many enemies. It became clear to me that unless we found a solution satisfactory to Congress, life insurance companies were in deep trouble. The original stopgap act of 1942, if applied to operations in the late 1950s, would have been a disaster for the life insurance companies because of changes in the methods of operations. And each stopgap proposal since then had been so worded that if no new legislation was passed, the act of 1942 would come into effect. Thus, the 1942 act was a sword of Damocles hanging over our heads.

Finally, with the help of many people within and without the company, I reached what appeared to me to be a solution. By that time, the disagreements on the joint tax committee were so deep and feelings ran so high that I decided to present this plan before the Ways and Means Committee independently and not as chairman of the committee. I explained this status very carefully and reminded the Ways and Means Committee that I was speaking only as president of National Life and not as chairman of the joint tax committee.

The proposal that I presented was not something that I had created. It had emerged from the cross-pollination of several minds earnestly seeking a solution. When it was presented to me, I had liked it. The more I considered the alternatives, the better I had liked it. The new proposal would provide more revenue than the government was getting under the most recent stopgap proposal but far less than it would have received under the 1942 act. With everybody disagreeing with everybody else, it seemed to me that we just had to have new legislation.

James Preble, an actuary by profession, was my assistant at National Life and had sat at my side during all the hearings and events to fill me in on the technical aspects of each proposal. I recruited him to assist me in preparing my written speech before the Ways and Means Committee of the House. Then we had made for us a large ten-by-eighteen-foot brown paper chart to help illustrate the contents of the speech. This we tacked up on the wall of the hearing room. My speech was given while about 250 life insurance presidents, vice presidents, and counsel were in the room. The response was swift and strong. The members of the Ways and Means Committee liked it, and the majority of those in attendance disliked it. Although some changes were made in details of the proposal, it was adopted by the Ways and Means Committee and went to the floor of the House, where it was passed. Then it was sent to the Senate where the fight began all over again. I presented the case anew, this time before the Senate Finance Committee, but not in as much detail as before the Ways and Means Committee. Eventually, the Senate Finance Committee approved the bill, and it went to the Senate floor, where it again passed. Shortly after, it was signed by President Eisenhower and became law. In the insurance world, the act became familiarly known as "The 1959 Act."

Over the last thirty years, the act has saved the policyholders of life insurance companies many hundreds of millions of dollars that would have been paid in taxes if no agreement had been reached. But now, as I write these words, the industry is again in turmoil, fighting with Congress and within itself. All this comes about because it is almost impossible to tax life insurance companies as other corporations are taxed on a net income basis because of the peculiarities of the operations, which themselves change from decade to decade. Enough changes in their operations have taken place that some much needed amendments were made just a couple of years ago, but now the industry must fight anew for the protection of its policyholders.

I could write about many other experiences that I had during my eighteen years as president of National Life. Most of them would be of interest only to those connected with the company. One of them, however, taught me a broad lesson about people that I have carried with me ever since.

Early in my presidency I arranged for a series of lectures to be given to the officers of National Life. The purpose was to expose us all to the latest developments on the subject of management. I had met and knew Professor Jack Edwards Walters of the Tuck School at Dartmouth. I had a high regard for him for many reasons, but among them was that he had been a successful executive in an industrial company before becoming a professor. At one of the lectures, Professor Walters announced that the subject that day was to be "Tolerance in Management." After lecturing for about twenty minutes, he said, "Now as part of my presentation, I'm going to give you all an intelligence test. Is there anybody here who's unwilling to take an intelligence test?" Not a soul indicated any unwillingness, although I'm sure not a one wanted to participate. "Now, I'm going to pass around these sheets. There are about forty questions. Some you will answer yes or no, others you will just underline, several are multiple choice answers, and some you will mark with a cross. It is all easy to follow. I'm going to take this alarm clock and set it for twelve minutes. When the twelve minutes are up, that's the end. You stop. Then I will orally give you the correct answers and you will grade your own paper. Afterward, pass the papers in."

I had never taken an intelligence test, so I did not know that in this kind of a test you should go right through, answer the ones that are easy to answer, and not puzzle over the ones that you are not quite sure about. If you do stop to puzzle, the time limit will do you in. Every question unanswered is the same in point value as a wrong answer.

We did as directed. We graded our own papers. We passed them in. When Professor Walters had collected the papers, he said, "Now, this is a standard test. It has been given all over the country. The average person gets about 25 to 28 points. A passable score is considered 20 to 25." Then he wrote the scores from the test papers on the board. Most of them ranged from 20 to 35. Two were marked 14. I was one of the 14!

Now he said, "Let me tell you that I don't believe in the validity of this test. That's because some questions are mathematical, some are philosophical, and some call for knowledge of the English language. In this room are all different kinds of experiences and education. The mathematically inclined ones will excel on those questions but not necessarily on the others, and so on. Now let me ask a question. Has anyone in the room seen this test before?" No one had. "Well, I want to tell you that I got this test from your own personnel department downstairs. It is the test given to the applicants for employment who are hired for your secretaries and assistants. Now do you understand what I mean by tolerance in management?" I did.

13

Deeper Into Politics

Ego is comprised of self-confidence, often overcon-
fidence, but it takes self-confidence to give
politicians the nerve to ask for public office and the
drive to discharge the duties of the office once
achieved. Self-doubters do not belong
in politics.

There has never been a time since I graduated from law school when I was not involved in some way in politics, except for the five years when I served as a superior court judge. Yet even then, I was a public advocate for improvements in the judicial system. For example, I advocated keeping the county courts open year-round instead of holding court only within specified terms, as was the case then.

Also while a judge, I advocated converting Vermont's municipal court system to a district system and spoke often in support of both these recommendations. Now, long after, the courts are in effect open year-round, and the district system we have now is not essentially different from the one I advocated. I take satisfaction that these things finally were accomplished, not by my doing of course, but by the inexorable passage of time and the change of events, principally the large increase in business resulting from our increasing population.

Before and after those years, however, I stayed busy with the chores of politics. I served at various times as a member of the City Republican Committee and the Washington County Republican Committee; as a delegate to the State Republican Convention, several times as chairman of its platform committee and one year as its chairman; as keynote speaker for the 1936 Young Republican State Convention; and as a delegate to the National Republican Convention in 1948, when Dewey was nominated for his second term, and again in 1972, when Nixon was nominated for a second term. During the 1948 National Convention I served as chairman of the subcommittee on resolutions and spent a whole week hearing more than a hundred witnesses testify on a variety of subjects. My most conspicuous early failure came in 1936, when I ran for the office of representative to the legislature from Barre City and was soundly defeated by the Honorable John W. Gordon, a lawyer and a former mayor of Barre City. John was a self-professed socialist who had acted as legal counsel to the two major labor unions representing the granite industry workers in Barre and who had worked with these two unions on political matters, too. He was a good mayor of Barre and ironically was numbered among the most conservative mayors of the city we had had up to that time. My father often told me the way to cure a socialist was to put him in a position of authority with real responsibility.

After this campaign I decided not to run for the legislature again as long as I was still practicing law. It is difficult if not impossible to run a top-notch law office and be a good legislator at the same time. The time required for one leaves little time for the other; hence, the usual result is a compromise in which neither job gets truly done. This is even truer today, when both these jobs are more complicated and more demanding.

During the 1940s, while I was serving on the board of directors of the American Bar Association, I became embroiled in politics again. The question of financial responsibility was a burning political issue within the association. I was on the side of fiscal responsibility, and hence when the issue was finally settled responsibly, I found myself as chairman of the finance committee. Thus I became stuck with the job of taking the necessary steps to produce a balanced budget at a time when money was tight. That is not a glamorous job ever, but it is even less so in such circumstances.

When Eisenhower ran for president in 1952, I took an early and active part in his campaign. When my political preference was announced in the papers, I received a number of letters from my conservative friends in the Vermont Republican organization, who were uniformly favoring Taft. Most of the letters began, "Have you lost your mind?" or with words to that effect. Even in those days, politics was not a kind and gentle exercise.

The gap between the Aiken-Gibson wing and the Proctor wing of the Republican party widened during the thirties and forties, and I found myself siding often with the Proctor wing. This gave me the image of a conservative, and on balance I guess I really was, and yet solving problems has always interested me more than mindlessly following a rigid political philosophy. This attitude often put me on the liberal side of issues. Such an apparent contradiction occurred in the mid-1930s, when I was president of the Vermont Chamber of Commerce. At issue was the Green Mountain Parkway. The Roosevelt administration proposed to build a skyway at federal expense running north and south the entire length of the state atop the Green Mountains. The Vermont Chamber favored the proposal, but the conservatives for the most part did not. There were two reasons why the Chamber favored it: it would have helped Vermont's situation, which was very bad at the time, and Vermont would have gotten a thruway without expending very much in the way of state funds. The parkway was vigorously opposed by several influential groups, and the issue became a hot potato. I joined the Chamber board finally and undertook to campaign for the parkway. My father, a conservative, opposed it. This debate was taking place shortly after radio came to Vermont. Station WDEV had a transmitting office in the Pavilion Hotel, and I consented to give a series of short speeches over the radio in support of the proposal. On one such occasion, my mother was listening to me on her radio at home. My father came into the house at a point about halfway through the presentation, listened a minute, and asked my mother, "Who is that damn fool?" She replied with some relish, "That, sir, is your son."

In later years I came to believe that my position had been wrong. The damage to the fragile soil at the high levels of the Green Mountains would have caused the state much trouble and ruined a large part of the beauty of the landscape. We were preoccupied with the unemployment problem and not then conscious of environmental problems, which we understand better now.

The result of all this activity is that I became by successive steps a more or less political animal. I enjoyed the action, and I enjoyed being at the center of things. Also, I was gaining experience and, occasionally, wisdom.

During my days in general practice of the law, for example, I was active in the Vermont dairy farmers' cooperative movement. I was drawn into the movement as a result of my acquaintance and friendship with Dr. Ernest H. Bancroft, a veterinarian of Barre Town, who was himself caught up in the cooperative movement by reason of his ties to so many farmers. The dairy farmers had experienced several crises in milk prices and had gradually organized milk marketing cooperatives throughout much of the state. Through Dr. Bancroft, I became legal adviser for the Granite City Cooperative Creamery of Barre and the Mt. Mansfield Cooperative Creamery of Stowe. Later I became Vermont counsel for the New England Dairies when it had its office in Boston, but I represented its membership through much of New England. In this way I was induced to fight the battle over the testing and slaughtering of dairy cattle afflicted with tuberculosis and later the same kind of battle over the program for the testing and slaughtering of cattle afflicted with Bangs disease. Both of these battles were fought vigorously within the farm community and the legislature. In both cases, legislation was passed, and the success of the program is seen in the fact that both tuberculosis and Bangs disease were stamped out in cattle in Vermont, and neither has recurred in any great numbers. In addition to preventing continuing huge financial loss to farmers, the legislative program eliminated a serious health hazard to humans who drank milk from afflicted cattle.

During the period in which I was representing the cooperative creameries, another serious crisis in milk prices existed in Vermont. The crisis existed because even though there were a number of milk cooperatives in Vermont, there were also a sizable number of independent dealers and creamery operators within the state who received milk from farmers in their geographical areas. Arthur Packard of Jericho was the president of the Vermont Farm Bureau, and because the state was still dominated politically by farmers, he was perhaps the single most powerful political figure in the state. At the time, Mr. Packard and a number of cooperative-minded farmers had undertaken to set up an overall cooperative bargaining agency that would encompass all dairy farmers in the state, both those shipping to cooperative creameries and those shipping to independent dealers. In this way, all farmers would be in a much stronger bargaining position for the price of their milk. Recruiting of membership for all dairy farmers was under way.

All went well until a group of independent dealers decided to fight back. They notified their milk producers that they would no longer accept milk from any farmer who joined a cooperative bargaining unit. This was a disastrous blow to the proponents of Milk Inc., as the new proposed cooperative was called. The announcement stopped the recruiting of membership in its tracks because farmers who were unable to ship their milk through independent dealers rarely had an alternative place to send their milk. I became aware of this problem late one night when the telephone rang in my home at 25 Tremont Street in Barre. I was in bed asleep. The ringing woke me, however, and I came downstairs to answer the telephone. It was Arthur Packard. He told me he wanted to come and see me.

I said, "It's pretty late, isn't it?"

"Yes, it is," he said. "But Deane, we've got a problem, a real problem."

So I told him to come ahead, and I put on a bathrobe to receive him. He arrived in about twenty minutes, and it was then well after midnight. Arthur explained the problem and then asked, "Isn't there some way we can use the law to stop this threat? If they get away with this, Milk Inc. is dead. We've just got to stop it some way."

I pondered the situation for a while, then gave him my opinion. "Arthur, there's no way you can stop that by court action. If it is stopped at all, it will have to be by passing an act of legislature making it illegal."

"Well," Arthur said, "let's explore that. What do you think could be done by legislative action?"

"Perhaps nothing," I said, "but it's the only course I can think of. Let me take a look at the *Vermont Statutes*. I've got a copy here in the house."

Upon leafing through the book I found that Vermont had a statute prohibiting milk dealers from paying different prices to different producers for the same quality and grade of milk. I read the statute over several times.

"Here's your answer, Arthur," I said. "If the legislature would pass a simple amendment to this provision it will become illegal to refuse to receive milk from farmers because they have joined Milk Inc., a milk cooperative. They would have to accept the milk." I read him the statute. "All we need to do to produce an appropriate prohibition is to insert right here the following words, 'and shall not refuse to accept milk of any farmer producer because of his being a member of a cooperative farm organization.' "

"Gee, that's great," said Arthur.

"Yes," I said, "but would the legislature pass such an amendment? Even if it would, could you get it done fast enough to do you any good?"

"Well, as to that, you leave it to me," he said. "I think I might be able to handle it."

I had my doubts but decided not to express them, knowing something of Packard's political power in the state.

"You get that amendment drawn up and typed and meet me at the Montpelier Tavern at nine o'clock in the morning," he said. "I'll have the directors of Milk Inc. there, and you present it to them. If they approve, I think I can get it passed."

"Okay," I said, wondering if I wasn't getting involved in a lost cause. It was two o'clock in the morning by then, and I went back to bed to get a few hours' sleep. I got up early, went to the office, typed out the amendment with copies, and met Packard at the Tavern as instructed promptly at nine o'clock.

At that time, farmers ran the state. Vermont had 251 legislators from 251 towns, and a good healthy majority were farmers or related to farmers. They were never against anything they deemed good for the farmers. All that is changed now, of course. Less than six percent of the voting population in the United States are farmers, and the percentage in Vermont is not much higher. There are few farmers in Vermont's legislature today.

The session with the directors of Milk Inc. went smoothly, as I was sure it would, and Arthur told them what ought to be done. They approved unanimously. Then I watched the smoothest job of lobbying the legislature I have ever seen. Arthur picked up the telephone and called the sergeant-at-arms at the statehouse, where the legislature was in session. He asked to speak with the chairman of the agricultural committees of both the Senate and the House. They were promptly called out of the session. The conversation went like this:

"This is Arthur Packard. We have a serious farm problem. Would you get the members of your committee and come down here to the Tavern for a short meeting at one o'clock?" After some slight demurring on the part of the chairmen, they each agreed to do so.

At one o'clock Arthur explained to them what the problem was. "Now," he said, "Mr. Davis will read the amendment that we think is necessary to get us through this crisis. We must have it passed and signed by the governor in forty-eight hours."

And that is what happened.

The bill was introduced in the House and promptly referred to the agriculture committee, which approved it unanimously. Second and third readings were waived without objections. The bill was then immediately passed by the House and messaged to the Senate under suspension of the rules, where the same action ensued. From there it was messaged directly to the governor, who signed it into law the following morning. By its terms, the law took effect immediately, which shows, among other things, that in the old days legislatures did not need to take unnecessary time to do justice!

I also learned that politics can be a brutal business. An incident that occurred at the 1948 state GOP convention during Governor Ernest Gibson's first term illustrates how easily friendships can be broken by political differences.

I was first introduced to Gibson in 1931 when he was a practicing lawyer in Brattleboro and I was a superior court judge holding court in Windham County. I admired the way he handled himself in court. Always a quiet, seemingly good-natured, smiling person, he was a tower of strength as a trial lawyer. He prepared his cases thoroughly, tried them well, and was eminently successful. During World War II, he had had active service in the Philippines, and when the war was over he was a natural candidate for public office. He ran for governor as a Republican in 1946 and won easily. We were friends up until shortly before his second term, although we did not always see eye to eye on political issues.

The incident that ruined our friendship occurred at the State Republican Convention just before his election to a second term in 1948. The convention was held in Montpelier. I had been appointed by the state committee to be chairman of the platform committee. This committee is charged with preparing resolutions expressing the position of the party on the issues it expects to raise or be raised in the forthcoming election and recommending them to the full convention for action. Frankly, I think it has become an outdated and meaningless exercise in party politics. Very few people other than those closely involved pay any attention to the platform of either party. Historically, candidates were supposed to be bound by the platform of the party under whose banner they ran, but today candidates do not feel any such obligation. Even in those days party platforms were usually a mass of generalities designed not to offend any segment of the voting population. As Dick Mallary, former Vermont congressman, once said, "What you don't put in the platform will never hurt you. What you do might." But at that time and in my position, I was still taking the platform seriously, or trying to.

The platform committee met several times at the Montpelier Tavern, and in accordance with custom invited the party candidates seeking state office to attend and express their views as to what the platform should contain. Governor Gibson was a candidate for a second term and attended and took an active and helpful part in the discussions. One plank he suggested raised a hot issue that was then current. It concerned a dam one of the power companies was building in Thetford for power and flood control purposes. Immediate and violent opposition to the dam was centered on the eastern side of the state but involved the whole state to some degree. Governor Gibson suggested a plank for the platform that read, "The party pledges that not one acre of tillable farm land shall be taken for power or flood control purposes."

In the political heat of the moment, this was thought to be good political strategy since being against the dam was like being for motherhood. There was one problem, however. The jurisdiction over dams on rivers that crossed state lines was by law a federal power superseding anything the state might wish to do. Hence, it seemed to me and to the rest of the platform committee that we should not as a party promise something we could not deliver. We had a spirited but friendly discussion, and finally all concerned, including Governor Gibson, agreed that nothing about the dam should go into the platform. The platform was typed and signed by all members of the committee.

The next day I left for a trip to Atlanta, Georgia, on behalf of National Life. I was not scheduled to return until late the night before the state convention opened. The morning after I returned, I went to my office early, and in the mail found a letter from Governor Gibson informing me that he had changed his mind about the power plank. Most of the members of the committee were not elected delegates to the convention and hence would not be at the convention and available to reconsider the issue.

The convention was scheduled to open at 10 A.M., and I had first read the governor's letter at 9 A.M. I hurried to the Montpelier City Hall, the site of the convention, hoping to see the governor before the session opened and to work out some method of handling the situation to prevent an embarrassing confrontation. I found a large crowd of people milling around the lobby at city hall trying to get their credentials approved and receive their badges of admission. In addition to the delegates, a large number of the public were seeking admission to the balcony to see and hear the proceedings. By the time I got into the hall, the proceedings were under way. Gelsie Monti, my longtime friend, was presiding as chairman. The governor was seated on the stage with the other dignitaries. I still felt no great pressure since, traditionally, the platform committee report is called for near the end of the convention. I was confident I would have a chance to talk to the governor at recess. But to my surprise and consternation, the chairman called for the report of the platform committee immediately after the opening formalities were concluded. I had to do some fast thinking. I decided my duty as chairman of the platform committee was to stick with the committee's report, so I went to the microphone, and moved its adoption. Then I returned to my seat on the floor of the convention.

The governor rose, walked to the podium, and announced that

189

he could not agree with the report. He said it was too long and more-over did not contain one very important plank which he had urged when he appeared before the platform committee. "In view of that I've written my own platform," he said. He pulled the draft of his platform out of his pocket and proceeded to read it. As I expected, his platform included the controversial plank reading, "not one acre of tillable farm land shall be taken for power or flood control pur-poses." Then the governor walked over to the secretary's table, dropped his platform on the table, and addressed the chairman. "I move that the platform of the platform committee be tabled and that my platform be adopted by the convention," he insisted. From the floor I requested permission to respond, which was granted, and I went to the podium. In as calm a voice as I could muster, I explained how the platform had been constructed, what the debate had been at the committee meeting, how the governor had been reluctant but ultimately agreed with it, what was contained in the governor's let-ter, and the fact that I had received it that morning. I explained that the committee's principal objection to the plank was that we as a party would be making a promise we could not possibly fulfill. I then resumed my seat on the floor. The governor rose again and now made a strong speech in favor of his platform and against the com-mittee platform.

I can't remember today anything he said in that speech, but I do remember how angry I was. Tension was mounting in the hall. You could feel it in the air. Again I strode to the podium, pulled off my coat, literally rolled up my sleeves, and in the strongest language of which I was capable disapproved of the convention going on record with a promise to the voters which by now they knew could not be fulfilled. Fortunately, I had with me a copy of the U.S. Supreme Court decision that had ruled on that point a year or so earlier in another state.

This put the governor and me squarely in opposition on a matter of principle. Gibson was a popular governor and a good one. He had been nominated for a second term, which made him the titular head of the party. I knew that the members of the convention would feel that they had to go along with the governor, but I really didn't care. I felt much better having said what I had. I returned to my seat and waited for the vote. Not another person in the hall spoke on either side of the question. I was sorry that this confrontation would necessarily embarrass the governor's friends as well as my own. To my utter surprise, the vote was 2 to 1 in favor of the committee's platform.

This ended our friendship. The breach was never healed, which as the years went by I deeply regretted. As I look back now, I wonder again, as I've wondered many times, was it worth it? Probably not. But how, in honor, could I have done differently?

It was, I believe, my frequent appearances at political meetings such as this and my demonstrated interest in public affairs that caused me to be drafted to undertake another mission, the results of which went a long way toward modernizing the administrative branch of Vermont state government and improving its efficiency.

Gertrude Mallary, a senator from Orange County, came to talk with me in the spring of 1957 about a bill she was preparing to introduce into the Senate. The bill would provide for a commission to study the administrative processes of Vermont state government to see if any changes could be made to improve efficiency or reduce the costs of administration. She had in mind an exercise similar to one that had occurred under President Hoover, which undertook a far-reaching examination of the workings of the administrative branch of federal government. It had been eminently successful and became known as the Hoover Commission. Since then, a number of states had appointed similar commissions to study the workings of their state governments. In the vernacular, they came to be known as Little Hoover Commissions because of the similarity of their goals and their methods. Senator Mallary was exploring with me the probable cost of such a study so that she might know how much should be included in the appropriation bill. I was ill-equipped to give her a truly informed opinion, but after talking with a few people to get their views, I picked the sum of $35,000 as an amount that should do a fair job. Sometime later, I read in the local newspaper that the legislature had passed the bill. The bill authorized the governor to appoint the members of the commission and set forth the goals of the study, and appropriated $35,000.

My next surprise was to receive a phone call from Governor Joseph Johnson asking me to become chairman of the commission.

Never having been very adept at saying no, I said yes. Moreover, I was greatly intrigued by the idea. It was a bipartisan committee balanced between Republicans and Democrats. The governor also appointed former mayor Dan Healey of Rutland, former lieutenant governor Ralph Foote of Middlebury, former state treasurer George Amidon, and Representative Laurence Hines from Franklin County.

We took two years to complete the study. As time went on, it became clear that the members had been well chosen. We worked together in complete harmony and were truly bipartisan. Only once during the two years did we ever split along partisan lines, and even then it was over such an insignificant issue that I cannot even remember now what it was. But for Vermonters for two years to discuss the myriad issues we did without ever considering our differing party affiliations was unique and something of which we were justly proud.

Our first step was to select a management firm with expertise in the area. We chose the nationally known Cresap firm. It became evident after our first two meetings that we would have to double or triple the appropriation if Cresap were to do the job. Since we did not wish to ask for more money, we decided to use the Cresap firm to map out a method for us to use, hire an executive director of the commission, then recruit volunteers to do the actual work. We members of the committee would spend our time discussing recommendations coming from these volunteers.

From a long list of interesting applicants for executive director, we chose Professor Rolf Haugen, a professor of political science at the University of Vermont, to oversee the project. He was also the university's director of the Center for Studies of State Government, which had a tremendous library of material on the subjects covering every state in the United States. We defined Professor Haugen's responsibilities as follows: "To oversee research, help select and recruit volunteers, handle assignment of special research items, draft agendas for the meetings of the committee, and to coordinate and review reports and recommendations from volunteers." His performance was superb.

The commission met every month, sometimes every two weeks, for two years. We never had a meeting without a carefully planned agenda covering relevant subjects of substance fully supported by research reports. In all, before the two years were over, we had the benefit of more than one-hundred different volunteers in researching the pertinent subjects. They came from many sources, but most from the faculty of Vermont's colleges and universities. The meetings usually lasted about a half-day, but toward the end of the two years of deliberations we sometimes met for a full day. Little time was wasted in the kind of aimless discussion that so often occurs in commissions of this kind. The methods we adopted were, in my opinion, largely responsible for the success that we had in the legislature. The key was the careful and painstaking construction of the agenda and the assignment of research proposals to our skilled volunteers.

At the end of two years we made a report to the legislature as we had been directed. The report recommended 135 ways to make Vermont's state government operate more smoothly and efficiently. We strongly urged as one central feature of the report that a Department of Administration be created that would consolidate eight existing agencies and distribute responsibility among eight divisions of state government. We also recommended that a cabinet form of executive management be established, that major departments be reassembled and streamlined to combine within a single agency all divisions that had similar or overlapping responsibilities, and that the state's budget and management procedures be overhauled.

Then ensued the slow, hard work of getting the recommendations passed by the legislature. I was invited to address a joint session of the House and Senate on the subject. I covered the report in considerable detail, and this helped to put the recommendations on the road to implementation. Some of the recommendations were within the power of the governor to implement without legislative action, but the more important ones were not. The legislature then set up a special committee of its own to study the recommendations and make reports to the legislature. I believe this action was the most important technique of all in getting quick and favorable action by the legislature. By the end of the first session, the legislature had passed the most important recommendation of all, which was the proposal for a department of administration within which would be gathered all of the service departments of the administrative complex.

The legislature also set up a permanent legislative committee with the responsibility of pursuing the objective of gradually passing such of the remaining recommendations as would meet the test of time. The joint Senate–House committee still exists.

Our report was printed and distributed to the legislature, to members of the administrative and executive branch, and to other interested parties and centers of influence within the state. The report became sufficiently popular that the state had to print it a second and third time to keep up with the demand. It became a sort of map or guide for all who had ideas about improving the administration of state government.

Later, when I was governor, I had the privilege of proposing to the legislature and leading the fight for the reorganization of major departments into agencies under one head. The recommendation was to gather together within each agency all the formerly scattered departments that were closely related to each other so that they could pursue common goals. The system allowed us to achieve greater governmental efficiency and furnished the basis for a cabinet system under the governor.

One other commission on which I served also deserves mention. Like the Little Hoover Commission, it also substantially changed our structure of town government and, too, our school system. This commission was appointed to hear the evidence and make recommendations to the legislature on appropriations to regional school districts for the purpose of helping them build new regional high school buildings to serve a group of towns. Perhaps you have driven around Vermont and noticed big, modern school buildings well out of town in the surrounding open spaces and wondered how these came to be. These are the regional high school buildings that resulted from our recommendations, which were passed by the legislature. Today they are an accepted part of our system and are more or less taken for granted.

The commission was the product of the leadership and action of John Holden, who was then Vermont commissioner of education. He had the view that the high schools of the state had become so outmoded and in some places were in such a poor state of repair that they no longer adequately provided a high school education. He believed they would have to be replaced, but that if towns were forced to rely wholly on their own funds to accomplish this, even the new high schools could not be built to accommodate all the new things in education that were available. He felt that many towns would be forced because of lack of funds to delay such construction, during which time pupils would be denied the full quality of education that was being enjoyed by the larger and more highly populated towns and cities. If the towns shared the costs of capital construction with other nearby towns, however, and if in addition the legislature granted some form of substantial capital construction aid, the tax burdens in each town would be sufficiently reduced to act as an incentive to towns to form regional districts and to undertake such needed construction. He felt the quality of education would thereby be substantially improved.

In 1951 the State Board of Education appointed a commission of twelve citizens to study the problem and to report. I was asked to serve as chairman and accepted. We served for about a year and made a report that became the basis for action in the legislature. We worked from a study that had been made the year before by the staff of the Vermont Education Board, which had concluded that more than a third of the state's 851 public school buildings were overcrowded. More than half of Vermont's public school children were housed in buildings rated as unsafe or unsatisfactory, an alarming number of these in makeshift quarters within school buildings, such as corridors and basements, or in rented quarters outside of the school buildings such as firehouses and churches. More than three-quarters of the children were housed in combustible buildings. The report concluded that 239 more classrooms would be needed to house clearly foreseeable enrollment increases. Total needs for school construction up to 1960 would require an expenditure estimated at $28,879,140, more than a third of which was above and beyond the unused legal bonding limit of the school districts needing the construction.

We took a year to conduct our own investigation of the problems and in 1952 reported to the board and to the legislature that a definite need existed for some sort of state assistance for school building construction. We recommended that the state guarantee bond issues voted for the purpose of financing the construction of elementary school buildings and that the state make outright grants to school districts called Union High School Districts for the construction of high school buildings.

My fellow commissioners and I were surprised and pleased by the action the legislature took on the basis of this report, supplemented by additional support from others interested in the problem. It voted to make grants not only for high school construction but also, because of lobbying on behalf of towns with meager resources, for elementary school buildings. The legislature recognized this as a political reality and now distributes grants on the same basis for both kinds of construction.

Vermont today has a substantial number of regional high schools, thanks to the foresight exhibited by Dr. Holden. Without his wisdom, the problem would not have been solved in time, the wasted time would have raised costs, and the delays would have been a hardship to many Vermont pupils who deserved a better education than the one they were receiving.

Looking back to those years of involvement in public and political affairs, I can see now how important they were in the pattern of my life. I enjoyed those activities immensely—partly no doubt, because I felt flattered to be asked. I never saw a good politician, including myself, who wasn't endowed with a generous supply of ego. Ego is comprised of self-confidence, often overconfidence, but it takes self-confidence to give politicians the nerve to ask for public office and the drive to discharge the duties of the office once achieved. Self-doubters do not belong in politics.

More important, each new experience of that kind broadened my knowledge and increased my confidence that I could handle the next experience. By the time I became governor, the sum total of those experiences had given me the ability to face the challenge of leadership with a fair knowledge of the state, its economy, its history, its people, and its problems. Also, I had acquired a knowledge of state government sufficient to offset my lack of having served in the legislature. Moreover, I had learned how to work with people in a way to get things done, which in politics is an indispensable prerequisite. And in spite of what the polls said, these activities had greatly increased my acquaintance throughout the state.

There is no question that the spark has been within me since that afternoon in 1913 when I went with my father to hear Teddy Roosevelt. Walking home with my father afterward, we discussed the meaning of the great man's words, and by the time we arrived home I had formed a new goal in life. I could see myself like Roosevelt battling in the political arena for right and for justice for the downtrodden. Of course I discovered many other goals in life after that, but always tucked away in the hidden recesses of the spirit was the spark of that exciting experience. Perhaps it accounts, in part at least, for the fact that never in all the later years have I said no when asked to join a political crusade, support a credible candidate, or get involved in any kind of problem-solving exercise that involved political action.

14

Marjorie

*Within two days of our marriage, I had Marjorie
on a horse for the first time in her life, and she has
been riding with me ever since. Our rides together
along the woodland trails have been especially
pleasurable because she has always loved the
woods and the world of nature.*

Marjorie Smith Conzelman and I were married in the Old South
Church in Boston on July 5, 1952. The daughter of A. Leroy and
Lena Smith, Marjorie grew up on a dairy farm on East Hill in Barre.
I first remember her when she was five years old and I was nine. She
was sitting in the Smith family pew in the Methodist church, her legs
too short to touch the floor, her eyes and ears completely concentrated on the pastor and what he was saying.

Marjorie attended the Cobble Hill school in Barre Town, a typical rural Vermont two-room school, four grades in each room. In
1922 she graduated as valedictorian from Spaulding High School
in Barre City, and in 1926 she graduated from Skidmore College in
Saratoga Springs, New York, again as valedictorian of her class.

She worked for a year in the book department and then as a
comparison shopper for R.H. Macy's in New York City. In 1927 she
married Lieutenant Clair McKinley Conzelman, a graduate of the
United States Military Academy at West Point, whom she had met

three years earlier on a blind date. Service at coastal artillery posts in the next fourteen years took them to Fort Totten, Long Island, then through the Panama Canal and across the Pacific to Fort Mills, Corregidor Island in the Philippines; to Fort H.G. Wright on Fishers Island off New London, Connecticut; to Fortress Monroe in Virginia; to Fort Sherman on the Atlantic side of the Panama Canal Zone; to Fort Barrancas in Florida; and finally to a second two-year duty on Corregidor.

Marjorie's interests and wide-ranging curiosity served her well during these years. Army officers and their spouses need to be flexible, innovative, and interested in the people and culture of the area where they serve in order to adjust to so many different customs and communities. On Corregidor, for example, when there were not enough teachers for the American school, Marjorie taught the third and fourth grade while a Filipino amah cared for her infant son Peter. She played tournament tennis in the Canal Zone and sometimes wrote skits or organized musical entertainment for the troops. In 1939 she had a rare opportunity to travel from the Philippines to China on the *Gold Star*, a small Navy ship based in Guam which stopped regularly in Manila en route to China and Japan. Its skipper turned out to be Commander Tuttle of Montpelier, Vermont, and he and his wife, Mary, were expert guides to sightseeing and shopping in the Orient. Although these years were full of moves and adjustments, Marjorie formed scores of close friendships with other army families. She continues to keep in touch with many of them to this day.

Ten months before Pearl Harbor, just as the Conzelmans' second two-year tour on Corregidor was completed and they were packed and scheduled to return to duty in the United States, orders were suddenly issued to evacuate all Army wives and children from the Philippines and to "freeze" all American officers. Marjorie and her children, Peter and Patricia, sailed from Manila on February 17, 1941. They landed at San Francisco, crossed the country by train, and reached her parents' Vermont farm in mid-March, hoping Major Conzelman's orders would be reissued as soon as women and children were safely out of the Philippines. In mid-summer of 1941 the *New York Times* published his orders, and Marjorie cabled him, rejoicing, only to learn that the orders had been canceled either by

Major General George Moore or by General Douglas MacArthur.

After the attack on Pearl Harbor on December 7, 1941, all weekly Clipper Airmail service to and from the Philippine Islands ceased. Unable to contact her husband and unsure when her family would be reunited, Marjorie decided to get involved with some phase of war service. When Governor Wills of Vermont set up the Vermont Council of Safety (Civilian Defense) under the direction of Albert Cree, she enlisted as a full-time volunteer and served for three years as one of Mr. Cree's administrative assistants. She traveled the state helping towns develop volunteer offices, setting up workshops, organizing training for child-care services, editing a Council of Safety newsletter, and giving hundreds of speeches to inform Vermonters about what they could do to support the armed forces. She also found herself in demand as a speaker on the Far East, especially on the Philippines and her travels to China and Japan.

The Japanese attacked the Philippines the day after Pearl Harbor. Soon after, they launched a siege of Corregidor that was one of the most brutal of the war. Marjorie's husband was a major serving as harbor defenses inspector and assistant operations officer on the staff of Major General Moore. The headquarters of the command was on Corregidor in Malinta Tunnel, which ran below the small island's highest hill and gave access to lateral tunnels that served as General MacArthur's headquarters, hospital quarters, and ammunition depots. Throughout the five-month siege, Major Conzelman regularly took the night shift on the Operations Desk, slept in the tunnel in the morning, and then visited all the batteries on "the Rock" in the afternoon. In March he was promoted to lieutenant colonel.

After the Japanese invasion, General MacArthur moved his troops as quickly as possible onto the Bataan peninsula to oppose the invading troops as they fought their way south. Without adequate air or naval power, reinforcements, or supplies, however, the U.S. troops could not withstand the Japanese attacks. When Bataan fell in April, seventy thousand captives were forced to begin the horrible "Death March" to Camp O'Donnell.

Across the two-mile-wide channel, U.S. troops on Corregidor held out without aid, supplies, or reinforcements for twenty-seven more days before the Japanese were able to cross the narrow expanse of water between Bataan and Corregidor and overwhelm the defenders. Colonel Conzelman, along with more than thirteen thousand others captured on "the Rock," became a prisoner of war.

Two years later, as General MacArthur worked his way north from Australia, the Japanese began moving surviving American POWs to Japan. On December 15, 1944, Colonel Conzelman was one of the 1,619 POWs crowded in the holds of the *Oryoku Maru* when it was bombed by American Navy planes near Subic Bay. Three hundred POWs were killed or were unable to get out of the holds, but Colonel Conzelman swam ashore with approximately thirteen hundred other officers and men and was recaptured by the Japanese. For six days these survivors were crowded on a tennis court at the Olongapo naval base without food or clothing. Later they were moved to Lingayen Gulf, and on December 28, they were shipped aboard the *Enoura Maru*. On January 9, 1945, in the harbor of Takao, Formosa, naval aircraft from the U.S. carrier *Hornet* bombed the Japanese freighter, scoring a direct hit on the peak hold. Colonel Conzelman was crushed by falling timbers and died of his wounds two days later. His body was buried in a hole on the sandy beach along with the bodies of two hundred other American prisoners. Only 425 prisoners reached Japan on a third Japanese ship, and of these 161 died within the next thirty days in Japan's bitter cold.

Because Japan did not report the deaths of these POWs until its surrender on August 31, 1945, Marjorie was hopeful throughout that her husband was still alive, perhaps in Japan. She only learned of his death a day after the surrender, when the information was released by the War Department. Much later she learned the circumstances of her husband's death from three Corregidor officers who survived all three death ships and finally returned to the United States after Japan surrendered.

Marjorie's only brother was also killed in the war. First Lieutenant Arthur Smith, pilot of a B-17 in the 8th Air Force in England, was killed on November 30, 1944, on his thirty-first bombing mission over Germany. The loss of her brother, the strain of her husband's three-year imprisonment, and her knowledge of the brutal conditions and starvation to which Colonel Conzelman had been subjected prior to his death threatened to overwhelm Marjorie. Only the necessity of helping her children face the loss of their father kept her from letting her grief and disorientation destroy her courage.

During the war I worked as general counsel at National Life and lived with my family on East Hill, a short distance beyond the Smith farm. I operated the farm as a dairy farm, raising Jerseys and Morgan horses. When gasoline rationing came along, it presented something of a problem to those of us who had to commute to our jobs. My father was then probate judge, and his office was in the courthouse in Montpelier. Barbara Smith, Marjorie's sister, who was also living on the Smith farm, was Vermont's children's librarian. Marjorie's office in civil defense was in the statehouse in Montpelier, and mine, of course, was at National Life, then in the old National Life building on State Street adjacent to the statehouse. We formed a four-car, four-person car pool to cope with the gas rationing and commuted together each day except when one of the four was traveling out of town, in which case the remaining members joined together in the car pool. These regular daily trips soon developed into a vigorous debating society in which all current issues of the day were covered from four different perspectives.

I had known Marjorie's family for a number of years, particularly her father, A. Leroy Smith. He was a prominent farmer, active in public affairs, and had served in the Vermont legislature as a Washington County Senator. I had acted as counsel for Mr. Smith a number of times and also had represented several of the organizations of which he was a member. I knew Marjorie's mother and her sister, Barbara, less well. I had not known Marjorie during my college years, as I was away from Barre during that time and she was in high school. Although she was two years behind Corinne in high school, they were friends and were thrown together quite often because of musical activities. Corinne played the piano and Marjorie the violin, and Corinne often accompanied Marjorie when she was playing the violin at school, church, or other places. They went together to the Methodist Institute, an annual affair that took place at Montpelier Seminary (now Vermont College).

Corinne and I often exchanged visits with Marjorie and her children after their return to the Barre area, and of course participated together in social events at the Methodist church in Barre, to which both families belonged. I came to know her children when I invited them to visit my farm, and I taught them both how to ride with somewhat better results than I had had with my own children. Marjorie's son, Peter, became a real lover of horses and riding.

Like many others in Barre, Corinne and I had followed the unfolding events of the war and its effect upon the Smith and Conzelman families. When Peter became proficient enough to go on trail rides with me, I talked with him at length about his fears and his hopes concerning his father. Both he and Patricia were suffering from an agony of uncertainty about their father, and when mail services from the Philippines to the United States ceased after Pearl Harbor, their fears and suffering increased manyfold.

In the spring of 1947 Marjorie and her children moved to Cambridge, Massachusetts. While her children attended nearby Phillips and Dean Academies, Marjorie assumed the position of executive secretary of the New England branch of the American Camping Association. She threw herself wholeheartedly into her work; she not only established a new office in Boston but also traveled extensively in the summer months to visit many of the 250 camps that constituted the New England section of the American Camping Association. She became a true believer in camping as an important part of the educational experience of youngsters, particularly those from urban centers who otherwise get few chances to experience the world of nature around them.

More than four years passed after Marjorie moved to Cambridge before I saw her again, although I did see her parents occasionally and usually asked after her and the children. Each Christmas we exchanged cards and, during the year, occasionally letters.

Sometime after Corinne's death in March 1951, while I was on a business trip to Boston, I phoned Marjorie at her office on Beacon Street and invited her to have dinner with me. She accepted. We had dinner together again several times during the next few months until we were corresponding fairly regularly. She was living alone in an apartment in Cambridge while her children were both away at college, and I visited her there several times. On one occasion she invited me to have dinner at her apartment. While Marjorie was cooking in the kitchen, her daughter Patty and I visited in the living room. Pat was telling me about her boyfriend, "Tony" Greeley, whom she had been dating during her senior year at college. She said to me, "If you'll help me catch Tony, I'll help you catch Mother."

By the spring of 1952 it was apparent that Marjorie and I were seriously interested in each other. By now both Tom and Marian were married and living in their own homes. Peter was attending West Point, and Patricia had just graduated from Wheelock College and was engaged to be married in July. When Patty insisted that Marjorie and I must not get married until she and Tony had returned from their Bermuda honeymoon because she wanted to be at our wedding, we decided it would be a fine idea to be married on the same day but not at the same time. And that's what we did. Patty and Sidney F. Greeley, Jr., were married at Christ Church in Cambridge at 4 P.M. on July 5, 1952. Following the reception at the beautiful home and grounds of the commander of the Watertown Arsenal, Marjorie and I were married at Old South Church in Boston at 8 P.M.. Our wedding, in contrast to Pat's, was completely informal and was witnessed by only family members and a few of the guests at Patty's reception who had received whispered invitations in the late afternoon.

After our wedding I began to witness the breadth and depth of Marjorie's interests. I discovered immediately that she liked to keep as busy as I did and that she pursued even her hobbies with energy and dedication. When she took up painting, for example, she studied under Stan Marc Wright of Stowe. Twenty-seven years later, she was still attending his classes. Her paintings hang throughout our house and are treasured keepsakes of many of her grandchildren. Since 1945, Marjorie has also extensively researched the incredible series of events, misjudgments, and failures of communication that led to the tragedy in the Philippines during World War II and to her first husband's death. She has collected enough information, much of it unpublished anywhere, to begin a book on the subject. Throughout this often painful work, she has proceeded with a thoroughness and intelligence that are hallmarks of her personality and with a hope of providing her children and grandchildren a picture of the father they never had the opportunity to know.

I am grateful that she made time to share my interests, too. As she was packing for our brief honeymoon at Wentworth-by-the-Sea,

I told her to bring along a pair of jodhpurs.

"What for?" she asked. "I don't know how to ride."

But I had chosen Wentworth for our two-day honeymoon because I knew the owner kept horses. He had assured me that he had a calm and quiet horse that would be suitable for a beginner, and he was true to his word. Within two days of our marriage, I had Marjorie on a horse for the first time in her life, and she has been riding with me ever since. Our rides together along the woodland trails have been especially pleasurable because she has always loved the woods and the world of nature. Our trail riding has added an extra dimension to her enjoyment of Vermont's beauty.

Gardening is another of her joys. She loves flowers of all kinds, but her special joy is gladioli. Each spring she plants approximately eight hundred bulbs, and each summer she takes great pleasure in cutting bouquets for the house and for friends.

She traveled the country with me when I was president of National Life and traveled Vermont with me throughout my gubernatorial campaigns and terms. She was an incomparable hostess, in part because she studied the problems of the company and of the state and could discuss them with a high degree of awareness and knowledge, and in part because she has possessed unusual poise in public.

But our years in the public eye were not always easy for her. I admit that it took me quite a while to get Marjorie's approval for my run for governor. I later found out that she was right in her objections because of the price we paid in energy and emotional trauma.

During the campaigns, she was tireless. She addressed hundreds of groups, often composed of people who were already familiar with her because of her war-time speeches, and she made a special point of speaking to women about the specific issues that she knew concerned them. I never questioned what she had to say and believe that because she listened so carefully to what I said and studied the issues carefully herself, she probably expressed my positions as well as I did myself.

I was most grateful for her ability to understand and to be with people when the mood was dark and grim. Her ability became even more important as the years of the governorship wore on. The governorship can be—and I believe usually is—a lonely and sometimes emotionally heartbreaking experience, and the companionship of an intelligent and understanding spouse, particularly one well informed and interested in public affairs, is a great comfort. Moreover, such a spouse can be, as Marjorie was, of tremendous help politically. Tom Candon, the able and canny Democratic House minority leader, called her "Davis's Secret Weapon." She wasn't so secret, but she surely was a weapon, for which I am grateful.

She was never more helpful, nor was I ever more grateful for her avid interest in foreign affairs—particularly in the Orient—than during my last year as governor, when we were invited to accompany seven other governors and their wives to a meeting in Japan. We had been invited by the National Association of Japanese Governors, and the trip was jointly sponsored by the U.S. State Department and the U.S. National Governors' Association. The purpose of the trip was to exchange information on current problems. The formal discussions lasted one full day, but our hosts arranged for us to travel as a party throughout Japan for seven more days as their guests. We had visited Switzerland the year before on a similar trip with a group of U.S. governors chosen by the U.S. Governors' Association and sponsored by the American-Swiss Association, but this was my first trip to Japan. Fortunately, it was Marjorie's fourth. Her previous visits were in 1930, 1939, and 1966, so I had with me not only an expert on Japanese history, customs, and culture, but one who could compare the differences over those forty-two years.

We visited many of Japan's scenic, historic, and religious places of interest. We enjoyed visiting the Horyuji temple, the oldest wooden building in the world, and were awed by the Daibutsu Buddha, the largest bronze Buddha in the world. Fifty feet high, it held all sixteen members of our party in the palm of its hand. We visited tea plantations and industrial plants, and we watched the feeding of the famous Doro beef cattle, supposed to be the most tender in the world, made so by massage and a diet of beer. We attended state dinners, musicals, and art exhibits, and even visited the official residence of Prime Minister Sato, who offered us a typical Japanese luncheon.

We visited Lake Biwa, Japan's largest lake, where people raise freshwater pearls. We went out in the rain in a boat and watched fish being dipped out of the lake into traps. Afterward we went to a pearl shop, where skilled hands performed the operation on the oysters necessary to grow freshwater pearls. The pearls are first removed from a live oyster. Then a strip of live oyster membrane is placed on each side of a three-year-old oyster's shell. No foreign body is implanted at all. At the end of six years, eight pearls are removed from each side, ranging in size from a grain of rice to a half-inch in diameter. No wonder Japanese are said to be patient people!

Everywhere we went on the trip, Marjorie was the focus of much attention. Cameras zeroed in on her from all sides. I wondered what this was all about and eventually found out that it was her white hair. Japanese people do not have white hair.

Marjorie greatly enjoyed watching Hazan Matsumoto, the famous Japanese artist, whose paintings were selling for $1,800. Before Matsumoto gave us a demonstration of her method of painting, she warned us that she might not be able to paint if she received no spiritual inspiration. But she knelt on the floor and painted in about thirty seconds a version of the old Zen priest who had stared so long at a blank wall in meditation that his arms and legs atrophied. Next she painted a waterfall in five seconds and after that an ethereal bird with only a few strokes.

Our last night in Nara was a surprise dinner and entertainment at a Japanese geisha house. Naturally, the American governors looked forward to this event with anticipation, and the wives even more so! When we arrived we were asked to take off our shoes in accordance with Japanese custom, and upon entering we were invited to sit cross-legged on the floor. The legacy of my childhood bout with infantile paralysis made that impossible for me without considerable discomfort. Eventually I was allowed the special privilege of sitting on the floor with my feet straight out in front of me. Soon each governor was attended by a beautiful geisha girl, who brought little glasses of sake and other treats in great abundance to keep the guests happy until the main courses were served. Since the governors' wives were also guests on this occasion, the tension lessened noticeably when it was discovered that the geisha girls were in fact the wives of the Japanese governors. Their faces were made up like geisha girls, and, with their hair also properly made up and the beautiful kimonos they wore, they were a sight to behold. I reminded Marjorie that she now had an opportunity to see how a man's needs should be attended to, as the geisha girls are known the world over for their skills in this respect. Marjorie's reply was that she already had more skills in this department than she desired to use. That ended the discussion.

Fortunately, I later had an opportunity to rebut. We were visiting Lois and John West, Democratic governor of South Carolina and later ambassador to Saudi Arabia. Theirs was a special friendship Marjorie and I had made among the governors of the country as a result of my regular attendance at governors' conferences. Several times we were guests of the Wests at their beautiful governor's mansion in Columbia. The staff employed at the mansion included a number of people who had been convicted of crimes and were serving sentences, several of them for capital crimes. They were educated, courteous, and efficient people, and it was an interesting and educational experience for us to get to know several of them.

An addition had been built on the mansion that served as accommodations for guests. Among the conveniences was a series of buttons that one could push to get whatever kind of service was desired. One called the butler, one the cook, others the maid, the chauffeur, the housekeeper, and so on. This made a great impression on Marjorie.

While driving home after one of our visits, I noticed that Marjorie was unusually quiet. I asked if anything was troubling her.

"I want a mansion," she replied.

"No way," I said. "We don't have mansions in Vermont. Not even for the governor."

"Well, can I have a button?"

"Sure, you can have a button," I answered.

"But if I have a button, what would happen when I push it?"

"Then you go out into the kitchen and get my breakfast," I replied.

"Just what I thought," she said. "No thanks—just forget it!"

She did get her button, however. When I left the governor's office, my staff threw a party and presented Marjorie with a large, elaborately decorated button.

There is no question that Marjorie's most intense interest is in her children, grandchildren, and great-grandchildren, and in this category she includes mine as well. Between us we have four children, eighteen grandchildren, and fifteen great-grandchildren (and more in prospect), and she showers her love and interest on them continually. A letter, a card, a telephone call to a family with a problem, an expression of joy at an accomplishment, or a message of concern to one who has suffered a setback, all demonstrate her love and interest. She is always there when help is needed and boundless in her outpouring of love. For my part she taught me much about the joy of close family relationships and has made our marriage a constant love affair for thirty-nine years. How lucky I have been!

•

15

My First Two Campaigns for Governor

●

A poll taken at this time by the Vermont Republican Committee disclosed that only about 45 percent of the people in the state had ever heard of me. It was fortunate that I got this message early in the campaign. I resolved then and there that the other 55 percent were going to hear about me, favorably or unfavorably.

B y 1967, I had served as president of National Life Insurance Company for seventeen years. I was sixty-seven years of age—two years beyond the normal age of retirement. I was in good health, loved my job, and would have been happy to stay on to the age of seventy, as some of the directors had asked me to. I was, nevertheless conscious of the increasing uncertainties of life and health that exist as one grows older and equally conscious that National Life had in place an age sixty-five mandatory retirement policy, applicable only to employees but eventually to be extended to officers. I informed the directors of my desire to retire and asked them to appoint a special committee to make recommendations to the board for my successor. National Life was in good condition, so altogether it seemed a good time to retire.

The board selected Dr. John Fey, who had been a member of the board of National Life for some years and then president of the University of Wyoming. Before that, he had served as a popular and capable president of the University of Vermont. He was a man with an attractive personality and a record of proven management skills.

At that time I held the title of president and chief executive officer. The board asked me to remain active as president and chief executive officer for a year and thus give Dr. Fey a chance to become fully acquainted with the company's personnel and operations before assuming the chief responsibility—to give him a chance to "get his feet under the desk," as the board expressed it. Dr. Fey, as I had expected, was an unusually quick learner; hence, well before that year was up, I was passing the major responsibilities over to him. At the end of the year he was made president and chief executive officer, and I became chairman of the board.

Not long after the press announcement of Dr. Fey's election as president, people began sounding me out and suggesting that I run for governor of Vermont. I was flattered but at first did not take the suggestion seriously.

It was not the first time I had been asked to consider such a run. I had been asked more than thirty years earlier, at the first statewide convention of Young Republicans. The convention, held in Barre, had been attended by 150 young men and women, all under the age of forty. Sterry R. Waterman was the first president. I gave the keynote speech. At the convention we adopted a state and national platform, which according to the press of the day was the first national platform prepared by a state convention of Young Republicans to be presented at the National Convention of Republicans. We Young Republicans of that day were flexing our muscles! Three days later, the Windsor County delegates discussed for over an hour whether to put up my name in 1938 as the Republican candidate for governor of Vermont. I expect that it was this piece of history that resulted in my name being mentioned as a possible candidate several times in the next thirty years. I was asked again in 1966 to run, but the request came during the transition of the presidency at National Life, and I could not give it serious consideration.

By the latter part of 1967, however, these requests to have me consider running were increasing in number. Political wheels from Burlington began coming to visit me at National Life and pounding the table for half an hour about how important they thought it was for me to run. Then the telephone calls and letters started coming.

Pretty soon I had at least two hundred requests before me. I began to give the idea more thought. I was conscious of full retirement impending and began to feel that life without action and responsibility would be a boring business indeed. My longstanding interest in state politics and my willingness to "do the chores" of politics and of the Republican party for many years had given me a general acquaintance with party regulars. My work and study as chairman of the Little Hoover Commission and of the committee to study aid for school buildings had not only increased my interest in state affairs but had given me some confidence that I could make a contribution as governor, if elected. And, of course, in all honesty, I must admit that the possibility of being governor of my state flattered my ego. None of us is immune to that kind of recognition.

But I did not underestimate the struggle I would face. The Democrats had greatly enjoyed their six-year control of the executive branch under Governor Philip Hoff and were not about to give it up without a fight. Hoff's election as governor in 1962 had been the first for a Democrat in Vermont in more than one hundred years. In addition, he was the first person, Democrat or Republican, to be elected to three two-year terms as governor.

I also recognized that there were at least two principal handicaps I would have as a candidate. First was my age. I was well beyond the age at which most people in the past had sought the governorship in Vermont. The only two I could remember whose ages were similar to my own had been Governor Smith of Rutland and Governor Weeks of Vergennes. Smith had been sixty-seven at the time of his election and Weeks seventy-three, and both men had served in a day when all top state officials tended to be older. In those earlier days, age was equated with experience, but the election of thirty-three-year-old F. Ray Keyser, Jr., as governor in 1960 had ushered in a young person's era in Vermont politics.

The working press—all quite young and eager and not lacking in youthful confidence—were sure that elderly politicians (meaning me) were a thing of the past. Calling attention to the remarkable increase in the number of young people in the state between the ages of twenty and forty-four, Stephen C. Terry, then a young reporter for the *Rutland Herald*, well expressed the views of his young associates in the press, when on January 2, 1968, he confidently opined that:

Vermont is becoming a state with younger people. It is vibrating with booming industry and a new optimistic attitude. This is being felt politically. It is the basis for the overwhelming appeal of the billboard ban. The Republican Party has the opportunity to win the General Election this year, but it must accent youth and be attuned to what's happening in Vermont. It can't do this by putting up an elder statesman as its candidate.

The second principal handicap I faced was that I had not come up through the chairs. I had not even served in the legislature, which is a good training ground for the governorship and a good basis on which to build a constituency and name recognition. For many years it had been a prerequisite experience for candidates for that office. Then I learned that my opposition in the Republican primary would be Attorney General James Oakes, an able, handsome, popular, and astute politician who had formerly served as state senator from Windham County. He had considerable support among Democrats and a strong constituency among Republicans. This development gave me even greater pause. I remember talking with Senator George Aiken during that period of uncertainty. He never supported other candidates as a matter of policy, and so, of course, I was not seeking his support, only his advice. He said, "I don't know where your support is. Certainly not in Windham County."

And then a wholly unexpected event occurred. A member of the House of Representatives from Randolph, without my knowledge, passed a petition among Republicans in the House and found that 82 percent supported me as the preferred candidate for the Republican nomination. Of ninety-one Republicans interviewed, sixty-four were for me, thirteen were for Oakes, and fourteen were uncommitted.

My interest grew. I decided to talk it over with Jim Oakes. I have always felt that there is a benefit in potential primary candidates talking things over face to face. Such a meeting often has the tendency to lower the level of strident rhetoric and discord even if both people decide to run. It gives each potential candidate a better idea as to how serious each other's intentions are, and it shows each that the other does not actually have horns. Moreover, it increases the probability that the losing candidate at the primary will support the winner at the election. I invited Jim to lunch. We had a very pleasant discussion and accomplished nothing except to confirm for ourselves that we were both determined to run. For by that time I was determined to run.

When I reached that decision at the end of January 1968, I decided to make an immediate announcement. I invited the press to meet me at the statehouse for the announcement and offered reporters a chance to interrogate me if they wished. Very few came. I suspect that they did not take my candidacy very seriously. I do recall that Vic Maerki, veteran leader among Vermont political reporters, attended and asked a number of questions. Walter "Peanut" Kennedy, who was then speaker of the House, showed up, announced publicly his support of me, and said a few kind words in my behalf. I read a formal announcement speech in which I promised, if elected, to slow down the pace of spending and not to propose new taxes until we could know the full cost of the commitments already made. I also promised that, if elected, I would not hesitate to ask the legislature for a sales tax if it became necessary to pay for those commitments. The press conference was soon over. The lack of enthusiasm and paucity of reporters made it obvious to me that I had to create more interest and excitement if I was to be a viable candidate. Nevertheless, both major newspapers of the state reported my formal announcement at some length.

Mine was not a very exciting political announcement or platform. It did serve, however, to set the tone of the forthcoming campaign because it put me in the role of a man who would slow down on new programs, and it opened the way for my opponent to cast me in the image of a "take stock and sit still" candidate, an image that usually makes a candidate look like a dull and uninteresting person. As it turned out, this was not a bad image to have at just that time. The state had just gone through five years of heavy spending from new innovative programs that resulted from the heavy influx of people into Vermont and the air of optimism that abounded from 1962 to 1967. The newspapers began discussing the probabilities of an Oakes-Davis contest in editorials, and letters from readers began appearing in the newspapers on one side or the other.

I began organizing my campaign and set up a campaign office immediately. I asked John Dinse, a widely respected and successful lawyer in Burlington, to be my chairman for the primary. He accepted and lent prestige and credibility to the campaign. I asked Lawrence Dawson to become operating chairman. Larry had had long experience in the field of public relations and fitted nicely into that spot. He was a strong manager of the campaign office, which we set up in the Tavern Annex on State Street. People began offering their services, and almost immediately we had a dozen or more full-time and part-time volunteers. At that time the Vermont law placed a spending limit of $7,500 on any candidate running in a gubernatorial primary. Today that is a laughable figure, but even then it was barely adequate for expenses. Certainly, there was no money available for staff.

A poll taken at this time by the Vermont Republican Committee disclosed that only about 45 percent of the people in the state had ever heard of me. It was fortunate that I got this message early in the campaign. I resolved then and there that the other 55 percent were going to hear about me, favorably or unfavorably. I knew that meeting people face to face was the only way I could accomplish it.

Almost immediately I had my first bit of hard luck. One morning, lifting my heavy double overhead garage door, I developed a hernia. I tried to carry on by wearing a truss but soon found that this was not feasible because I was doing so much driving. Although I knew the press was waiting for an opportunity to suggest the infirmities of my age, I decided to take the bull by the horns and have an operation to correct the problem. Furthermore, I prepared a press release about it and asked one of the volunteers to hand-deliver it to the Crow's Nest, the name given to the space on the upper floor of the statehouse occupied by reporters from the major newspapers. A young lady from the campaign office delivered the press release as requested. As she was leaving the Crow's Nest, however, she suddenly remembered a previous promise to get some information for one of the reporters. She went back to explain why she had not yet been able to accomplish this. As she approached the doorway of the Crow's Nest, the reporters had just finished reading the release, and she heard one of them exclaim, "Now we've got him!"

The operation was performed, and I went home in a few days. In another few days, I was back on the road. But of course, this brief hospitalization lent fuel—temporarily, at least—to the fire of the claim that I was too old.

One morning shortly afterward, I woke up at home and looked out the window to see a large Dodge motor home parked in the driveway. I went out to investigate and found no one there. Further investigation disclosed that the vehicle belonged to my brother Ralph, who was then living in Florida. Without my knowledge or any prior arrangement, he had driven the vehicle to Vermont, left it in the driveway for my use during the primary campaign, and started back to Florida without even stopping to see me. As it turned out, I used it both for the primary and for the first general election campaign. It was of tremendous help. We could pull off the road whenever we wanted to for a nap or a lunch or even to hold an interview. We decorated the motor home with DAVIS FOR GOVERNOR in large multicolored letters so that it would not go unnoticed anywhere it was driven or parked.

On one occasion shortly before the primary, our campaign bus was parked on the grounds of the Connecticut Valley Fair in Bradford, and Marjorie was "tending bus" while I spent my time touring the cattle barns where the farmers were to be found. A visitor to the bus, who turned out to be the wife of a farmer, said she was looking for me and would like to talk to me. Marjorie told her where I was and assured her that I would return shortly. Marjorie invited her into the bus for a cup of tea. The lady said, "Mrs. Davis, my husband read in the newspaper that Mr. Davis is interested only in the big farms and the big farmers and that he has no interest in small farmers like us."

"Well, I can tell you, Mrs. Brown, that that is not true," Marjorie said, "but I'd much rather you heard it from my husband. If you can wait, I'm sure he'll be glad to talk with you. And also, Mrs. Brown, you must know that not everything you read in the newspapers is fact."

Just then John Mahoney, a reporter for the *Rutland Herald,* who was following us for a week, returned to the bus. Marjorie introduced him to Mrs. Brown and said, "John, I've just been telling Mrs. Brown that not everything you read in the newspapers is a fact."

"But Mrs. Davis," John replied, "the facts are not always the truth."

Still later in the week, John provided me with another reason to chuckle. John was one of those reporters who never forgot to use my age in his press reports. Invariably, he even added a year. We had had a long and tiring day. After we had been at the fairgrounds a little while, I said, "John, I have an appointment over at the agriculture building to talk with some farmers. Do you want to come?" He looked at me with a pathetic expression and replied, "Mr. Davis, I'm really bushed. Do you mind if I go in and lie down in the motor home for a bit?"

"Sure, John," I replied, "you young people have got to get your rest in this business."

He never mentioned my age in the newspaper after that.

But age remained an issue, lurking in the background throughout the primary campaign. It was always heartening, therefore, to see young people become involved in my campaign. I recall receiving a letter from John Nicholls, now a practicing lawyer in Barre but then a law student in Boston, informing me that he would like to work for me in the primary. I replied, thanking him, but advising him that I could not hire him because of the $7,500 limitation on spending. He replied to my reply immediately, asking, "Where did you get the idea I expected a salary? I just want to be in the campaign." I had a similar letter from Charles "Chuck" Butler, a former Vermonter who was then a student in Arizona, offering his services. I kept these two young men nearby, partly because they were so useful doing countless things and partly because they could open a path for me to reach younger voters. They also took turns driving and maintaining the motor home and passing petitions.

I would not want to overlook the contributions of the youthful and energetic Davis Americans or the Davisettes. The Davis Americans were the Renaud sisters from Winooski: Rachel, Denise, Patty, and Alice, the younger daughters in a family of fifteen. These talented young women wore red, white, and blue costumes, including the characteristic Davis straw hats, which had become a hallmark of the campaign, and appeared at dinners and other functions where there were sizable audiences. They sang beautifully and their voices harmonized extremely well. In addition they were heard daily on radio and television singing "The Team For the Times," a musical number written specially for the campaign.

The Davisettes were a group of young ladies, eight in number, who wore special matching costumes and straw hats and kept things hopping doing countless chores, including hostessing at dinners and putting on bumper stickers, always with an engaging smile that captured attention. It was our belief that any candidate who decided to use bumper stickers had to win the sticker war. A mere scattering of bumper stickers did more harm than good, making you look like a loser. These young ladies were a major factor in our success in getting many more bumper stickers than my opponent.

Passing petitions also became an important part of our early strategy. The law required that candidates file petitions signed by voters before the candidate was qualified to have his name on the ballot. The number of needed signatures was fixed by statute as a percentage of population and was quite small. Some candidates did not bother to get more signatures than those needed to satisfy the minimum requirements of the law. I believed that passing a petition could become a very effective campaign tool, so we kept passing petitions long after we had the legally required number. Each official petition had places for twenty-five voters to sign, but we cut the petitions in order to leave only ten spaces for signatures. We felt that if the petition contained only a few spaces to be filled, people would more readily agree to pass them. And it worked that way.

Furthermore, if we gave people petitions with twenty-five spaces to be filled with signatures, they were quite likely to procrastinate on passing the petition with the result that when the day of filing was at hand, they wouldn't send in the petition at all because they were embarrassed by not having passed it as they had agreed. We adopted the practice of sending a personal letter signed by me to each person who had passed the petition thanking him or her for the effort. I also signed and sent a personal letter to every signer of the petitions as the petitions came in. We were most agreeably surprised at the effect of this practice. We received many letters of commendation from the recipients. I believe, also, that the practice has a tendency to hold the signer more committed to the candidate. In Vermont I regard it as a campaign tool of major importance. Because the work to gather the signatures and send the thanks comes at the start of the campaign, it helps to build a constituency at a time when a candidate most needs it.

I did all the things that conventional candidates do. I spoke to

Rotary, Kiwanis, and other service clubs, and to meetings of Republican voters; I went to coffee klatches; I tramped the streets and shopping centers shaking hands and shook hands at the gates of the larger manufacturing companies. This walking the streets and shaking hands I found very difficult for the first two weeks, but I soon settled into the routine and enjoyed it. In the shopping centers I found that if I could get inside the stores with the permission of the management, it worked out much better than meeting people outdoors. Something about the closeness of being inside got the attention of people more definitely, and I had some most interesting and profitable experiences in this way. I found, too, that if I went into a store, it was mandatory to shake hands not only with the boss but with all the staff, too. It is better not to go in at all than to miss anyone.

Once, when I was campaigning in Washington County, I stopped in East Calais village, where a small group of people had been assembled to meet me. A middle-aged gentleman dressed in collar tie and hat reminiscent of the early twentieth century stepped up to greet me. It was a time when my age and conservatism were being regularly discussed in the press.

"Mr. Davis," he said, "I want to welcome you to East Calais. I've heard a lot about you and read everything I could in the papers and listened to you when you spoke on radio and television. And Mr. Davis, I saw right away that you were my candidate because you see, Mr. Davis, you and I believe in the same things. There is one great American that I have the greatest admiration for. I believe just as he does, and I know from listening to you that you do too. So I'd like to present you with a book about him and his political views that you and I share." Walking a bit closer, he handed me a book saying, "That man, Mr. Davis, was William McKinley, and I know you and he are soul brothers." At that the small crowd roared with laughter. That man was Marjorie's uncle, Victor Smith.

Late in the campaign I found there was a special value in going where other candidates did not. I followed a practice of going into the country and picking an area of average-looking farmhouses and making a call. Sometimes these calls lasted fifteen or twenty minutes. I found people were delighted to talk with me. And I'm sure that after I left many of these told of their experience to others in the neighborhood. At any rate, I ended up with a good vote in the rural sections.

As the primary campaign progressed, I found that the press was getting more interested and showed up in more places where I was scheduled to be. We began the practice of sending all members of the political press our schedule each day. Some of the press who showed up were obviously most interested in seeing if I would put my foot in my mouth. All candidates run this risk, but inexperienced candidates who are inclined to talk too much run the greatest risk. I was no exception. One example makes the point and is, I believe, the worst mistake I made during my several campaigns. A reporter asked me if I believed that a man could live on fifty-six dollars per week. This was the minimum Vermont wage at the time. I replied that it would depend upon where the man lived and how he lived, whether he grew his own vegetables, kept hens and a cow, or not. I said that I knew of two men who each had less than fifty-six dollars a week but got by because they lived a kind of subsistence life. The next day one newspaper's headline read, DAVIS BELIEVES FAMILIES OF FOUR CAN LIVE ON FIFTY-SIX DOLLARS A WEEK.

This is the kind of political baggage a candidate picks up by talking too much, and it was a goof I had to live with not only through the primary campaign but through all four campaigns. In some of the plants I went into, I found workers wearing buttons that read $56.00 A WEEK—LIKE HELL. A seasoned campaigner would not have answered the way I did, but in the early part of the campaign I was naïve enough to believe that it was necessary not only to be 100 percent truthful but to be fully frank. It took a few experiences such as this one to teach me that while 100 percent truthfulness is a must at all times, complete frankness is not always a political virtue.

In order to get a broader, sounder, and up-to-date perspective on the campaign, I arranged for an advisory group to meet at my home every week to discuss the happenings of the week before and establish an agenda for the next week. Composed as it was of some of the best thinkers in the legislature and a few longtime members of the state Republican committee, this group was invaluable. My advisers were especially helpful in briefing me on the recent history of some of the most often-discussed issues.

By June, our organizational methods had apparently impressed the *Rutland Herald*. It printed a detailed description of my organization and methods of campaigning under a large headline that read DAVIS BASING CAMPAIGN ON CLOSE-KNIT, WELL-OILED ORGANIZATION. This set the stage for other papers to frequently characterize the campaign as "well oiled."

I had hoped that the sales tax could be avoided as an issue in the primary campaign. Eventually it was because Jim Oakes's position paralleled my own. He simply said that if substantial revenue were needed, Vermont would need to consider a sales tax.

Gun control was perhaps the most emotional issue in the primary campaign. In my travels I found much feeling on both sides. The rapid rise in crime in which guns were involved prompted many people to support the registration of all guns. Sportsmen, farmers, and many members of labor unions felt equally strongly that gun control was an unwarranted restraint upon personal rights. I felt that the registration of guns would do little, if anything, to control crime and hence took a firm stand against gun control, including registration. Jim Oakes favored it.

Oakes also was in favor of a guaranteed annual income. I opposed it and pointed out that it would be a practical impossibility to separate those who were justly qualified for it from those who were not.

One other social program also became an issue. Governor Hoff had started a program of bringing five-hundred young black people from out of state to Vermont annually to mingle with Vermonters, particularly young people, and to participate in informational and educational programs. Oakes supported this program. I said I had misgivings about it but would support it if it proved to be successful.

Throughout the primary campaign, I took the position that the two principal problems facing the state were how to finance a proper level of public education and how to lower property taxes. I could not see that Oakes's position on these two matters differed essentially from mine. The central issue in the campaign really came down to whether the people of Vermont wanted a governor with financial and administrative experience who would make fiscal responsibility the principal goal of his administration, or one who would favor a more activist administration—which would of course involve more rapidly rising state expenses.

We finished the primary campaign without taking a single poll. The only polls I knew of then were the polls taken by the Vermont Republican party and the polls taken by Professor Vincent Narramore, a professor of political science at St. Michael's College. The Narramore polls had been started years before and were based on the theory that the town of Salisbury was a bellwether town because its voting results had been essentially the same as the rest of the state for quite a while. On September 9, the day before the primary, Professor Narramore announced to the press that Davis would win "handily." The *Rutland Herald* reported that in the Narramore poll, 70 to 75 percent of the votes went to Davis.

On September 10, primary election day, nearly sixty thousand voters cast ballots. It was a good turnout judged by primary election day standards. I attracted approximately 62 percent of the total vote against Oakes's 38 percent and carried every county in the state except, as Senator Aiken had warned me, Oakes's home county of Windham, where Oakes had a two-to-one victory. Both Jim and I were surprised at the extent of my statewide victory, and he admitted so to the press, but he also immediately announced that he would support me in the coming general election. He lived up to that promise completely and was able to carry with him most of his supporters. His help was of inestimable value and deeply appreciated by me. As it worked out, he was subsequently appointed to the second judicial circuit of the United States, a court which among lawyers is considered the second most prestigious court in the country, after the United States Supreme Court.

Most of the newspapers of the state commented editorially on the primary results in the governor's race. The *Bennington Banner*, which had strongly supported Oakes, carried the analysis a step further. The editor had this to say:

> Many Democrats are elated this morning because they feel that Davis will be the easier of the two G.O.P. candidates to defeat in the November election. Davis's strong showing in the primary should give them second thoughts. The vote yesterday was considered heavy, so the outcome has greater significance than it would have if there had been only a light turnout. Davis

has proved that he can win the support of a vast majority of Vermont Republicans. If the voters' mood remains conservative he can probably do better in November. Lt. Gov. Jack Daley, who tends to be rather conservative himself, is no shoo-in; in fact he must now be considered an underdog in the light of Davis's impressive primary victory.

I saw considerable evidence that this view was shared by other members of the liberal press, and I took heart. I was beginning to be taken seriously as a candidate.

Now I faced Lieutenant Governor John Daley, a former high school teacher in Rutland and now the Democratic gubernatorial nominee. Daley had served his city as mayor. He was a popular, handsome, gregarious young man with a most pleasing personality. He had wide name and face recognition as a result of several campaigns and his service as lieutenant governor in the Hoff administration. With the primary over, he was now ready to campaign in earnest and started immediately. So did I. We had a total of eight weeks to slug it out before Election Day.

For the most part, Democrats rallied around Jack Daley and put on a forceful campaign. But the Democrats tried to get political benefit out of the passage of the state welfare program, which for the first time took from the towns responsibility for caring for their poor. They seemed to forget that the program had been passed at a time when the legislature was controlled by a Republican majority. At the same time, they had to live down the $7 million deficit that existed at the end of the Hoff administration. Compared with the size of some recent deficits, $7 million would be regarded as peanuts, but it was not regarded so at the time. In the end, the sales tax was the only real issue, and the Democrats played it for all it was worth.

My platform remained essentially the same: to restore a balanced budget and to bring more efficiency into state government in the administrative branch. But I introduced a new issue, too.

My travels about the state and my discussions with concerned citizens had persuaded me that some kind of development controls were going to be necessary if we were to preserve our heritage of "unspoiled Vermont." No one seemed to know just how this was to be accomplished; nor, to begin with, did I. I did know that any legislation that would provide adequate control would run counter to Vermont's long history of individualism. And I also knew that one of the fiercely held aspects of that individualism was the belief that no one could tell a Vermonter how to use his land. Since the solution was not apparent, I spent my time trying to dramatize the problem, and I did my level best to describe the values to Vermont of retaining that unspoiled heritage. I found wide agreement on this point.

I carried on this general election campaign much as I had the campaign for the primary. Now I had the help of the organized Republican party throughout the state. The party officials were confident that we could and would win and supported me with enthusiasm.

By now, I had learned a few things about political speaking at luncheon and dinner meetings. I had learned that brevity and speaking to the point are virtues in political dialogue. I learned once again that getting close attention is necessary in good communication and especially in political speaking. I gradually developed a technique to respond to these necessities. Before we sat down at a luncheon or dinner meeting, I would arrange with the chairman to pass out small index cards (which I always brought with me) to the audience and to explain that the speaker had requested everyone in the audience to write a question and pass the card back to the head table before the end of the meal and before the speaking. It was a simple matter, as these cards dribbled back during the meal, to pick out the ones I wanted to answer. I soon found that, invariably, one or two questions were asked by large numbers of people. These questions were the ones I wanted to answer because they showed me instantly where the widest interest was. From the other questions I selected a few that I wanted to answer and discarded the rest. In this simple manner my speech was automatically prepared, subjects selected, and quickly organized. I knew that I would have the close attention of the audience, and it made speaking at these affairs a sheer pleasure.

I began, too, to develop a healthy respect for coffee klatches. I met fewer people at a time at this sort of gathering but could talk to them much more intimately and effectively. We encouraged the hostesses to invite both supporters and nonsupporters. We found, too, that these coffees usually produced one or more people who were motivated to get out and do some actual campaigning. Some of our best missionaries came from this source.

Both parties had held their conventions on September 21, 1968, for the purpose of adopting a platform and to fire up the troops. The Republican platform stated that Republicans would consider a sales tax "but only as a last resort." Some of the more conservative Republican delegates tried hard to have the whole issue of a sales tax eliminated from the platform, and I understood why: having it in would certainly not attract us any votes and it might drive some potential voters away. But I was getting more nervous daily as I considered the meager figures and information I had relating to increasing state expenses, and I felt it was only fair to state the truth. After all, it was only what I had been saying in the primary campaign. I made this position clear to the convention, and the delegates voted to leave the plank in.

The Democratic platform was silent about the sales tax. I always wondered about this because Daley and almost every other prominent Democrat queried on the subject was outright opposed to any form of sales tax. Moreover, the Labor Council, which met on the same day, listened to a speech from Daley, promptly endorsed him for governor, and passed a resolution declaring that it would "oppose any type of sales tax, since such a tax would be detrimental to the working people of the State of Vermont."

Daley set the tone for the remainder of his campaign in his speech at the Democratic Convention by lashing out at what he called the " 'stand pat' doctrines of the Republican party." The *Times-Argus* reported that "in a slam at Republican Deane C. Davis's call for 'taking stock,' Daley said 'they would have the people of our state take stock, as they put it, and would arrest and stifle the new spirit that has been kindled in our state.' "

This was merely a continuation of the primary campaign theme Oakes had used to describe me as a "do-nothing governor" or a "caretaker governor." William A. Hunter, the Democratic candidate for lieutenant governor, developed the theme further by dubbing me as " 'Old Double D,' stands for 'Don't Do.' " Hunter further told the convention that "the days of the aristocrats governing Vermont are over." It was never wholly clear to me whether the Democrats were caught up in and believed this time-worn propaganda or whether they genuinely failed to see the financial troubles ahead if they persisted at a galloping speed to spend money on new programs.

An amusing sequel to Hunter's "Double D" designation was the brainchild of Al Moulton, who was then chairman of the State Republican Committee. Moulton promptly offered a prize and welcomed everyone in the state to enter a contest for the best definition of the meaning of "Double D." This quickly turned the tables on the Democrats as definitions poured in with suggestions such as "Distinctively Deserving" and "Dump Daley." The press, of course, picked up the contest and kept the whole thing alive. The winning entry was "Dependable Deane," which earned its creator a free dinner at a Montpelier restaurant.

Three days after the convention, Daley took his "blitzkrieg campaign" into Brattleboro. This was Oakes's home town, and according to the press reports, Daley hoped to swing disenchanted Oakes supporters to him. His lack of success was soon apparent. Thirty-three former Oakes supporters met with me for lunch on October 7 in Brattleboro at my invitation. Speaking at the luncheon, Brattleboro realtor Richard Sykes, one of Oakes's strongest aides in the primary campaign, said, "I have not seen a Republican in Windham County who is not solidly behind the entire Republican ticket and especially your candidacy. The Democrats are only engaging in some wishful thinking if they expect any help from Oakes Republicans in Brattleboro. I am sure that we heartily agree with Jim Oakes himself, who has made it very clear since the primary that he believes it is imperative for the future of Vermont to elect Mr. Davis and the Republican ticket."

Daley had other trouble, too. The campaign was hardly under way before the Democratic candidate for lieutenant governor, William Hunter, found himself in public disagreement with the party's gubernatorial candidate. Daley had proposed in a well-publicized speech that industrial growth could be expanded "especially around the present industrial cities." Hunter took issue with this view and said that he "did not want to keep growth confined to the larger population centers in the state which already have industrial development." He favored "an even flavor by spreading growth throughout the state."

It became clear almost immediately, however, that the sales tax was going to be the most potent issue—perhaps the only potent issue. Gun control, education, property taxes, crime, economic development, clean water, and the environment were all among the issues I expected to confront, and I was not disappointed, but all these other matters were discussed primarily in the hope of winning minor points by each side. Nothing was as important as the sales tax issue.

I had a strong compulsion to speak out clearly on the sales tax early in the campaign. I hoped against hope that new needed expenditures and new revenues would somehow balance each other out, but I was not at all sure they could or would. The only honest thing to do was to tell people what I felt about a sales tax even if it was dangerous politically to do so. I had a chance to do this at a meeting of students at Johnson State College in early October. I knew Daley would be speaking to the students the next day, and this would give a chance for the different positions to be clearly expressed. I used the opportunity to state my position as fully as I could. "The property tax is the most regressive tax you can have," I told my audience,

and while it is possible for a sales tax to fall heavily on those least able to pay, it is possible to avoid this with proper exemptions, such as food, clothing, drugs, and medicine. This is the only kind of sales tax we should even consider.

The hope of getting by without additional sources of revenue is getting dimmer. The sales tax is the only real, untapped source of revenue left, and I don't know whether the next legislature will pass it or not. Lieutenant Governor Daley will tell you tomorrow that he will veto a sales tax. I don't say that because I don't think anyone who looks at the state's fiscal situation realistically can say that.

We have reached the time in the history of Vermont when all the good things that need to be done far exceed our capacity to do them. We have gone a long way in providing services in an attempt to cure our social ills in order to make life more pleasant. If you take the local taxes and add the state taxes and compare it on an income basis with any state in the union, Vermont is the highest tax-paying state in the nation. But this is bound to happen if we want the same level of services offered in the other states.

Then I called attention to a projection by the Department of Administration that the state would receive an additional $26 million in the next biennium because of natural growth, and I said I hoped this was true. "If the revenues increase," I said, "we could get by in the next biennium, and no new sources of revenue would be needed."

I thought I had expressed myself clearly and directly. I thought I had made clear the relationship between the growing financial needs of the state's expanding programs, especially its new welfare program, and the crisis Vermont was facing in inadequate revenues to meet those needs. I thought I had made it clear that if revenues did increase as the Department of Administration projected, Vermont could escape a sales tax, but that if, and only if, revenues fell below projections, the state would need to fall back on its last resort—a sales tax. I thought I made all this clear. As I learned later, I thought wrong.

On that same day, I put myself on record regarding conservation and environmental control while speaking in Brattleboro to the Windham County Farm Bureau. In part, I said, "I will further expand and find new ways to improve our efforts in conservation, carrying pollution control to the headwaters of our streams and rivers, and securing the less tillable land at higher elevations for the preservation of wildlife."

The reference to pollution control and securing less tillable land for wildlife was an indication of my growing concern for environmental control, but I was still not sure what was the best way to go about it. The issue was either unimportant to Daley or he was similarly unsure of what direction to suggest. He rarely mentioned it.

By early October, it was noticed that Daley had changed his strategy at least in one respect. He began to speak only from prepared text. This was exactly contrary to my practice, as I spoke always "off the cuff." I think this made me a more effective speaker, but it also made me more vulnerable to making political gaffes. I know I fell victim to this in early October when both Daley and I appeared before the students and faculty at Mount St. Joseph's Academy in Rutland. I responded to a question, which was itself slanted, concerning the desirability of large industry in Vermont. I replied, "I think we can absorb a certain amount of large industry in our larger cities. I think IBM is pretty big for our state's digestion, however." I was right—IBM was pretty big for the state's digestion, and it made radical changes over a large area surrounding Burlington—but I did not intend to say, nor did I mean, that IBM was not good for Vermont. Daley and Hunter, however, immediately picked up my remarks and made political hay with them for quite a while.

Fortunately, the small and inevitable slips every candidate makes did not obscure my central themes, nor did they cost me the support of thoughtful voters. On October 8, State Republican Chairman Al Moulton released a Becker poll taken in Vermont that showed me running ahead of Daley. Four days later, newspapers carried the news that the *Rutland Herald* and the *Times-Argus*, which had supported Oakes at the primary, now supported me in the general election. A week later the *Burlington Free Press* in a short editorial announced its support of me, "because Davis's qualifications outshine those of his opponent."

Sometime after the Becker poll figures had been released, and perhaps because I was attracting so much apparent support, rumors began to circulate that the State Democratic Committee had taken its own poll. The press questioned Chairman Esposito about the rumors. He admitted that such a poll had been taken and that, according to instructions, the figures had been given only to Daley. Daley then admitted to receiving poll figures and said that the figures showed that he and I were running nip and tuck. Quayle and Company, the professional firm that had taken the poll, promptly wrote a letter to the *Burlington Free Press* in which the pollsters said that the results showed Davis leading Daley by "a significant margin." This may have hurt Daley some as it was at about that time that I could feel my campaign workers begin to show more confidence and enthusiasm.

Another minor incident of the campaign which helped to add a bit of fun was the formation of the Davis Morgan Posse. A group of friends, all Morgan riders, put together a small posse, seven in number, of Morgan horses and their riders. All wore hats bedecked with ribbons reading DAVIS FOR GOVERNOR. I led the posse riding my favorite mare, Ru-Lee Darling Dee, in appearances at Enosburg Falls, Barton Fair, Bristol Fair, South Royalton, the Connecticut Valley Fair at

Bradford, and at Montpelier. It was an excellent attention getter. Ru-Lee was a high-stepping, spirited mare, and she helped to show that I was not as old and tired as my opponent would have people believe. On one occasion, I invited one of the reporters to ride with us. He graciously declined.

The last of the fun went out of the campaign on October 25, however, when my worst fears were realized. All through the campaign I had been saying that I did not advocate a sales tax, but if the needs of the state required it, I would not hesitate to recommend a sales tax. Now State Budget Director Ronald Crisman released a press statement indicating that spending requests from department heads for the next biennium were expected to be $66 million higher than projected revenue.

The good news was that my campaign would be helped by this announcement. It would show that my forecasting skills were accurately tuned. The bad news was that no longer could I escape the specter of having to recommend increased revenue. I tried for a while to comfort myself by hoping that maybe the recommendation could be held off one more year, but it was a forlorn hope.

One day before the election, I predicted that I would carry the election by a 55-45 percent margin. Mavis Doyle, writing in the *Burlington Free Press*, conveyed my prediction and went on to say that "all polls taken in Vermont substantiated Davis's prediction." Veteran reporter Vic Maerki, writing the same day in the same paper, was even more forceful in his projections.

> If Republican Deane C. Davis isn't elected the next governor of Vermont tomorrow, a lot of political reporters will be asked to turn in their typewriters, and the professional pollsters will be asked to return their fees.

On Election Day I took the day off from campaigning because I knew it would be a long, tiring night waiting for the returns. Marjorie and I took a short horseback ride, then went to our usual voting place at Montpelier City Hall. A lot of people were hanging around the voting booth hall, eager to talk with us, and we spent an hour or so chatting with them. I felt relaxed all day because I was so glad that the ordeal was nearly over. For eight long weeks I had been getting up at dawn, driving up and down and across the state, shaking hands, making speeches, answering phone calls, attending coffee klatches, appearing on radio and television, and conferring daily with campaign workers at headquarters. I had had hardly a moment to be alone or to be quiet, and it was a great relief to know that it would be over one way or another before we slept that night.

The media, as had been the custom, set up facilities around the state to collect and analyze the voting figures as they came in during the evening.

It seemed to me that the evening had hardly begun when one of the major national networks announced that I had won the election. The figures at that point, while showing me ahead in most counties, did not seem impressive enough to me to conclude that I would win. I told the crowd of supporters gathered at the Tavern in Montpelier that it was too early to take that statement seriously. But they paid no attention to my words of caution and began celebrating in earnest, assuming that I had won. As the figures began to pile up, they became more boisterous. Shortly the telephone rang, and it was Lieutenant Governor Daley conceding defeat and extending courteous congratulations. Not long after, the telephone rang again and it was Channel 22 in Burlington asking if I would come to Burlington to be interviewed on television. Marjorie and I grabbed a car and drove to Burlington, where both of us were interviewed. I remember nothing of either the questions or the answers. However, I do remember driving back from Burlington to the celebration in progress at the Tavern and running over in my mind an inventory of the problems ahead that would surely face me as governor. All of a sudden these problems looked much bigger than they had during the campaign. I confess now that in the excitement and the fatigue of the evening, there was a moment when I seriously asked myself whether I had the necessary strength, knowledge, or wisdom to do the job. But my doubts evaporated almost immediately upon arriving back with the celebrants at the Tavern. I got considerable amusement from the fact that the percentages as the tabulating wound down were exactly as I had predicted. Marjorie and I left the party early and went promptly to bed. We slept the sleep of the just and awoke late in the morning refreshed. From then on for the next four years, I was too busy to have any self-doubts.

Both Daley and Hoff were most gracious in conceding defeat, and both called upon Vermonters to get behind the newly elected governor and do everything they could to further the interests of the state. Also, Governor Hoff went to great lengths to help in the transition from his administration to mine, for which I have always been grateful.

The day following the election, as I had promised I would do if elected, I submitted my resignation as chairman of the board of National Life.

A few days later, I asked my longtime secretary Edna Cheever to come and be my secretary in the governor's office. She had opposed my running for the office and had tried to get Marjorie to oppose it too. In spite of that, Edna, who by then had retired, worked hard for my election through the primary and first general election campaign. I said, "Of course you understand that you are going to be my secretary in the governor's office?"

"I am not!" she said.

Surprised and a bit chagrined, I asked, "Do you mean that?"

"I certainly do," she replied.

"Well, at least you can tell me why," I said, to which she responded, "Just because you want to make a damn fool of yourself, it doesn't mean that I have to."

Shortly afterward, Marjorie and I left for Florida for a brief vacation. When we returned, I began holding hearings to try to learn in detail all about the problems and needs of the various departments. The hearings filled three weeks and were an educational experience for me—but a grim one indeed. Each succeeding day it became increasingly and distressingly clear that there was no escape from providing for a substantial addition to the tax revenue. And the size of the shortfall was such that the new money would have to be found within one or both of the two broad-based taxes—that is, the income tax or a sales tax. I called together sixteen of my supporters, some of whom were legislators, some officers in state government, and a few others whom I called for special reasons. We met at the Holiday Inn in Burlington, and I took the greater part of a day to lay out all the figures before them and to remind them that I had pledged a balanced budget. I pointed out again that personal and corporate income tax was one of the highest in the country; hence, there was no point in trying to rely entirely on increases in the income tax to solve the problem. I asked them for an honest and frank opinion, and I got it. You'll have to go to a sales tax, they responded.

That night I decided to recommend a sales tax. Furthermore, I decided that I would not put off the evil day. I would announce my intention in my inaugural speech. I did this for two reasons. First, because every governor has more clout at the start of his term and second, because everything the legislature could or would do in the session just beginning would depend on whether a sales tax was passed. It would be a waste of the legislature's time to sit by for weeks or months if it did not resolve the question of the state's available funds immediately. And I made a third decision that night. Ironically, it was the hardest decision I would make as governor. However, I had a pretty fair idea of what the backlash would be from the proposal of a sales tax, and even before I was sworn in, I decided that I would not run for a second term.

16

First Gubernatorial Term

*. . . I pointed out that environmental issues were
becoming increasingly important not just in
Vermont but around the country. People were beginning to realize that humans are indeed an inescapable part of the intricate system of life and
growth that begins with air, soil, and water . . .*

On January 9, 1969, I was sworn in as Vermont's seventy-second
governor. I stood at the rostrum of the House of Representatives Hall
to take the oath of office. There, too, stood Chief Justice James S.
Holden, waiting to administer the oath of office to me; Lieutenant
Governor Thomas L. Hayes, who was presiding over the joint ses-
sion of the House and Senate; Speaker of the House Walter Ken-
nedy; and the other members of the "Team for the Times":
Attorney General James M. Jeffords, Secretary of State Richard C.
Thomas, Auditor of Accounts Robert T. King, and State Treasurer
Frank H. Davis.

In the well of the house directly in front of the podium sat outgoing governor Philip H. Hoff, able, handsome, and charming as
ever; his wife Joan; and their daughter Gretchen. Four other former
Republican governors and their wives were also there: Lee Emerson
of Barton, Joseph B. Johnson of Springfield, F. Ray Keyser, Jr., of
Proctor, and Harold Arthur of Burlington, all of whom were accom-

panied by their wives.

A large contingent of my family attended, too. My son Tom and his wife Dolly were there, as was my daughter Marian and her husband Frank Calcagni; my two sisters, Ruth Nims and Helen Murray, and my brother Ralph; Marjorie's two children, Peter Conzelman and Patricia Greeley, accompanied by their spouses; Marjorie's sister, Barbara Smith; my ten grandchildren and five of Marjorie's. Patricia, at my request, sang a soprano solo of "America the Beautiful." After the oath was administered by the chief justice, a nineteen-gun salute announced the inauguration of a new administration.

As I stood there during the preliminaries, I recalled that this was a pageant I had witnessed several times before but had never, of course, participated in. At first I felt a sense of unreality. Then my mind flashed back to my growing-up days on Allen Street in Barre. I saw and heard again in memory my father and mother and was achingly aware of all the sacrifices they had made for their nine children. They were always so proud when their children spoke pieces in public or won other minor honors. Most of all, I remembered how much my father hoped at the end of his life that his children and grandchildren would achieve some of the things he had once hoped to achieve. How much I wished that my father and mother could have been there!

Behind me were six weeks of formal budget hearings, three weeks more than had been scheduled. I had opened the budget hearings to the press, and at first they had attended in sizable numbers, but the reporters soon became bored with the mass of detail. Even to me, the long hearings were a tiring exercise, but they were tremendously educational and thoroughly worthwhile as each department head presented his requests and answered searching questions from me and several associates. At the time this procedure for handling budget matters was unique. At the end of the hearings, I was a sadder but wiser man. It was clear—not only to me, but to my advisers—that substantial new revenue would be needed.

Long and careful thought was given to making drastic cuts, and of course we did trim the budget substantially. But nothing that we could realistically do would have obviated the necessity for new revenue. Vermont had just completed six years of setting up new programs. The state was in the midst of an immigration boom, and revenue was increasing quickly, which gave people courage to begin new programs. Welfare and education, the two largest areas of expenditures, were expanding rapidly, as were their needs. It was not a time when it would be politically possible to cut programs drastically, at least to the extent necessary to overcome the need for a new source of revenue.

It was also perfectly clear that only one source of revenue other than a sales tax should be considered. This was the personal and corporate income tax. But Vermont's income tax was already the highest in the nation compared with other states' taxes on the basis of income, and the state needed to have continued industrial development to serve the increasing employment needs of its residents. High income taxation, either of persons or corporations, would only retard our improvement in that respect.

I agonized over whether I should recommend a sales tax to the legislature. I considered just serving up the financial facts and asking the legislature to choose the new sources of revenue, or perhaps deciding on none at all. But I realized that failure to recommend which source of new revenue should be pursued would be viewed as cowardly. And it would have been. Finally, I elected to bite the bullet and recommend a sales tax. I was fully aware of the political reaction that would follow such a recommendation. When I reached my decision, I did not sleep for two nights.

Before I announced my decision, however, I decided to invite Representative Thomas Salmon, whom I had long admired, to come to my office to be briefed on what my proposals were to be. I did this because I had confidence in Representative Salmon, then the minority leader in the House, and I felt that it would encourage cooperation on the part of the Democratic party members in the House if they could believe that I would play fair with them, no matter how much we might disagree. I did not expect them to endorse the sales tax. The Democrats had long opposed it, and of course there was a great deal of political mileage for them in opposing the sales tax. Representative Salmon asked if he could bring someone with him, and I told him to bring anyone he wished. He brought Representative James D. Shea of Winooski and Representative George H. Sloan of Rutland—both prominent Democrats. They came, and I explained the sales tax and some other prominent features of the inaugural address.

On rereading that inaugural address today, I am surprised at the number of state problems it covered. In the first part of the speech alone, I described for the legislature sixteen areas of concern that were pressing for attention, but I had concluded, of course, that the first and overriding necessity was to put Vermont's financial house in order, and that is what I emphasized. I told the members of the legislature that in the present biennium, state appropriations for the general fund totaled $141.6 million while departmental requests for the next biennium totaled $243.2 million, an increase of more than 73 percent. I also told them that in the budget hearings we had cut $50 million from departmental requests; that we had eliminated every nonessential item we could find; and that we had not included in the budget even one of the 877 new positions requested by department heads. I pointed out that to raise state aid to local school districts to 40 percent of actual costs would cost an additional $17.4 million. I warned them that to maintain only our present commitments to the University of Vermont, to the state colleges, to the regional correction system, to our mental health programs, to our vocational education programs, and to state employees would call for increased spending in startling amounts.

I proposed then to present a one-year budget. Lean as we had been able to make it, it nevertheless called for $17 million more than the state's projected revenue. Finally, I made the proposal that had been keeping me up nights. I announced that, "reluctant as I have been to come to this conclusion, after exhausting all other possibilities and only as a last resort, I must ask you to face together with me the prospect of a tax program adequate to meet our needs." I went on to detail a 4 percent sales tax with food exempt and a provision for graduated refunds to people earning less than $12,000 of annual income. I also proposed increasing the corporate income tax by 20 percent.

As I came out of the Hall of Representatives after delivering my inaugural speech, Governor Hoff walked up to me and congratulated me on my action and the kind of sales tax I had proposed. But on the whole I expected a bad reaction to this proposal, and I was not disappointed. Immediately the press jumped on the words "last resort," suggesting that because I had made the recommendation in my first inaugural address the proposal was obviously not a "last resort" but indeed a "first resort." The reporters seemed to ignore their own newspaper record of the dozens of times when I had flatly stated that if Vermont needed additional revenue, I would recommend a sales tax. But that's politics, which after all runs on emotion to quite an extent. The phrase even became fodder for my first political cartoon, which showed a picture of me speaking on television with the caption, "Well, we'll have to begin with our last resort—a sales tax!"

But there were some early supporters of the sales tax, including some, besides Hoff, who surprised me. Mayor Francis Cain of Burlington, a Democrat, made a public statement in favor of the tax, and both the *Burlington Free Press* and the *Rutland Herald* carried editorials favoring the tax and my action in proposing it. Gerald Witherspoon, tax commissioner in the Hoff administration, was another supporter. Governor Hoff had recently forwarded to me the results of a tax study committee, appointed by Hoff and chaired by Witherspoon, which had recommended a sales tax. Now Mr. Witherspoon came over to talk with me about the sales tax and expressed his approval of such a tax for Vermont.

One interesting bit of comfort, if not support, came from one of the most distinguished and scholarly Democrats in the House. He came to my office during the peak of the controversy and said, "Keep it up. And keep your chin up. You're absolutely right." But of course in the end he had to vote against the sales tax, as did almost all Democrats in the House and Senate.

Two weeks after my inauguration speech, I again appeared before a joint session and delivered my budget message. Here I went into the specifics. My message carefully detailed the figures and the reasons behind them.

I proposed a one-year budget for fiscal year 1970 that pared more than $20 million in requests from department heads and yet that still called for expenditures of slightly more than $96 million, an increase of 16 percent over the year before. Nearly half these expenditures would be earmarked for social welfare and education. To bring home how dramatic these increases were, I compared the proposed budget with the general fund expenditures of three years before, when expenditures proposed for welfare were 80 percent less and expenditures for education were 120 percent less. Why was this? My answer was, "Commitments." During those three years, bold, new and expensive programs were inaugurated by the legislature. Now the moment of truth had come. It was time to pay our bills.

Dramatic as the increases were, they would not have startled anyone who had truly studied the state's financial problem. History shows that when any government provides generous new programs for its citizens, a considerable time passes before the full cost of those programs can be seen. This is because it takes a long time for all who are eligible for the benefits to catch on to them. Only eventually (but also inevitably) does everyone eligible for benefits make his way into the system. The rapid but delayed increase in welfare costs confirmed my worst fears in this respect. I never wanted to leave the impression that I was opposed to these increases in welfare and education, but I was fearful that Vermont was running blindly into a financial corner from which it would be most difficult to extract itself, and I was concerned and determined that the state should operate on a balanced budget and pay for these programs as it went along.

Again in the budget message I pointed out the arguments for a sales tax. I told the members of the joint session that if they could find a better source for new revenue, I would applaud their efforts.

The first reaction in the legislature was one of shock. The press interviewed many members of the legislature to get their reaction to the sales tax proposal. About an equal number were forthright enough to say they were for a sales tax as to say they were opposed, but the largest number were hedging a bit until they could appraise the reaction among their constituents. Consequently, they usually responded to the effect that if a sales tax were truly needed, it should have this or that amendment or that they would have to study the figures some more.

This was a good, safe answer for a politician on such a sensitive issue as a sales tax. I fully recognized that the pressure back home from constituents would be formidable. Hence, a real selling job had to be done if the sales tax was to pass, and I realized that it was my job to do that selling. In the days and weeks ahead, I tried my best to sell my position on the sales tax and took every opportunity that was offered to speak on the subject. And many that weren't offered!

The legislative session was a long, dark period when I struggled to persuade legislators that the proposal for a sales tax was fair and that it was the only practical source for the additional revenue we needed. I had little time to move forward with other needed actions, but I realized that until the question of the budget was resolved, no real planning could be undertaken.

Finally the sales tax was passed by the legislature on April 22, 1969. I signed it immediately. Thus, by its terms it became effective on June 1, 1969. It was not exactly as I had proposed, but the terms were close. The legislation reduced the rate from 4 percent to 3 percent, and the refund provision was altered. The ceiling was lowered determining the breakoff points above which no refund would be paid. In its main respects, however, the bill as passed embodied the provisions that I had proposed.

Finally the state was living up to the commitments that previous legislatures had made to welfare. Moreover, it had substantially raised the level of state support for public education and thus given some relief to property owners from skyrocketing property taxes in the towns and cities. Now I was ready to turn to other problems and issues. But since I had asked for, and received, a one-year hold-the-line budget, with the exception of expenditures for welfare and education, no funds were available with which to inaugurate the kind of new, bold, and expensive programs that had made the past few years so dynamic. To some people, this seemed like a period of inaction. Some legislators, as well as party politicians, equated a "do-something" administration with spending programs. There was considerable criticism of my administration during this period for this reason.

There was plenty to do, however, even if there was no new money to spend. Personnel matters and ironing out differences of opinion always take much of a governor's time. A long list of people are always waiting to see the governor, especially a new governor, to take his stripe or to try to enlist his interest in some pet project. Moreover, and despite what my critics were saying, we had several planning projects that required increasing amounts of my attention as ideas worked their way toward proposals. And then, of course, I faced an ever-growing list of invitations to appear at special functions around the state. These were particularly time-consuming because of the travel involved. Yet in Vermont, they are very much a part of the governor's job, partly because they have been made so by tradition. They are also an effective way for the governor to communicate with the voters, a task that is so essential to good government. The lobbying I did on these occasions for the principles behind the famous Act 250 exemplifies this. It would have been impossible to get such a radical change in the law enacted during a single session of the legislature had there not been widespread support for the basic ideas. Much of that support was the result of discussions around the table and in informational talks during my visits at special-occasion dinners around the state. Consequently, during this so called "quiet time" I found it impossible to keep up with my correspondence. Eventually I purchased a small dictating machine. I carried it with me in the car together with a pile of correspondence and dictated my replies while the driver worried about travel problems. When things were really busy, however, there were simply not enough hours in the day to accomplish everything that needed to be done.

One of the things that kept us hopping throughout 1969 was student unrest. It was a year of student unrest pretty much over the country, and Vermont was not excluded. Nor was the movement confined to students. It was really a youthful protest movement, but it was most often manifested on college campuses, and it took many forms. Here in Vermont young men and women engaged in marches, meetings, Vietnam War condemnation protests, and meetings to condemn ROTC. In the climate of those days the military was despised by large numbers of students, and to an almost equal degree, so were officials of government, both state and federal. Sometimes these confrontations were threatening enough to border on violence, and college administrators, as well as state and local government officials and police departments, were concerned lest the movement get out of hand. I do not recall that it ever did get seriously out of hand anywhere in Vermont, but feeling ran high. To deal with the situation, I appointed Charles Butler as an assistant in the governor's office to help create and maintain a liaison between the governor's office and the most vocal of college youth. Butler was a recent college graduate and had many friends and acquaintances among the vocal groups and in general, I believe, shared their views. Through arrangements made by him, I attended several meetings of statewide protest groups and a few other strictly local groups. In addition, I held one meeting at the statehouse, which was attended by most of the presidents of colleges within the state and by representatives of the young college students.

At the very height of the student protests in Vermont, at the request of President James Armstrong, I went to Middlebury College to speak to the students. Ironically, on the very day I was holding my "rap" session with the Middlebury students, I had, on the request of Governor Peterson of New Hampshire, authorized the head of our state police to assist in evicting fifty students who had taken over the administration building at Dartmouth College. The New Hampshire State Police had previously sent troopers to help quell a disturbance at Grafton, Vermont, and at another time twenty-five New Hampshire State Troopers had stood by in Hanover as insurance against a disturbance which was threatened but never materialized at Norwich University.

The Middlebury meeting was held in the beautiful college chapel, which was filled with students and faculty. A contingent of some twenty-five or thirty students paraded up and down the aisles with large placards expressing various messages of protest against war and government in all its forms. The students marched up and down the aisles during the proceedings, and since they did so quietly, no attempt was made by the college personnel to prevent them. Tension, however, was running high. In the middle of my speech, a loud shot reverberated through the chapel. It sounded as if it had come from a small aisle or entryway about ten feet from where I stood on the raised platform but out of sight to most of those in the audience. The expressions on the faces of people in the audience were ones of extreme shock and concern. I turned to look in the direction from which the shot seemed to have come. Seeing nothing unusual, I went on with my speech. After the speech President Armstrong told me how impressed he was with my composure. "You didn't miss a syllable or a gesture of your speech," he said. I had a feeling that it was not a shot at all, but a firecracker set off by a student prankster.

I've always liked people, so I did not find the chores of campaigning for governor quite as onerous as some others have. I particularly enjoyed visiting the county fairs. The smells of the barn have always been a tonic to me, and fairs were comfortable places to talk to Vermonters about the issues that were important to them. (DCD)

The most effective gimmick to boost my name recognition during my first campaign for governor was the Davis Morgan Posse. Seven friends and fellow Morgan riders joined the Posse and rode with me throughout the state. I always rode my spirited Ru-Lee Darling Dee, a high-stepping mare who turned heads and showed people that I was not as old and tired as my opponent would have people believe. (DCD)

Marjorie and I traveled to Burlington the night I won my first term as governor to appear with journalist Vic Maerki and outgoing governor Philip Hoff on Channel 22. Hoff was as charming as ever, despite the defeat of the Democratic nominee. We were joined by the Davis Americans, four sisters from Winooski who had sung at major functions throughout the campaign. (DCD)

Family Watches as Davis Takes Oath as Governor

On January 9, 1969, I was sworn in as Vermont's seventy-second governor. During the ceremony, my mind flashed back to my growing-up days on Allen Street in Barre. I saw and heard my father and mother in my memory and was achingly aware of all the sacrifices they had made for their nine children. How I wished they could have been there. (courtesy of the Burlington Free Press and the Vermont State Library)

"Well, We'll Have To Begin With Our Last Resort — A Sales Tax!"

My first inaugural address became fodder for my first political cartoon. The press seemed to ignore the dozens of times during the campaign that I had said that I would not hesitate to propose a sales tax if Vermont needed additional revenue to meet its obligations. It was a rough start to my first term.

Vermont's first Green Up Day was on April 18, 1970, three days after the adjournment of the legislature that passed Act 250 and Act 252. Green Up Day brought 70,000 Vermonters out, young and old alike, to help clean up the state's highways and roads. I spent the day flying by helicopter over the state and touching down to lend a hand and share a word of encouragement whenever I saw a work crew. (courtesy of Robert Babcock, Jr.)

The boat ad was created during my second campaign to counter the low ratings I endured because of the sales tax. In the ad, a voice-over explains that I didn't want to impose a sales tax but had to in order to provide funds for the state's burdened budget. It was an instant success and has since been called the most effective television ad in the history of Vermont politics.

Marjorie and I had much to celebrate at my second inaugural ball. The first term had been a difficult one, filled with political and legislative battles, and the succeeding campaign had been in many ways more challenging than the first. A little breathing space was welcomed by all. (DCD)

My wife Marjorie has taught me much about the joy of family relationships and helped keep our large and far-flung family close. This is my daughter Marian, with her husband Frank Calcagni, and their son, Tom. (courtesy of Tom Calcagni)

This is my son Tom, with his wife Dolly, and their children: front row (L to R), David, Richard, Dan, and Dawn; middle row, Timothy, Linda, Corinne, and Julie; back row, Michael. (DCD)

When I married Marjorie, I gained two stepchildren as well. This is Marjorie's son Peter Conzelman, with his wife Roberta, and their children: front row (L to R), Peter, Jr., Cathy, and Clair; back row, Betsey and Susy. (DCD)

This is Marjorie's daughter Patricia, with her husband Sidney Greeley, and their children David, Stephen, and Thomas. (DCD)

Marjorie rode a horse for the first time on our honeymoon at Wentworth-by-the-Sea in 1952. She quickly became a very capable rider, and in the years since we have shared innumerable happy woodland rides through the Vermont countryside and occasional more formal riding excursions. (DCD)

When our grandchildren were young, Marjorie and I bought three Shetland mares and their foals on impulse, even though we knew Shetlands are generally too difficult for children to handle easily. It was a brief experiment, but all of our grandchildren were offered this and other opportunities to learn to ride. Tom's daughter Corinne was one who really enjoyed riding. (DCD)

Ronald Reagan and I first met each other at a 1968 Republican governors'
conference in Palm Springs, California. I came to admire and respect him enor-
mously and urged him to run for president as early as 1972. We both laugh now
at his answer: "I'm too old." But politics is only one of our mutual interests. We
both love horses, too. (DCD)

George Aiken got the short avenue to the west of the statehouse and I got the short avenue to the east. Governor Davis Avenue was dedicated by Governor Madeleine Kunin in July 1988. Marjorie and Tom attended the ceremony with me and were present for the unveiling of my street sign. (courtesy of Craig Line)

In the years since I retired, I have been approached by many people—mostly students, journalists, and potential office seekers—for interviews. In the summer of 1989, I was photographed in the stable behind my house for a public television series by Chris Graff on Vermont's six living former governors. (courtesy of Vermont Educational Television)

I think every governor has a different job to do. The job depends upon the needs and conditions prevailing at the time. Often when the going was rough on the campaign trail, I paused to consider whether the struggle was worth the gain. But when I left office I had the strongest feeling ever that it had been worthwhile. Eminently so. (DCD)

After the speech some of the protesters invited me to come over to one of the college buildings near the chapel, where they wanted to talk with me. When I got there, I found about fifty students waiting, including those who had been protesting in the chapel. We all sat around on the floor for an hour and a half discussing their concerns.

The meeting at Middlebury was notable because the questions raised there were searching ones and pretty much covered the gamut of the issues large and small that concerned the protest movement of the times. I tried hard to answer those questions. I acknowledged the existence of a "generation gap," which I defined as an inability to discuss problems from the same perspective, and confessed that the gap was widening and was probably already even wider than I supposed, despite my efforts to discover bridges for mutual understanding. I illustrated the generation gap in my own case by saying that I had been brought up to believe the people owed a duty to defend their country but that I saw this feeling in few young people today, although I had never met a returning Vietnam war veteran who didn't share my feeling. I wasn't claiming that youth in that day were unpatriotic. To be unpatriotic, they would have had to recognize the rightness of defending the country and then refuse to do so. But the current attitudes made it very difficult for the generations to understand each other. I told them that police action is justified when there is promise of sufficient violence to cause serious injury, but that even in those cases, the decisions were painful and difficult to make. I also said that ROTC made sense to me as a good way to train officers for the nation's civilian army, but that each college had the responsibility to decide whether ROTC was good for it or not.

It was a particularly spirited meeting even for that era, but I was able to walk away at the close of the meeting intact and feeling that I had spoken honestly with the protesters. At a few of the other meetings, some of the protesters became quite belligerent. In spite of the frustration, vehemence, and occasional outright hostility, however, I enjoyed the discussions and argument with the young people—although even today I don't know whether I accomplished anything or not. I would like to believe that giving these young students a forum where they could express themselves and get publicity had the effect of lowering—somewhat, at least—the level of the vehement rhetoric of the times, but who knows?

One of the other heated issues of my first year in office was one that recurs in Vermont and never seems to be permanently resolved. Certainly few Vermont issues have been charged with more emotional content for as long as this one has. It concerns the management of the deer herd. The issue goes back to 1866, when the legislature apparently first undertook deer herd management. Since then, at increasingly shorter intervals, the issue has popped up repeatedly and has had to be dealt with at the highest levels, including the governor's office and the legislature. Vermont may well be the only state in the United States where the issue assumes this importance. It first arose during my administration in 1969, and though it recurred several more times during my four years and absorbed a lot of time and energy, it always seemed to find only temporary solutions.

Stripped to the ultimate simplicity, the question is whether the size and health of the deer herd is best managed by strictly protecting does from hunters or by permitting open season on females and antlerless deer for varying periods of time according to the prevailing conditions of feed on the ranges. According to the wild animal biologists, the best way to maintain the largest herds consistent with food conditions on the deer ranges from year to year is to delegate the authority and responsibility for establishing open season on does and antlerless deer to the Fish and Game Department. An impressive body of scientific and practical evidence supports this conclusion, but a sizable number of deer hunters in Vermont do not agree. They do not believe that open seasons on females can contribute to larger herds, either in the short run or in the long run, and they are valiant defenders of their political point of view. Moreover, they recognize that they have more wallop with a politically sensitive organization like the legislature than they have with the Fish and Game Department and Board. And so the argument waxes and wanes. I have never been very successful when opposing the position of qualified professional scientists on any issue, and consequently I found myself on the side of the professionals, favoring delegation to the Fish and Game Department, under the supervision of the Fish and Game Board. But I was no more successful in finding a permanent solution to the issue than were any of the governors before or after me. The issue still festers.

One of the bright spots for me in the spring of 1969 was a program I inaugurated at the suggestion of Stella Hackel, who was then commissioner of employment security. The number of dropouts from public schools was rising, and we hoped we could somewhat stem the tide. The program was simple. The state Department of Education was keeping a list of the names of the dropouts reported by school principals. Our plan provided that these names would be sent to me by the department, whereupon I would write a personal letter to each former student expressing the state's interest in him or her, pointing out the demonstrated value of a public school education, and encouraging the young man or woman to seek counseling as to the best way to handle whatever problem stood in the way of his or her education. That counseling, the letter would say, was available through the facilities of the Department of Employment Security. I did not try to oversell the idea of going back to school, but I laid great emphasis on the desirability of seeking counseling to help them make the right decision, whether it was going back to school, taking some special outside classes, or seeking employment. Help was available through the same department. I gave them specific information on where to go for counseling and whom to see in their geographical area. I can't say how effective the program was because we had no way of keeping exact statistical records of results, but the letters of appreciation I received from parents and students alike proved that for the times it was of great benefit.

In March I received through the mail the first of several threats on my life. Such threats to governors occur in most states at one time or another. Usually they are the work of crackpots and do not truly represent any real danger. But they are annoying to deal with because the state police, who have responsibility for such situations, never know for sure what kind of person they are dealing with. Sometimes, the state police throw a tight security guard around the governor until the investigation reveals more clearly who and what they are dealing with. I recall taking a horseback ride one Sunday on the road from Montpelier toward East Montpelier Center. After I had turned around and started back, I was puzzled and surprised to meet the governor's car coming toward me. A state trooper had been quietly following me on that ride! Fortunately, I had only four or five of these threats, none of which was serious, during my four years in office.

In May following the adjournment of the legislature, I inaugurated what we called the Statehouse on Wheels. This visitation project was designed to bring the statehouse to the residents of Vermont and to make it easier for people with complaints or problems to communicate directly with those who presumably could do something to help them. Not only or even primarily because of geographical distance, but because of psychological factors, some Vermonters were hesitant to come to Montpelier and seek out those who could help.

We tried it out first in the southern part of the state, which historically has always felt more remote from the statehouse and from state government in general. We went on three successive days to Rutland, Brattleboro, and Bennington. The "statehouse" that went along, in addition to myself, included Al Moulton, assistant to the governor; Harvey Scribner, commissioner of education; John Gray, commissioner of highways; John Wackerman, commissioner of welfare; Lawrence Wright, commissioner of taxes; Robert Wilson, commissioner of development; Joseph Newlin, an assistant in the governor's office; and occasionally the newly elected attorney general, James Jeffords.

The meetings were widely publicized in each town or city and were usually held in a building used by local government. They were set up in such a way that each of us had a special room in which to meet with the people so that the discussions were private. Wherever we went we found a sizable number of people waiting to see us. Most were waiting to see me, usually because they just didn't know which official had jurisdiction over their problem, but after a few words of explanation, encouragement, or introduction, I could usually refer them to the particular commissioner who could best serve them. In this way I could handle from thirty-five to forty-five interviews a day and still squeeze in a luncheon or some other kind of appearance where I had a speech to give.

Most of the discussions at these meetings were quite serious, but occasionally a bit of humor would creep in. I remember one farmer who called on us while we were in White River Junction. He vociferously denounced snowmobiles, both in general and in particular, and complained bitterly that snowmobiles running with their mufflers wide open woke him up in the middle of the night. I listened patiently, then explained that this was a matter for the state's attorney of his county, who would decide whether sufficient cause existed to prosecute the offending parties. The farmer thanked me profusely and left, but as he reached the door, he turned. A broad smile broke out on his face and he said, "Governor, before I leave, I just want you to know that when Mother and I can afford it, we're going to have one of those contraptions."

On the southern tour we saw selectmen of local townships, retail operators, people concerned with highways in their own area, and social action people, among many others. We decided quickly that the visits were sufficiently successful to warrant taking the State-house on Wheels to the northern part of the state as well, which we did in August. There we visited Newport, St. Johnsbury, and St. Albans. While the kinds of problems we encountered there were often different, our general method of handling the meetings was the same as in the southern part of the state.

One of the questions that students often brought up at these meetings was whether a student should be elected or appointed to the board of trustees at the University of Vermont, since it was a state-supported institution. I had misgivings about this because I felt it might be more conducive to increasing rather than diminishing conflict, but this did not make me hesitate about answering questions on this subject. I said that I thought students should have free access to present their points of view to the board at any and all reasonable time and that it was reasonable for students to elect a representative to express their viewpoints from time to time. But my own view of human nature is such that I thought that electing a student to the board would eventually be followed by a demand that more students be elected so that their voice would be louder. This point of view may have been a symptom of my age and conservatism, but I was not swayed by anything I heard then.

I was also often questioned during this period about aid to parochial schools. Clear evidence existed that some of the parochial schools were having a hard time financially. Some had already closed, and it looked as though others might. So I answered these questions by saying that if we could handle the legal barriers to such action, I would be in favor of giving financial aid to parochial schools. I received many letters from Vermonters criticizing this stand, including some from old and dear friends, but I still think it was a logical and reasonable point of view. The practical situation is that the responsibility for furnishing elementary and secondary education is the responsibility of the state, and where parochial schools exist, the taxpayers are getting a free ride so far as the cost of educating those attending them. I understand and wholeheartedly agree with the constitutional doctrine providing for separation of church and state, but I think we have carried the interpretation of that clause to unreasonable conclusions, and this is one of the areas that I think supports my view. Another is the recent judicial interpretation relating to prayer in schools.

All of us who participated in these visitations felt they were a success. We learned a lot, met many interesting people, and indeed were able in many cases to do something about the problems with which we were presented. Certainly, the people whom we were able to help thought they were worthwhile.

Only the press was never quite sure what to make of these visits. We repeatedly insisted that our motive was not political, and it was not. But the fact is that every time we were able to help someone resolve a specific problem, I did gain a political advantage regardless of the continuing simmering statewide troubles over schools, highways, welfare, and the sales tax. It can be argued, of course, that anything a governor does is political, but it is also true that the best way to be political is to do things that help people. In any event, these visits did give me what the *Rutland Herald* called "an immense political boost."

In the latter part of June 1969 I persuaded the cast of Up With People to come to Vermont and give one of its widely known and greatly admired concerts. I had become interested in Up With People through my grandson, Thomas Calcagni, who had been a member of the cast at one time and who with his wife, Stephanie, had later served with the administrative staff, traveling extensively around the country arranging concerts. The organization intrigued me for several reasons, the most important of which was that the cast members, recruited from all socio-economic levels and different ethnic and national backgrounds, were lively, handsome, vital, and enthusiastic young people who demonstrated through their abilities that they had the power to lift people up by communicating the up-beat side of life in this world. Everywhere the program traveled, it picked up recruits.

The concert took place on June 25 at the Barre Auditorium, which was larger and better equipped for voice renditions than was any hall available in Montpelier. Twenty-five hundred people attended, filling the hall to capacity. The concert was a whopping success, and I was greatly pleased with the enthusiastic reception that the performance received. I was particularly pleased because I thought that the enthusiasm and spirit of these young Americans demonstrated that we could expect to look forward to a happy solution to many of the nation's problems.

One problem in Vermont in particular forced itself upon me throughout the winter and early spring of 1969 with an insistence that could not be ignored. This was the problem of poorly planned development, particularly in the southern part of the state. By mid-spring, it had reached a proportion that presented a true emergency.

In May, I decided that we could no longer put off the attempt to solve the sticky problem. I reached this conclusion only after much study and soul-searching. The heavy vacation home and commercial construction in southern Vermont was threatening our environment and alarmed a large number of people in the state. I made several trips to Windham County, where the danger was most evident, and visited the towns of Wilmington, Dover, Stratton, and others to see firsthand what was going on. I talked with many people who had varying points of view, from planners to town officials to bankers to realtors to developers to legislators to other concerned citizens.

During this period the nature of the emergency was underscored by an incident unfolding in the Town of Stratton. There it became public knowledge that the International Paper Company (IPC), through one of its subsidiaries, was about to construct fourteen hundred recreational homes on a huge tract of land the company owned. Workmen were already busy bulldozing roads, cutting trees, and doing other preliminary work. At the time Vermont had no law on the books or any other clear legal means to prevent this action. The town was up in arms, as were many other towns around the state that had become interested and active in environmental protection.

What could I do? What should I do? I decided to go directly to headquarters. I called Ed Hinman, president of IPC, and asked him to come to Montpelier with such number of his associates as he cared to bring for the purpose of discussing this development. I had some difficulty in locating him by telephone but finally reached him in a remote Canadian village, where he was on a fishing trip. I was grateful for the promptness of his action. He came to Montpelier with five of his top associate officers. I told him as courteously as possible but in no uncertain terms that Vermont would not stand for a development of this size in such a small town because of the effect upon the environment and the quality of life in the state. I must give great credit to President Hinman and his associates for the manner in which they received this ultimatum. After an afternoon's discussion, the president and his associates withdrew to hold a meeting of their own, at the conclusion of which President Hinman came back to my office and told me that the company would halt the development until and unless the plans were approved by the State of Vermont. He told me further that IPC would engage a qualified development planner and would not start the development until we were completely satisfied. I drew a long breath of relief. The result was that the development was never restarted during my term of office.

This experience convinced me that speed was essential if we were to prevent large-scale, improper, poorly planned development in Vermont. We had to have new legislation to deal with the problem, but this would be a puzzling and difficult job to accomplish. I fully realized that any proposal to impose adequate development restraints would run squarely up against one of the most fiercely held traditional "rights" of Vermonters—a tradition that had been in force ever since the original pioneers came into Vermont and hacked out homes amid the primeval forests of the region. This was the right to use one's own land as one saw fit. I knew that such legislation could not possibly be passed, much less at the first session, unless somehow we could build widespread public support for the principle as well as for the legislation not only among legislators but among people throughout the state. Moreover, it was clear that we would need the best minds we had available in the planning and legal fields to draw up the proposed legislation. If and when we should wind up with a piece of legislation to propose to the legislature, I wanted it to have not only the appearance but the substance of soundness as well. And I wanted it to hit the problem head-on. In this way we would have something that was politically marketable, while from a strictly practical point of view, we would have a large number of people, strong individuals all, who would fight for their own product. And this is exactly what we set out to do.

To begin with, I set up a statewide citizens' meeting that we called the Vermont Conference on Natural Resources, to be held in the statehouse. It was a technique that Governor Hoff had used before. We sent out invitations to a large number of Vermonters, including those who were known to be inclined to support such legislation as well as those who might be expected to oppose it. We hoped to awaken widespread interest and support by giving the public the facts concerning the danger to our environment, and we hoped to involve as many people as possible in formulating the cure. Barry Commoner, an internationally known environmentalist and expert and activist in the field, was engaged as the principal speaker. He made one of his usual rafter-shaking presentations, after which the conference members broke up into a number of work sessions, each involving a separate component of the total problem. These groups worked hard and long during the day, and by the end of the conference the sentiment was nearly unanimous to request the governor to set up a special commission to hear all the pertinent evidence, to seek the testimony of experts in the field to make recommendations to the governor for action, and to prepare legislation for presentation to the legislature. The sentiment was nearly unanimous that the need for action was so clear that we had to move with speed. The conference participants left with a strong sense of urgency, of being personally involved, and with a determination to push forward to solve the problem. Afterward, they became a vital force in spreading the word, in building support throughout the state, and in supporting the legislation when it was finally drafted. Our own state planning department was hard at work on the problem, and with the help of that staff we were able to recruit Walter Blucher, a land-use planner of national stature who was then living in Arlington, Vermont, to help us. The state planning department also did a superb job of furnishing backup services whenever they were needed, and I shall be eternally grateful to them for their assistance to me personally during this trying and controversial period.

I acted promptly on the recommendations of the conference and on May 18, 1969, issued Executive Order 7, which authorized a Governor's Commission on Environmental Control, to consist of a blue-ribbon group of Vermonters. I appointed seventeen members plus John Hansen, an ex officio member, who was then an assistant attorney general. James Jeffords, the attorney general, also become personally interested and contributed greatly to the work of the commission. The chairman was Representative Arthur Gibb of Weybridge, a former banker and investment counselor, who was well educated and had broad experience in many fields of activity, including an enviable record in the Vermont legislature, both in the House and in the Senate. He was a man of great personal charm and was well known for his judicial and fair-minded temperament. To assist the commission I appointed an advisory board of twenty-nine members, all of whom had excellent records of past achievement and strong credentials. They were knowledgeable in the various sciences and had expertise in environmental work or related fields. They set to work diligently and quickly, conscious of the enormity and urgency of their task.

My appointment of this and several other important study commissions during 1969 prompted some of the press and indeed some of the legislators to ridicule these commissions. This is understandable. In the long history of study commissions, only a small percentage of their reports are ever translated into legislative action, and indeed study commissions have often been used as a way to sweep troubling political questions under the rug. But this need not be so. I had learned by my service on the Little Hoover Commission and on the Committee to Study State Aid to Public School Buildings just how effective study commissions can be when the reports are promptly followed by strong advocacy and support before the legislature and its appropriate committees. I knew that what is too often lacking is a determined effort to follow through with the legislature. So I stuck to my point in spite of the ridicule. The problems we were studying were not routine ones and in some cases necessitated plowing new ground. Moreover, I felt we needed the extra political support that the activity of study commissions furnishes. Their reports and activity in the end provided powerful support as the matters ran the gauntlet of the legislative process.

As 1969 ended, I was able to appraise my one-year, hold-the-line budget and the early results of the sales tax. I was pleased to see that the new revenue from the sales tax was coping adequately with the sharp increase in expenditures that Vermont was experiencing because of commitments the legislature had made in previous years. In fact, the sales tax was bringing in revenue faster than I had projected. As a result, the state would have some surplus to apply toward the deficit of the last few years. All in all, I found Vermont to be in a position at the beginning of 1970 where I could report to the legislature that the fiscal program was working. Vermont was now in a position to face up to new programs crying for attention.

In preparing my message for the opening of the legislature in 1970, I was aware that an unusually large number of issues needed to be addressed. Among those were state aid to education, housing, pay increases for state employees, the relationship between the state and the cities and towns, and law enforcement. The recently revised formula for computing aid to education was causing critical problems, both politically and fiscally, for many of the state's school systems. The Vermont Housing Planning Commission, which I had appointed a year earlier to study the barriers to affordable housing, was now ready to make specific suggestions to solve some of the problems it had uncovered. State employees were clamoring for pay increases, and rightly so—their recent raises had not kept pace with the rapidly rising rate of inflation or with pay levels in the private sector. In law enforcement it was clear that necessary facilities were badly needed to provide adequate communication among state police officers, county sheriffs, and town and city police officers. This inadequacy was seriously hindering law enforcement officers in their ability to address a 42 percent rise in major crime in the state in the previous year alone.

I made recommendations in each of those areas, but I chose to focus attention in my address on four other major areas of concern. Each was a complex issue. It was apparent that it would be impossible in a single "State of the State" address to give these issues the attention they deserved without overwhelming the legislators with detail. Moreover, the length of such an address would stretch beyond the limits of a normal attention span. Consequently, I arranged with the leadership of the legislature to deliver my address on four separate days in early January. Thus it was possible for me to cover the subjects much more thoroughly in an atmosphere that was conducive to attracting closer attention by the legislators on each separate subject. As far as I know, this was the first time any such procedure had been used by any governor of Vermont.

In my first message to the joint assembly, I discussed how Vermont was proceeding in its efforts to eliminate poverty. I pointed out to the legislature that Vermont, in comparison with her sister states, did indeed stand tall in showing a willingness to support social welfare programs, and that during the next fiscal year, the state would have available approximately $40 million in state and federal funds to fight hunger and poverty. This compared with approximately $20 million that had been spent two fiscal years earlier, when the state had begun to implement its new welfare system. The real challenge, I told them, was whether we had the discipline to make sure these monies were being used for those in real need who were unable to provide for themselves. I saw no need to change the 1967 Social Welfare Act. The philosophy of helping those in proven need was embodied in the act, I said, and it was a worthy goal from which Vermont should not retreat. But at that time in Vermont, as in most every other state in the nation, critics of state welfare operations were complaining about inefficient use of funds and wasteful policies. I reported that during my first months in office, I had received hundreds of complaints from citizens who, in one way or another, had criticisms of the system. I told the legislature that I felt, therefore, that it was incumbent on me to heed those complaints and to undertake a thorough investigation of the operations of the welfare department.

My second message addressed Vermont's concern about its environment. In introducing the topic I pointed out that environmental issues were becoming increasingly important not just in Vermont but around the country. People were beginning to realize that humans are indeed an inescapable part of the intricate system of life and growth that begins with air, soil, and water, and that includes myriad forms of life and activity upon which we are all mutually dependent. I referred to the Environmental Institute at Ripton, Vermont, which a year earlier I had persuaded the New England governors of the New England Regional Commission to fund with federal funds. This was an educational facility where teachers would be taught the basics of ecology and related subjects so that they, in turn, could teach the young. I announced that the institute would open for business during the coming summer. I then made precise recommendations for legislation to control land use in the fragile higher elevations; to restrict pesticides; to control water quality in the state's lakes, ponds, rivers, and streams; to regulate mobile homes; and, most important, to control land development.

I devoted my third message to the issue of reorganizing the administrative branch of state government. My ideas stemmed from my two years as chairman of the Little Hoover Commission, known officially as the Commission to Study State Government, which in 1959 had made 135 recommendations for ways in which state government could be streamlined and made more efficient. Although many of the recommendations had been adopted in the decade since and had proven themselves, more could still be done. My current concern was that the total cost of state government had grown from $60 million in 1960 to $225 million in 1970; that the number of state programs had grown from 150 to 275 in the same period; and that the number of state employees had grown from 3,500 to more than 6,000 during that decade. My proposals were to bring the staff operating those 275 programs into eight different agencies, grouped according to similarity of operations or other relationship to each other, with a secretary at the head of each agency. Furthermore, separate boards and commissions would be brought within some department for budgetary purposes. This would provide a clear line of authority and responsibility running from the governor down through each of the component parts. It would narrow the span of control to approximately eight people and make it possible for the first time in Vermont for a governor to have a true cabinet. Proposals such as mine had been tested successfully in other states, and I believed it was time to give Vermont's government a chance to govern.

My fourth and final message, on January 15, was my budget message. Budget messages have a special capacity to be boring. Of

255

necessity they must be full of figures, and figures do not lend themselves to oratory. Legislators usually listen with more politeness and patience than real interest, but budgets are a very necessary part of the whole management of government and hence must engage the attention of both governors and legislators if good government is to prevail.

I must say, however, that it was a much more enjoyable task in 1970 to present the budget than it had been the year before. The legislature and I, working together, had passed the sales tax and had held the line on increases in expenditures during the previous year. This had put the state back on a financial track that allowed it to pay its bills, to live up to its promises to education and to welfare recipients, and to start paying off the deficit that my administration had inherited. Moreover, the economy was performing well; revenue from the sales tax was more than we had expected.

The budget I proposed for fiscal 1971, based on anticipated revenue, was $109 million—$12 million less than requested by the state's departments and agencies, but still the second largest increase in the state's history. The reason for the dramatic jump was not hard to find. Inflation was partly to blame. More significant, the legislature in the 1960s had committed the state to a broad range of social services, the costs of which were only now coming home to us. I told the legislature that I had heard suggestions that Vermont should abolish its sales tax, and that I was sure bills would be introduced for that purpose, but I also said that I was sure no one who spent any time studying the figures would reconsider that issue.

All the newspapers in the state treated my extended message kindly, but I still had my critics. In the weeks ahead, my proposals to reorganize the administrative branch of government, for example, were bitterly fought by department personnel fearful of losing their "turf." The hue and cry was raised that I was trying to interpose another level of government. This opposition should not have surprised anyone, and it didn't surprise me. One has to view these proposals in the perspective of the state's history. At the time when our state constitution was adopted, there was widespread acceptance of a principle that runs directly contrary to the principle of centralization. The principle was brought here by the passengers on the *Mayflower* and was based on their experience in Great Britain, where, as had happened in many other countries, a centralized government had abused power. As a result of that experience, the founders of our country were guided by the principle that wherever power is given to an individual, it should be offset with power to someone else who can circumvent the exercise of that power. Their concern was not efficiency but freedom, and they had seen centralization as a threat to freedom.

But my critics failed to take into account that conditions had changed since the eighteenth century. The tremendous intrusion of government, both state and federal, into the affairs of people calls for quite a different kind of government if government is going to be able to govern at all. Citizens had long since repudiated the principle of noncentralization by asking their governments to take responsibility for many affairs that had once been the responsibility of private citizens. One need only look at the growth of government programs in Vermont in the 1960s to see how willingly Vermonters had centralized their government. Furthermore, these critics failed to take into account the very practical benefits that would result from the creation of these new "superagencies." Good government does not just flow from good organization. It depends upon good people. But even good people—indeed, the best people—cannot function effectively in these modern times without adequate and workable organization. During the first three months of the legislative session, I spent a lot of time answering these critics and pushing for my organizational proposals.

I also had my hands full with the investigation into welfare abuse. The complaints that had prompted me to call for an investigation had either to be proven or disproven, I felt, if the system was to work for the benefit of both the state and the deserving recipients. Otherwise, bad feeling was bound to increase. Accordingly, I asked William French, head of the Department of Administration, to undertake the comprehensive review that I had proposed to the legislature. To assist him, I appointed a bipartisan committee of Vermonters that included some of the seasoned legislators. In the course of that investigation, Mr. French, with my approval, engaged the Pinkerton Agency to make some of the checks that were carried out. The Pinkerton Agency was an acknowledged expert in the field, and I had every confidence in its thoroughness and discretion. However, some of the organizations for the poor took vehement exception to this investigation and branded me as an enemy of the poor. Their vehemence and even their conclusions surprised me. I felt, and had so stated at every opportunity, that the state should not be niggardly with the truly needy but that it should forcefully resist all forms of cheating. In light of this and in spite of the opposition, therefore, I felt the investigation must go on and be completed. And it was. It was carried out fairly and efficiently, and although it did not uncover a large number of abuses, it served its purpose well, which was to discover whether there were abuses.

And there were some. We discovered, for example, that hippies living in large groups in various places around the state were entitled to food stamps if they ate at a shared table because this arrangement qualified their commune to be considered by the federal government as a "family." For an outlay of three dollars, they were receiving $626 worth of food stamps. As a result, we established in Vermont a policy that a welfare recipient must have a bona-fide residence in the state and live in an abode that is adequate for year-round living. Many of the hippies of that time came into Vermont in the summer but went south before the snow fell. The purpose of the new regulation was to eliminate from welfare and food stamps any groups that came to Vermont in large numbers in the summer, lived in old broken-down buses, abandoned houses and barns, tents and ramshackle tarpaper shacks, then hitchhiked back to the Sun Belt when cold weather came. This regulation and others to prevent abuse were implemented as the result of the investigation and raised another whole storm of protest among certain groups. This may have hurt me politically, but I don't know. I suspect that it helped me as much as it hurt. I do know that after the report was made public, reports of welfare abuse slowed to almost none. At the very least, the investigation appeared to assure most people that the system was running as well as it could.

One major program grew out of a theme I had not emphasized in my annual message but could have. Certainly, it addressed a major need. This was the creation of the Vermont Municipal Bond Bank as a separate authority to help the state's towns and cities finance their bond issues at reasonable rates. The need at the time for such a bond bank was acute. Conventional banks were overloaded with municipal borrowings, and towns were finding it increasingly difficult and costly to finance their own operations, especially the large number of new schools. Obviously what was needed for all towns large and small was ready access to the national money markets on terms reflecting high credit ratings. As governor, I wanted the state to help, but I hoped we could do so without significant strain on the state budget. Peter Giuliani, who was then chairman of the ways and means committee and a seasoned legislator, came up with the ideal plan. He also spearheaded the architecture of the plan, and the resulting legislation was passed during the 1970 legislative session.

The solution was to create an independent state agency whose function would be to acquire and consolidate diverse individual town bond issues and fund the consolidated debt by issuance of bonds sold in the larger amounts. These have greater interest for the large financial institutions in the national capital market. The first of its kind in the country, the Vermont Municipal Bond Bank a year later liquidated the existing crisis with its first issue. In the years since, the bond bank has processed issues aggregating more than $300 million, saved Vermont towns and school districts substantial amounts of interest, not recorded a single loss, and not cost the state's general fund a single penny.

Without question, however, it was environmental issues that preoccupied my time and interest throughout the 1970 legislative session. Over the previous ten months, the Governor's Commission on Environmental Control had met fifteen times with the advisory members. John Hansen, the assistant attorney general who served ex officio on the commission, was extremely active studying and researching the legal phases of the various proposals and led in the actual drafting of the bills that were forthcoming. Attorney General Jeffords was also much interested in the commission's work, volunteering his own time and the strength of his office to help develop the legislation. The commission finally issued its first report January 19, 1970, less than two weeks after my special environmental message to the legislature.

During the remainder of January, all of February, and the early part of March, I spent a lot of time both behind the scenes and publicly pushing for the environmental bills and the government reorganization bills. I had hoped to get action on some of the reorganization proposals at the first session, but I was absolutely determined to get my environmental bills passed, the most important of which were Act 250 and Act 252. I feared that we would lose momentum on the environmental legislation if we did not make substantial progress in 1970. I let it be known that I would call for an extension of the legislative session if necessary, and in my mind I had determined that if the legislature failed to pass the bills, I would call a special session solely for that purpose.

Three weeks before the end of the session, action had been taken on only two bills. One had passed the House and one the Senate. Opponents were having much success in setting up roadblocks, and in addition to the central acts of 250 and 252, bills were languishing that would limit pesticide use, restrict development at elevations higher than twenty-five hundred feet, and create zoning for floodplains and lake shores. The principal opposition came from lawyers representing developers and from conservatives who labeled Act 250 as "statewide zoning." Consequently, for the remainder of the session, I put all the steam I could behind the passage of the whole package of my environmental legislation.

Just before the legislature adjourned, I had to deal with the problem of an oil spill in Lake Champlain. At first I thought it was a political nuisance, but later I changed my mind and saw it as a fortunate political circumstance. The spill had been discovered in early March just offshore from Burlington. I did not hear about it until early April, when I immediately asked the Highway Department to send a crew to make a close inspection and to investigate. Its report disclosed that the spill, which had been caused by a minuscule leak in one of the tanks of an oil distributor located onshore, now involved about ten acres of the lake. At first I had some trouble persuading the oil distributor to cooperate, but when I announced that unless the oil distributor cleaned it up immediately, I would ask the Highway Department to do the job and bill the distributor, cooperation immediately ensued. This instance was significant because it showed that my water pollution bill, which had just been passed by the legislature, could and would work.

My work with the legislature was briefly interrupted when I flew to California to participate on national television in the program *The Governor and J.J.* The program portrayed a fictional governor facing the problems a governor faces while in office, and it starred the popular actor Dan Daley as the governor. To add an additional touch of interest, the writers occasionally invited a genuine governor to participate by staging a short visit between the real and the fictional governors. I received a call from the network inviting me to appear on the show. I found out later that Nancy Reynolds, Governor Ronald Reagan's secretary, had suggested my name to the network. At first I was a bit reluctant to accept because of my responsibilities at the legislature in its closing days, but I asked for a day to think it over. Finally I accepted, having been persuaded by the popularity of the program and its tremendous audience. I thought I could get some real publicity for Vermont.

The network sent me a script, which I memorized, but when I arrived I had a feeling that I would do much better if I could speak extemporaneously, as I have never been comfortable speaking from manuscript or from memory. As soon as I arrived, I went to the office and talked with the assistant director of the show and asked permission to extemporize. The answer was no. But a bit later I went to the barbershop for a haircut, and there in the chair next to me was Dan Daley. I introduced myself, and during our discussion I told him of my request, which the assistant director had turned down. He replied, "You go ahead and do it your way. Just don't say anything to anybody." So that was the way I did it, and it came off fine. In this manner I was able to talk about Vermont, its beauties, its economy, and its skiing. The newspapers had carried news accounts of my forthcoming appearance, so we had a large Vermont audience that night as well as an excellent national audience.

My grandson Thomas Calcagni was in California at the time working for Up With People, and he came to the hotel and stayed overnight with me and watched the show. When I returned to Vermont the next day, having flown seven thousand miles in order to be seen on television for five minutes, I found that the legislature had adjourned its evening session to permit the members to watch the program.

Finally, after a truly strenuous session lasting thirteen weeks, the legislature adjourned in the early hours of Sunday morning,

April 15. What an historic session it had turned out to be! Three of the agencies I had recommended in the government reorganization bill had been established. Henceforth, Vermont would have an Environmental Conservation Agency, an Agency of Development and Community Affairs, and a Human Services Agency. In addition, the legislature authorized the creation of the cabinet system, which was a major step in bringing our state administrative branch into the twentieth century. Acts 250 and 252 were enacted, as were a number of associated environmental bills, including one that banned DDT and another that endorsed the stringent Health Department regulations controlling land development. To top it all off, the legislature had passed my recommended budget with only minor changes. Truly, legislation had been passed that would affect the fundamentals of state government and the quality of life in Vermont for the indefinite future. I had reason to be happy, and I was.

With barely time to catch our breath, we held Vermont's first statewide state-sponsored Green Up Day a short three days later on April 18, 1970. As a celebration of the environmental bills just passed, the timing could not have been better, but it was luck, not planning, that led to the happy coincidence. A year earlier, Bob Babcock, Jr., who was then a full-time reporter for the *Burlington Free Press*, had been driving to work in Montpelier from his home in Waterbury when he had become appalled by the devastation resulting along the interstate from the spring runoff and the unsightly litter that had thus been revealed. Upon arriving in Montpelier, he had come to my office and proposed the inauguration of a statewide effort, supported by the state Highway Department and large groups of volunteers, to clean up the highways of the state. I had been immediately intrigued by the idea. It seemed to be just what we needed to excite Vermonters and to focus attention on the environmental movement.

Promptly, I set up a top-caliber steering committee to coordinate this ambitious project. The state highway personnel were enthusiastic, and their enthusiasm quickly spread to other state agencies eager to be involved. As citizens about the state began hearing of the project and offering their services, it became apparent that we had a bear by the tail and that we had better make it a success. Failure would do as much harm as success would do good. We decided not to put on a hastily thrown-together program during the spring of 1969 but to take the necessary time to plan and organize. We set the date for the first Green Up Day to be one year later, on April 18.

At my request, the *Burlington Free Press* gave Bob Babcock a leave of absence to work full time organizing the project. He served as co-chairman of the steering committee with Ted Riehle, Jr., and they and their committee did a masterful job of planning and executing the project. Support came from all over the state and from citizens' groups as diverse as college students, high school students, Girl Scouts, Boy Scouts, 4-H clubs, teachers, and school administrators.

The more we worked and planned, the more excited we all became. When April 18 finally arrived, we were thrilled to see more than seventy thousand Vermonters out on the roads picking up and hauling trash and supervising the action. A large number of them were young people, whose enthusiasm was contagious and whose work was invaluable.

As a measure of safety, we closed the Vermont interstate highway system from 9 A.M. to noon. Each exit and entrance was manned by a Vermont state police officer or a deputy sheriff, a constable, or a member of a local police force to deny access to travelers, to direct them to alternate routes, and to explain to them what was going on. At first some of the travelers were angry or annoyed, but they became immediately cooperative and complimentary when the project was explained to them. A Green Up litterbag and a bit of literature was given to each traveler. Later, we received many letters from people from out of state who had been traveling that day, complimenting the state for the program. During the day I flew over the state highways and some of the town roads in a helicopter, touching down wherever we saw a group of workers on the highway. It was an exciting day for all of us.

The results went far beyond our expectations. Four thousand truckloads, amounting to 20,000 cubic yards of trash, were removed by the Highway Department from the interstate and other state roads. Another 20,000 cubic yards of trash was removed from town roads. Ninety-five percent of the 24,000 miles of interstate and state roads was cleared, and an estimated 75 percent of the 8,300 miles of town roads was cleared.

I believe this was the largest statewide voluntary citizens' effort ever organized in Vermont. It greatly enhanced the pride of Vermonters in their state. It inspired many Vermonters to refrain from thoughtless littering on their highways. It set the stage for continuing cleanup programs that have given Vermont a national reputation for having the cleanest roads in the United States. It also set the stage for the passage of the bottle bill and a long list of other environmental legislation that has earned Vermont a name for itself as a state where its residents care passionately about their land.

17

Once More,
Into The Breach

*The boat ad turned the bitterness of the sales tax
into a laughing matter. It reaffirmed for me a lesson I had learned long ago: Never overlook the
power of humor as a communication medium in
politics or anywhere else. It has the power, at
times, to turn hate into laughter.*

In Vermont, politics emerges early in election years. My campaign
for a second term as governor began in early March 1970, when I
publicly stated my intention to run. I made my decision in spite of
and in contradiction to the decision I had made in late 1968 not to
seek a second term. I had felt at that time, after proposing the enactment of a sales tax, that it and I would be so unpopular that I could
not be reelected.

But by early 1970 my travels around the state had convinced me
that an increasing number of people had finally come to understand
that a sales tax was necessary if Vermont was to operate on a balanced budget. And most thinking people, when the chips are down,
believe a balanced budget is necessary and wise for state government. Also, I wanted to finish reorganizing the administrative
branch of state government.

I made my decision knowing that I had the support of the Vermont Republican Committee, which had endorsed my candidacy

without my knowledge early in 1970. Historically, this was an unusual and highly controversial practice and, I think, on the whole a poor one. I believe that it causes so much resentment among supporters of candidates not endorsed that it is likely to cause a split in the party at general election time.

However, I had also made my decision despite the press's continued reports of my unpopularity. The Democrats, as well as some more liberal and independent-minded Republicans, thought my reported lack of popularity gave them an obvious chance to recover the governorship. As if to prove the press right, candidates soon got in line to oppose me.

Shortly after my informal announcement, Senator Leo O'Brien of Chittenden County announced his candidacy for governor on the Democratic ticket. There were also indications that former lieutenant governor Daley, against whom I had run in 1968, was considering another try. If he chose to run, he would have to face O'Brien in the Democratic primary. But it was well known that former governor Philip Hoff, a strong leader in the Democratic party, favored O'Brien. This seemed to reduce the odds that Daley would run.

Then on March 27, 1970, the *New York Times* reported that Lieutenant Governor Tom Hayes had told its reporter that he would run for governor in the primary against me. The article also stated that Hayes had not decided whether to enter the Democratic or Republican primary or to run as an Independent. The author of the article, the highly regarded R.W. Apple, wrote that "this statehouse struggle is the result, in large measure, of the Republican Party's increasing conservatism in a state where liberal Republicans were once dominant."

This informal but definite announcement that the lieutenant governor would run for governor came as no surprise to me. I had assumed for some time that he would. By April 1970, our personal and political differences went back at least several months.

In October of the previous year, Lieutenant Governor Hayes had spoken at an antiwar rally in Burlington on Moratorium Day. Later, he had flown to Washington to march in the November demonstration organized by the New Mobilization Committee to end the war in Vietnam. I was personally opposed to the Moratorium and to the protest marches but had carefully and purposefully refrained from making them a political issue. I respected the lieutenant governor's opinion and supported his right to speak publicly against the war and to engage in antiwar marches, but I was disappointed that he did not talk it over with me. After all, we had run on the same ticket. I felt that because he was a Republican and had the image of a Republican, as well as the support of Republicans in Vermont, our political destinies were inescapably tied together.

Just two weeks after Hayes made his informal announcement to the *Times,* he formally announced that he would seek the governorship. He also announced that he would run on the Republican ticket. This was a critical political and strategic decision for Hayes to make, and therefore, I imagine, a difficult one. His sympathies by that time seemed to be more in line with Democratic than with Republican philosophy. While political parties as such seem less powerful today than they once were, it is still necessary to have the support of a major political party to win. In any event, waffling in public as to which party you will go with just before entering upon a campaign is not good politics. What usually happens is that you irritate too many in both parties. The better procedure is to make the break and talk about the reasons later.

However, Hayes's declaration finally ended the newspaper speculation as to whether he would run as an Independent, a Democrat, or a Republican. Perhaps a Narramore poll released a few days earlier had convinced him that he would have great difficulty winning as an Independent, but it also showed him, if polls such as this have any validity at all, that he could play a pivotal role in the general election. The poll had reported that if the race were a three-way race, the results would be O'Brien 42.5 percent, Davis 40.3 percent, and Hayes 17.2 percent. If these results came to pass, the election would be thrown into the legislature for resolution because the state constitution leaves the decision up to the legislature in races where no candidate receives a majority of the vote. The Narramore poll also reported that there was a strong anti-Davis sentiment resulting from the sales tax.

I was not disturbed by this poll because I do not think poll results of one town can be extrapolated to represent accurately the sentiment in the state as a whole. Professor Narramore had long defended his poll by arguing that the town of Salisbury was a "bellwether town" that had never been wrong, but that was no longer true after the Davis–Oakes primary contest and the Davis–Daley contest in 1968. Furthermore, I well understood that any poll, no matter how scientific and no matter how valid at the time it is taken, is only an indication of voter preference on the day the poll is taken. I well knew that I would have to campaign hard to overcome the voter resistance caused by the sales tax, but I was confident that once we got the campaign going, I could win over a substantial number of voters who were still unhappy about the sales tax.

During March and April, the newspapers gave considerable space to the Hayes–Davis contest for governor, and by May 1 the campaign was really under way. I had appointed John Nicholls of Barre as manager of my campaign office in the Tavern Hotel in Montpelier, and John Dinse, a well-known and able lawyer in Burlington, had accepted the job as campaign chairman for the 1970 primary campaign. Both of these men had worked actively for me during my primary campaign against Jim Oakes in 1968, John Nicholls as a campaign volunteer and John Dinse as campaign chairman. I thought highly of them both and was happy to have them on board for this, my third campaign fight.

On May 1, the *Times-Argus* carried a long article with a headline that read, DAVIS WRITES HAYES OUT OF THE G.O.P. IN A BURST OF POLITICAL ANGER. This was something of an overstatement for two reasons. First, I couldn't write Hayes out of the party even if I wanted to; moreover, Hayes had pretty much written himself out of the party by his public statements and his own actions. However, the incident that produced the headline occurred at the end of a regular press conference on other matters when a reporter asked me why a poll taken by the Becker Research Company for the Republican State Committee had not been made available to Hayes. The truth was that I did not know why it had not been made available to Hayes. I had had nothing to do with that decision of the Republican State Committee, but if I had been asked, I would have had no objections to its being given to Hayes. In fact, I would have advised it. But I also said that Hayes, in my opinion, was not a Republican, and that any man who leaves his party the way he did and comes back all of a sudden simply to run on the Republican ticket proves the truth of my statement.

Our differences soon became more acute and more public. In

May 1970, while I was in New Mexico attending a governors' conference, five students at Ohio's Kent State University engaged in a mass protest against the war in Vietnam and Cambodia were killed by rifle fire from National Guardsmen. With this tragedy, the fire of the Vietnam protest burst into full flame. In my absence, Lieutenant Governor Hayes, as acting governor, ordered the American flag at the statehouse lowered to half mast. His action brought instant and vehement protests from all over the state. Telegrams and telephone calls by the scores began pouring in to me in Santa Fe. While I believe Lieutenant Governor Hayes sincerely felt that what he was doing was right and also that he was getting pressure from his own constituency, I was convinced that the great majority of Vermonters did not share his perspective on the tragedy. I know that I did not. The only thing to do was to come back to Vermont and restore the flag to full mast, which I did. From then on, no doubt existed but that there was a serious rift between Tom and me.

As the summer wore on Hayes and I engaged in sporadic politicking, but it was not much of a campaign. Both of us made political speeches when invited and statements to the press, attended coffee klatches, and made customary appearances, but there was no real, forceful, organized effort on either side. I purposely left my real campaigning until after the primary, as I always expected to win the Hayes contest.

The most active campaigning was being done in the Democratic primary by O'Brien and Daley. Daley had finally declared himself a candidate for governor in early summer. I had no doubt that O'Brien would win the primary and that he would be a formidable opponent in the general election, but in the meantime, he and Daley were running vigorous campaigns, not so much against each other as against me.

It was partly for this reason that we inaugurated in the middle of July a novel campaign activity called the *Davis Digest*. It was the brainchild of Al Moulton, who was then my special assistant and whose political acumen is inferior to none. The *Digest* was a newsletter that we regularly sent to our campaign workers, to members of local and county Republican committees, and to other centers of influence. Its objectives were to answer, clarify, or deny public statements made by Hayes, O'Brien, or Daley, and to call attention to the accomplishments of the Davis administration up to that time. It was successful on both counts.

As confident as I was, my margin on primary day, September 8, was a big surprise even to me. I finished with nearly 80 percent of the 39,697 votes cast, carrying every county in the state by a substantial margin. Hayes lost in every town in his own county of Addison, including his home town, Middlebury, where the voters gave me a whopping win. I won in every town in my own county of Washington. In the city of Montpelier, where I lived, the vote was 89 percent for Davis and 11 percent for Hayes.

The *Burlington Free Press* called it a "massive defeat," and it was. But in retrospect, it seems to me that the Hayes campaign had weaknesses. First, he ran a campaign almost exclusively against me with no clear affirmative program detailing what he would undertake to do if elected. Second, he ran in the Republican primary after publicly declaring that he might run as an Independent. It was a statement not designed to please longtime, hard-working Republicans. Third, the sales tax had found more friends in the Republican party than in the Democratic party, and he ran against the sales tax.

Of course, I was happy at the outcome of the primary, but I was not jubilant. I had a nagging feeling that there should never have been a contest between Hayes and me, that it was totally unnecessary and totally undesirable from everyone's point of view. I liked Hayes and always had, and I recognized his many talents. Furthermore, I never quite understood why Hayes had made the decision to run. He was too intelligent a man to have been led into that exercise. I suspect he got some bad advice from a few of the working press, with whom he was philosophically attuned and with whom he was collaborating closely at the time.

On the same day that I defeated Hayes, Senator O'Brien easily defeated Daley in the Democratic primary.

Two days after the primary, the *Burlington Free Press* reported that while I was basking in a Republican organization unified behind me, Lieutenant Governor Hayes was considering joining the Democrats. According to the newspaper, Hayes was going to meet with the Democratic leaders and discuss throwing his support to O'Brien in return for any of the political plums that would fall from the tree if O'Brien should win. The report was given some credence on September 16, when at the close of a news conferences Hayes severed his ties with the Vermont Republican party. "It is now obvious," he said, "that there is now no place in the Republican party for a liberal candidate as an active political figure." In the days ahead he did support O'Brien, and several years later, when Tom Salmon became the next Democratic governor, Hayes was appointed a superior court judge.

The O'Brien–Davis campaign was, as I expected, a much more spirited and vigorous affair than the primary campaign. It began with pledges by both candidates to wage a strong campaign, and both candidates lived up to that promise. For my part, I opened this new phase of the campaign the day after the primary at Woodstock at a Republican Unity meeting by saying that "Leo O'Brien was the chief legislative spokesman for the Hoff administration, and if the voters want to go back to the days of record-breaking deficits and uncontrolled spending, they will have a chance to in this election." This was the theme that I intended to pursue in the campaign, and I did. O'Brien, for his part, immediately countered by charging me with "shirking executive responsibility" in connection with welfare. "There is no excuse for this heartless threat to families already struggling with minimal incomes depleted by inflation and recession," he said. It was clear that the portrayal of me as a "heartless" enemy of the poor was to be one of his themes throughout the campaign. Not surprisingly, the sales tax was the other critical issue.

Both parties held early platform conventions, the Democrats on September 12 and the Republicans on September 19. The Republican platform, among other things, promised no new or additional taxes for the coming year, state funding of public education at 40 percent, protection of the environment, and support for equal pay for women. The Democratic platform charged me with "overtaxing the people" and "distorting the state's needs to justify a sales tax." It also labeled the welfare policies of my administration "callous and insensitive" and claimed that the sales tax was archaic and unfair.

The campaign had hardly gotten off the ground when Professor Narramore released figures from a poll that had been taken in Salisbury on August 29. Why these figures had been withheld when the rest of the figures of the poll had been released just before primary day was not explained. The poll showed O'Brien leading me by 68.9

percent to 31 percent. Narramore's release stated that he had checked seven other cities and towns, had adjusted the findings to better reflect the probable statewide results, and in so doing had come up with adjusted figures showing O'Brien leading me by 59.1 percent to 40.9 percent. According to Narramore, "the sales tax is the monkey on the Davis back."

When asked what my reaction was to these figures, I replied, "I don't particularly like the results, but I haven't started fighting yet." O'Brien, naturally cheered by the figures, urged his supporters to keep working.

Meanwhile, while the debate raged on over the state's welfare program and the investigation I had authorized, the commissioner of welfare resigned. The press interpreted Judge Wackerman's resignation as an indication that he was not sympathetic to my position on welfare. That may have been true, but it if was, he never said so to me. What he did say to me was that he had been having health problems and that the pressure of the job was more than he wanted to bear. I could understand that—it was indeed a pressure job. But perhaps he also interpreted our investigation of the welfare department as a criticism of him. It was not and never had been. He had rendered excellent service as a public official, both as a municipal judge and as commissioner of welfare.

For Judge Wackerman's successor I chose Joseph Betit. A former commissioner of welfare in Alaska, he had an enviable record of achievement in that position. Philosophically, Betit was a strong conservative, and this was anathema to the liberals, who used the appointment as gasoline to throw on the fire of the controversy already in progress. Betit did indeed "run a tight ship," but a fair one. And the liberals were not exactly stranded without a voice. A majority of the welfare board to whom the welfare commissioner reported in those days were liberals, so there still were occasions when on controversial matters, a majority of the board would overrule one of Betit's decisions. But apparently this was not enough to satisfy everyone. During the O'Brien campaign, the Organization for the Poor voted to demand from both Senator O'Brien and me a statement as to whether we would fire Betit after the election. Richard Blum, director of Legal Aid, had already demanded Betit's head. O'Brien promptly and wisely, I thought, stated that he would make no committments one way or the other concerning appointments until he was elected. I responded by reaffirming my full support of Betit and stating that as long as I was governor, I would not fire him. I then countered that firm stand by pointing out that my proposed budget for 1971 included a 67 percent increase in expenditures for welfare over the amount budgeted before.

The poor were not my only critics. Labor leadership had long opposed me politically, I suppose because I had been president of National Life for sixteen years and was thus categorized by labor as an employer. It seems impossible for professional labor leaders to view employers as anything but enemies of labor. I have no such bias and never had. During my sixteen years as president of National Life there were two attempts to unionize National Life employees. In each case the campaign never got off the ground, which says something, I think, about the history of National Life's treatment of its employees.

The top labor organization in the state is the Vermont Labor Council, which is made up of delegates from other labor groups from all over the state and functions as the leadership group, recommending candidates for public office to members of the labor unions. It makes these endorsements after inviting the candidates for major office to address the membership of the council. Just why the candidates are invited is not too clear to me because the council's decisions are made long before the meeting. But its influence upon the votes of the membership of labor organizations is nowhere near as great as it pretends. Nevertheless, the council's influence is sufficient so that a candidate would rather have its support than not. In all three of my previous campaigns—the Oakes primary, the 1968 general election, and the Hayes primary—the council had favored my opponents.

So of course, I had no illusions when I received an invitation to appear before the council and speak on September 18. I went not to seek its support but because my refusal to attend would be interpreted as fear. Moreover, it gave me a chance to straighten out some of the misconceptions that are always thrown around in a political campaign.

The newspaper said I received a "chilly" reception, which is an understatement, but the person who introduced me to the group did give me credit for my willingness to make an appearance. I was introduced by then-president of the council Ralph Williams, a truly dedicated labor leader, who said, among other things, that I showed "great courage" for approaching labor even though I was "entering the lion's den without a sword." I replied that Williams probably meant that I was showing more courage than judgment! But I told the members that I came not expecting to receive their support but to make sure everyone understood the difference between my views and those that had been attributed to me. I went on to tell them where I stood on each of the major issues of the campaign. Afterward, I felt well rewarded for the effort that I had made when the *Burlington Free Press* reported that "observers were surprised at the punch in the governor's speech, which has carried the most impact of any he has made in the gubernatorial campaign."

One of the issues that concerned labor and many others in the early fall of 1970 was a housing shortage. O'Brien publicly called upon me "to put moral pressure on the banks" to put more money into the housing mortgage field in an effort to relieve the state's shortage. He unfairly claimed that I had ignored the preliminary report of the Vermont Housing Planning Commission, when in fact I had appointed the commission and supported its thorough work. The report concluded that banks were shying away from home loans because of the Vermont law placing a ceiling of 7.5 percent on home mortgages. At the time, banks in Vermont could get a better return on their customers' deposits outside of the state. I agreed that the ceiling should be lifted, and I had long opposed ceilings on bank rates since all it did was to drive money out of the state when market rates were higher outside than inside Vermont. But I did not believe in teasing banks to do something that I thought a breach of duty on their part. Their duty to their depositors and to their stockholders is to invest their depositors' money at the most advantageous rates. In 1970 that meant investing out of state. Furthermore, I well knew that such a "moral" approach would not amount to anything, and I did not want to be in the position of looking like a political opportunist. So I said so publicly. O'Brien replied, "Whoever first said that Deane Davis cares more about money than he does about people was proven correct again." It was an old and worn theme by now that was probably most effective among those who already believed it.

Leo O'Brien and I also wrangled over the land use tax issue. The "land use tax" was a proposal to tax open land in actual farm production at its use value as farmland rather than at its market value for developers.

The farmers then as now were having a hard time making ends meet. One of the factors contributing to those "hard times" was taxes, which were rising steeply and rapidly due to development in Vermont. Yet it was clear public policy in Vermont that farms should be saved as an important understructure for the economy and to preserve the cultural and social values of farm life and the aesthetic value of the lands. I never believed that having a land use tax would singlehandedly save Vermont's farmland, but I did believe that it was justified under the circumstances and might help farmers who wanted to continue farming. A proposal for a land use tax first came up in 1968, when an act was introduced in the legislature. I was in favor of it then and continued to support it in 1969 and 1970. Several other states had similar legislation with varying results. The bill was highly controversial. I was not saying that those who opposed it either in 1968 or 1970 were necessarily wrong. What I was saying was that O'Brien was inconsistent when in 1970 he claimed to be a firm supporter of the land use tax while in 1968 he had forcefully opposed it. It was only one of the inconsistencies that I pointed to in answering O'Brien's charge that I was guilty of a credibility gap for proposing a sales tax in early 1969 after I had said in late 1968 that I would do so only as a "last resort."

During October, Senator O'Brien attempted to make an issue out of the fact that I did not put more money in the budget for the Development Department. It is true that I had only minimally increased that department's budget, but that was because Vermont needed such large sums of money to finance the education and welfare budgets and because the state was preoccupied with environmental problems at the time. But this issue never got anywhere. After all, long before I was elected governor I had won my spurs in economic development. I had been president of the old Vermont Association and was later one of the founders and first president of the Vermont Chamber of Commerce, which superseded the old Vermont Association. This record was fairly well known. Furthermore, economic development was not a glamorous issue because the majority of Vermonters had little interest in the subject at the time. To those who were interested, I was able to point out that during the first year of my term of office in Vermont, 178 plants had expanded with a value of $30 million. An additional eleven new corporations had come into the state. That value of plant expansions was twice as much as for any previous year on record. The issue soon died. In fact, it never really got born.

There were many other issues and other planks in both the Republican and Democratic platforms, but the campaign was fought largely on the welfare and sales tax issues.

Every event, major or minor, relating to welfare that could even remotely be considered adverse to me was touted by O'Brien as further indication that Davis was a cold-blooded, steel-eyed man with ice in his veins and malice in his heart toward poor people. Even the administrative changes I ordered in the Welfare Department to correct the flaws and loopholes which our investigation had uncovered came under fire.

This type of politics is not new. It has been present almost since the beginning of human history. It is considered smart politics, when the conditions permit, to appeal to the basic human impulse of jealousy. It is an emotion that easily turns to cordial dislike and sometimes to hatred. Even affluent people respond to it as an indication of their essential virtue. Politicians understand this to be a part of the human condition. I understood this and so, of course, did O'Brien.

Looking back to those days, I am convinced now that all that hullabaloo did me as much good as it did harm, probably more. The "war on poverty" is far from being won, and I'm not sure it ever will be. But one thing I am sure of: Welfare can never be satisfactorily measured and distributed by formula alone. A greater element of governmental discretion must be mixed into the distribution process if we are to distribute welfare funds economically and efficiently on the one hand and make the dollars do their utmost at the same time. Fairness has been equated with formula in the past, but welfare cases just don't fall into neat little cubicles. The human element with its infinite variety of differences calls for discretion.

The sales tax was another phony issue, for several reasons. For one thing, the only logical objection to a sales tax is the aspect of its regressivity. That is, unlike the personal income tax, the tax rate does not increase as the tax base of the taxpayer increases. Thus, a sales tax is more of a burden on low-income people who must buy essential items, such as food, in about the same quantity as more affluent people. But that whole argument fades into insignificance when, as in the tax we passed in 1969, food is exempted and progressive refunds are provided for people with low incomes. When I originally proposed the sales tax, I proposed a rate of 4 percent and asked that refunds be provided to anyone earning less than $14,000. The legislature, for reasons the legislators considered good and sufficient, cut the rate to 3 percent, limited the progressive refund feature to those earning no more than $7,000, and increased the personal income tax by a small percentage. By the time of the campaign, more than forty-two thousand people had applied for and received refunds.

Years ago, when sales taxes had no such refund features, labor leaders and many others quite understandably adopted the philosophical position that sales taxes were bad taxes because they were not progressive. Years later, they still stick to that point in spite of the refund feature that now makes that argument illogical.

The sales tax was also a phony issue because its repeal would have made it necessary to raise personal income taxes by 30 to 35 percent, and yet the Vermont income tax was already close to the highest in the nation. Furthermore, to have raised the personal income tax that much would have practically eliminated new or enlarged industry in the state. It has long been shown that a low personal income tax is one of the features that most attracts industry to locate in a place. The best example of that is right here in Vermont's own backyard, where the state of New Hampshire has enjoyed outstanding industrial development in part because it has no state income tax at all. Vermont needs now—as it did then—a modest increase in industry to provide the necessary jobs for a healthy growing economy.

But perhaps the best proof that the sales tax was a phony issue is shown by what has happened in the years since. We have had two Democratic administrations in Vermont since the enactment of the sales tax in 1969. Neither administration has shown the slightest interest in repealing the sales tax. On the contrary, the first Democratic administration to succeed mine, Governor Salmon's, tried to raise the sales tax to 4 percent but failed.

But the sales tax is a hard tax to defend politically because of the myth of regressivity, which has been attached to it for so many years. No governor ever really wants to recommend a sales tax, and I didn't either. Governors, including me, do it only because there is no other way out. That was true in Vermont's case. Today, every state in our union but four has a sales tax. This proves that there must be something good about a sales tax.

Throughout the first part of the campaign I was trying to find a way to explain the sales tax to the people, and I was frustrated because I was not succeeding. It was like shoveling smoke. Most people were either for it or against it—and that was that. The trouble was that I was trying to reach people by using logic. And then two things happened: the boat ad, and Senator O'Brien's use of the phrase "economically feasible."

The boat ad was the brainchild of a young man in Wellesley, Massachusetts, named Sam Miller, who had a small advertising business of his own. He did contract work with the Becker Research Company, the well-known polling firm. Miller, in his twenties, was an unusually capable, perceptive, and imaginative person, and a very high-minded young man, too. When he was asked to help us with some ideas on communication, he explained that he only accepted retainers in political campaigns after he was convinced that the candidate truly merited election.

"How do you determine that?" he was asked.

"In several ways, but principally by spending time with the candidate in his usual routine," he replied.

So it was agreed that he would follow me for one whole day. And he did. It included my usual daily activity in the office, on the campaign trail, and at home. I even let him feed the horses with me. At the end of the day, sitting outside with me before dinner and talking, he agreed to work with us. I still don't know how I passed the test, but because of Sam Miller's creativity, the boat ad was born.

The boat ad was a television commercial in which I am pictured in a small, ancient rowboat bearing the word *Vermont* in large letters on its stern. The boat is in Lake Champlain in South Hero. I am wearing old jeans, a western jacket, a sloppy western hat, and western boots, the garb I customarily wear around the stable. The boat is half full of water, and I am standing knee-deep in it, furiously bailing the water with a bucket and tossing it over the gunwales into the lake. For what seems like a long time but is only a few seconds, only the sound of the sloshing of the water is audible. But that sound is enough to let people view the scene and consider its significance before the voice comes on. Then the voice of an actor overrides the visual scene, explaining that Governor Davis didn't want to impose a sales tax but had to in order to provide the necessary funds to give adequate aid to education, to care for the poor, to support our police system, and so on.

The ad was unlike anything I had ever done before. Marjorie had misgivings about having me appear on television in clothes that were decidedly ungubernatorial. I was exhausted by the filming. At one point the cameraman and producer launched into a long discussion about some technical points of the filming and neglected to tell me that the camera had stopped. I bailed vigorously until I was ready to drop. Over the course of that day, I'll bet half the water of Lake Champlain came in through that dinghy's holes and was pitched back over the gunwales.

We first saw the ad at a private viewing on Sunday morning at WCAX-TV in Burlington. Marjorie thought it lacked dignity. I thought it was just plain corny. But after several of my advisers argued strongly that the ad vividly portrayed why the sales tax was necessary, I agreed to put the ad on the air. The decision was made to air the commercial later that day during WCAX's popular interview show, *You Can Quote Me.*

This ad was an instant success. Almost immediately the telephones starting ringing in the office and at home. Half of the callers thought the ad was wonderful and half thought it was terrible. But the inescapable fact was that *everybody* was watching it, and in one way or another it was communicating with Vermonters at all levels. The truth of this came the very next day when I was campaigning in St. Albans. As I was walking up the city's broad main street, a tall, lanky Franklin County farmer waved from the other side of the street with a hearty, "Atta boy, Governor. Keep bailing!"

It even touched children. A woman in St. Johnsbury wrote to me while the ad was running and told me that one evening while she was babysitting for her four-year-old grandson, he had run in from the other room where he was watching television.

"Granny, Granny, we've got to help Deane Davis," he had cried.

"We have?" his grandmother asked. "Why?"

"His budget is leaking," the concerned child replied.

Years later, people still remember that ad. Not long ago, I went into a Montpelier hardware store to buy an inconsequential item and came to the cashier's desk to pay for it. When I had paid for the item, the young lady at the cash register asked with a mischievous look in her eyes, "Governor, did that boat ever sink?" We chatted about how she knew of the ad, and she told me that she had watched the ad every night it was shown. She appeared to be about twenty-five years old, and if that is correct, she would have been only ten years old at the time she was watching it.

Several experts have since told me that the boat ad was the most effective television ad in the history of Vermont politics. I have also been told that it was used in Great Britain in an hourlong commentary on American politics. I don't know whether either claim is true, but I do know its message was clear: I needed the sales tax to keep Vermont afloat.

The boat ad turned the bitterness of the sales tax into a laughing matter. It reaffirmed for me a lesson I had learned long ago: Never overlook the power of humor as a communication medium in politics or anywhere else. It has the power, at times, to turn hate to laughter. I've seen it in the courtroom many times. Before this ad, universally in Vermont, when people were purchasing items that were subject to tax, the cashier would quote the price and then say, "plus fifty-six cents for Deane." These remarks subsided after the ad began running. They did not disappear, of course, but the ad brought about a marked change in the frequency with which they were uttered. People were now seeing the tax in a new perspective.

Practically upon the heels of the boat ad came a second incident that dealt another blow to the anti-sales tax argument. Throughout the first part of the campaign, I had been earnestly striving to get Senator O'Brien to categorically say whether he would recommend a repeal of the sales tax if he were elected. Obviously, if the sales tax was a bad tax, it should be repealed. But O'Brien always dodged the question, usually by further discussing how bad the tax was. I could not seem to get him to make a square-toed answer, and I needed a yes or no, because either way he would be vulnerable to follow-up questions. If he answered yes, he would have to indicate how he would provide the money for extra aid to education, to support welfare, and to fund other major items in the budget. If he answered no, then he would destroy the logic of his case and point up the insincerity behind his opposition to the tax. The bald truth was that the Democrats liked the sales tax and never repealed it even when they were in a position to do so. But the Democrats didn't want to be politically blamed. I didn't want to be blamed, either, but I could see no solution without it. Naturally, because I had been forced to make a commitment, I wanted O'Brien to make one too.

Around the middle of October we both appeared on the same platform at a political meeting in Essex Junction. Again I pressed him for a yes or no answer. As usual, O'Brien tried to talk about other things. I was unusually persistent and kept asking him for an answer. The audience caught on to his hedging, and a group of students began chanting, "Answer him, answer him, answer him!" Finally, to avoid giving a direct answer, he replied that he would recommend the repeal of the sales tax "when it became economically feasible." I thanked him for his answer and turned to the audience to say, "I want you all to know that I intend to recommend repeal of all taxes—when it becomes economically feasible." The audience howled. Everyone had caught the ridiculousness of O'Brien's answer. Thereafter, whenever Senator O'Brien and I were on the same platform, I told the audience that he had promised to recommend the repeal of the sales tax as soon as it became "economically feasible" and that I intended to recommend repeal of all taxes—when it became economically feasible. This always brought a laugh, and I never saw another audience that didn't grasp the significance of the situation. Vermonters now knew that the sales tax was inevitable and that there was no other choice. Now everyone could put into correct perspective and meaning my words "last resort," which I had used in 1968 and which had dogged my footsteps for so long. Vermonters knew that 1969 was the last resort. "Last" had never meant in point of time, it had always meant in point of fact.

During the latter part of October, editorial endorsements of me began to come in. Naturally, I was glad to receive them. This list was longer than I expected, but every one of them was deeply appreciated. Those that I can remember include the *Burlington Free Press*, the *Rutland Herald*, the *Times-Argus*, the *Vermont Sunday News*, the *Valley News*, the *Newport Express*, the *Caledonia Record*, and the *Addison Independent*.

Despite this support, as the election came down to the wire the Narramore poll announced that the O'Brien–Davis contest "was too close to call." Actually his figures showed, as he admitted after the election, that O'Brien carried a slight lead over me. In contrast, the Becker Research Company, which had taken several polls for us (none of which were released during the campaign), showed on October 11 that I was leading O'Brien 48 percent to 40 percent, with 12 percent undecided. Naturally, I concluded that the election could go either way. As usual, my supporters gathered early in the evening at the Champlain Room at the Tavern to watch returns as they came in.

The results surprised everyone, including me. I drew twenty thousand votes more than Senator O'Brien and won with a twelve-point lead.

Many newspapers engaged in postmortems to try to explain why an election everyone predicted would be close turned out the way it did. Perhaps the most logical and credible explanation was made by John Becker, president of Becker Research Company. He had taken polls for us and had been under contract to give advice from time to time. Now he pointed out in an interview with the Vermont press that the strong tide of opinion against me had shifted significantly after the boat ad began appearing in September and after O'Brien's "economically feasible" remark in our debate in October. I would certainly agree that those were the two most important events to turn the tide of public opinion.

Several things about the election results pleased me after the grueling six-month campaign. I carried every county in the state, even the city of Burlington, which is heavily Democratic. Also, I carried many towns that were also heavily Democratic. But few things touched me as much as Senator O'Brien's generous concession. During the evening of the election day, Senator O'Brien congratulated me on the result and showed that he was a broad-minded, decent, and indeed magnanimous individual. He issued a formal statement, part of which read,

> I congratulate Governor Davis and pledge my support to him in his second term. We have differences, but we share much in common, in particular a deep love for Vermont and a faith for Vermont's future. Deane Davis is a tough fighter. He served Vermont well and will continue to give to us good sound government. I respect him and I like him personally . . .

I could have said the same things about Senator O'Brien. I respected and liked him personally. He went on to be commissioner of agriculture under Governor Salmon and did a very good job indeed. He is an able man and a good one.

18

The Second Term

*Seventy-one governors had stood before similar
gatherings in Vermont's long history to mark the
end of their administrations. I am sure that each of
them did so with a certain amount of nostalgia
and regret. I was no exception. Yet I had a feeling
of satisfaction, too, for I had accomplished the
principal goals that I had declared during my
campaign for governor.*

After the grueling campaign, Marjorie and I took a ten-day vacation in Florida. We had a happy and relaxing time. There was a beach in front, a heated swimming pool in back, and one of the best trotting-horse racetracks in the South nearby.

While resting in Florida, I had a chance to contemplate how foolish we are in Vermont to stick to the two-year term for governor. Only three of the fifty states retain the two-year term. Residents of the other forty-seven states have decided that requiring a governor to run for reelection every two years makes it practically impossible for him to give his best either to the state's business or to his campaign. Of course, this is also true of a governor running on a four-year term, but at least in those states he is guilty of such neglect only half as often.

When the two-year term was fairly common throughout the country, the job of governor in other states and certainly in Vermont was nowhere near as demanding as it had become by the 1970s. In the past the business of the legislature in Vermont was usually disposed of in a three-month session, and the governor was a full-time governor only while the legislature was in session. The budget was prepared and voted on only once in two years, and the scope of state government was only a fraction of what it has become. Outside the legislative session, governors spent only about one day each week in the governor's office, and very little supervision of the administrative staff was required of them. Those days are long since past and will not return. To perform the governor's job today and run for re-election at the same time requires a person with an iron constitution, inexhaustible energy, and nerves of steel. And even when a governor is possessed of all those characteristics, both the state's business and the campaign cannot help getting shortchanged to some degree. Every former governor with whom I have discussed this issue is strongly in favor of the four-year term.

My second term was quite different from my first. During the first two years the sales tax; Acts 250 and 252 and associated environmental legislation; and the reorganization of the administrative branch with the creation of a cabinet system had dominated the scene. These issues were highly controversial, substantially changed the direction of state government, and were fought valiantly on both sides. A little breathing space was welcomed by all.

The task of putting into effect legislation of this fundamental character does not end with the enactment of the law. It became the task of my executive department to put the machinery and people together to make the laws work. Consequently, a large part of my time and energy for the second two years was spent doing just that.

But during the campaign I had taken some strong positions on a number of issues, and now I felt a duty to present them to the legislature. By the time Marjorie and I returned to Vermont, I had just over six weeks to prepare my legislative program, hold my budget meetings, and make major decisions that would frame the state's budget for the coming year. Much work also had to be done on my administrative reorganization program, which remained one of my priorities and which, because of a bill passed in the previous session of the legislature, put me in a unique position in Vermont history. Now that the reorganization had received legislative approval, I had more power than any governor before me. Within seven weeks I would have the power, as no other Vermont governor had had before me, to hire and fire all department heads as well as the authority to create a second superagency, the Human Services Agency. Moreover, I had the power to submit to the legislature a complete reorganization plan that would take effect automatically as long as it was not rejected by the House or Senate within ninety days.

In the meantime, I had two other matters to attend to. The first set me apart from all the governors who had preceded me in that it involved moving the governor's office out of the statehouse—the historic and symbolic seat of power. The move was necessitated by extensive remodeling and redecorating of the statehouse, but it was also inevitable. The traditional governor's office in the statehouse was most inconvenient for the transaction of business. It consisted of a large room—unnecessarily large—with two tiny adjacent offices. It was designed in the days when the governor's principal job was to be in the statehouse while the legislature was in session or when other ceremonial events were in progress. It did not fill the needs of a governor in modern times who spends fifty-two weeks a year in the office and who has a staff of eight to ten people. All except two of our staff had to be housed in small rooms in the northern wing of the statehouse, a considerable distance from the governor's office. The arrangement was most inconvenient and inefficient. Moreover, the legislature badly needed the space that we were occupying in the north wing for committee rooms.

Irving Bates, director of state buildings, and I discussed new ways to handle the situation. In his usual able and innovative manner, he suggested that I continue to use National Life's former office on Baldwin Street for daily work; that I use the statehouse offices while the legislative sessions were in process and for ceremonial occasions; and that a new office for the governor be constructed on the top floor of the Pavilion for the year-round working office. In the new arrangement, I could have all my personal staff close to me and some of the other departments that work closest to the governor nearby on the same floor. For the first time in the state's history, a distinction would be made between the governor's business and ceremonial offices, but anyone who had ever managed an office would see the wisdom of the new arrangement. Generally, people understood that Vermont was changing and the government had to keep up.

The other matter was nearly two years old and still waiting to be resolved. For all that time, Vermont had been trying to force the International Paper Company to remove approximately three hundred acres of sludge from Lake Champlain near its plant in Ticonderoga, New York. Many people inside as well as outside state government were involved in the struggle, including Attorney General James Jeffords, who took a very active part. Already the sludge had so reduced the oxygen level in the water above it that trout were unable to live. We had valid fears that unless the situation were corrected, it might actually kill the lake. If this happened, it would take many generations for the lake to be brought back. During the past summer, I had arranged a meeting with Governor Nelson Rockefeller of New York and Edward Hinman, president of International Paper Company, who agreed to test removing a small quantity of the sludge to see if it could be pumped without damaging the lake. We thought this would settle the matter, but we were disappointed. IPC took the position that sudden removal might cause ecological damage to the lake. Our engineers said this was nonsense. We appealed to Senator George Aiken for help in trying to convince the U.S. Department of the Interior to step into this case and order the sludge removed. Senator Aiken did his usual masterful job, and on November 19, 1970, Interior Secretary Walter Hickel ordered the state of New York to come up with a detailed plan for the sludge removal within three weeks. Thus Vermont took one more major step along the road of protecting its land, water, air, and total environment.

I also had a pressing personnel problem. William French had been serving as my secretary of administration, but my agreement with him when I recruited him from his job as manager of the Vermont division of the New England Telephone Company was that he would serve only two years, after which he would return to the telephone company to protect his pension. Now I needed to find a replacement. This is probably the second most important job in the state, next only to the governor's. The relationship between the people holding those two positions has to be close and mutually confidential. I turned to Richard Mallary, then of Fairlee, who had an extensive career in the Vermont legislature. He had served as a representative to the House for several terms, had been elected and reelected as Speaker of the House, and had then been elected to the Senate. In the fall of 1970, he had just been reelected as a senator from Orange County. I felt he could serve me in important ways because he understood the state's problems and issues as well as or better than anyone else in the state and he could be relied upon for much day-to-day advice. Also, he would make an excellent emissary between the governor's office and the legislature, whose members had great confidence in him. To my great joy, I was able to persuade him to give up his senatorial seat and accept the job, where he proved to be outstanding.

As I had done before, I broke my 1971 joint message to the legislature into multiple parts in order to cover the topics I wished to address in sufficient detail to make all the important points. Several of the programs and initiatives I wanted to propose were social as well as economic ones.

In the area of welfare, for example, I had discovered on the campaign trail that there was widespread disgruntlement with the rapidly growing incidence of common-law marriages that permitted a wife to continue to receive money from the state for the support of herself and any children she and her former husband may have had even if her new husband was capable of supporting all of them. Consequently, I recommended legislation that would require men living in families receiving welfare to support the whole family. I also recommended that penalties be increased against a husband who deserted his family, that the state be authorized to enforce the order of the divorce court in alimony and child-support payments, and that fines in such cases be paid to the Welfare Department. Finally, I recommended legislation that would require adult children whose parents were receiving welfare to support their parents if their financial situation was adequate to do so. While there were sizable amounts of money involved in these issues, the more important purpose was to try to cut down on these practices themselves, all of which were socially undesirable.

Education also remained an issue. Parochial schools were having a particularly hard time in Vermont. Several had closed, victims primarily of the constitutionally mandated separation of church and state that banned the use of public money to support parochial schools. Now other closings seemed likely. When these schools closed, all the students would be suddenly thrown into the local public schools, putting further stress on the already burdened public system. I have always thought that if a parochial school were certified by the Department of Education, there would be practical advantages to everyone concerned in helping the parochial school rather than risking the closing of the school and the sudden introduction of these children into the public school system. Few towns could afford this full burden. Recent court rulings supported my position and had opened the door to the possibility of some public support of parochial schools. Based on these new interpretations, I recommended that existing law be amended to make it possible for local school districts, if they wished, to provide books, supplies, and transportation to parochial schools.

I also urged an amendment to the property tax rebate program. In 1969 the legislature had enacted legislation providing a modest rebate for low-income senior citizens on their property taxes. Approximately fourteen thousand Vermonters had received refunds in 1970, and the program was working well with only slight effect upon the budget. I recommended that these amounts be increased an average of 50 percent and that partial exemption on Vermont personal income taxes be granted. It was a situation where I felt we could do much for a deserving segment of society with only moderate expenditures.

But the real issue for the 1971 session of the legislature was once again money. The sales tax had made it possible for Vermont to meet its spiraling commitments to public education and welfare, but the pressure for more money for new programs and for the expansion of old programs was relentless. Few people understood the dimensions of this new appetite for money, growth, and improvement, or its basic cause—the rising tide of immigration into Vermont that had started in the early 1960s and that has continued unabated into the 1990s. Prior to this mass immigration, frugality in government had been the prevailing Vermont philosophy.

But these modern immigrants brought with them new attitudes based upon their experiences in the areas whence they came. A large majority of them came from areas of great population density, where a different political attitude and experience prevailed, and where at their insistence state government had taken responsibility for correcting every social problem. It was a philosophy that was possible, even probable, because those areas were much more affluent and taxes came more easily. Now, when problems in those areas grew larger and more difficult to solve, many people sought escape. Along the Atlantic seaboard, Vermont soon became appealing. People were attracted to its open spaces, greening landscape, pastoral beauty, simpler lifestyle, and what seemed like an opportunity to take a greater part in community living. But though these people sought simpler living, they wanted some things that Vermont didn't have: better schools, better roads, better health care, better mental institutions, better airports, a more modern and generous welfare system, better police systems, and many other things. To these people, many aspects of the state's infrastructure seemed inadequate and needed fixing, and of course much of it did. But these people wanted it now. Consequently, state government set about giving it to them. Tax collections were automatically higher. Vermont had no need to pass new taxes. More people brought in more taxes, and a more abundant economy resulted in larger personal incomes. Inflation contributed too. Nothing pleases a politician more than to have more money to spend without having to pass new taxes. In this atmosphere, no wonder we wanted every seemingly good public service from our state government that we saw in other larger states. In our enthusiasm, however, newcomers and old-timers alike sometimes forgot or at least ignored the fundamental fact that Vermont is an extremely small state and that despite rapid and abundant immigration, it is destined to remain that way. This was why in the 1970s, 1980s, and 1990s money has once again become one of the principal problems of Vermont state government. Our reach still exceeds our grasp. The unhappy task I had as governor was to proclaim this doctrine to a legislature that very naturally wanted to see us move ahead to new and higher things.

My budget message was presented on January 21, 1971. By way of prelude I told the legislature that it was a sobering duty to present my message because of the nature of the budget and times. Although the budget had to be an austerity budget, it nevertheless projected the second highest annual increase in revenue in Vermont history. The irony was that the state's needs and demands had grown so fast that it was necessary to have austerity in the midst of reasonable growth.

I outlined the state's per capita expenditures in 1969 and compared them in detail with those of other states in nine major categories. This comparison found us varying between third and sixth highest compared with other states. On a comparative average income basis, Vermont would have finished still higher. We were fifth in taxes in Vermont on a per capital basis, while Vermonters were thirtieth in average income in the nation! Certainly no one could accuse Vermont of shirking its duty to support government or to provide good education for its young people or welfare for its deserving poor!

My budget showed projected revenue for the next year of $119 million, $9 million more than the year before. Budget requests were $138 million. We had only about $9 million more to spend in the next fiscal year, $4 million of which was needed just to take care of things that were beyond our control. That left only $5 million for discretionary spending. I recommended that the legislature stick to my $119 million budget, and I am proud that the legislature adopted that budget almost to the dollar.

One of the bright moments early in my second term was the dedication of the new Pavilion Office Building. The question of what to do with the old Pavilion Hotel had bedeviled me during my first term, and I was glad to see the matter finally and so satisfactorily resolved. The hotel had been built in 1876 on the site of an earlier hotel. Over the years it had been the home of legislators, lobbyists, Supreme Court members and their staff, lawyers practicing before the courts of Montpelier, politicians, distinguished visitors, and just about everyone from out of town who came to the capital city on official or political business. It was an imposing structure, which as Senator Edward Janeway said, "had a shabby gentility that goes with an old building but a dignity and charm that got to you." It came to be called The Lady of State Street.

Long before I took office the fight had started over the building's future, a fight that had gathered momentum and bitterness as time went on. One side wanted to preserve the building. The Pavilion had a rich tradition, probably unequaled by any other building in Montpelier. Opponents wanted to tear it down and erect a modern building on the site. They pointed to its crumbling foundation and deteriorated structure. A majority of experts agreed with the opponents: it was not feasible to try to preserve the building.

I had never taken a public position, but in 1970 I knew that time was running out, and I must decide one way or the other. Politically, whichever way I decided would be wrong, for hundreds of people were lined up on both sides of the issue. Finally, as the cab driver once said, "I decided to throw away principle and do what was right." Before I could make a decision, however, Angelo Pizzagalli came to see me with a proposal. Angelo, one of Vermont's well-known and respected contractors, offered to tear down the building, save all usable materials, and rebuild the structure on the same exterior design as the old hotel. The inside of the hotel would be remodeled with new materials as a modern office building for the use of state officers and departments. I was intrigued at once but wondered about cost. He said he would do the work for a price not in excess of already quoted prices for tearing the building down and erecting a modern building or trying to rehabilitate the old structure. What a relief his offer was. His firm built the building, both sides were completely happy, and Vermont and Montpelier got what it needed: all the charm and tradition of the old structure and a solid new building in addition. Dedication ceremonies were held March 26, 1971, and I had the pleasure of cutting the ribbon.

January 1972 marked the opening of my fourth year in the governor's office. I was quite aware that it would be a different year in several respects, the most significant one being that at some point, probably early in the year, the legislature and even the public would begin to look at me as a lame-duck governor. My muscle with the legislature would show gradual signs of deterioration. This happens to all governors during their final months in office. This did not bother me since my study of the legislative and gubernatorial history and legislative psychology had fully conditioned me to the event, but it suggested to me that I should adjust my program to take into account this approaching alteration in my status.

I also knew that I was not ready to decide whether to seek a third term. The best thing to do, consequently, was to leave the question open, at least until the 1972 legislative session was completed. I answered all questions about running for a third term by saying that I would face the decision in the spring. While it would be natural for many to conclude that at the age of seventy-one I would not seek a third term, they still could not be sure. The consensus was that I could win a third term if I decided to run. Several papers expressed that view. The *Times-Argus* said, "It is acknowledged that if he does choose to run again, Davis will be unbeatable." I don't know whether that was a valid conclusion, but it was helpful to have the experts think so.

All governors pick up a certain amount of so-called "political garbage" as they go along. The longer their term, the more "garbage" they carry, particularly if they propose and support controversial programs and even more particularly if they support them forcefully. I was no exception. The sales tax, the environmental legislation, and the reorganization of state government had all left wounds of greater or lesser severity. They were all controversial, but the sales tax and my welfare position were unusually controversial. Moreover, they were politically sensitive issues, and I had pursued them with vigor, determined to win.

Entering 1972, I decided that my legislative program would be less comprehensive than in any of the three preceding years. It would consist mostly of changes in legislation already enacted or of proposals for things that just had to be done.

Unlike previous years when I had made multiple personal appearances before the legislature at the opening of its session, I made but a single personal appearance at the start of the 1972 session. I even went so far as to file my budget message in writing a week later, on January 13.

For a welcome change, I was able to point out to the legislature that there were clear new signs of improvement in the health of the Vermont economy. The state's fiscal condition had turned the corner during the preceding summer, and the present Vermont indicators enabled my economic advisers to predict a growth rate of 8.5 percent. If valid, this rate of growth assured a substantial growth in revenue during the next fiscal year. I was also able to assure the legislators that Vermont had made substantial progress in the past year in enacting the legislation passed in the past three years. State government was more flexible and responsive to the needs of the public, thanks to the reorganization of the administrative branch. Nowhere was this more evident than in the area of environmental protection.

With considerable pride, I reported on the achievements made by the Agency of Environmental Conservation and the state Environmental Board. The quality of our air was improving, and much progress had been made in the building of sewage treatment plants. In the short time since enactment of Act 252, sewage treatment plants had been begun or were in process in nine communities and twelve industries. Already portions of the Winooski River and other waterways previously unfit for swimming were close to meeting full standards for active recreational use. Nearly one hundred open burning dumps had either been closed or were no longer polluting. Building and other forms of construction going on in the state were of manifestly better quality. Decisions on permit applications were being made with greater dispatch and efficiency. This was, I thought, an excellent start toward implementing Acts 252 and 250.

I reminded the legislature that our planning for the future must not neglect the economy. We had estimated that forty thousand additional jobs would be required in Vermont during the current decade. More than three-quarters of those jobs could be provided by expanding enterprises already operating in the state, and because of this the new Agency of Development and Community Affairs was directing its economic development section toward increasing services to existing businesses. The agency had established a foreign trade counseling service and a link with the federal government contract bidding activities. As a further service the agency was providing engineering and technical assistance to firms having problems with pollution abatement. In addition, the agency was continuing its industrial development efforts, which too had been redirected toward service-oriented industries of high quality, such as peripheral computer products, medical electronics, and pollution abatement equipment, all of which had high potential in the marketplace.

Finally, I shared with the legislature the news that the state's welfare costs had grown from $209 for every household in the state in fiscal 1970 to $354 per household per annum in 1972. This was on a per capita basis, not on an income basis, and was the seventh highest welfare cost in the fifty states, despite heroic efforts on the part of the social welfare department to contain costs. We had established a quality control unit to detect and deter abuse as well as to recover funds owed by absent fathers. It was working well, and we expected to recover soon a quarter of a million dollars, a sum that we estimated would rise to one million dollars per year in the near future.

Compared with some of the news I had had to report in the previous three annual messages, most of this news was good. If the economic rate of growth my economic advisers had predicted for the coming years were achieved, it would be particularly fortunate. The revenue was sorely needed. We were still living in the early 1970s, both in Vermont and in the nation, in an upbeat frame of mind, and all signals were go whenever a good new liberal program was presented.

Moreover, I had my own agenda with which I was eager to move ahead. The times seemed especially right to move ahead aggressively on environmental issues, and I proposed that the legislature take steps to solve the problems caused by nonreturnable containers and strip development. The former was a blight upon the state's landscape and a drain on its highway funds, and the latter was sapping towns and villages of their economic vigor and destroying their integral charm and attraction. I also called for a clarifying amendment to Act 252 that would have held in abeyance the municipal fines prescribed under the "pay to pollute" policy as long as a municipality had on record a plan approved by the Water Resources Department outlining a schedule for taking and completing the steps that would bring it into compliance with the law.

There were three issues that had to be faced without question, however. All were controversial, and all were critical to the state's future. Any one of them would have been sufficient to keep the governor's job interesting for the length of the legislative session and beyond.

The first was land use. Act 250 provided by its specific terms for the creation of three statewide plans to be developed and approved by the legislature. The plans would outline the use of land in the state, generally identify its capability for different kinds of use, and if not directly then indirectly detail the uses for which it was ill suited. The three plans described in the act were an Interim Land Capability Plan, a Capability and Development Plan, and a final Land Use Plan.

During the discussion and studies preceding the drafting of Act 250, our principal counselor, Walter Blucher, had warned us of the indispensability of a Land Use Plan to the successful and efficient enforcement of Act 250. Twenty years later, I am still very conscious of those stern warnings. For example, as recently as 1986, the state was involved in a controversy concerning the manner and limits of protecting Vermont's upland waters. The issue is an extremely important one, and one that I believe would not have arisen if Vermont had had a Land Use Plan in place that made clear that the fragile ecology of land above fifteen hundred feet is simply unable to support certain kinds of construction. With such a plan in place early on, developers would have shied away from developing those areas, and Vermont in the 1980s would not have had to invest heavily to correct the problems caused by poorly planned development.

Originally, we conceived that a workable final plan would be approached in three successive steps. We fully appreciated the political difficulties in getting legislative acceptance of such a plan. It was viewed by many as statewide zoning—which in one sense it was— and *zoning* had become a bad word in the legislative lexicon. Vermonters have always resisted intrusion by government into their affairs, particularly where their real estate is concerned. Moreover, people quite reasonably feared that the values of real estate would be affected by a Land Use Plan. Values would have been affected, some for the worse and some for the better, but on the whole I felt strongly that the Land Use Plan was a necessary restraint that Vermonters should be willing to accept for the good of the whole state.

At the time of the 1972 session we were only at a preliminary stage of the three-part program. I reported to the legislature that the interim plan had been completed and had been adopted by the Environmental Board, and that I expected to sign it shortly. However, I reminded the legislature that Act 250 had mandated all three plans. According to the legislature's specific direction, it was the legislature's responsibility to approve both the succeeding Capability and Development plan and the Land Use Plan. I also reminded the legislators that our original schedule called for the last two plans to be submitted at the 1972 session. Clearly, the process was far more complex than we had realized when Act 250 had been drafted; it seemed prudent, therefore, to revise the goals and to work toward completion and submission of the plans to the legislature by January 1973.

The second critical area of concern was education. Between 1962 and 1972, Vermont expenditures, both state and local, for education had increased 400 percent while enrollment had increased by only 40 percent. If projections by the Department of Education proved correct, state and local annual expenditures would need to increase to $180 million by 1975, while enrollment would continue to increase by only 3 percent per year. I told the legislature frankly that in deep sincerity, I did not believe Vermont could raise that sum except through confiscatory taxes.

Education is clearly one of the state's most important obligations. People believe in good public school education and within reason are willing to support it. But we do have to be realistic and recognize that there are limits to the amount of money which local or state governments are able to raise in support of what the educational system feels is necessary for a good education.

I told the legislature that I thought Vermont faced two serious questions, both of which lie at the heart of the conflict over the state's role in financing education. One is narrow and essentially technical in nature: Can it be clearly demonstrated that sizable increases in educational expenditure produce commensurate increases in the quality of education? Educators, I'm sure, would tell us that this is a difficult—even unfair—question, to which the unsupported answer is probably yes. And yet I believed then and believe now that we must find some kind of broad measuring stick to determine the success or failure of the state's system in providing a suitable education for our young people. Furthermore, that measuring stick must be one that the public with the help of the educators would be able to understand.

The other question was—and I believe still is—an important question of public policy: At what point do the costs incurred in the pursuit of a desirable, even imperative, goal such as the education of our young people become so heavy that the pursuit becomes damaging to the public interest? For example, our real estate property tax is driving land into development and is a substantial factor in the erosion of agriculture. It strikes hardest at the elderly and others who are on fixed incomes. Are we serving the public good when we wind up thereby driving the parents and grandparents of our young people from their homes and land? I thought not then, and I think not now.

Perhaps there are no completely satisfactory answers to those two questions, but I thought we ought to make a sincere effort to find out.

Moreover, there was building up in the country a judicial doctrine that threatened our system of financing support of public education. It had begun in California and was spreading to other states, including the New England states. It was based on the premise that every child in a state is entitled to an equal education. Vermont had adopted that principle many years ago when it began giving towns and cities aid for education with the specific goal of equalizing education among the so-called "rich" and "poor" towns—that is, to help iron out the differences between towns with many children and minimum taxable real estate and towns with much taxable real estate and proportionately fewer children to educate. The towns have fought over the state aid formula for years, and they always will, I suspect, until by some magic we discover and enact a different and perfect way to fund education that reserves the authority to run the schools to local school districts. In the early 1970s, however, the California court held that if one town was not able to raise as much money as another town for support of schools, and that as a result equal education was not available in the poor and affluent towns, then the applicable government was required to find another system of funding education that would result in equal education for all.

The combination of these funding dilemmas in public education was sufficiently complex and disturbing that I felt it was time for the legislature to appoint a distinguished commission of government officials, legislators, and citizens to consider the problem and to propose alternative programs at the 1973 session of the legislature.

Like education, the third critical problem I believed Vermont was facing was not new. The state's one maximum-security prison, at Windsor, had been quite inadequate for years and was long overdue for replacement. In 1970, the legislature authorized in excess of $5 million for a new prison in Windsor, but when the bids were opened, we discovered that skyrocketing costs had made the project impossible with even that high level of funding. I pointed out to the legislature that the philosophy and public policy in the United States with reference to prison management had changed greatly in the previous few years. More and more emphasis was being placed on community correctional centers and work-release programs. Vermont already had one such institution in St. Albans, which was proving to be quite successful. I told the legislature that the Corrections Department would recommend one central facility for the state with 140 beds, within which would be a close-confinement section for those who required maximum security. The emphasis within the institution, however, would be upon altering the attitude and behavior of inmates as well as on improving their education and skills.

I strongly favored the Corrections Department's proposal and called the legislators' attention to Vermont's progressive history in handling its prisons. I reminded them that when Vermont first set up its style of handling probation and parole, it was the second complete system of probation and parole established in the world. By 1972, the need to construct a new correctional facility was acute. Rising costs were only making it more difficult.

The legislative session was hardly under way when the discussions started as to whether I would run for a third term. There was considerable speculation about whether I would run for a third term and considerably more speculation about who would succeed me if I declined to run. The press had much to say about my desire to pick my own successor. Actually, that was not true. Naturally, I had ideas as to who among those available would be best for the times, and I was also quite interested that whoever did run should be, in general, at least, convinced that the programs I had inaugurated were good for the state. I had several young men in mind who I thought would make excellent governors. Among them was Luther F. Hackett, whom the press said was my hand-picked candidate. When Hackett did decide to run, I was pleased and frankly said so. I thought he would make an excellent governor, but I did not pick him, nor did I push him to run. Had I chosen to, however, I can see no reason why a lame-duck governor should not be allowed to express his opinion just like anyone else inside or outside of state government.

I did not have much time to become involved in the debate, though. The start of the legislative session gave rise to the usual assortment of fires that needed to be tended and doused. One of the first that required my attention and among the most sharply contested issues of the 1972 session was the question of what to do about the 15 percent surtax on income tax. The surtax had been passed in conjunction with the sales tax in 1969 and was designed to destruct automatically when the $7 million deficit I had inherited from the immediate past administration was paid off. In the 1972 budget I had finally been able to plan for the final installment on that debt, and now, without some action of the legislature, the payment of the last of the deficit would trigger the end of the whole surtax. But the spiraling costs of education suggested to me that it would be more prudent to amend the surtax provision and repeal it in three steps, five percent per year. By thus showing our intentions to lower taxes and support education, I felt the taxpayers, or most of them, would understand Vermont's situation and be content. But Marshall Witten, the able and charismatic chairman of the House appropriations committee, did not want to give up even one-third of the surtax revenue. Another group wanted to stick by the original goal and eliminate the surtax completely. This would have meant the loss of approximately $6 million in revenue. To compensate for this, the group proposed a similar-size cut in programs uniformly across the board. I regarded both of these proposals as unwise and the second proposal as irresponsible in addition.

For three weeks the controversy raged. Finally, while I was in Washington attending a governors' conference, I learned by telephone that both of these differing proposals had so many supporters that the result was in doubt. I left the governors' conference and flew home immediately. I called a hurried meeting of the leaders of the Republican party in the legislature and did my level best to persuade them away from either one of these propositions and to adopt my original proposal. Eventually, the leaders agreed and called a caucus of all Republicans in the House, where my position was explained to them. The question went immediately to the House floor, and the House voted down both of the other proposals and in favor of mine 88 to 51, a vote that was almost strictly along party lines. The newspapers called it a victory for me—and it was, of sorts—but I regarded it as only doing the governor's job, which day to day serves up as many defeats as victories. Furthermore, there is altogether too much emphasis put on victory or defeat. This tends to complicate the task of getting legislative action that solves problems correctly.

The proposal I described in my State of the State message concerning municipal and industrial pollution fees also ran into some problems in the legislature, particularly in the Senate. Two alternative proposals were made that I felt would be disastrous, one by Attorney General Jeffords, a staunch and valiant supporter of environmental protection, and another by Bob Babcock, Jr., a representative of Vermont Tomorrow, an environmental lobbying group. I was fully in sympathy with their goals but adamantly opposed to their methods. The Babcock proposal would have charged the fees and refunded 90 percent of them to the polluter (municipal or individual) with a provision that the money be used for pollution abatement. The Jeffords proposal would have cut the fees in half but forced the payment while plants were being built and until the abatement was fully achieved. The fees for either of these proposals would have run into big money at a time when municipalities were having plenty of economic trouble. To burden them further at the very time they were incurring heavy costs in purchasing equipment and building plants for pollution abatement would be the straw that broke the camel's back. In contrast, my proposal was simply to waive the fees when a plan was in place with scheduled dates for beginning and finishing as long as the polluter complied with the plan.

The Senate Committee on Natural Resources found itself unable to achieve a consensus, so the chairman, Arthur Jones, called the entire Senate into session as a committee of the whole to hear the arguments on all sides. I prepared a written statement and appointed Robert Williams, secretary of environmental conservation, as my representative. The point of my presentation was that to impose gigantic fees while there was still no true noncompliance was to court disaster. Fortunately, enough senators quickly saw the light. I breathed a sigh of relief.

In Vermont, governors spend much time and energy attending local events around the state. Chicken-pie suppers celebrate every conceivable event of a public nature, from crowning queens to honoring local dignitaries. Before I was governor, I had watched other Vermont governors doing this and thought it a waste of time. Being governor changed my perspective, however, and I am now fully committed to the view that this tradition is worth preserving. Certainly, it takes a lot of energy and time, but it is worth it because it gives a governor a real opportunity to keep in touch with the people of the state whom he is supposed to be serving. It gives him a chance to explain things (at times), and more important gives a chance to a lot of people to explain things to the governor. The tradition is worthy of preservation in Vermont. In larger states it would be impossible just because of sheer size. I'm glad Vermont is small.

I had other opportunities to be impressed by the unique relationship Vermont has with its governors. A wide variety of intensely personal problems find their way to the governor's office that in other, larger states, because of the sheer numbers of the problems, never would.

I recall sadly the case of two children who were lost in the woods in the Town of Orange. The woods were spread over a huge area, much of it covered by a thick and almost impenetrable underbrush. When news of the lost children was reported over radio and television and in the newspapers, it sparked immediate and widespread interest; hundreds of people flocked to the scene and offered their services as volunteers. The state police were called in and took charge of organizing the search, which at one time included five-hundred people. For days the press reported every detail of the search. After days of fruitless searching, the state police commissioner and others concluded that the children were either dead or had wandered away from the area, and the search was called off.

Within a day or two a tired, grim-looking man appeared at the governor's office without an appointment and asked to see me. Upon questioning the man, my receptionist learned that he was the father of the two children. She came immediately to my office, where I was holding a conference with a half-dozen or so individuals, and told me about the man. I asked the conferees if they would be willing to interrupt our meeting long enough for me to see the children's father. They quickly agreed and left the room, and the man came in. He had with him a detailed hand-drawn map of the terrain that showed its various characteristics. He was sure that the children were still in the wooded area and believed that they were in the most impenetrable part of the wilderness. It was obvious the man was near collapse from lack of sleep, fatigue, and worry. He wanted me to do something to get the search started again. I will never forget the look in that man's eyes as he made his plea. I felt that the state police were probably right and that further search would be useless, but how could I be sure? So I let my heart rule my head and called the commissioner and asked him to put the search back together again for a new try and to concentrate on the section of the woods where growth was thickest.

I wish I could report that the added search was successful and that the children were found alive and well. Unhappily, I cannot. Their bodies were found weeks later by hunters. I am sure, however, that every one of those searchers felt better for making another try. I know I did. When the father left the office, he said to the receptionist with tears in his eyes, "You know, that wouldn't happen anywhere but in Vermont. Anywhere else, I wouldn't have been allowed to see the governor."

There are indeed advantages to living in a small state.

As March began the speculation and discussion accelerated as to whether I would seek a third term. A strong public feeling was growing, however, that I would not run again. The people who held that conviction were right. I was not ready to make a decision, but by that time I was leaning strongly on the side of not running.

Finally, in early April as the legislature adjourned, I made up my mind. I held a small press conference to announce my decision not to run again. I gave the reporters a written statement and answered a few questions. Boiling it all down, I said that I had accomplished what I had set out to do. I had put the state's financial house in order, I had reorganized and streamlined the administrative branch of state government, and I had established the legal administrative structure that would enable Vermonters to preserve and enhance their environment.

What I didn't say at that time was that Marjorie had noticed and was concerned about my increasing deafness and felt I should quit. Moreover, I was missing a fuller family life. I felt that Marjorie had paid a pretty stiff price for my opportunity to serve as governor. And then, too, I kept looking at the calendar.

I don't think anyone was greatly surprised by my statement not to run. As time passes, I have become even more sure that it was the right decision.

Around the middle of May I resurrected my Statehouse on Wheels. I took a group of top administrative personnel to Windham County for a couple of days. The southern portion of Vermont has long had a feeling that state government is not sufficiently aware of or interested in its problems and needs. We went there partly to try to offset some of this feeling and partly because Windham County was where ski development and hasty, unplanned development had first become a critical political issue. While the problems of development led the list of concerns in this area, southern Vermonters had their full complement of other issues, too. One in particular was a proposal by federal transportation authorities to construct a four-lane east-west thruway essentially over what is now the scenic Route 9. The proposal was not popular. For that reason, I took with me all the major agency heads as well as the state highway commissioner, the planning director, and his two executive assistants.

I agreed with the opponents of the new four-lane highway that such a highway in that location would destroy much of Route 9's scenic charm. I agreed with them that the proposed highway would be merely a link in a chain bringing people from the East Coast across Vermont into New York State. If the federal government truly desired an east-west thruway across Vermont, I suggested that it would be better as well as less expensive to improve the highways from Rutland to Bethel and from Montpelier to St. Johnsbury, after which Vermont would have a cross-state highway serving a far greater number of the state's residents and out-of-state travelers, too. Fortunately, the federal government's proposal was ultimately abandoned.

On this trip south, we surveyed ski areas and visited with town selectmen, chambers of commerce, town planning officials, developers, local businessmen, and any and all citizens who had a problem to bring before us. As in the past, the traveling statehouse was greeted warmly and gratefully wherever we went. It proved itself once again to be a valuable vehicle in keeping government in touch with the people it serves. As more and more local problems have become partly the responsibility of the state, nothing has been done to set up formal arrangements for intercommunication between state and local governments except the formation of the League of Cities and Towns. The Statehouse on Wheels is just one informal manner in which these joint problems may be aired.

As the 1972 election season started warming up, so did politics. Attorney General Jeffords and Luther F. Hackett had both announced their candidacy for the Republican primary nomination for the office of governor. This in turn prompted announcements by Kimberly Cheney, Robert West, and Stan Lium for the Republican nomination for the office of attorney general. Local Republican groups started holding political meetings to plan for the coming contests, and I was often asked to attend. Since I was not to be a candidate for any political office, I felt an obligation to assist the Republican effort, and, consequently, I accepted these invitations when they did not conflict with any other engagement or responsibility.

At these meetings I embraced the opportunity to take some soundings on my proposals for an equalized state education tax. The proposal emerged as a result of galloping costs of education, skyrocketing increases in town property tax appraisals, and the growing disparity between the ability of towns to furnish "equal education" in all town school districts. The proposal called for a base statewide per-pupil allotment paid for by a statewide property tax, pursuant to a statewide property appraisal. I knew this proposal would have to find favor with other statewide office seekers and by town and school officials in many towns before it would have any chance of succeeding. Before the summer was over, I knew that Vermonters were not yet ready for such an approach. The reasons were complicated. Some Vermonters thought the proposal was complicated, although it was far less so than the Miller formula, which would be eliminated. Others objected because it seemed like another tax. It was, but not an additional one. Still others—perhaps the most—objected on the ground that localities would lose control of their schools. Of course it was a step in that direction, although I took pains to point out that under a statewide property tax to finance public education, Vermont towns would still retain the power to spend the money and to determine how it should be spent.

In 1972, however, support was just not there for such a far-reaching reorganization. It still isn't, but every session of the legislature brings to light more and more problems concerning the financing of public education. Today I hear increasing numbers of politicians suggest a statewide property tax as the solution, or at least as a major part of it. I believe in the long run that this solution is inescapable.

By August, two issues dominated Vermont's political scene. The hottest one was the Republican primary contest between Attorney General Jeffords and Fred Hackett. Close behind were the problems and issues concerning Windsor State Prison.

The 163-year-old edifice had itself become a problem. Doing his best to solve the problem was Robert G. Smith, who was surely sitting in the hottest seat in Vermont during 1972. Particularly in August of that year, his seat was even hotter than the governor's, which usually has a temperature reading higher than any Fahrenheit thermometer sold in Vermont.

Smith's seat was hot because he was the man responsible for keeping prisoners secure and properly fed and cared for in an antiquated facility; for placating the guards, who were quite properly complaining of overwork; for resolving the inmates' complaints of bad housing conditions; for persuading a sizable proportion of the public that Vermont was keeping abreast of trends in correctional philosophy; and for reassuring the people of Windsor and surrounding areas who were disgusted with and alarmed by the apparent lack of security at the prison.

It was in such a climate that on Saturday, August 26, 1972, a large prison break occurred, the second mass escape in four months. Eight prisoners escaped in broad daylight. The prisoners had sawed through bars on a window. No guards had been overpowered. The break had been accomplished out of sight of anyone. Everything indicated that the cause of this escape was simply the antiquated prison building, and hence the antiquated control methods that were used in such a building. People asked, of course, how bars could have been sawed without a guard seeing it. The answer was the timing. The guards were being called and the visiting room was full. And, of course, in a building like that, there are many places that are not visually covered every moment of the day. That level of security would be impossible to achieve. Even in a modern prison, it is impossible to cover every window in the building every minute of every day, although today closed-circuit television makes it possible to have surveillance in all such areas and new carbide steel is impervious to cutting with any type of blade.

An unconfirmed story quickly circulated that one woman had been threatened by two of the prisoners shortly after their escape. The residents of Windsor were both scared and mad, and that's a bad combination, though not at all an unusual one. Fortunately, four of the eight prisoners were recaptured by Sunday, but this did not allay either the fear or the anger of the people of the area, who had already experienced a mass escape of nine prisoners in the preceding April.

It was obvious to me that this was a hot potato. By Saturday night, Commissioner Kent Stoneman had issued with my approval a set of temporary regulations and procedures that both tightened immediate security at the prison and launched a long-range review of procedures.

Just a week before the prison break, I had announced to the press that the New England Regional Commission had authorized a study to determine the feasibility of building a tristate maximum-security prison to serve Maine, New Hampshire, and Vermont. Correction officials from the three states had already met and agreed that a tristate facility would be a good answer to the maximum-security problems of the three states, among whose Vermont's were the worst. I was strongly in favor of the study and hopeful that it might turn out to be our solution.

Now, at the request of the Windsor selectmen, I convened a meeting in my office of local Windsor officials, selectmen from surrounding towns, a few legislators, and Corrections Department officials. Windsor residents had a host of complaints. The local police had not been notified of the escape for three hours. The prison siren had not been blown, as was the custom when prisoners escaped, although it seemed less important to prison officials now that a two-way radio communication system connected all town enforcement officers in the state. And corrections officials had not notified the town that the state planned to build a drug rehabilitation center at the prison farm. In no uncertain terms, the local Windsor officials let us all know that they no longer cared to have a prison facility in their town.

As a lame-duck governor, there was little I could do to cure the Windsor problem except to try to get something concrete ready for the 1973 legislature and to improve the administration in Windsor if possible. I decided that some changes could be made and soon announced to the press that a shake-up in the Windsor staff was in the works. Responsibilities and duties were being increased and reassigned. Among those reassigned was Robert Smith, who initially took a thirty-day leave from his job as warden because of high blood pressure; he eventually moved to a job with less pressure. He was a victim of complex circumstances and did, I think, the best job he could, considering the pressures on him from all sides. I liked and respected him for his long and faithful career and his devotion to his job. But even with these changes, I expected troubles to continue until a new maximum-security prison could be constructed or Vermont instituted some other program to handle hardened criminals.

For the next two and a half months, the central issue in the state was who my successor would be. On the whole, the Jeffords-Hackett campaign did not produce any world-shaking debatable issues. Sporadic attempts were made to get some fundamental debates started, but most of them fizzled out. Both candidates were doing a creditable job on the hustings, shaking hands, attending coffee klatches, speaking at Rotary, Lions, and other service clubs, and doing modest amounts of radio and television advertising. But the real issues of the primary were personality, experience, general political philosophy, and whether I was supporting Hackett. If one can judge by the reams of newspaper columns, the latter issue won by a mile.

Long before August, the press had made up its mind that I favored Hackett. The press was right. I liked and respected both Attorney General Jeffords and Fred Hackett, but as governor I had worked more closely with Hackett, both as a close personal adviser and as chairman of the most important committee in the House, the appropriations committee. The chairman of the appropriations committee has to be an extremely knowledgeable person. Every department and program has to be scrutinized by that committee; consequently, legislators who serve on that committee get an uncommon education in state government and come to know people and issues to a degree that members of other committees seldom do. Moreover, the work is such that it gives a discerning person a perspective that is quite unusual.

This was just one of Fred Hackett's strengths. It was also one of the reasons I had used him as an adviser and come to respect him for his ability, his knowledge of state government, and his general political know-how. In addition, he served as a member of my Advisory Committee on Economics, a distinguished group under the chairmanship of Raymond Saulnier, former chairman of President Eisenhower's similar committee. I came to believe that Hackett fitted the times and the current needs of the state admirably and that he would make a good governor if elected.

Contemporary political wisdom was that a retiring governor should not endorse a candidate because it would be an unfair use of his office. Under these circumstances, I religiously answered the press each time I was asked that I did not and would not endorse either candidate. I knew of no other way to handle the matter, then or now. But in my heart I saw no reason why I should not have a preference the same as any other voter.

Then, in a debate between Jeffords and Hackett, Jeffords claimed that my administration had tried to prevent him as attorney general from suing the contractor for damages over the collapse of a roof at the Vermont State Hospital in Waterbury. I promptly issued a formal statement denying this, saying that Jeffords was making reckless allegations that were untrue and that did the attorney general no credit. The *Rutland Herald* and the *Times-Argus* immediately responded by declaring that I had "broken the neutrality in the Republican primary campaign." Afterward, Jeffords backpedaled, claiming that underlings in my administration and not me had tried to prevent him from bringing suit against the contractor. But despite my best efforts to stay out of the primary contest, the lines had now been drawn, and the controversy only fueled the debate over my role in the election.

In retrospect, it is difficult to know how, or if, I influenced the election despite my efforts to appear neutral. Clearly, Jeffords was apprehensive that I might publicly endorse Hackett; at one point he even asked for an appointment with me to assure himself that I would not do so. The newspapers painted Hackett as both courting my support and working to dispel suggestions of any close relationship between us. What was the result? All the charges and counter-charges probably helped both candidates as much as they hurt them.

Unquestionably, all the press coverage focused attention on the Republican primary. When it came time to cast their ballots, 88 percent of all the Vermonters who voted cast ballots in the Republican primary. In the end, most newspapers in the state endorsed Jeffords, but Hackett carried the vote by seven percentage points. His opponent for governor in the 1972 general election would be Thomas P. Salmon of Bellows Falls.

The campaign that followed was a bruising one. Salmon, of course, had the support of the Vermont Labor Council, which, except in special cases, always supports Democrats. But I do not know how much its support really means in Vermont, where the union workers are quite independent and often have strong views that clash with those of their own leadership. I had learned that in 1970, when I saw labor union leaders and members split over the issue of welfare.

I suspect that the two things that influenced the election most were disgruntled Republicans and Independents who were Jeffords supporters in the primary and the comparable skills of the two candidates in campaigning. Salmon is an extremely intelligent, articulate, handsome individual with loads of charm. Hackett is likewise an extremely intelligent individual with his own kind of charm. But in the hustings on the campaign trail, I think Salmon probably surpassed Hackett in getting favorable attention and holding it. During the campaign, Frank Smallwood, a political science professor at Dartmouth and a very discerning individual, said publicly that "Salmon is a much more exciting campaigner than Hackett. Fred just can't fire up the voters." This factor is hard to assess, but it very definitely is a factor, and the voters make the decision.

Another incident should also be figured into the equation, although, like charisma, it is a difficult factor to assess with assurance. This was the question of who would chair the State Republican Committee. After the primary, Jeffords became a candidate for the job, which is a paid position, but the newspapers said that Hackett and I did not approve. I do not recall ever being asked, but I would not categorically deny that I was. I do know that it would have been unusual to have been asked my opinion on that question because those kinds of questions are usually kept pretty close to the chests of the state committee members. However, Hackett was asked, and he did not approve. The newspapers made a big thing of this, and it may well have further irritated Jeffords supporters, who were already disgruntled because he had failed to win the Republican nomination for governor.

During the week before the election, the campaign reached the boiling point. Informal polls—including one by Vincent Narramore in Chittenden County—began to show that if anyone had an edge, Salmon did. Every expert was projecting a close election. At long last I called a press conference to publicly state my support for Hackett, but there were Davises on both sides of this election. My son Tom, a longtime Democrat, was working hard for Salmon. During the last week I noticed that Salmon was using Tom Davis much more, taking him along on the campaign trail and making sure that he was introduced as my son. It was good strategy. Salmon even praised my environmental work. I know Salmon was sincere in this statement, but I expect that under the circumstances it was good politics, too. During this same critical period, Senator Aiken, who traditionally kept himself removed from political endorsements, publicly threw his support to Hackett on the ground that Nixon was going to be elected president and Republicans would be needed to support him.

And then, at exactly the right time, a dozen Republicans went public with a signed advertisement in support of Salmon. The ad was circulated among the major newspapers in the state. I believe this ad had the effect of encouraging further disaffection among Republicans and hence was an important factor in the race.

The result of the election was a surprisingly big win for Salmon, who carried the election 56 percent to 43 percent.

Governor-elect Salmon and I promptly met and discussed a variety of matters involved in the transition. We got along fine, as I knew we would. My son, Tom, was offered and accepted the job of secretary of human services. It was a good appointment. Tom had already proven his administrative capacity as head of the Office of Economic Opportunity. He had studied social questions in depth in college, and his disposition and temperament has always been toward the underprivileged. He did a fine job in my opinion, and I was proud of him.

On the day before Governor Salmon took office, he and the

commissioner of motor vehicles came into my office together and presented me with a new number plate on which the message x GOV was printed. Both were Democrats, so I jokingly asked, "Now, how long is this number plate good for?" The commissioner replied immediately, "For life." I have tried several times since to give the plate back, but the commissioners have refused to take it.

On Thursday, January 5, 1973, I mounted the rostrum in the House of Representatives to say good-bye to the Joint Assembly of the Senate and House of Representatives. Seventy-one governors had stood before similar gatherings in Vermont's long history to mark the end of their administrations. I am sure that each of them did so with a certain amount of nostalgia and regret. I was no exception. Yet I had a feeling of satisfaction, too, for I had accomplished the principal goals that I had declared during my campaigns for governor. Even the deficit I had inherited from Governor Hoff had been paid off, with close to half a million dollars left over to be put toward reducing the state's bonded indebtedness.

I think every governor has a different job to do, depending upon the needs and conditions prevailing at the time. I think it was well for two reasons that I was too old to have any further political ambitions. If, during my term of office, I had entertained those ambitions, I might very well not have fought for the sales tax. Moreover, instead of fighting for Act 250 and Act 252, I might well have settled for a compromise that would have kept everybody reasonably happy but that failed to address the problem head on. I made enemies on both of these crusades. Often when the going was rough on the campaign trail, I paused to consider whether the struggle was worth the gain. Yet standing there on the rostrum to say good-bye, I had the strongest feeling ever that it had been worthwhile—eminently so. The hardest test any of us has to pass is the one we ask ourselves: Have we met our own standards of conduct? These are the questions that recur in the middle of sleepless nights.

Of course, I had regrets and disappointments—indeed, many. But most of them were not all that important. The greatest was my inability to complete the passage of the statewide Land Use Plan that had been proposed in Act 250. The plan had generated so much controversy and the task to write it was so gigantic that I was unable to submit a finished plan until the eve of my departure from office.

New faces, a new governor, new problems, new issues, and new legislators always bring new directions and new programs that cause old unfinished ones to lose their prominence and attractions. I knew the statewide Land Use Plan was in this kind of jeopardy, and although Governor Salmon joined me in signing the recommendation for legislative enactment, the plan never made it out of committee at the 1973 session. Nowhere does the past become the past faster than in changes of administration.

Was the enactment of a Land Use Plan important? Indeed it was. It would have given a sense of direction to the district environmental boards, which hear and make decisions on applications for land development. It would have made decisions more uniform across the state. And, I believe, it would have given legal stability to the whole of Act 250. The disappointment was mine, but the loss, I believe, was the entire state's.

In the afternoon, after my farewell address, I attended the inauguration ceremony for Governor Salmon and then the traditional reception for the new governor, which lasted until late in the afternoon. Afterward, our state trooper driver drove us one last time to Poultney, where we planned to spend the night with Marjorie's sister before starting another trip to Florida. On the way to Poultney, we came within an inch of a head-on collision when a car suddenly appeared from a side road. Only the quick reaction and skill of the trooper avoided a crash.

I left the office of governor thinking of the things I had wanted to do that remained undone and knowing that I would miss the excitement of my association with the legislators, the members of my staff, and the people I had worked with in the administrative branch of state government. But my overriding feeling was one of relief. There is great comfort in living a private life, in not watching all the details of one's life displayed on the screen and in the newspapers. Almost twenty years later, my strongest memory of that week is of Marjorie's obvious joy that we were about to start our lives anew as private citizens.

19

Winding Down

It gives me much to think about to find myself
now, as I began life, part of a large, busy, and
loving family. And now, more than I was able to
when I was younger, I appreciate how fortunate I
am.

I looked forward with keen anticipation to the final day of my second term. I was satisfied with what had been accomplished, but I was tired, physically and emotionally. Personal privacy is a great privilege, though those outside public life seldom realize it. After the rigors of two primaries and two election campaigns, four years of fourteen- and sixteen-hour days, thousands of miles of travel up and down and across the state shaking hands and making speeches, hundreds of meetings with staff, state officers, legislators, and public interest groups, and innumerable chicken dinners, I was not only ready but eager to recapture the joys of private life.

The day I left office we drove south for an overnight stop in East Poultney with Marjorie's sister, Barbara. We then journeyed to Pompano Beach, Florida, where Don Martin of Montpelier had loaned us his comfortable condo on the beach. All I could think of as we drove merrily along through the winter countryside was the prospect of sleeping till noon and spending the rest of the day in the sun, my vision of the way to wind down.

And it worked. My recovery was swift and complete. After ten days of late rising, regular meals, and complete rest, I found myself unable to sleep past seven o'clock in the morning or even to stay in bed. I needed to know what was going on in the world, and I needed exercise.

Fortunately, I had taken my bicycle along on the trip. While searching for a suitable place to ride in that congested area I spotted a new Catholic church nearby. Investigating further I found that adjacent to the church and adjoining manse was a five-acre paved parking lot. Since this space appeared to be unused except on Sundays, I thought it would be perfect for my purpose. I decided to approach the resident priest and ask permission, but I had a few doubts about whether he would welcome my use of the parking lot for such a mundane purpose. Imagine my surprise when the door of the manse opened in response to my knock, and there stood Bishop Robert F. Joyce, a long-time friend from Vermont who was filling in while the resident priest was on vacation! He assured me the new parking lot needed breaking in and that both he and the church would be grateful if I would use it.

The Pompano racetrack, whose track, stables, and grandstand are among the best on the east coast, was also nearby, so my attention soon gravitated in that direction, too. I looked up Dr. Davidson of Essex Junction, who spent a month each year racing his trotters at Pompano, and found him at the racetrack in a mobile home with his family. For the next two weeks I enjoyed watching the horses as much as he enjoyed driving them. The pungent smell of the barns and the sweat of horses have always been great medicines for me, and I credit my time at the track for my quick recovery from exhaustion.

But I was not permitted to concentrate exclusively on biking and horses. Douglas Kitchell, senator from Caledonia County, phoned me after Marjorie and I had spent about three weeks in Pompano Beach. He had a strong interest in matters of public health, and this had prompted him to join a group of like-minded Vermonters in forming a unique public health organization called the Cooperative Health Information Center of Vermont (CHICV). Funded by the federal public health authorities, CHICV was formed in response to a growing belief that health care was too expensive and did not meet the needs of large numbers of the Vermont public. Its goal was to produce a sophisticated data base that would document the distribution of medical and hospital services in Vermont. This information would make it possible for federal and state authorities to make informed decisions as to what, if anything, was needed to meet the state's medical needs.

Senator Kitchell, speaking for the board of trustees of CHICV, asked me to assume the presidency of the organization on a half-time basis, at least during its formative period. I explained to him that I was trying to wind down after four years of governorship. But he persisted in his low-key, charming way. I had to admit that I was interested in the offer because it was an opportunity for me to educate myself about a field that I had a strong interest in but little knowledge. After a couple of days of thinking it over I accepted the offer, though somewhat reluctantly, with the understanding that I would start April 1 after my return from Florida to Vermont.

The data base was to consist of medical records and financial and hospital utilization data gathered regularly and continually from all Vermont hospitals. After analysis, the data would be assembled for quick and easy comprehension and reported regularly to the individual hospitals and to federal and state health authorities. My role was to preside over the selection of staff, to visit hospitals around the state and assure their staffs that we were not out to cut their throats, and to act as a legislative liaison, which of course brought me back in touch with people I knew well. Nothing was mandatory as far as the hospitals were concerned. In fact, at that time it was not even a legal requirement that the hospitals furnish the information. Understandably, some were reluctant at first to participate, but every Vermont hospital eventually joined the program. This voluntary action on the part of every hospital earns the management of Vermont's hospitals high marks for their dedication to public service. Few organizations of any kind react with enthusiasm to government looking over their shoulders at the details of their operations.

In the beginning the emphasis was on collecting data on hospital utilization and medical procedures, although a certain amount of financial information was also collected. CHICV remained active until federal funding was no longer available, whereupon the extensive data base was turned over to the Vermont State Department of Health. Sometime later the Vermont legislature enacted legislation to establish the Hospital Data Council to continue the work of CHICV and enlarge its scope. The new legislation included a provision which made the furnishing of the information by the hospitals mandatory. It also specifically provided for budget review by the council and for recommendations to be made by the council with respect to each hospital's budget, but it did not require the hospitals to adopt the recommendations.

When we began, I didn't know where we would come out. I don't think anybody did. At the time, public pressure for government intervention in the area of health care was so strong that something had to be done. We hoped to provide the data that would create intelligent choices about what that might be.

Is the process working? It is probably too early to draw a valid conclusion. But this interesting experiment in a new kind of relationship between the hospitals and the state through the Hospital Data Council does show promise. There is more than a pious hope that it can succeed without mandatory legal requirements. It provides for a credible method for receiving input from the state, the public, and consumers without mandatory state price fixing. It relies heavily on a spirit of cooperation on the part of all concerned, especially the hospitals. I hope it will succeed. If it fails there will be a hard-fought political battle over whether mandatory price fixing should be legislated. Already the chairman of the Hospital Data Council has called publicly for authority for the council to enforce its recommendations. In my opinion a hard-fought political battle in this sensitive area would be unfortunate and might lose more ground than it gains.

When you retire, people naturally assume that you do not have enough to do. And if you retire from elective office, it is soon apparent that you have picked up an incredible number of obligations to people with long memories. Now they come to collect. They ask you to be on this committee or that, to be chairman of this or that, to fund-raise, or to commit yourself to crusades to save the world. Not surprisingly, most former politicians are the kind who can't say no— that's one reason why they became politicians.

I was no exception. Before the first year of my retirement was over, I was astonished to find myself serving on the boards of seventeen charitable and philanthropic organizations. These included boards with aims as diverse as the Boy Scouts and the Vermont Symphony Orchestra. But they were all worthwhile causes that I was happy to support.

Moreover, I was serving on the boards of directors of four business corporations. One of these was National Life. I continue to serve on the board two decades later, thus continuing an association that spans half my long life.

Now, also, troops of people came to interview me. The numbers surprised me. Many—in fact more than 150—have come to interview me on the history, philosophy, and workings of Act 250 and Act 252 alone. Most of these were students writing theses on environmental subjects or writers of articles for magazines, but some have been candidates seeking information on the subject. Though time consuming, these interviews please me because I believe unreservedly in the merits and present and future worth of Act 250 and Act 252 to the state of Vermont.

I also still had my duty to the Republican party, which meant giving modest financial support to the party and its candidates. Understandably, Republican candidates feel justified seeking financial support from former office holders. I did the same thing. Candidates at all levels also come, as I once went to the elders of the party, seeking advice, that, too often, I feel incompetent to give. Others come seeking the use of my name either on campaign literature or in some other way. To each I offer what I can, but I do not support a candidate financially or otherwise unless I am willing to support the candidate publicly. I also make it clear to all candidates that I won't run around the state and engage in soliciting votes or making political speeches.

I stayed active in the Republican Party after I retired from the governorship not just because of a lifetime's habit but for philosophical reasons. I believe in a strong two-party system, and I am concerned about its future. Both the Republican and Democratic parties have long histories of serving the country well. But we are seeing an increase in splinter parties today even as we see party membership and party loyalty declining in both major parties. If this trend continues, it can only result in the rise of spoiler candidates who, in small states like Vermont, can be elected without commanding the votes of a majority. It would serve our democratic system well if we could strengthen the two major parties by requiring party registration, by requiring voters to declare their party before voting in primaries, or by devising any other means that would accomplish this result.

All of this activity quickly destroyed any illusion I had that retirement would give me unlimited leisure time for relaxation. But I had no complaints. I was doing what I really wanted to do.

The post-gubernatorial years did bring me more time to enjoy my children and grandchildren. It also gave me time to mend some fences. When Corinne died, Marian was living at home waiting out the return of her husband from army service in Korea. Tom was at the University of Vermont, living in his campus fraternity house during the week and coming home weekends to our Nelson Street house in Barre. Their mother's death was a tremendous blow to both children. Corinne was a wonderful mother and developed a very special closeness with both children, sharing their hopes and dreams as well as their problems. I recognized this, but found myself powerless to step into the breach and become even a passable substitute for her after her death.

The times did not help. When his mother died, Tom was taking political science courses at the University of Vermont and learning the more modern views of political philosophies. These seemed quite foreign to what I had been taught by my father and others of his generation. Of course, the political center was slowly but definitely shifting to what we call the left. I was slow in following it, so when Tom came home on weekends we spent a major portion of our time together in political arguments. I laugh about it now and understand that the dogmatism in my arguments only caused Tom to work harder to prove me wrong and thereby strengthened his viewpoint.

Somewhere along about that time Tom made a definite decision to become a Democrat. At first I was disappointed and hurt by his decision. I have nothing against Democrats, but they just aren't Republicans. Five generations of Davises had been Republicans, and I had grown up in the days when most people inherited the politics of

319

their parents.

As I had time to reflect upon this situation, however, I began to see it from a different perspective. I am proud of Tom for the courage he showed in making his own decision and never wavering from it. The fact that I did not agree with that decision only emphasized the courage and independence it took to make it.

Also, as time went on we found that we had many things in common. Tom has used his many acquaintances in Vermont to help keep me informed on the political issues of the day, and this has fueled our continuing and increasing interest in the problems of state and federal government. These days, since both of us have served in government, we discuss current events and problems from a more practical and mature point of view and find that we often agree. I have discovered that our approach to these problems is surprisingly similar—both of us are more interested in problem solving than in political philosophies.

In the last few years Tom and I undertook a widespread search for an elusive Davis ancestor. We developed a mild interest in genealogy and learned more about my great-great-grandfather, John Davis, who came to Vermont in 1802. John Davis built a "pitch" on what became the family homestead on Pike Hill in Corinth, and with my great-great-grandmother cleared the land and raised five healthy, rugged children in that remote and lonely area.

Tom and I added what we gathered to the information my father had collected and passed along to my brothers, sisters, and me. He told us that we were descendants of a number of *Mayflower* ancestors through my paternal grandmother, Alantha Chandler Davis. All of the ties were through the Chandler line, which I am sure accounts for my middle name being Chandler.

My daughter, Marian, and her husband, Frank, eventually moved to Ocala, Florida, where they purchased and operated a book store for a number of years. After they sold the store, Frank took a sales position with a nationwide company that markets all of the merchandise used by book stores except books. He serves a wide marketing area and enjoys his work immensely. Marian handles the accounting for a large retail clothing firm. We keep in touch by telephone and occasional visits.

I have another son and daughter, Marjorie's children Peter and

Patricia. Together they eventually brought nine grandchildren and more recently six great-grandchildren into the family fold. I love every one of them as if they were my own, and as with my own grandchildren and great grandchildren, I take keen interest in the myriad of happenings in their lives. Fortunately, many of my grandchildren and Marjorie's grandchildren either live in Vermont or within a four-hour driving radius of our home in Montpelier, so we get to see them frequently. Three of my step-grandchildren worked for me during summer vacations when they were teenagers. This was a wonderful opportunity for them and a wonderful experience for Marjorie and me. At that time I was seriously raising Morgan horses, and they all became proficient riders. Clair, Peter's oldest son, went on to West Point, where he made the prestigious West Point riding team. My granddaughter Corinne fell in love with horses, and after she married persuaded her husband to take up the sport. Today they have two good horses at their home in Williamstown, Vermont, where they care for them personally and trail ride together.

It gives me much to think about to find myself now, as I began life, part of a large, busy, and loving family. And now, more than I was able to when I was younger, I appreciate how fortunate I am.

In the summer of 1974, two years after leaving the governorship, I was thrown from a horse while riding in a parade at the Addison County Fair. I suffered a compression fracture of a vertebrae and a bruised ego. The compressed vertebrae kept me from riding for two and a half months. Marjorie tried to console me by pointing out that there is no way to save face when dismounting a frightened steed in front of a crowd of two thousand people, but I still felt the indignity of the fall and the growing frailty of my advancing years.

The following January Marjorie and I flew to California to preside at the annual meeting of the American Morgan Horse Association. I was president of the AMHA and Polly Bee, one of the directors, had asked me to come to Seaside to marshal a big parade which was to be held a couple of days prior to the AMHA meeting. This annual parade includes a four-mile march over cement streets and is always attended by huge crowds along the route. Polly had agreed to furnish me a well-trained, calm, and sensible horse to ride in the parade. Upon arriving at the starting point, I found the horse waiting as agreed. Bands were playing, flags were fluttering, balloons were flying, firecrackers and pistols were crackling, and confusion reigned supreme. The horse, thoroughly upset, was circling nervously while two men struggled to hold him. Finally able to get aboard, I started on our four-mile trek while the horse continued to prance and circle as his nervousness increased. By this time it was hard to tell who was most nervous—the horse or I. Only six months recovered from my accident at the Addison County Fair, I struggled to restrain the horse and keep my seat. You can bet that the Addison County Fair incident was in the front of my mind and that the cement streets looked much harder than the grass at the Addison County Fair.

About halfway along the parade route I suddenly heard a loud voice calling "Guvanah, Guvanah." I looked to discover where the voice was coming from, and I was startled to see, in the front line of spectators, the Reverend Johnson, the black minister who was the centerpiece of the Irasburg affair that captured Vermont headlines for months both before and after I took office in 1969. A large contingent of family and friends was with him, all of them vigorously waving flags and balloons. The Irasburg affair began when a young man home on leave from the army and a couple of his pals drove by the Reverend Johnson's house in Irasburg in the small hours of the morning and discharged a firearm several times at the house with the obvious intent to scare the occupants. There were more developments in the story, but the affair lost its newsworthiness after the minister returned to his native California. Now he was obviously harboring no grudges against Vermont. He wanted to chat. I finally maneuvered my prancing horse near enough to have a word or two with him and then resumed my wild ride.

The parade ride finally ended uneventfully, and I proceeded to my next assignment, which was to present Ronald Reagan, governor of California, with a certificate of lifetime honorary membership in the American Morgan Horse Association. I had met Governor Reagan many times at governors' conferences, and Marjorie and I had ridden with him in the California mountains so we knew what an ardent horseman he was. I found him at the statehouse in Sacramento but was puzzled to see crowds of people, including scores of

TV and newspaper reporters and cameramen, milling around outside the governor's office. I had some trouble getting into Governor Reagan's office, but when I finally did, I asked him, "What's all the excitement out there?" "Oh," he said, "this is the first day of the new fiscal year and the legislature (heavily Democratic) won't give me a budget, so no one working for the state in any capacity can be paid."

"Well," I said, "you look pretty calm in here. What are you going to do about it?"

"I'll wait a few days, and then I'll go on television and ask the voters to get after their individual legislators," he answered. "They'll come around. They think they can embarrass me, but when it's all over they will be the ones who will be embarrassed. They'll come around," he said.

For a week I watched the newspapers closely, and, sure enough, his prophecy came true. He made his speech on television, and in a few days the legislature passed a budget similar to the one Reagan had submitted. Reagan knew his California voters, and he had an abundance of patience, a quality of great value to a governor.

Governor Reagan and I stayed in touch, and some years later he asked me to be his campaign manager in Vermont for the Vermont Presidential Primary. I accepted happily, but his request made me chuckle. In 1972 I had attended the Republican National Convention in Miami as chairman of the Vermont delegation. One of Reagan's friends was giving him and Mrs. Reagan a party on one of those harbor boats that is permanently tied up and never goes anywhere. Marjorie and I were invited to the party and attended briefly but left early because a meeting of the Vermont delegation had been scheduled for early in the evening at convention headquarters. As we left Reagan followed us out, and we chatted informally for a few minutes. I told him that I hoped he would be the next president after Nixon. He shook his head and said, "It can't work out. I'll be too old." But as it turned out he was not too old to be elected in 1980 and again in 1984.

During the summer of 1976 Marjorie and I rode regularly, enjoying the beautiful scenery and terrain we have in this area. One day in late September we rode for three hours, which was a bit longer than usual. I was trying to clear some of the hanging branches that were beginning to clutter one of our best-loved trails and was leaning and reaching to cut branches with my brush clippers for almost an hour. I do not remember feeling particularly tired, but the next day I began having peculiar fleeting pains in my back and arms. Marjorie tried to get me to call my doctor late that night, but I resisted. Instead, I lay in bed reading *Shogun*. The description of Lord Toranaga's heart problems came suspiciously close to describing my own symptoms. Without mentioning this to Marjorie, I slipped out to my den where she couldn't hear and called Dr. Dale's residence. I found he was out of town, so I called Dr. Burns, who was covering for Dr. Dale while he was away. I expected to be told that the symptoms were unimportant, in which case I would be able to tell Marjorie, "I told you so." I told Dr. Burns the story, and his staccato reply was "Get up to the hospital in eight minutes, and I will meet you there." I include this rather odd sequence of events to suggest that it may not always be wise to try to diagnose our pains and twinges even if it is late at night and we are loath to disturb the doctor.

For three months Dr. Dale tried to control my weakened heart with medication. This did not succeed. Finally, in late December, Dr. Dale sent me to the Medical Center Hospital in Burlington for an angiogram. The angiogram showed several blockages, and Dr. Coffin, who performed the angiogram, strongly advised bypass heart surgery within thirty days. Dr. Dale concurred after seeing the test results. Because of my advanced age and general condition I wanted to go to Ohio to the Cleveland Clinic, which had originally developed the technique and had an excellent reputation in the critical first days of aftercare. Dr. Dale called the Cleveland Clinic and was told that it would be three months before I could be admitted.

A few days after this report I was sitting in our living room wondering what to do next. The telephone rang, and the caller was Gordon Foster, a friend in Green Valley, Arizona. He inquired about my health, and I told him the story, probably at unnecessary lengths.

"Oh," he said, "so you want to get into the Cleveland Clinic. Well, the administrator of the Cleveland Clinic, Dr. Wasmuth, is sitting here right across the table. I'll put him on the phone."

I told Dr. Wasmuth the whole story as far as I knew it. He asked many questions, after which he asked me to have Dr. Dale call him. Dr. Dale did call and filled him in with the medical details. Within an hour Dr. Wasmuth called me and told me that arrangements had been made at the clinic for me to be operated on January 5 provided I passed all the required tests, but that I would have to be in Cleveland on January 2nd to begin the tests. I had four days to get ready.

Everything worked out as planned, and two weeks after the operation I was home. Marjorie and I spent February and March of 1977 at the beach on Siesta Key in Florida, where I religiously walked the beach and practiced giving up the fatty foods that without doubt contributed to my heart condition. During this time I had occasional problems with heart rhythm but no pain. I read a lot of good books and wrote *Justice in the Mountains*, which was published in 1980. By the first of May I was back on a horse, just as the doctors had promised. At last I had found a way to wind down.

That summer and fall I was involved in a lawsuit that named my law school roommate and my partner in the Boston shoeshine parlor, Gelsie Monti, as the defendant. The suit was brought by a disgruntled client of Monti's who claimed malpractice in connection with a lawsuit that Monti had handled for the plaintiff. By that time Monti was eighty-two years of age and critically ill in the McFarland nursing home in Barre. Monti simply refused to accept any lawyer other than me to defend him.

At that time I had not tried a lawsuit for thirty-five years and felt my incompetence keenly. I did my best to dissuade Monti, but my protestations and refusals fell on deaf ears. Finally it became apparent that my persistent refusal would terminate a life-long friendship. So, with great trepidation and much against my better judgment, I agreed to handle his case. Another lawyer, Edwin Free, Jr., offered his help and associated himself with me in the case. But I did set one condition on my taking the case.

"What's the condition?" Monti asked.

"That you let me plead insanity in defense," I replied. "I can prove that you are insane simply by showing that you picked me for your lawyer."

Monti saw no humor in that.

The case was tried in Washington County Court with Judge

Edwin H. Amidon presiding. The court ruled that no proof existed of any damage to the plaintiff on the malpractice claim and entered judgment for Monti on that count. The case was appealed by the plaintiff to the Vermont Supreme Court, where it was heard on briefs, and shortly thereafter the Supreme Court affirmed the judgment of the trial court. Unfortunately, Monti died before the Supreme Court decision was released and never knew that he had won.

Trying this case under those circumstances was an educational experience for me and taught me how much the rules of practice and the law itself had changed in thirty-five years. For some time after my retirement from National Life I had harbored the illusion of returning to law practice. This experience completely cured me of that illusion. I recognized that time had passed me by.

Now, at the age of 90, I find the time has come when I can enjoy sitting in front of the fire. I don't feel old—just older. I count my blessings. I enjoy my children, my grandchildren, and my great grandchildren and their visits, which are frequent but not frequent enough. I reminisce and see and feel and enjoy special times, special friends, and special events all over again. I still ride horseback but not as fast or for as long. Everything else seems to move at a faster pace—including time and the world around me.

Again and again, I relive a week-long ride I took in the California mountains with the Ranchero Visitadores. Every year, five hundred men carry on the tradition of the Spanish ranchers of lower California, who long ago each spring rode in large groups to gather and reclaim their cattle. The ride started in Santa Barbara in the courtyard of the Santa Barbara monastery, where the five hundred riders sat on their horses while the ride was blessed, and a chorus of priests sang beautiful and intensely moving religious songs. I remember the warm companionship we shared during the day. Each night we gathered after a sumptuous dinner to enjoy a show by professional entertainers flown in by helicopter from Hollywood. Each night, after the entertainment and even before we had finished tucking ourselves into our sleeping bags on the sand, we were sound asleep, sleeping the sleep of the just. We woke every morning at six o'clock to the glory of a new day and drank in the clean, bracing mountain air. After we had showered and shaved under make-shift showers and eaten a big breakfast, we mounted our horses for another day's thirty-five mile ride. The world seemed like an impossibly wonderful place and life a marvelous gift from God.

For two of the days my riding partner was Art Linkletter, and I listened with fascination to his comments about his life and experiences. A nineteen-piece orchestra accompanied us, and in addition to its entertainment at night at dinner and after dinner in camp, its members serenaded us on the trail every now and then as we rounded a curve or went over the ridge of a hill. The beauty of that Spanish music defies description, and I still hear scraps of it in my head at the most unlikely times.

I remember, too, "Man and His World" at Expo '67 in Montreal, when the board of directors of the American Morgan Horse Association asked me to assemble twenty top Morgan horses and antique carriages to take part in the segment called "Man and His Horse." This was the first dramatic production with horses ever held out of doors, and it included several hundred horses selected from, among others, the Northwest Mounted Police, the Queen's Guard from England, and a band of top riders from the Barbados. We spent one week in rehearsals and two weeks in the spectacular itself, where on some nights we drew audiences of twenty-five thousand spectators, filling the grandstands.

My life has been long and full, and my memories are many.

Sitting in front of the fire at home not long ago, I noticed that Marjorie was looking at me, not speaking, with a quizzical expression on her face.

I asked, "What are you thinking?"

There was a long pause. Then she said, "I love you."

She claims that my only response was, "In that case, I will turn up my hearing aid."

There's no place like home.

20

What's Ahead for Vermont?

The people of Vermont are, on the whole, tolerant,
open-minded, and moderate, and they have a
sense of self-worth and dignity that commands
respect. Perhaps they are a bit contrary at times,
but they are also realistic, whether in business or
politics.

Ninety years have passed with incredible speed, years that provide perspective and make me realize what a priceless privilege it has been to live in Vermont during the exciting and rapidly changing twentieth century. In the last decade of the century, the winds of change are still blowing strong. I hear many people wondering how much of Vermont's quality of life will endure.

Around me, I believe I see forces now at work that will determine what Vermont will look like twenty-five or thirty years hence. I claim no expertise in this field and have not the gift of prophecy. I speak only as a Vermonter who has lived all his life in Vermont and who has been an interested observer of the events that changed its past and are now shaping its future.

But first: What is this Vermont quality of life that so many love but fear will not endure? I believe there are three principal areas that distinguish Vermont from many other states: landscape, community, and philosophy. Together, these constitute the Vermont quality of life.

Many people find the difference is primarily a matter of landscape. They see friendly hills, wooded terrain, gurgling brooks. They feel the solitude of quiet places. They revel in the pastoral scenes of cattle grazing on lush green meadows against a background of wooded hills and beautiful farmsteads charmingly composed of white houses and red barns. Although constantly changing, Vermont's landscape has always consisted of a relatively sparse population, plenty of woodland areas, open land, and a considerable degree of isolation.

Features of the landscape that set Vermont apart from the other rural regions are the upland meadows, the diverse nature of the forests, and the absence of visible commercialism. The upland meadows in particular, combined as they are with small villages and a variety of forest types, yield a patchwork-quilt quality to the landscape not found elsewhere. The drive from White River Junction to Montpelier over I-89, for example, provides a panorama that illustrates this quality.

The state's woodlands, due to the gradual regrowth of trees from former pastures and the lack of extensive commercial forestry, are a natural mix of northern and southern hardwoods with a variety of softwoods. The rolling nature of the topography also gives Vermont's forests an unusual diversity that contrasts with the more homogeneous forests of many rural regions of the United States. There are few states where oak and beech join with the northern spruces, firs, and birches, where pine, maple and aspen interact on hillsides and where elms and maples guard the fence rows.

Many other features of Vermont's landscape are not unique but nevertheless serve to add to the beauty of the state. Church steeples and village greens, for example; silos attached to barns, which in turn are often attached to houses; covered bridges over sparkling water; cellar holes framed by lilac; and the four distinct seasons of the year are integral to the state's natural identity. So, too, are the dirt and gravel roads, shaded as they are by canopies of trees and flanked by stone walls that seem to wander without purpose through the rolling hills and occasional cemeteries.

Vermont's landscape is a pleasing combination of all these features. Only the entire picture, not a piecemeal description or single spot, captures the quality. And where but in Vermont does one encounter highways kept clean by an annual statewide program called Green Up Day, in which the work is done by volunteers?

Like the landscape, the Vermont community is a bit different from that found in other rural areas. The difference includes the absence of a rigid class system, the ability of the state to function as one community, and the small-town structural relationship of the state as a whole. From the time of the state's early constitution, Vermont has had an established pattern of opposition to elitism and artificial privilege that has enabled numerous immigrant groups to integrate rapidly into the community and to participate in community affairs at all levels. One of the best examples is Barre. Once wholly an Anglo-Saxon community, Barre, with its granite quarries, attracted skilled Europeans, Canadians, and Italians in large numbers. In only a few decades the melting pot had worked perfectly. This tradition remains strong today in Vermont and is reflected in the general acceptance of blacks, back-to-the-land settlers, and a host of retirees, as well as the many working migrants from urban suburbia and megalopolis.

I do not deny the existence of some prejudice. But I have found that the overwhelming majority of Vermonters do not share it, or they successfully cover it up. The fierce pride felt by native Vermonters does not prevent them from accepting new people and new ideas. Anyone who doubts this need only consider the 1985 session of the legislature when the House of Representatives—composed of a majority of Republicans—elected a Democrat as speaker, the most important office in the House. The new speaker had been born elsewhere and had only recently moved to Vermont. Some measure of how his new ideas were accepted may be gleaned from the fact that he was reelected as speaker in the following legislative session. More recently, Vermont elected a Jewish woman born in Europe as governor. She hardly fits the traditional portrait of the old New England WASP, but for that matter neither do the Vermonters who elected her.

Then, too, the Vermont quality of life to many—indeed, to most—is partly a matter of the state's history. Most of our forebears, young men and women, were settlers from lower New England. According to the sentiment of the time, they regarded ownership of land as an indispensable condition by which first-class citizenship was to be obtained. Settling on lands widely separated, they sought to better themselves by mastering their own problems. They revered the tradition of self-reliance. Yet these self-reliant Vermonters had a strong sense of neighborly duty and spirit. They helped raise each other's barns and cabins, and later, when the farms had become more modern and tillable, they "changed works" and did the chores for neighbors when sickness or death struck.

This neighborliness became an integral part of early Vermont life. It was passed on from generation to generation. It prevails today to a remarkable degree, not only on the farms where it started but in village life throughout the state. It is evident in gardens people grow, the vegetables they share, the cup of flour passed to a friend or neighbor, and the families drawn together through the church, kindergarten, Cub Scouts, the village basketball team, and the activities of the local high school.

Bill Paine, Vermont's deputy commissioner of agriculture, has described the highest sense of community in Vermont as "the silent communication among folks who've known each other for years. The example might be the visiting hours at the undertaker's when person after person comes, smiles haltingly, hugs members of the family for perhaps the only time ever, sits awhile, and leaves quietly without saying a word."

The people of Vermont are, on the whole, tolerant, open-minded, and moderate, and they have a sense of self-worth and dignity that commands respect. Perhaps they are a bit contrary at times, but they are also realistic, whether in business or politics. Consider their support of the environmental movement in Vermont to control the use of natural resources, which philosophically runs counter to their traditional sense of land ownership. They recognize, however, that something has to be done to protect the state's land and waters from the ravages of unplanned development, and what has to be done, Vermonters will do. They acted with moderation but with decisiveness when the legislature enacted Act 250, to regulate land use and development, and its companion, Act 252, to protect the waters of the state. They are also liberal-minded, in the literal sense, not in the New Deal sense. Vermont was the first state to attempt to achieve popular apportionment, which was initiated in 1821. Later,

Vermont became the first state to outlaw slavery, and in recent times, it was the first to ratify suffrage for eighteen-year-olds and one of the first to ratify suffrage for women.

For generations Vermont was considered a great state to visit but a hardscrabble place in which to live. It produced great men and women, many of whom went elsewhere to pursue their careers, including two presidents of the United States. It has long provided vacation retreats for many Americans of ability and distinction.

For the greater part of the twentieth century Vermonters have been trying in different ways to lure migrants from other states in the belief that economic progress would solve the state's problems. Years ago, when Vermont's population was approximately a quarter of a million, I listened to Senator Harry Daniels, a canny Vermonter from East Montpelier, speaking on the floor of the Senate. He said, "All we need is to bring another 250,000 people into Vermont, and our troubles would be over." He was expressing the majority view at the time. Since then we have learned better. Vermont now has the extra 250,000 people, and its problems have multiplied many times over.

What happened? After a hundred years of economic stagnation, the picture has suddenly changed. In the early 1960s, for a variety of reasons, people began looking at Vermont differently. People wanted to come to Vermont not only to visit but to live and work and make their permanent homes. During the last twenty-five years Vermont has experienced its largest immigration since before the Civil War. During the decade 1960–1970, alone, the population of Vermont increased by 14 percent, and by the end of the next decade, it had increased by another 15 percent. During these years, Vermont was one of the fastest-growing states in the United States, and the pace of this increase left Vermonters a bit breathless. At first, this migration was greeted enthusiastically by Vermonters, but by the end of the first decade of growth, some were having second thoughts. Increasingly today, Vermonters are expressing a wish to close the door or at least to slow down the pace of immigration.

It is difficult to know precisely why migrants come to Vermont in such large numbers. Little hard evidence exists except one scientific study based on in-depth interviews with sixty-four people who moved into northeastern Vermont during the 1960s. There are also some excellent articles that have been published in Vermont during the same period, some of which quote sample migrants on their motivation. But over the last twenty years I have been privileged to talk with a large number of these new Vermonters, and I have some strong convictions as to what motivated most of the migrants in the years 1960–1980. All of them shared a common attraction for the widely heralded beauty of the Vermont landscape, but it is doubtful that any came for that reason alone. They came because they were unhappy with big city living. Most came from high density areas, either from inner cities or suburbia. They were unhappy with the pollution, the dirt, the unsightliness, the crowding, the traffic, the noise, high living expense, and the high incidence of crime prevailing in their former homes. They were of all ages, income levels, and educational backgrounds. They were managers, plant workers, doctors, lawyers, engineers, musicians, artists, teachers, and professors. None of them had been forced to move. All came of their own free will, for reasons that were adequate for them.

Among the younger group, I often heard "loss of control" over their lives as their reason for leaving, and many referred to the "class distinction" that exists in the city. Others said that they wanted work that was more directly related to the "public good." Individually and as a group, they showed a clear desire to assert independence in their daily lives. Older migrants, on the other hand, usually had adequate income or resources. Many of all ages used words like "quiet," "peaceful," "a chance to think, to feel, to meditate and to enjoy" to explain their choice. Both old and young preferred to live in the smaller towns and villages or on the fringes of the larger towns.

Even after making full allowance for the infinite variety of reasons that motivated the younger migrants, I got the feeling that these younger new Vermonters wanted a chance to be more directly involved in community affairs. They wanted to have a voice in what happens and a part in influencing the community around them. This was probably the strongest single reason so many came and are coming to Vermont.

Perhaps the best test of why they came is to see what they did after they arrived. They became involved in community affairs, including town and village, public and private activities. They became candidates for school boards, selectmen, and the legislature. A smaller number became candidates for higher state offices. Often they were successful. At one time in the 1980s, nearly half the members of the legislature were not born in Vermont. That rough ratio also held true with the higher offices in the administrative branch of state government.

On the whole these new Vermonters were able, well-educated people who sought a chance to express themselves and to work for change and improvement in public affairs. The vision they had of Vermont was of a place where they could best achieve their dream of a good and active life.

Only after this migration was well under way did Vermonters begin to worry about the speed with which the state's farms were declining. And they had good reason to worry. Between 1960 and 1970, six thousand Vermont farms were lost. Many of these were dairy farms. Recently, Professor Fred Webster of the University of Vermont, an acknowledged expert on Vermont agriculture, predicted that of the state's remaining 2,600 dairy farms, only about 1,100 would remain by the end of the century. I remember when there were more than 32,000 farms in Vermont.

But farm statistics like these can be quite misleading. Usually today we are talking about a different kind of farm than existed in 1950. Moreover, we have to agree on a definition of a farm in order to make helpful statistical comparisons. The one now used for most purposes is an enterprise that produces a gross income of one thousand dollars or more from sales of agricultural products alone.

Agriculture has been evolving in Vermont since the state's settlement. Certainly, since the dissolution of the sheep industry in Vermont, dairy farming has been almost constantly changing. At first, butter and farm-separated cream were sold as cash products from subsistence-type farms. With the growth of manufacturing in cities and suburbs in southern New England, Vermont farmers began supplying whole milk. First, it was shipped in ten-gallon cans and later in tank cars attached to passenger trains on their overnight runs to Boston and New York City. Early in this century, men and horses were the main sources of motive power and doers of heavy work on the farms. During the 1920s and 1930s, however, tractors and electricity revolutionized farming. Commercial farms with these new sources of power crowded out the old subsistence operations, and the mass exodus of rural people to cities and villages climaxed with the Great Depression of the 1930s. Only the complete restructuring of our economy after World War II enabled all the people released from agriculture to enjoy full employment and a higher standard of living.

A quick glance at the degree to which dairy farming has changed over the long run may be gained by an anecdote told by Professor Webster. Speaking of a little valley outside Randolph, Vermont, where his grandfather lived and farmed, Professor Webster describes how all the milk produced in the valley by seventeen operating farms was picked up for transportation to the creamery by one man and a pair of mules each day. Since a pair of mules could not draw more than a ton of weight, the limit of production of these seventeen farms was something less than a ton. Today in that valley only two farms survive, and each produces approximately four tons of milk per day!

Back in 1950, Vermont was producing 1.3 billion pounds of milk per annum. Today, Vermont produces 2.4 billion pounds of milk per year on less than 20 percent of the number of farms operating in 1950. By the year 2000 it is estimated that Vermont will still be producing at least two billion pounds of milk per year, even though half of the state's farms may be lost in the coming decade.

How could this be?

The disappearance of the sheep industry in Vermont meant that only the land best suited for pasture and cultivation of other crops was kept open. Later, the introduction of improved horse-drawn farming equipment made it possible for each remaining farmer to keep more cows. When the gasoline-powered tractor became available early in this century, the number of cows the farmer could keep suddenly tripled. The last two decades of high technology drastically affected not only the dairy farmer but his customers as well. Farmers could not only carry more cows but could produce three or four times as much milk per cow without a proportionate increase in feed. High-tech improvements made it possible to upgrade farmers' herds by using artificial insemination with semen from the best bulls in the country. And now embryo transplants are being used on a few farms and hold promise for even greater herd improvement. Applied chemistry is also an important aspect of dairy farm operation today because it improves the diet and health of dairy cows.

Why then are the number of Vermont farms declining? There are several reasons. First, not all farms are situated on land suited to take advantage of the possibilities of greatly increased production. On some the soil is too fragile, too rocky, or too poorly drained. On others the tillable land may be too steep to use the latest and most efficient farm equipment. On others the farmer does not wish to undertake or cannot undertake the higher capital investment or the tight management systems necessary to increase the size and efficiency of his farm operations.

The family farms that are successful—and there are many—are operated as true business enterprises by the families who live on the farms. The farms require capital, hard work, and a highly skilled level of management. Finally, farms are being sold for development, as a consequence of pressure from immigration and the high demand for housing. If farmland is situated in the right place, has the proper soil for building, and possesses other characteristics that make it suitable for development, it brings an extremely high price. Often these prices make it more practical for a farmer to sell the land than to use it for farming. Thus, the actual number of farm acres in Vermont in the future will be determined as much by the economics of what else the land is good for as by the demand for land for agriculture.

Experts believe that dairy farming will prevail in Vermont for a long time to come, but in a different form from what it is now. Evolution is continuing. Nowhere near as many farms, acres, cows, or farmers will be involved. There will be increased emphasis upon higher production per farm and per cow, concentration on the best systems of management, pressure to specialize, attention focused on improved marketing techniques, and continued use of the new technology as it comes along. Vermont will be producing approximately as much milk as it is now and perhaps even more on fewer farms. Two examples where improved marketing has already achieved great ends are at the Cabot Cooperative Creamery, which does a natiowide business on behalf of its five hundred farm members, and Ben and Jerry's Homemade, Inc. The Cabot Cooperative pays its members a substantial premium over the average price for milk because of better packaging, superior management, and maintenance of high quality. Ben and Jerry's combines skillful management, a superior product, and continuing improvement and enlargement of its marketing methods. This is a sign of the future in distribution of dairy farm products. There are others, less well known, and there will be more.

Bill Paine has an interesting formula for farm success. "A successful farmer is one who listens well," he says, "not to somebody talking to him, but to what Mother Nature is trying to tell him, and who adapts new techniques, new research, and new equipment to the conditions he can't change." He adds, "A farmer to be a success has to have a belief in some form of Higher Being. You and I don't make the corn grow."

Paine tells, for instance, of the farmer who experimented with growing soybeans when most people thought soybeans could not be efficiently grown on Vermont soil and in this climate. Today that farmer grows all his feed for his milking cows. Another farmer is experimenting with the feeding of liquid whey, a waste product that costs him nothing except the cost of transportation. These examples merely demonstrate the independence and innovation of those farmers who are able to do something less costly, more efficiently, or on a different scale from their neighbors.

Hobby farming in Vermont has greatly increased. It is responsible for the first turn-around in the total number of farms in the category of those producing income of one thousand dollars or more. In that category, the number of farms in Vermont increased by nine hundred farms in the period 1982–1988. Granted, these hobby farms are for the most part small operations, although a few are of substantial size. Most of these smaller hobby farms are operated by new Vermonters who hold down full-time salaried positions and carry on the farming operation mainly for recreational purposes and what Governor Richard Snelling calls "psychic income." But these farmers are there and must be taken seriously. In the aggregate they make a significant contribution to Vermont's quality of life. Most important, they help maintain Vermont's open spaces and thereby help preserve the beauty of the landscape.

These hobby operations are not confined to dairy operations.

Indeed, most are not dairy at all. Sheep, horses, and market gardening for specialty products predominate. One such farmer who comes to mind is a college professor who grows turkeys. Each November he has to take a few weeks off to get his turkeys to market. Another college professor has eight hundred head of sheep. A businessman who spends most of each week in New York carries on a sheep operation. He says it keeps him active and moving. He does not expect to make any money out of the operation, but he is trying hard just to show that he could. Again, he appears to be looking for "psychic income."

It is a great comfort for me to know that family farming is here to stay for the predictable future. That assurance makes it possible for me to imagine what Vermont will look like in the future. Dairy farms will be smaller in number but larger in size, with more cows, higher production per farm acre, and more profitability for the family farm. From an overall economic viewpoint, agriculture will not be as important to the state's total economy as it was in the past. It will produce as much as it does now, but because of the remarkable increase in recreation, tourism, manufacturing, and service operations, it will contribute a smaller percentage to the economy of Vermont as a whole. The farms least suitable for increasing production or too close to urban areas will gradually continue to be sold for other purposes, primarily housing and service facilities.

The current rate of migration must at some point subside to a more reasonable and sustainable rate. More high-technology industries will come to Vermont but doubtless at a more leisurely pace to match the labor supply. Sufficient open spaces will be kept to maintain our attractive landscape. A larger proportion of the increasing population will take root in the rural sections of Vermont and in the smaller towns and villages, which will contribute greatly to the ability of these towns and villages to render increased municipal services to their inhabitants and make more of the towns and villages even better places to live.

As Art Ristau has pointed out, the Vermont of today is a man-made landscape, made and preserved by the farmers past and present. Vermont of the future will likewise be man-made. It will be just as beautiful and even more orderly, as long as the environmental ethic continues to prevail.

Index

Index

Davis, Corinne Eastman (first wife),
124, 127
descriptions of, 112–13, 117–18
illness and death of, 118–23, 203,
319
"I Thought I Had Cancer," 121
lessons/advice from, 158
"Love Song: 1950," 123
married life with Deane Davis,
115–23, 202–3
poetry and, 115, 123
at Spaulding High School (Barre,
Vt.), 38, 40, 112–14, 202
Davis, Deane C., 58, 66–67, 83–86
Act 250 and, 241, 260, 262, 285,
294–96, 312–13, 318, 331
Act 252 and, 260, 262, 285, 294,
295, 312, 318, 331
age issue and, 212–13, 215, 217
as alderman in Barre, 99
American Bar Association, on the
board of, 182
American Morgan Horse Association and, 321–22, 327
birth of, 21, 47
boat ad and, 278–80, 282
at Boston University College of
Liberal Arts, 76–77
at Boston University Law School,
34, 40, 55, 65, 70–82, 84–85,
87, 88, 90–91, 93–96, 112, 114
bottle bill and, 264, 295
as Boy Scout, 31–32
Boy Scouts, on the board of, 318
childhood of, 1–40, 47–54, 59,
60, 62–65, 92–93, 112–13,
141, 207
at Church Street School (Barre,
Vt.), 33
as city attorney of Barre, 99
Committee to Study State Aid to
Public School Buildings, as
member of, 194–96, 212, 252
Cooperative Health Information
Center of Vermont
(CHICV), as president of,
315–17
crime/law enforcement/prisons
and, 227, 253, 278, 290,
298–99, 306–8
as dairy farmer, 154, 202
dairy farmers' cooperative movement and, 184–87

deer herd management and, 244–
45
in Delta Theta Phi, 78
development and, 223–24,
226–29, 249–53, 255, 260,
262, 275–77, 285, 294–7,
304, 312–13, 318, 331
education issues and, 221, 227,
237–40, 245, 247–48, 253,
256, 271, 275, 279, 281,
288–91, 297–98, 300, 305–6
environment and, 227, 228, 241,
249–52, 254–55, 259–60,
262–64, 271, 275, 285, 287,
293–96, 301, 311–13, 318, 331
at Epworth League, 48
Executive Order 7, 252
formal education of, 5, 33–40, 48,
54–55, 59, 60, 65, 70–82,
84–85, 87, 88, 90–91, 93–96,
112–14
with Fuller Brush Company,
82–83, 86–87, 89, 114
at Goddard Seminary, 34
government reorganization and,
191–94, 255, 260, 262, 265,
285–86, 293, 303
as governor, 194, 205–8, 232–314
Governor and J.J., The,
appearance, 261
governor's office moved, 286–87
as grand juror in Barre, 99
gubernatorial campaign (first),
174, 205, 211–30, 268, 273,
314
gubernatorial campaign
(second), 205, 265–85, 314
gun control and, 221, 227
heart surgery for, 324–25
at Hermanson and Silverman,
90–91
highway cleanup project, 262–64
housing issue and, 253, 254,
274–75
income tax and, 232–33, 236,
277, 300
as insurance lobbyist before U.S.
Congress, 177–78
as insurance lobbyist before
Vermont Legislature, 150–53
Japan, trip to, 206–8
Justice in the Mountains, 325
labor unions and, 273–74, 277, 310